WASSER STRUM
P9-AER-570

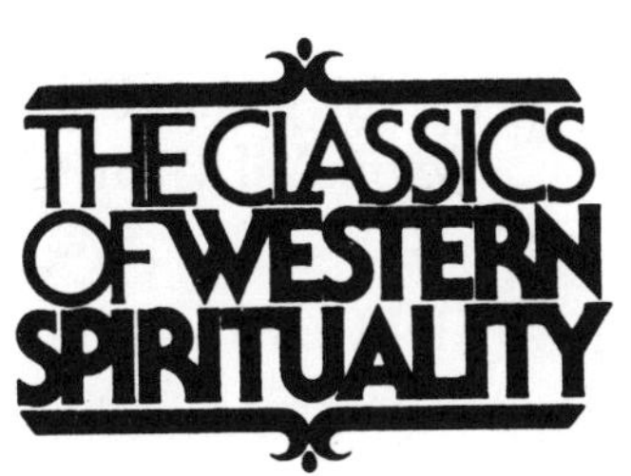
THE CLASSICS
OF WESTERN
SPIRITUALITY

THE CLASSICS OF WESTERN SPIRITUALITY
A Library of the Great Spiritual Masters

Bishop Kallistos of Diokleia—Fellow of Pembroke College, Oxford, Spalding Lecturer in Eastern Orthodox Studies, Oxford University, England.

George A. Maloney—Spiritual Writer and Lecturer, Seal Beach, Calif.

Seyyed Hossein Nasr—Professor of Islamic Studies, George Washington University, Washington, D.C.

Heiko A. Oberman—Professor for Medieval, Renaissance and Reformation History, University of Arizona, Tucson, Ariz.

Raimundo Panikkar—Professor Emeritus, Department of Religious Studies, University of California at Santa Barbara, Calif.

Jaroslav Pelikan—Sterling Professor of History and Religious Studies, Yale University, New Haven, Conn.

Sandra M. Schneiders—Professor of New Testament Studies and Spirituality, Jesuit School of Theology, Berkeley, Calif.

Michael A. Sells—Emily Judson Baugh and John Marshall Gest Professor of Comparative Religions, Haverford College, Haverford, Penn.

Huston Smith—Thomas J. Watson Professor of Religion Emeritus, Syracuse University, Syracuse, N.Y.

John R. Sommerfeldt—Professor of History, University of Dallas, Irving, Tex.

David Steindl-Rast—Spiritual Author, Benedictine Grange, West Redding, Conn.

David Tracy—Greeley Professor of Roman Catholic Studies, Divinity School, University of Chicago, Chicago, Ill.

The Rt. Rev. Rowan D. Williams—Bishop of Monmouth, Wales.

EARLY ISLAMIC MYSTICISM

SUFI, QUR'AN, MI`RAJ, POETIC AND THEOLOGICAL WRITINGS

TRANSLATED, EDITED AND WITH AN INTRODUCTION BY
MICHAEL A. SELLS

PREFACE BY
CARL W. ERNST

PAULIST PRESS
NEW YORK • MAHWAH

Cover art: AIDA MUŠANOVIĆ, a graphic artist, was born in Bosnia and earned her B.F.A. degree at the Academy of Fine Arts at Sarajevo University. A survivor of the aggression in Bosnia, she came to the United States, where she co-organized the internationally shown project *Sarajevo '92,* the art/print portfolio created in the besieged Bosnian capital under war conditions. The image on the cover of this volume depicts the prayer niche (*miḥrāb*) from the "Colored Mosque" in Foča (pronounced Fó-cha), in southeast Bosnia-Herzegovina. The mosque, one of the masterworks of South Slavic architecture, was constructed in 1551 C.E. It was called the Colored Mosque (*Aladža džamiya*) because of its stunning colors both on the interior and exterior. The artwork shows the section of the *miḥrāb* known as *muqarnas,* the "stalactite" forms that connect the square to the curved areas of the mosque and are symbolic of the connections between heaven and earth. The mosque was destroyed by Serbian nationalists during the "ethnic cleansing" of Foča in the spring of 1993. It is to all such destroyed Bosnian monuments that the artist pays homage in her artwork.

Library of Congress Cataloging-in-Publication Data

Early Islamic mysticism: Sufi, Qur'an, Mi'raj, poetic and theological writings/translated, edited, and with an introduction by Michael A. Sells.

p. cm.—(The classics of Western spirituality; #86)

Includes bibliographical references ( ) and index.

ISBN 0-8091-0477-6 (cloth: alk. paper).—ISBN 0-8091-3619-8 (pbk.: alk. paper)

1. Sufism—Early works to 1800. I. Sells, Michael Anthony. II. Series.

BP188.9.E2 1996

297'.4—dc20

95-52973

CIP

Published by Paulist Press
997 Macarthur Boulevard
Mahwah, New Jersey 07430

Printed and bound in the United States of America

Contents

EARLY ISLAMIC MYSTICISM

CONTENTS

Editor and Translator of this Volume

MICHAEL A. SELLS is Emily Judson Baugh and John Marshall Gest Professor of Comparative Religions at Haverford College and Chairperson of the Haverford Department of Religion. He served in the Peace Corps in Tunisia and studied Arabic language and literature in Egypt. He received his Ph.D. from the University of Chicago in 1982. His research interests are Arabic poetry, the Qur'an, Islamic spirituality and Western mysticism.

Among his published writings are *Mystical Languages of Unsaying* (University of Chicago Press, 1994), a study of the mystical language of Plotinus, Eriugena, Ibn 'Arabi, Meister Eckhart and Marguerite Porete; *Desert Tracings: Six Classic Arabian Odes* (Wesleyan University Press, 1989); "Sound and Meaning in Surat al-Qari'a" (*Arabica* 40.3, 1993); "Bewildered Tongue: the Semantics of Mystical Union in Islam," in Moshe Idel and Bernard McGinn, eds., *Mystical Union and Monotheistic Faith* (1989) and numerous articles on Arabic poetry, Qur'anic language, and the mystical writings of Ibn 'Arabi, Marguerite Porete and Meister Eckhart. He is co-editor and contributor to the *Cambridge History of Arabic Literature, Andalusia Volume.*

Dr. Sells is a founder and president of the Community of Bosnia Foundation, dedicated to supporting a multireligious Bosnia-Herzegovina.

Author of the Preface

CARL W. ERNST, born in 1950 in Los Angeles, is Professor and Chair of the Department of Religious Studies at the University of North Carolina-Chapel Hill. He has also taught in the Department of Religion at Pomona College in Claremont, California. He received his A.B. degree in Humanities and Religious Studies from Stanford University in 1973, and his Ph.D. in Comparative Religion from Harvard University in 1981, having specialized in Islamic studies and Greek philosophy. Dr. Ernst has been on research tours in India, Pakistan and Turkey with support from the Fulbright program (1978–79, 1986), the American Institute of Indian Studies (1981) and the American Research Institute in Turkey (1990). He has also received translation and research grants from the National Endowment for the Humanities (1989–90, 1993). His research has focused on early Islamic mystical texts, the development of Islamic culture in South Asia and the social and institutional history of Sufism.

His publications include *Words of Ecstasy in Sufism; Eternal Garden: Mysticism, History, and Politics in a South Asian Sufi Center; Manifestations of Sainthood in Islam* (edited with Grace Martin Smith) and *Rūzbihān Baqlī: Mysticism and the Rhetoric of Sainthood in Persian Sufism.*

DEDICATION

*THIS VOLUME IS DEDICATED
TO THE PEOPLE OF FOCA IN
BOSNIA-HERZEGOVINA,
AND TO ALL THOSE WHO BUILT,
WORSHIPED WITHIN, ADMIRED,
CARED FOR, AND LIVED WITHIN
THE SHADE OF ITS COLORED MOSQUE.*

ACKNOWLEDGMENTS

With gratitude to Mahmoud Ayoub, Emily Camp, Carin Companick, David Dawson, Anthony Dugdale, Carl Ernst, Seemi Bushra Ghazi, Erica Gelser, Emil Homerin, Connie Kim, Alexander Knysh, Paul Losensky, Kevin McCullough, Birch Miles, Elizabeth Penland, Aida Premilovac, Usma Wahhab, Ashley Walker, and Krista Woodbridge for their comments and corrections to earlier versions of this work. With special gratitude to Joan Powell, Shirley Stowe, James Gulick, and Trudy Swain at Haverford's Magill Library for their assistance in helping me obtain the Arabic texts.

Preface

Islamic mysticism is one of the most extensive traditions of spirituality in the history of religions. From its origins in the Prophet Muhammad and the Qur'anic revelation, the mystical trend among Muslims has played an extraordinary role in the public and private development of the Islamic faith. This variegated movement has spanned several continents over a millennium, at first expressed through Arabic, then through Persian, Turkish, and a dozen other languages. Yet it would be a mistake to say that Islamic mysticism is well understood today. Modern European scholarship has consistently approached Islamic mysticism as a separate category called Sufism. This English term (like its French and German equivalents) suggests by the "ism" word ending a kind of school of thought or ideology, which many scholars supposed was an external addition to the stern and legalistic image that they assigned to Islam. The colonial prejudices and racial theories of the nineteenth century encouraged the notion that Islam was a "Semitic" religion that, like Judaism, was considered to be anti-spiritual. Orientalists believed that any genuinely mystical reverberations in Islamic culture were necessarily imported from an external source, generally Christianity, yoga, or Buddhism. Thus Sufism was a term often viewed in a positive light, precisely to the degree that it was understood to be contrary to Islam.[1]

In the twentieth century a new factor arose that would further obscure the picture of Islamic mysticism. By the end of the first world war, most Muslim countries had been conquered by European, Russian, or Chinese armies. The flames of nationalism were fanned by colonial rule, and eventually resistance movements were led to independence by Western-trained

1. These tendencies can all be seen in the first European study devoted to Sufism: Lt. James William Graham, "A Treatise on Sufism, or Mahomedan Mysticism," *Transactions of the Literary Society of Bombay* 1 (1819), pp. 89–119. This piece was originally written at the request of another colonial official and Orientalist, Brigadier-general Sir John Malcolm, in 1811. Many of the same attitudes can be found, nearly unchanged, in works on Sufism published within the past few years.

secular leaders who espoused socialism and similar ideologies. As in the West, the secularizing ideologies of modernism provoked a reaction; invoking the sacred symbols of the past, fundamentalists in Muslim countries (like their Jewish, Christian, Buddhist, and Hindu counterparts) attempted to resist the nation-state and remake the world in their own authoritarian image. Islam became a battle cry, a symbol in a contest for power, in which Iranian mullas shrewdly made use of the eager mass media outlets of the West. In all the hue and cry about Islamic fundamentalism, superficial journalistic coverage has missed an important point: alongside of secular modernism, fundamentalism's other principal opponent has been Sufism. Fundamentalists claim that they alone are entitled to use the term Islam; centuries of Muslim tradition that fail the fundamentalist test are rejected as "innovation," in a highly selective reading of history. Sufism is attacked for offering an alternative to the authority of fundamentalists. The Islamic Republic of Iran does not permit Sufi organizations to function, and the Kingdom of Saudi Arabia absolutely forbids reverence at the tombs of Sufi saints in Arabia (which have all been destroyed in any case). Fundamentalists commonly aver that Sufism has nothing to do with Islam. The dervish orders of Sufism are illegal in Turkey as well, but that is part of a different story; Atatürk banned the orders as part of the secularization of the Turkish Republic in the 1920s.

So where does Sufism lie, and what is its relation to Islam, between the constructions of European Orientalists and the denunciations of modern Muslim fundamentalists? What of the modern Sufi groups in Europe and America that consist largely of non-Muslims? To this problematic category one can add certain emigrants from Muslim countries, who bitterly denounce the Islam that has been used for political purposes, and who passionately deny that their beloved Sufis could have anything to do with it. Sufism has become a contested term. To define Sufism in such an absolute fashion, whether to claim or to reject it, amounts to little more than a political exercise based on contemporary culture clash.

While the confrontations of modern ideologies are doubtless significant in their own right, their pretense of primordiality obscures the earlier historical processes of the Islamic tradition. Spirituality, as Michael Sells points out, has been a basic aspect of Islamic religious practice, which does not stand in opposition to legal duties but provides them with meaning. Current research increasingly shows us a picture of Islamic societies in which mystical accents could be found, with multiple inflections, at all levels. While hagiographic literature sometimes presents Sufis in (usually victorious) rivalry with Islamic religious scholars ('ulama'), it can also be demonstrated that many premodern religious scholars were attached to Sufi circles. Likewise, most identifiable Sufi masters were also distinguished in various aspects of traditional Islamic scholarship. At a recent international conference on the subject of "Sufism and its Opponents," it quickly became clear that, prior to the nineteenth century, mysticism in itself was never a controversial subject separable from the texture of Islamic religious life, though particular mystics and Sufi organizations have at times fallen into political confrontations.[2] Even jurists renowned for their criticism of mystical excesses, such as Ibn al-Jawzi and Ibn Taymiyya, were themselves initiated into Sufi orders and fully familiar with mystical literature.

With this anthology, Michael Sells offers a different way of reading the Islamic mystical tradition. For this volume, he has chosen a handful of authors and texts from the earliest period of Islamic mysticism. This is not to say that this selection exhausts the possibilities or focuses on some kind of primordial essence. Rather, he has thoughtfully chosen some foundational points, which have served as a basis for much of the later elaboration of mystical thought in Islamic civilization. These texts belong to a period when early Sufis labored with the richly textured vocabulary of Arabic to fashion a language for the soul. Sells rightly emphasizes the extraordinary role of the Qur'anic revelation in forming a template for that inner language. But alongside the Arabic word of God there was another literary idiom, resonant and subtle, created by the poets of the Arabs. Highly conventional and densely packed with artifice, the pre-Islamic Arabic odes have often been dismissed by Western scholars as the recondite and atomistic products of the nomadic Semitic mind. Sells persuasively demonstrates the esthetic power of the odes, and he shows the deep continuities they share with early Arabic Sufi poetry.

The mystical authors represented in this collection have scarcely been translated into English previously, although some have formerly appeared in scholarly French and German versions. The anthologies of Islamic literature produced in this century by English translators have included at most some snippets of Sufi poetry, along with a few stories. Scholars of Islamic studies who deal with mysticism have emphasized the importance of the Qur'an commentaries of Ja'far al-Sadiq and Tustari, the ingenious synthesis of mysticism and scriptural authority in Sarraj, and the acute psychological analysis of mystical states by Qushayri. Commentators have frequently

2. The papers from the conference on "Sufism and its Opponents," held at the University of Utrecht in May 1995, are being edited by Fred de Jong and Bernd Radtke and will be forthcoming from E. J. Brill.

drawn attention to the moral insights of Muhasibi, the powerful ecstatic sayings of Bistami, and the bold poetic declarations of Hallaj. Surprisingly, hardly any of these works is available in a complete and reliable English version. Those translations of Sufi authors that were available in more or less complete forms (Arberry's versions of 'Attar and Niffari, Abdel-Kader's rendering of Junayd) were flawed by inadequate textual editions or lack of literary sensitivity. Reading these translations was too often like trying to hear a symphony on a bad car radio with static interference. General anthologies of mystical literature were forced to settle for including a few of these inadequate versions along with standard selections from St. John of the Cross and Plotinus. *Early Islamic Mysticism* is, then, a breakthrough. For the first time, readers have access within a single volume to some of the finest writers in early Islamic mysticism. To this largely Arabic collection a single piece in Persian has been added, ably translated by Paul Losensky and Michael Sells, containing 'Attar's powerful portrait of the foremost woman Sufi, Rabi'a of Basra.

The most difficult, and perhaps the most impressive, achievement of this anthology is its literary resonance. Translation is under the best of circumstances a frustrating profession, especially with poetry, but careful honing and a sensitivity to the music of words have allowed Sells to create some of the finest available literary translations of Arabic prose and verse. He frequently experiments with English equivalents for Arabic terms, striking a balance between familiarity and strangeness to lead the reader into new insights. There is a freshness and directness of style here that brings a thousand-year-old spiritual tradition to life for the contemporary reader. The translator and the publisher are to be congratulated for making available such a treasury of rich mystical texts, which can serve as the first usable collection illustrating the range of early Islamic spirituality.

Note to the Reader on Translation and Familiarization

The Sufi writings from the seventh Islamic century (thirteenth century C.E.) are among the more widely known writings in mystical literature. English versions of Rumi (d. 672/1273) are among the best-selling poetry collections to this day in the English-speaking world. The writings of Ibn 'Arabi (d. 638/1240) have received a rebirth of attention in the last decades, with new translations and editions and the founding of an international society of Ibn 'Arabi studies that publishes its own journal and books, and sponsors at least two international scholarly conferences per year.

The earlier period of Islamic mysticism is equally rich, but access to these earlier writings is far more difficult. Many of the more influential figures of early Islamic mysticism are known to us primarily through sayings that were passed on orally for generations before finally being compiled in various sources. Because early Sufi sayings are embedded in various, partially overlapping compilations, it is difficult to select a version of a particular figure's sayings for translation. Also, early written texts that are available are often unedited or untranslated. In addition, the early Islamic texts presumed a readership of Muslims imbued with the Qur'an, the traditions of the Prophet Muhammad, the Islamic poetic heritage, and the intricate vocabulary of the Sufis. To present this remarkable material to the nonspecialist demands a strategy in translation, commentary, selection, and arrangement.

This volume offers selections from the major figures of early Islamic spirituality, beginning with the Qur'an. In addition to a general introduction, introductions to each text have been provided, along with interpolated introductory comments where such comments are necessary for the nonspecialist to become familiar enough with style, allusions, and terminology to engage the writings. In order to make the distinction between text and commentary clear, all critical and introductory comments are in italics. These introductions are meant to serve as a guide to the reader not familiar with the developed vocabulary, literary conventions, poetic heritage, and common traditions that the early Sufi writers assumed their audience would know. Brief biographical sketches occur with the introduction to each author.[1]

The first goal of the translations is to render the literary qualities of the original texts into as clear and natural English as possible. A strategy of familiarization is needed for key dates, terms, names, and features that are so distinctive to the tradition that no single English correspondence can do them justice. With dates, I use first the Islamic date, with the Hijra, Muhammad's flight from Mecca to Medina in 622 C.E., as the beginning point. The C.E. date, based on the Christian calendar, then follows: for example, Sarraj (d. 378/988). With more common terms, I have employed a formal transliteration in the first instance of their usage (e.g., the *mi'rāj*, the account of Muhammad's journey through the seven heavens to the divine throne), and used the anglicized version thereafter (Mi'raj). With less common but frequently occurring key terminology (e.g., *fanā'*—the annihilation of the ego-self in mystical union), I have kept the formal transliteration and placed the Arabic in brackets when it is important to know that a particular Arabic term has been used.

With frequently used names, I have used the formal transliteration for the first appearance in a chapter devoted to the personage in question (e.g., Abu Naṣr as-Sarrāj), in formal lists of authorities, and in the index, but elsewhere I have used the informal and untransliterated form (Sarraj). With names of prophets and other figures familiar from the biblical tradition, I have used the English version of the name in the introduction (Moses, Abraham, Jesus), and the informal Arabic version (Musa, Ibrahim, 'Isa) in the body of the text.

It might seem easier to simply choose one set of terms or another. There is a compelling reason, however, for asking the reader to become familiar with both English and Arabic names. There are many Musas, Ibrah-

1. The effort to make accessible the richness and depth of the sayings and writings is a task that leaves no space for extended discussion of the very difficult issues of biography, historicity, and hagiography that surround early Islamic mystical figures. Such an investigation would require a volume on its own.

ims, and 'Isas (or Eissas) in the English-speaking world. These names relate directly to the Qur'anic texts presented in Chapter 1. Yet many readers may be unaware of the cognates. Readers unversed in Arabic names deserve to have access to the manner in which the Qur'anic tradition overlaps with and diverges from the biblical tradition. Such access will allow them to see how traces of the themes in the early mystical texts of Islam are reflected in names used in everyday life.

I also use the familiarization principle in varying translation styles for key terms regarding deity. I have varied the translation of the Arabic *allāh* between "God" and an anglicized version of the Arabic, Allah. By varying the two, I hope to emphasize the distinctiveness of the Arabic notion of deity, while avoiding the presupposition that the Qur'anic Allah is some "other being" posed in opposition to what in the West is called "God." I have attempted to bring across faithfully the epithets used after references to deity, such as *ta'ālā* (Most High), *subḥāna* (Most Praised), *'azza wa jalla* (Almighty),[2] and after references to revered personages such as Muhammad (God's blessings and peace upon him) or Sufi "friends-of-God" (May God have compassion upon them) in a manner that is faithful to the original but also relatively natural in contemporary English idiom. The goal requires a fine line in translation between a distortion of the distinctive Islamic idioms into preset forms from the Western tradition and an alienation of the reader through continual emphasis on nonessential differences.

The two principal Islamic references to ultimate reality are a critical issue in walking this fine line. The word *allāh* is treated by early writers as a proper name. *Al-ḥaqq,* a term that means "the true," or "the real," can be used as a simple substitute for Allah, but more often refers to what in English has come to be called "the absolute," "the ultimate," or "ultimate reality." To collapse the two words into a single translation such as "God" would be to lose a key tension in early Islamic writings between the personal deity that speaks through the Qur'an and the concept of ultimate truth or reality. To say there is a tension between these two terms is not, of course, to say that the two terms refer to two different things; such a notion would be absurd in early Islam. The two terms represent different ways of referring, however, and those different ways of referring create much of the richness

2. These terms are actually in the form of verbal interjections that would be very unwieldy to repeatedly translate into English with word-for-word literalism. Thus *ta'ālā* would mean "who has been raised or affirmed Most High" or "may he be raised or affirmed most high."

and texture of the early writings. In the translations below, Allah is rendered as "God" or "Allah," and *al-ḥaqq* is rendered as "the real."

Certain crucial words, terms, or concepts bedevil the translator. An Arabic root like *w/j/d* can form itself into several related words that mean a variety of things (finding, ecstasy, existence, experience). Frequently the writer plays on all these meanings at the same time, with some emphasized more strongly in one instance and others in another instance. To attempt a completely consistent translation, with a one-for-one parallel of each Arabic word with an English equivalent, would be to betray this word play. The alternative is to shift the English according to the primary sense. In cases where the play on the secondary sense is of critical importance, signals are given through notes or by placing the transliteration of the Arabic in parentheses. With this crucial vocabulary, it is the very impossibility of any simple solution to translation that allows the familiarization principle to work most effectively. Through parenthetical Arabic terms, introductory comments, and notes, in modulated degrees of technical complexity, the reader unfamiliar with Arabic is allowed access to key concepts of early Islamic spirituality that are constructed around particular clusters of related words and Arabic word play.

In rare cases, I have invented a new term. The neologisms are used only when the customary translation of a term is inaccurate and has led to false comparisons or misinterpretations. Thus the term *wali* is translated here as "godfriend" or "friend of God" rather than "saint," for example, and the term *'abd* as "godservant" rather than "slave." Neither Arabic word contains an equivalent to "God," but in both cases the deity is assumed to be the grammatical indirect object of the person-in-question's friendship or service. To leave out this assumed reference would leave the reader unfamiliar with such conventions more confounded than enlightened.

A final word should be said on the relationship among introductions, commentary, and translation. Here again, I have tried to walk a path between two extremes. One approach is to simply present what purport to be purely neutral translations with purely factual glosses. Such a mechanical solution is dubious. Literary translation demands a series of delicate compensations and decisions based on an interpretation of which sense of a word is most essential in each usage, and how it can be reconstructed in a completely different language world. There is no simple word-to-word correspondence in literary texts. Second, even if such a mechanical presentation were possible, it would not be meaningful for anyone but specialists, and specialists might as well read the original texts in the original languages.

The other extreme is to place the translations within the translator's particular vision or version of what spirituality is or should be, and how it must be understood. This extreme can entail the bending or distortion of a complex and varied tradition to fit a single, particularized perspective.

The translations, commentaries, and introductions in this volume all represent a particular point of view. That point of view is one that tries to respect and celebrate the diversity within the Islamic mystical tradition and the distinctiveness of that tradition, as well as the universal appeal of much of that tradition. The introductions, commentaries, and notes do not attempt to be interpretation-neutral, but they do endeavor to leave the reader clues and evidence of where and how interpretive moves were made in the process of translation, and to offer the reader the possibility of bringing alternative interpretations and perspectives to bear on key issues. With this goal in mind, key Arabic terms are included within the notes and, in cases of particular terminological difficulty, within the text itself.

Introduction

♦ ♦ ♦

SPIRITUALITY AND EMBODIMENT IN ISLAM

In his early Sufi commentary on the Qur'an, the Baghdad mystic Sahl at-Tustari depicts the essence of the Prophet Muhammad in cosmic terms as a pre-creative column of light:

> God Most High, when he wished to create Muhammad (the blessings and peace of God upon him), manifested some of his light. When it attained the veil of majesty, it bowed down in prayer before Allah. Allah created from the position of prayer a great column like a glass of light, as both his interior and exterior. In it is the *'ayn* (very being, essence, source, eye) of Muhammad, God's blessings and peace upon him. He stood in service before the lord of the two worlds for one thousand thousand years with the dispositions of faith, the beholding of faith, the unveiling of certitude, and the witness of the lord.[1]

From the position of prayer *(sajda)* was created "a great column like a glass of light as both his [Muhammad's] exterior and interior," which is the very being of Muhammad. In this image of a primordial position of prayer (created before the human body, on which such a position is based), Tustari has dramatized a feature of Islam that will be continually assumed by the texts within this volume, the symbiotic relationship between spirituality and embodiment.

The position of prayer, placed by Tustari beyond even the essence of the Prophet, implies a body. That body is oriented toward a particular point and positioned in a state of submission (the word *Islam* means surrender or submission and for this reason the ritual prayer is often viewed as an epitome of such surrender). With Tustari's image, this pre-eternal position of submission and orientation suggests not a surrender to some delineated and delimited authority, but more perhaps—as will be seen from the rest of Tustari's text in Chapter 2 in this volume—an opening up, to and toward the source of being.

As with Tustari's direct reference to the Islamic position of prayer, the other authors represented in this volume also make direct references to Islamic ritual practice. More often than not, however, the spiritual element in Islamic ritual practice is not an explicit object of commentary, but is instead assumed by authors as the common world of their audience. That common world of Islamic life and practice, developed out of the Qur'an and the traditions of the Prophet Muhammad, is called the *sharī'a*. As a corrective to a common assumption that law and spirituality are opposed to one another, and to the reflection of that assumption in the view that shari'a and spirituality must be opposed to one another in Islam, this introduction will begin with a remark on the spirituality of Islamic ritual practices, which function as a subtext within the texts presented in this volume.

The brief survey below begins with the spirituality of the "five pillars" of ritual Islam: the prayer *(ṣalā)*, the fasting during the month of Ramadan, the obligatory contribution *(zakā')* toward those less fortunate in society, the pilgrimage *(ḥajj)*, and the Islamic Witness *(shahāda)*, which is embedded in the call to prayer; other aspects of Islamic ritual practice will also be mentioned.

The goal of this discussion is not to suggest that the texts presented in this volume are meaningful only to practitioners of Islam, but rather to elucidate the ritual context assumed by the writers and original audience of these texts. An understanding of that context will allow a better understanding of allusions in the texts themselves and should strengthen, rather than weaken, the appreciation of the texts in interreligious and extra-Islamic contexts.

Islamic Spirituality and the Shari'a

Prayer

The issue of prayer dramatizes vividly the misunderstandings common in discussing Islamic spirituality and its relationship to the shari'a. The word *prayer* is used to translate at least four very different activities in Islamic spirituality: (1) the ritual prayer *(ṣalā)*, an aspect of which was mentioned above; (2) personal entreaties and petitions to the deity *(du'ā)*; (3) meditative remembrance *(dhikr)*, in which certain key Qur'anic phrases or divine epithets are continually invoked, aloud or silently; and (4) *munājāt*, devotional conversations between the lover and the divine beloved. When Muslims use the English word *prayer* it is most often the first type of prayer, the ritual prayer, that is meant.

Ritual prayer in Islam is based on bodily movement. The worshiper faces the *qibla*, the direction of Mecca at one of the five precisely specified times of day, simultaneously with all other Muslim worshipers. During the prayer, which can take place in public (particularly during Friday services), or in private, the worshiper makes a set *(rak'a)* of physical gestures: bowing forward, sitting in on the back of the legs, touching the ground with the tip of the forehead. Interspliced among the *rak'a*s is the recitation of Qur'anic phrases.

Because the ritual prayer is the more public and obligatory act translated into English as prayer, it has become a touchstone for generalizations about the alleged exteriority of Islamic worship as opposed to spirituality of prayer in other traditions.[2] As the Tustari passage explicitly demonstrates, however, and as most of the texts in this volume assume, Islamic ritual prayer is not opposed to spirituality, nor is there anything "unspiritual" about a practice that focuses on bodily movements rather than interiorized verbal petitions. The physical movements *(rak'a*s) of ritual prayer enact the simultaneous orientation of all worshipers—body and spirit—toward the center point of the Ka'ba in Mecca and harmonize the body and spirit within that orientation.

Ramaḍān

Ritual prayer breaks up the day, obliging the practitioner to rise before dawn and to interrupt work or social occasions in order to reorient the body and soul toward the ultimate. The fasting *(ṣawm)* for the month of *Ramaḍān* even more radically impinges on the common flow of space and time. Daytime becomes a time of austerity, with complete abstinence from food, drink, and sex. Nighttime becomes a time of communal celebration.

The last days of *Ramaḍān* culminate in the night of destiny *(laylat al-qadr)*, a vigil reenacting the night Muhammad was gifted with the divine word and marking a moment of close intimacy between the divine and the human.

Zakā

The tithe is enjoined on all Muslims as a contribution to the less fortunate. The word for tithe, *zakā,* is based on the concept of purification. The tithe institutionalizes the Qur'anic virtue of generosity, and is a social embodiment of the caustic Qur'anic denunciations of acquisitiveness ("as if a person's wealth could make him immortal," 104:3). Through constant generosity and sharing, and through avoidance of all predatory economic practices, wealth is purified.

The Pilgrimage (ḥajj)

The pilgrimage to Mecca and its ancient shrine, the Ka'ba, brings together many aspects of embodied spirituality. While passing through the stations of pilgrimage, the pilgrim reenacts the founding events of Islamic life. Through the formal sacrifice of a sheep, for example, Abraham—the builder of the Ka'ba—is remembered for his sacrifice of a sheep in place of his son. Simultaneously, Muslims around the world offer a sacrifice on the great holiday (*bayram* or *'īd),* a sacrifice that links them to the pilgrims near Mecca performing the same act. On the plain of Arafat, there is a simultaneous *re*enactment of Muhammad's final sermon and *pre*-enactment of the final day of judgment or moment of truth *(yawm ad-dīn)* as the Islamic community chants "*labbayka*" (Here I am, lord). The circumambulation of the Ka'ba, therefore, is a movement around that point where the world and the transcendent meet, the axis mundi. The Ka'ba itself represents the three archetypal moments in the Qur'an when the world of time and the world of eternity come together: the creation (the stone of the Ka'ba is viewed by tradition as a relic of the original creation), prophecy, and the day of judgment.

The Islamic Witness

The call to prayer resonates over Islamic communities five times a day, breaking through daily preoccupations and demanding a moment of reflection and self-composure before the ultimate. The call to prayer includes within it the Islamic Witness or Testimony *(shahāda):* "I witness that there is no god but God and Muhammad is his Prophet." The first statement of the Witness, "there is no god but God" *(lā ilāha illa llāh),* is a quote from the Qur'an and in its recited form is a distillation of the distinctive features of Qur'anic cadence. The refrains of the call to prayer, wafting over the Islamic community, are perhaps the most immediate and typical feature of

Islam that a voyager to an Islamic society will encounter. These chanted cadences resonate over each community five times per day, breaking through daily preoccupations and demanding a moment of reflection before the ultimate. The verbal, recited affirmation of the oneness of God is another aspect of the "orientation" of the human, through all aspects of the body and soul, toward one point.

The Ta'ziyya and Veneration of the Prophet's Family

Beyond these five pillars of ritual Islam are a series of other important practices and observances. In Shi'ite Islam, a key observance is the *ta'ziyya*, the reenactment of the martyrdom of Husayn—the grandson of the Prophet and the third Shi'ite Imam. This passion play, in which the innocent Husayn, his followers, and his family are depicted as they are ruthlessly killed, one after another, becomes the occasion for an extraordinary meditation on the tragic aspect of human existence. It reaches the highest pitch of intensity when audience members no longer perceive themselves as watching a representation of an event that took place centuries ago, but rather become, as it were, participants in that event, co-participants with the actors. The Ta'ziyya does not replace the other five pillars for Shi'ites, but assumes nevertheless a crucial position in the embodied spirituality of the community.

While Sunni Muslims do not observe the Ta'ziyya formally, they venerate the figure of Husayn and remember the tragedy of his martyrdom in their own way, through celebrations of the birthday (Mawlid) of Husayn, his sister Zaynab, and other key members of the prophet's family. The Mawlids of Zaynab and Husayn bring millions of non-Shi'ite Egyptians into Cairo for intense celebrations, circumambulations of shrines, and Sufi *dhikrs* or meditation ceremonies.

Baraka Islam

The "visitation" made to a saint or the shrine of a saint to receive blessing *(baraka)* is a controversial but very widely practiced aspect of Islamic culture. Throughout much of the world, local shrines serve as centers for visitation and the transmission of baraka. This baraka, a divine blessing and a kind of sacred force, can be interpreted in many ways. It can be used for healing or for spiritual illumination. Despite the efforts of certain Islamic groups, particularly those based in Saudi Arabia, to exterminate the practice of shrine-visitation as un-Islamic, it is one of the most typical features of Islamic societies around the world.

The Prohibited (ḥarām) *and the Allowed* (ḥalāl)

Throughout the early Islamic writings there are references to Islamic regulations on the prohibited and the allowed. This critical distinction within Islam marks all human behavior and gives every aspect of behavior, however small or common it might seem, a relationship to the sacred. All foods, for example, fit into one of three categories: prohibited foods (such as wine and pork or any meat not prepared with the proper sacrificial forms and prayers), allowed foods, and foods that might be ambiguous (meat whose preparation is unknown).

Both popular and scholarly treatments of Islam in the past two centuries have been dominated by a paradigm that has placed "spirit" (as exemplified for many by the Sufis) against "law" (as exemplified by the kind of ritual practices and prohibitions reviewed above). Although Islamic mystical writers are scathing in their criticism of those who carry out ritual practices for egoistic reasons (see Chapter 5 in this volume) or without true devotion, they find no inherent contradiction between spirit and law. Indeed, they build their own traditions, practices, and sensibility on the ritual markings of categories of prohibited and allowed, as the texts below will suggest.

The Embodied Word

In Islam, the word of God is not a person, but rather a text, the Qur'an. It is a text that is both embodied and performed within Islamic societies. The Qur'an is composed in a highly distinct classical Arabic style. When Muhammad was asked for a miracle like the miracles of prophets before him such as Moses and Jesus, he was inspired with new Qur'anic pronouncements. These Qur'anic messages made the following argument: This Qur'an is the miracle. If any human being can compose anything like it, Muhammad is invalidated as a prophet. Although some have tried to meet this Qur'anic challenge, Muslims find the composition of the Qur'an, in its original Arabic, to be something beyond the ability of any human to produce, and thus a miraculous word of God communicated to and through the messenger of God, his Prophet Muhammad.

To understand the way the Qur'an is embodied, it is necessary to note the method of its composition and the way it is learned and taken to heart by its audience. Because "composition" of the Qur'an is tied intimately into the original Arabic sound patterns and meaning patterns, most Muslims believe the Qur'an is untranslatable. For people around the world, a major first step into Islamic life is the learning of sections of the Qur'an in Arabic, by heart, orally, through repeated recitation. Although it is established in a written canonical form, the Qur'an is preeminently an oral and performed text. It is recited on public occasions and in groups. Cassettes of highly trained reciters chanting the Qur'an are used and played by Muslims around the world. In addition, the format of the Qur'an is nonlinear, with stories scattered in fragments throughout rather than told in single episodes. The nonlinear format encourages a continual, cyclical pattern of recitation in which the stories, scattered in various places, are woven together in a nonlinear way through constant performance. The Qur'an is a word that is continually embodied in the rituals that are grounded in it and that are occasions for its performance.

The Qur'an is embodied not only in shari'a rituals and the cadences of Qur'anic reciters, but also in the patterns of Qur'anic calligraphy, one of the central Islamic arts. Calligraphy is a form of meditation, with a state of lucid calmness being the result of training in Qur'anic calligraphy, and a necessary precondition for the best calligraphic art. Qur'anic calligraphy is not so much an "embellishment" as it is a central mode of art, a writing of the divine text in calligraphic patterns and in the stone calligraphy that graces the entrance of Islamic buildings. Finally, the mosque itself—the central artistic achievement within the Islamic world—is constructed around the Qur'anic principles, with the prayer niche *(mihrāb)* facing Mecca, the large hall for group performance of ritual prayer, the minaret for the recitation of the call to prayer and Islamic Witness, and the dome that symbolizes for many Muslims the cosmos of concentric spheres through which Muhammad ascended during his Mi'raj to receive the divine revelation.

♦ ♦ ♦

FOUR PHASES OF ISLAMIC SPIRITUALITY

The texts in this volume represent four phases of classical Islamic spirituality.

1. The pre-Sufi phase includes the Qur'an, the central ritual elements of Islam, and the accounts of Muhammad's Mi'raj.

2. The early period of Sufism includes the sayings and writings of the early Sufi masters such as Hasan of Basra, Dhu n-Nun of Egypt, Rabi'a of

Basra, Bistami, Muhasibi, and Junayd of Baghdad, the legacies of whom have come down to us largely through collections of their sayings in the works of later writers. This phase extends from the time of Hasan of Basra (d. 110/728) to that of Niffari (d. 354/965).

3. The formative phase of Sufi literature shows Sufism as a self-conscious mode of spirituality embracing all aspects of life and society. This phase begins with Sarraj (d. 378/988) and extends to Qushayri (d. 465/1074).

4. The Sufi synthetic works of the seventh century of Islam by ʿAttar, Rumi (d. 672/1273), and Ibn ʿArabi.

The Qur'an and pre-Sufi Spirituality

It would be unfair to the Qur'an to try to summarize Qur'anic spirituality in this brief overview. Instead, we might focus more narrowly on the theme of the spirit within the Qur'an, saving other aspects of Qur'anic spirituality for Chapter 1. In the Qur'an, the spirit *(ar-rūḥ)* is associated with three primordial moments: creation (as exemplified by the "inspiriting" of Adam when the creator breathes into him the spirit of life, and by the conception of Jesus through the spirit); prophecy (exemplified by the spirit as the necessary accompaniment and aid in prophecy and in the famous passage on the "night of destiny" in which the spirit of prophecy descends); and the moment of truth or day of judgment in which the spirits return to the celestial analogue of the Kaʿba.

The Qur'anic language of spirit is the context in which these three archetypal moments are united, as well as the point at which the signs of reality—the polarities of day and night, male and female, odd and even—are brought together. The spirit in the Qur'an is never an isolated, disembodied entity. It is evoked always and only as a mediator between the eternal and the temporal, the divine and the created. It is found within the act of interpreting the signs *(ayas)* embedded within the Qur'an and within the world. The Qur'an continually returns to the notion of a universe of signs embedded within signs, meanings within meanings, deeper realities within other realities.

At the final moment of truth, the spirit returns to its source and the meaning of the signs becomes explicit. At this final moment, there is a reversal: What seems secure (the mountains, the heavens, the earth, the instinctive nursing of a calf by its mother) is torn away, and what might seem ephemeral, "a mote's weight of generosity or a mote's weight of evil"

(99:8), is revealed as having absolute reality. The heavens are stripped away, the stars are strewn, the seas boil over, the tombs burst open, and each person is asked "what she has given and what she has held back" (82:1–5).

The story of the Mi'raj (Muhammad's ascent through the seven heavens to the divine throne) becomes a central paradigm for Sufi understandings of the mystical journey. Based on a very brief mention in the Qur'an, the Mi'raj account was elaborated in the hadith and sira (biography of Muhammad) literature and collated with key passages on Muhammad's reception of the divine word. Muhammad is taken on a night journey from the sacred enclosure at the shrine in Mecca to the "house of sanctity," identified by later writers as the temple in Jerusalem. From there he is taken through the seven heavens and is greeted by, and in effect validated by, the previous prophets who now occupy those heavens (Adam, Jesus, Joseph, Idris, Aaron, Moses, and Abraham). At the culmination he sees the lote tree of the furthest boundary, the divine throne, the house of life (the celestial counterpart to the Ka'ba). Finally, he receives divinely ordained prayers for his community.

In addition to the Qur'an and the Mi'raj traditions, the rich heritage of Arabic poetry and later other poetic traditions (Persian, Ottoman, Urdu) became central modes of Islamic expression. The tradition of the pre-Islamic Ode supplied key aspects of Sufi lexicon, sensibility, and emotive nuance. The most important poetic heritage of Islamic spirituality is the remembrance of the beloved. The remembrance of the beloved includes a series of subthemes: drunkenness, love-madness, perpetual wandering, the secret shared between lover and beloved, the stations of the beloved's journey away from the lover, and the meditation of the ruins of the abandoned campsite of the beloved, ruins that are signs of both the beloved's presence and her absence.

The final element in pre-Sufi spirituality was the emergence of early ascetic tendencies and theological controversies, both of which centered around the figure of Hasan of Basra (d. 110/728). Hasan's probing of the key Qur'anic tensions between divine predestination and human responsibility and between the all-one deity and the plurality of its attributes (the Seer, the Hearer, the Compassionate) led to a new movement of theological inquiry. At the same time, Hasan's ascetic piety became a symbol of resistance to the new imperial culture. While grounding itself in the Qur'an and shari'a, this ascetic piety began to develop a set of supererogatory or free devotions, that is, devotional forms beyond what is enjoined by the shari'a: asceticism, fasting, meditations, and spiritual pedagogy.

The Emergence of Sufism

Qur'anic spirituality, embodied in the performance of the Qur'an and in the signs and symbols of all aspects of the world, never stressed asceticism, and indeed, for some early thinkers, was not compatible with asceticism. Certain ascetic practices, such as the fasting in Ramadan, are integrated within the shari'a, and indeed, it would be hard to find a more rigorous practice than Ramadan enjoined upon an entire community of believers within a major religious tradition.

But the ascetic life as a withdrawal from society was not encouraged in early Islam. Muhammad, whose life is considered a model for Muslims, lived fully within society, married, had children, fought in battles, and set up a government. The ascetic impulse in the second century of Islam has been attributed to a reaction by Muslims to the corruption caused by the vast new wealth of the expanding Islamic empire, to influences from Christian ascetics in Syria and Egypt, and to influences from Indian asceticism. Whatever its origins, the asceticism of the second century of Islam is a major issue in the development of a group of Muslims who came to be known as "Sufis," a name that comes, according to many, from the wool *(ṣūf)* clothes they wore. While Hasan of Basra represented a movement toward integrating ascetic piety into Islamic spirituality, it was the next generation that more clearly articulated the roles and limits of ascetic piety, its relation to Qur'anic spirituality, and its relation to key theological issues of divine predetermination and affirmation of divine unity.

The tension between world-affirmation and world-transcendence (not rejection) is dramatized vividly in the life and sayings of Rabi'a al-'Adawiyya (d. 185/801), a freed slave from Baṣra.[3] Rabi'a becomes the touchstone for a developing set of values that were to be the ethical ground of Sufism. The values included the affirmation of the divine unity interpreted as a relational absolute in which only the divine beloved is a matter of interest, or even consciousness; trust-in-God, interpreted as a refusal of all need for the goods of creatures; and acceptance, interpreted as a relentlessly active acceptance of divine will to the point of refusing to ask the deity for anything other than "its will being done."

These values were consolidated in Rabi'a's radical affirmation of the virtue of sincerity. In one story, she is portrayed as running down the path with water in one hand, fire in the other. When asked why, she states that she will douse the fires of hell and burn paradise, so that no one will ever love the beloved for any other reason than sincere love, devoid of fear of punishment or desire for reward.

Rabi'a's focus on the affirmation of divine unity as more than a verbal affirmation, as something to be performed throughout a person's entire life, vividly clarified the limits of asceticism. When asked if she hated Satan or loved Muhammad, Rabi'a answered neither, that she had room only for one concern, love of the divine beloved. Similarly, when an ascetic began showing his contempt for the world, Rabi'a answered dryly that anyone who spent so much time rejecting something must be very attached to it indeed; one whose only concern was love of the one beloved had no room for distractions such as rejecting the world.

Complementing Rabi'a's affirmation of divine unity as a way of life was the rigorous and psychologically relentless critique of the human egoism offered by mystics such as Muhasibi (d. 243/857). Muhasibi spent a lifetime examining the subtleties, seductions, and self-delusions of egoism. He divided egoism into numerous subcategories such as conceited self-display, vanity, self-delusion, and pride, each category with its own carefully delineated definition and set of subcategories. Muhasibi's moral psychology has been influential on all sectors of Islamic culture, but it was particularly important in the emergence of Sufism.

While Rabi'a, Muhasibi, and other early thinkers were integrating new modes of practice and self-scrutiny into Islam and developing Sufism as a modality of Islamic life, other thinkers were writing Qur'anic interpretation from the perspective of this new Sufi modality. The figure Ja'far as-Sadiq (d. 145/765), the sixth Imam in Shi'ite thought, became the center for a rich variety of intellectual movements within early Islam, from philosophy to Shi'ite jurisprudence to alchemy. The Qur'anic commentary attributed to Ja'far is one of the earliest specifically mystical or Sufi commentaries. In it, the prophetic visions of Muhammad and Moses are viewed as archetypes for the Sufi mystical experience of *fanā'*, the passing away of the human ego-self in union with the divine beloved. The Qur'anic commentary of Sahl at-Tustari (d. 283/896) also had a significant impact on Sufi thought. Tustari's notions of the primordial light of Muhammad and the pre-eternal covenant between humans and the deity were to exercise influence over centuries of Sufi thinkers.

Out of the same Iraqi circles as Tustari came Junayd (d. 297/910), perhaps the most famous of the early Sufis within Islam. Junayd's sayings and writings focus on the trial or test *(balā')* that the Sufi must undergo to encounter reality, and the overpowering, even violent nature of the manner in which such a person is seized, overwhelmed, and obliterated by the divine presence. Junayd's articulation of the annihilation of the ego-self in union with the divine became a centerpiece of Islamic mystical thought. Junayd and other early Sufis grounded this concept of mystical union in the famous divine saying: "When my servant draws near to me through obligatory and free devotions . . . I become the hearing with which he hears, the seeing with which he sees, the hands with which he touches, the feet with which he walks, and the tongue with which he speaks."[4]

While the Baghdad and Basra regions of Iraq were experiencing a flowering of Sufi thought, the Iranian region of Khurasan was becoming another center of the new movement. As is the case with many early Sufis, we know the sayings of the most famous Khurasan mystic, Abu Yazid (or Bayezid) Bistami (d. ca. 261/875), only through oral traditions. The Bistami we know varies radically according to the collector of the sayings. In some accounts, he is a radical ascetic and shari'a absolutist. In other portraits, he is willing to break the laws of ritual purity as a way of calling blame upon himself, to keep himself and his followers from falling into the trap of venerating his own person rather than the one deity. The different Bistamis are in fact complementary; in neither case does Bistami reject the Qur'anic polarity of sacred/prohibited *(ḥarām)* and allowed *(ḥalāl)*. Rather, he pushes the polarity to its extreme, and his famous mystical utterances emerge from that polarity.

Hallaj was another master of the mystical utterance, including the famous "I am the real." This statement was interpreted by defenders of Hallaj in the same way that Bistami's famous saying "Glory be to me" was interpreted by his defenders: as the divine voice speaking through the mystic whose ego-self has become annihilated in his love of the divine beloved. Hallaj had studied with Tustari and Junayd, but he eventually parted ways with them. He insisted on confronting society with the more radical Sufi paradoxes, rather than using them more discreetly within a select circle of followers. His execution in Baghdad in 304/922, for complex reasons involving political intrigue as much as theology, became one of the most famous events in the history of Sufism and is debated down to the present day.

One of Hallaj's surviving works includes a memorable interpretation of Iblis, the closest spirit-being next to Allah, who refused the divine command to prostrate himself before the newly created Adam (Sura 2:30–33; 38:71–75), and thus was expelled from heaven for disobedience and became the cursed Satan. In Hallaj's text, Iblis defends himself by saying that he was an absolute monotheist and that he could never bow before any other being than the one deity, even at the divine command. Drawing on the poetic tradition, Iblis presents himself as the loyal lover who will not abandon loyalty to the beloved (in his case his monotheism) even at the cost of annihilation, or worse, eternal separation from the beloved. Drawing on the sophisticated theological disputes over human free will and divine predetermination, Iblis claims that Allah had eternally known that Iblis was an absolute monotheist and would never bow before an "other-than-God" and thus had eternally forewilled Iblis's self-sacrificing disobedience to the command. Finally Iblis suggests a dynamic coincidence of opposites in which farness and nearness from the beloved have become the same for one totally consumed by love for the beloved. Although Hallaj's writings on Iblis are not a standard part of Sufi curriculum, they were influential within Sufism (through the commentaries on them by Ruzbehan Baqli [d. 606/1209]), and have remained a source of interest and creativity within the Islamic world, as well as attracting the attention of artists and scholars from outside the world of Islam.

The final second-period figure represented in this volume is Niffari (d. 354/965). Unlike Tustari and Junayd, Niffari does not appear in the official chain *(silsila)* of Sufi masters, and thus is not a central figure in institutionalized Sufism. Yet his sayings, collected by later followers, are among the more distinctive and compelling examples of Islamic mysticism, and have been widely appreciated within Islam and by non-Islamic readers as well.

The Formative Period of Sufi Literature

Islamic spirituality entered a new phase with Abu Nasr as-Sarraj (d. 378/988) and his *Book of Flashes*. By Sarraj's time, tensions were felt within Sufism (between various followers of Tustari and the followers of Bistami, for example), and between the Sufis and other Muslim intellectuals—as would only be natural given the explosive growth and power of the Sufi movement in the preceding 200 years. Sarraj helped inaugurate the systematic explication of Sufism as a way of life by carefully and explicitly grounding it in the Qur'an and the shari'a. He also placed the paradoxes and ecstatic utterances of the Sufis into context and attempted to harmonize the tensions between followers of Junayd and followers of Bistami. Sarraj articulated the virtues propounded by Rabi'a and Muhasibi (trust-in-God, active acceptance, critical self-examination) into a dialectical movement of seven stages along the Sufi path. He also integrated the various reflections of Sufi mystical experience into a psychology of extraordinary states—from bliss to awe to terror—that could come upon the Sufi without warning or will.

Other major works followed immediately. Sulami (d. 412/1021) preserved the great early Sufi interpretations, including those of Tustari and

Ja'far mentioned above. His *Ranks of the Friends of God* portrays the early Sufi "godfriends" in a style that uses the full hadith *isnād* (chain of authorities) for each saying, and continually reinforces the grounding of Sufism in the shari'a. By using the *isnād* form for the sayings of the Sufis, and by beginning each chapter with a formal hadith of the Prophet, with full *isnād*, Sulami integrates within Sufism a formal chain of authority. He places Sufi tradition within the context of a "passing on" of tradition through a chain of personal human contacts.[5] The *isnād* format also allows the codification of early Sufi tradition in a manner that can be taught through the schools.

Culminating early Sufism is the work of Qushayri (d. 465/1074). In addition to a Qur'anic commentary, Qushayri composed a Risala (treatise in letter form) that took the earlier writings of Sarraj, Abu Talib al-Makki (d. 386/966), and Sulami to a new level of literary and philosophical intricacy. One short section of the treatise is perhaps the most lucid introduction to Sufi thought ever written. In it Qushayri places twenty-seven key Sufi concepts within an intricate analytical framework, with each concept shown in its range of possible meanings and in both negative and positive lights. The section brings to a new level the Sufi synthesis of the poetic tradition with the mystical experience of passing away. Finally, Qushayri gives an in-depth analysis of the major concepts discussed in this introduction and present in all of the selections in this volume. Because early Sufi language demands a familiarity with these key concepts, I have placed Qushayri's work toward the beginning of this volume.[6] Qushayri will prepare the reader for the critical Sufi terms, and serve as a glossary for future reference when those terms need to be reviewed.[7]

The Age of 'Attar, Rumi, and Ibn 'Arabi

After Qushayri, a number of developments occurred within the wider Islamic world and within Sufism that radically altered the nature of Sufi literature. Al-Farabi and, most influentially for Sufism, Ibn Sina (Avicenna, d. ca. 428/1037), brought an entirely new modality of thought to Islam, partially modeled on Aristotle and other Greek thinkers. The further development of rationalist philosophy by Ibn Rushd (Averroes, d. 595/1198) led to a reaction against such philosophy by the Sufi writer Abu Hamid al-Ghazali (d. 505/1111). Ghazali succeeded in gaining widespread acceptance for Sufism at the expense of the philosophers. Despite the fact that he was trying to refute the philosophers, al-Ghazali was forced to use the categories of the philosophers in his refutations and thus helped give them wider circulation.

Within Sufism, much more organized structures were beginning to take shape, culminating in the system of brotherhoods, united around a single Sufi master and selection of texts and practices, more developed "free devotions" of Sufi Dhikr, *samā'* (musical audition), and dance, along with a systematization of the relationship between disciple and pupil.

The writings of 'Attar (d. 627/1230), Ibn 'Arabi (d. 638/1240), and Rumi (d. 672/1273) reflect this vast new world of thought, practice, and institution. For the most part these writings lie outside the purview of this volume. There is one exception, however, and to explain that exception it is necessary to take up the vexing and fascinating question of chronology.

Early Sufism and Non-Chronology

What has been offered here has been a brief and selective overview of some of the major figures of early Sufism. However, because many of the sayings of the early Sufis were passed on orally for generations or even centuries before being written down, it would be impossible to offer a chronology of early Sufism and equally impossible to present early Sufi texts in chronological order.

The mystical utterances of Bistami, for example, were collected and commented on by Junayd in a book attributed to him. Junayd's book on Bistami was lost, but Sarraj collected the Bistami utterances and Junayd's comments from the oral tradition, placed them within his own commentary, and placed the entire work within a section of his *Book of Flashes*. The sayings are attributed to Bistami (d. ca. 261/875), but Sarraj is not convinced Bistami actually said all of them. They were passed on in a book by Junayd (d. 297/910), but that book was lost. Sarraj (d. 378/988) collected them from the oral tradition and placed them in his work. Where in a chronological presentation would we put such a work?

An equally dramatic illustration concerns Rabi'a (d. 185/801). The vast majority of the sayings and anecdotes of Rabi'a occur very late. Indeed, it is not until 'Attar that we have a relatively full presentation. Thus one of the earliest Sufis has her sayings preserved in the writings of the fourth period of Sufi thought. In choosing selections for this volume and in choosing the arrangement of those selections, any notion of strict chronology was out of the question. The volume is meant to focus on the early period of Sufism, yet many of the sayings of one of the earliest Sufis, Rabi'a, are preserved only in the work of a much later writer. The issues of oral tradition, written tradition, and modes of transmission are simply too complex for easy boundaries. To exclude Rabi'a and the fascinating issues her sayings raise concerning mysticism and gender on the basis of the criterion of composition of the written text would be to reinforce the written over the oral in a way that does not reflect the way Islamic tradition works and does not offer any particularly cogent value of its own.

The selections here have been chosen and arranged with an effort at partial chronology (according to the date of the author of the sayings, not the compiler), but with special attention to the principle of familiarization described in the Note to the Reader. They are meant to allow a progressive entry into the intricate world of Sufi vocabulary, each selection building on the previous selection.[8]

EARLY ISLAMIC MYSTICISM

SUFI, QUR'AN, MI`RAJ, POETIC AND THEOLOGICAL WRITINGS

1

Sources of Islamic Mysticism

♦ ♦ ♦

THE QUR'AN

Introduction

From the perspective of Sufism, it makes little sense to single out a few passages from the Qur'an as mystical; Sufis view their thought and way of life as Qur'anic in every sense. Examples below will show that even those Qur'anic passages that might seem resistant to mystical interpretation can be the occasion for powerful Sufi exegesis. Any passage in the Qur'an could be—and was—integrated into the Sufi view of life—or, conversely, the Sufi view of life was grounded in the Qur'an as a whole. Indeed, Sufi literature is woven around a core of Qur'anic language. As is common in many varieties of Islamic literature, in Sufi writings the Qur'an does not need to be formally "cited"—a simple Qur'anic phrase would be enough to generate a successful allusion to the verse or passage from which the phrase was taken.[1]

On the other hand, there have been a number of passages of the Qur'an to which the early Sufis came back to time and time again. Below are English renditions of those passages.[2] Explanatory comments introduce various kinds of Qur'anic discourse, with the Qur'anic renditions following. The commentary at this point is meant to introduce the reader to these passages in their Qur'anic context, to allow Qur'anic passages to be appreciated in their own right. The specific role these passages play in Sufism will be highlighted throughout the later chapters of this volume.

The passages below focus on the following key moments: creation, prophetic inspiration, and the day of judgment or moment of truth. Each of these moments offers particularly close contact between the human and the divine. Each becomes a paradigm for Sufi thought and praxis. A number of other Qur'anic passages are particularly important to the Sufi tradition, from the passages on the central revelation of unity (tawḥīd) *to the famous "Light Verse."*[3]

One of the more beloved passages of the Qur'an is the first section of the Sura of the Compassionate, which repeatedly links human understanding to divine munificence in bestowing existence and well-being. This passage is one of the primary sources of Sufi thought. A series of rhetorical questions is addressed in the dual grammatical form to two unnamed listeners: "Which of his signs will you deny?" This grammatical dual form (ān) *combines with other words that end naturally with the same sound to form an intense end-verse assonance throughout the sura. To give some indication of this, I have begun the sura by highlighting the first two end-words,* al-Raḥman *(the Compassionate) and* Qur'an, *using English qualitative accent marks to show how an English version of the assonance might sound.*

From the Sura of the Compassionate (al-Raḥmān): 55:1–34

The Rahmán
Who taught the Qur'án
Who created humankind
And taught them the declaration
The sun and the moon in their reckoning
The star and the trees bowed low in prayer
Heaven he raised up and the balance set down
  Do not oppress in the balance
  Mark the proper weight and do not cheat in the balance
And the earth he placed down for humankind
In it are fruit and date palms with unfolding calyxes
And the kernel in the blade of grain and the fragrant herb
Which of the signs of your lord will the two of you deny?[4]

He created the human being from wet clay like that of a potter
And created the jinn from smokeless fire
Which of the signs of your lord will the two of you deny?[5]

Lord of the Easts and lord of the Wests
Which of the signs of your lord will the two of you deny?

He brought the two seas together until they met
Between them a barrier never to be breached
Which of the signs of your lord will the two of you deny?

From it are taken pearl and coral
Which of the signs of your lord will the two of you deny?

His are ships set up upon the seas like landmarks
Which of the signs of your lord will the two of you deny?

Everything upon it passes away
Only the face of your lord endures, majestic and giving.
Which of the signs of your lord will the two of you deny?

Those in the heavens and the earth beseech him
In every day he is in a [different] condition
Which of the signs of your lord will the two of you deny?

We shall make time for you, O you two weighty ones![6]
Which of the signs of your lord will the two of you deny?

O tribes of jinn and tribes of humankind,
  if you are able to break through the regions of the heavens and earth
    then break through!
  you will not break through without sovereign power!
Which of the signs of your lord will the two of you deny?

The Creation of Adam and Adam's Status as Regent

In Islam, Adam, despite his weakness and fall, is considered a prophet (nabī). *The Qur'anic accounts of the creation of Adam center on several key elements: Adam's being created as a* khalīfa *(caliph or regent) of Allah on earth; the molding of Adam out of clay and the divine's breathing into Adam of the spirit* (rūḥ); *the objection of the angels to the creation of a creature that would "corrupt the earth and spill blood."*

In the following passage, Allah announces his intention to create Adam as a regent (khalīfa) *on the earth. When the angels question the creation of a being who will "corrupt the earth and spill blood," the divine voice asks if they know "the names." They reply that they know only what they have been told. After Adam teaches them the names, they are commanded to prostrate themselves, that is, assume the position of Islamic ritual prayer* (sajada) *before Adam. One of the heavenly company, Iblis, refuses and as a result is ultimately exiled from the divine presence and becomes known as Satan,* ash-shayṭān.[7]

The exact nature of the special knowledge of Adam, the knowledge of the names, is a matter of rich speculation within Qur'anic commentary. Do the names represent the names of the angels? Or do they represent the names of all creatures?[8] *In Sufism, the names are often thought to represent the divine names, the various manifestations of the divine in the forms of predications used in the Qur'an (the all-hearing, the all-seeing, the compassionate, etc.). However the names might be interpreted, Adam is seen as containing, despite his human mortality and weakness, a special kind of knowledge or wisdom, which for some Sufis will become the archetype of mystical knowledge* (ma'rifa). *The angels' objections to the creation of Adam and Iblis's refusal to bow before Adam showed not only his pride but also his ignorance of Adam's true qualities. Some other Sufis will offer a different evaluation of Adam and Iblis. They will view Iblis's refusal to bow before Adam, at least in part, as an affirmation of pure monotheism, the refusal to bow to anything other than the one God, even at the risk of exile, torment, and separation from the divine beloved.*

In the two passages on Adam's creation that follow in this section, Iblis's refusal to bow before Adam is woven into a direct reference to Adam's special place in the cosmos because of his having been molded from clay by the "two hands" of God, and because of his having received the spirit (rūḥ) *breathed into him by the deity. There are sudden shifts of grammatical person, typical of Qur'anic discourse, so that the deity is referred to at times in the third person singular, at times in the first person singular, and at times in the first person plural, "we." In addition, the passages start out with a relative clause, "when," which is never completed, another particularity of Qur'anic discourse.*

The Creation and Regency of Adam, Sura 2:30–34:

When your lord said to the angels:
I am going to place a regent *(khalīfa)* on the earth,
and they said: Will you place one there
who will corrupt it and spill blood,
while we recite your praises and exalt you?

He said: I know what you do not know.
  Then he taught Adam all the names
and showed everything to the angels, saying:
tell me their names, if you are sincere.
  They said: praise be to you,
we know only what you have taught us,
you are the all-knowing, the most wise.
  He said: O Adam, tell them their names,
and when he had told them the names,
he said: did I not tell you that I know
what is hidden in the heavens and earth,
and know what you disclose and know what you hide?
  Then we told the angels
to bow before Adam
and they did, except for Iblis,
who was scornful and acted proud,
and became an unbeliever.[9]

The Creation of Adam and the Pride of Iblis, Sura 38:71–75:

  When your lord said to the angels,
I am going to create a person *(bashar)* from clay.
  When I have shaped it
and breathed into it of my spirit,
fall bowing before it.
  All the angels fell bowing together
  Except Iblis who acted proud
and became an unbeliever.
  He said: O Iblis
what has prevented you from bowing
before what I created with my two hands?
Are you too proud or are you too lofty?[10]

MARYAM, 'ISA (JESUS), AND THE SPIRIT (19:16–27)

Jesus, along with Muhammad, is singled out in the Qur'an for his special relationship to the spirit (rūḥ). *Like Adam, he was brought to life directly through "inspiriting," that is, the deity's breathing into him of the spirit. He can perform miracles, such as bringing a bird back to life, and is thereby associated also with the life-force itself. The passage selected below shows how Jesus' very conception was through the spirit. It also gives one of the more dramatic and beloved discussions of a female figure in the Qur'an, a figure who was to become a paradigm for female Sufi saints such as Rabi'a. In the passage, the spirit comes to Maryam in the form of a* bashar *(human being). Though the term* bashar *is not gender-specific, Maryam acts as if it were a male she was confronting.*

And recall in the book Maryam,
when she withdrew from her people to a place facing the East

And veiled herself from them. We sent her our spirit which
took on the likeness of a fully formed human being.

She said: I take refuge in the Compassionate from you. Would
that your intentions were pure!

He said: I am only a messenger from your lord, sent to bestow
upon you a son without blemish.

She said: How can I have a son when no person has touched
me and I have not been unchaste?

He said: So it is! Your lord said: for me it is easy! We will
make it a sign for humankind and a mercy from us—and the
matter was decreed.

She conceived him and withdrew to a distant place.

The birth pangs drove her to the trunk of a date palm. She
said: I wish I were dead and forgotten!

A voice called to her from below: Don't grieve. Your lord has
placed a stream below you.

Sway the tree trunk toward you and ripe dates will shower
down around.

Eat and drink and be comforted. If you meet any human, say:
I have consecrated a fast to the compassionate and cannot
speak today to any human being.

She carried him forth to her people. They said: Maryam, you have
brought forth a wonder!

The Prophethood of Muhammad

Another key passage in the Qur'an for Sufism is the first section of the Sura of the Star (53:1–18), in which Muhammad's prophetic visions are depicted. The sura begins with the divine voice swearing by the setting star that "your companion" has not gone astray. The reference to "your companion" is clearly a reference to Muhammad as the receiver of the vision in question. This vision is also called an inspiration (waḥy) *and is explicitly said not to be rooted in desire* (hawā), *which the Qur'an associates with the inspiration of the poets. The object of vision is never actually described. Instead, the text evokes the process of vision by tracing a movement along the highest horizon and then a descent and drawing near of what is seen at the distance of "two bows' lengths." The passage ends with an affirmation of the validity of the vision (the heart of the prophet "did not lie in what he saw"). This affirmation becomes a proof text for Sufism's claim that the locus of spiritual vision and mystical knowledge is the heart.*

Sūrat an-Najm (The Sura of the Star) *53:1–12*

By the star when it sets
Your companion has not gone astray nor is he deluded
He does not speak out of desire
It is nothing less than an inspiration inspired
Taught to him by one of great power
And strength that stretched out over
While on the highest horizon
Then drew near and descended
At a distance of two bows' lengths or nearer
He revealed in his servant what he revealed
The heart did not lie in what it saw
Will you then dispute with him on his vision?

In a second passage that follows directly on the first, the divine voice, speaking of Muhammad again in the third person, describes another vision ("He saw it again a second time"). Here, "the lote tree of the furthest limit" (sidrat al-muntahā) *is placed in or near the enigmatic "garden of sanctuary"* (jannat al-ma'wā). *We are told almost nothing about the tree, except that it was "enveloped" or "shrouded." Of key importance is the "gaze" of the Prophet, which neither "turns aside"* (zāghā) *nor "overreaches"* (ṭaghā). *This one verse was to become the paradigm for Sufi understanding of the mystical gaze and the proper state of the Sufi in contemplation.*

When the Qur'an states "He saw it again a second time," the antecedent of the pronoun (hu, *it/him) is unstated, and thus the referent of the "it" is not determinable from the passage. The identity of the referent becomes a matter of controversy within the tradition, with the debate centering on whether the deity can be seen in this world. Those for whom the vision of the divine can occur only in the afterlife tend to interpret the it/he as referring to the messenger-angel Gabriel. This key passage and the debate over vision of the deity in this life can always be heard beneath the highly complex Sufi discourse on the nature of Sufi witnessing* (mushāhada) *and vision* (ru'ya).[11]

Sūrat an-Najm, 53:13–18

He saw it descending another time
At the lote tree of the furthest limit
Therein was the garden of sanctuary
When there enveloped the tree what enveloped it
His gaze did not turn aside nor did it overreach
He had seen the signs of his lord, great signs.

The passages on Muhammad's vision were collated by early Muslims with the Qur'anic verse (17:1) recalling the Prophet's night journey (isrā') *from the sacred place of prayer* (al-masjid al-ḥarām) *to the furthest place of prayer* (al-masjid al-aqsā). *The verse begins with a direct discourse in which the deity speaks of itself as the one who took his servant (Muhammad) on the night journey. Then the Qur'anic voice speaks of the divine in the first person plural ("we have blessed") and Muhammad in the third person singular ("in order to show him our signs"). At the end of the verse, however, it is the divine that is referred to in the third-person plural (he is the All-Hearing* [as-samī'], *the All-Perceiving* [al-baṣīr]*).*

Although this rapid switch in voice can be confusing for the reader encountering the Qur'an for the first time, one soon becomes habituated to the way in which these person-changes occur. As mentioned above, some of the surprise and initial ambiguity can be cleared up by capitalizing pronouns referential of the divine, but such a procedure ultimately obscures the voice-and-person interplay that is at the heart of the Qur'an's sense of intimacy.

> Glory to the one who took his servant on a night journey from the sacred place of prayer to the furthest place of prayer upon which we have sent down our blessing, that we might show him some of our signs. He is the all-hearing, the all-seeing.

This cryptic Qur'anic verse was elaborated on in the sayings (the hadith) of the Prophet Muhammad. According to these sayings, Muhammad was taken on a night journey from Mecca to Jerusalem on a divinely sent creature called Buraq, and from Jerusalem made his Mi'raj (ascent) in the company of Gabriel, through the seven heavens (and in some accounts down through the seven layers of hell). Through the association of the night journey verse with the vision passages, accounts of the Mi'raj *will often locate the lote tree of the furthest boundary or the garden of sanctuary, either explicitly or through allusion, within the itinerary of the heavenly journey.*[12]

Also associated with Muhammad's prophecy is the short, exquisite sūrat al-qadr *(sura of destiny or power). In highly lyrical form, the night of the Prophet's revelation is evoked, with the spirit* (rūḥ) *coming down during that night or upon that night. Constructed around this sura is the beautiful ritual of the night of* qadr*, one of the last odd-numbered nights of the holy month of Ramadan. The festival of the night of qadr is often the time for a child's first attempt at fasting during Ramadan. It is also the occasion of a vigil during which the individual, family, or community will stay up throughout the night in order to be close to the revelation of the destiny for the following year. The night of* qadr *comes at the end of a month of celebration and fasting, during which the normal rhythms of day and night, eating and sleeping, are transformed. The observance of the night of* qadr *can involve a full evening and night of prayers and meditation. This night might be considered one of the more mystical moments of Islamic life, even among those who do not consider themselves Sufis. Its celebrants consider it a moment when the divine and the human are particularly close to one another, when the relationship between the two is particularly intimate.*

Surat al-Qadr also contains within it an acute version of the gender dynamic found throughout the Qur'an, but most often lost in translation. In this sura, the phrase "night of fate" is grammatically feminine, and the re-

sultant pronouns and feminine gendered verbal inflections are patterned throughout the sura in a delicate balance with masculine grammatical constructions. There is an undertone of implicit personification of the night as a woman, but that personification is never complete. Because the personification is not complete, translators do not feel justified in using the English feminine pronouns, but when the neuter is used, the gender balance—one of the most delicate aspects of both Qur'anic and Sufi discourse—is lost. Below are two translations, one that uses the standard "it" to translate the pronouns, and one that uses the masculine and feminine pronouns in order to show the gender dynamic. The sura is built around an end-verse assonance ending in r; *in the first translation below, the original Arabic terms* qadr *and* amr *indicate this assonance and preserve the crucial ambiguities of the two key words.* Qadr *can mean either destiny or power, and its precise sense in the sura seems to lie in between these two English choices.* Amr *can mean "command" or it can be used in a much more general way to indicate any matter, situation, or state of affairs. In the second translation, English terms have been chosen in order to give a fluent reading in English.*

The Sura of Destiny (al-Qadr, Sura 97)
The Sura of Qadr

VERSION 1, UNGENDERED:

1. We sent it down on the night of *qadr*

2. And what could let you know what the night of *qadr* is

3. The night of *qadr* is better than a thousand months

4. The angels and the spirit come down on it by leave of their lord from every *amr*

5. Peace it is until the rise of dawn

VERSION 2, GENDERED:

1. We sent him down on the night of destiny

2. And what could let you know what the night of destiny is

3. The night of destiny is better than a thousand months

4. The angels and the spirit come down within her by leave of their lord from every command

5. Peace she is until the rise of dawn

Moses and Joseph

The story of Moses is scattered throughout forty-four passages of the Qur'an, in typically nonnarrative fashion. However, certain short pericopes concerning Moses have become central to the Sufi tradition. In the first example here, Moses becomes the disciple of an unnamed teacher who engages in a series of acts that baffle Moses. In later tradition, this teacher is known as Khidr or Khadir. Khidr becomes a key figure for Sufis, particularly when their activities might seem baffling from a more conventional point of view. Just as Khidr's actions were baffling even to so great a prophet as Moses, so the Sufi's actions might well seem, from the outside, puzzling or even outrageous. Khidr also becomes the teacher (shaykh) par excellence for any Sufi not attached to a particular teacher at the time.

The story begins with Moses seeking the "confluence of the two seas." There is a mysterious episode in which Moses and his squire (fatā) *have forgotten a fish they were planning to eat. The fish has made its way back to the sea, and they retrace their steps to find it. This episode has been interpreted by some as a reference to the waters of immortality, the fish coming alive again in them and escaping to the sea.*[13] *At any rate, when they retrace their steps, they come across a mysterious stranger that the divine voice (speaking through the first person plural) describes as "our servant." This servant has been singled out for a "special knowledge," or "knowledge of [the deity's] core being,"* ('ilm ladunnī). *Moses joins up with the mysterious teacher, who agrees to let Moses accompany him as long as he does not ask about his actions. He then proceeds to engage in three outrageous acts. When Moses asks him about each act in turn, the stranger finally leaves the prophet Moses behind. Before leaving him, however, he gives Moses the* ta'wīl *or inner interpretation of his actions. Like the theologians* (mutakallimūn) *and the Shi'ites, many Sufis practiced an inner interpretation that would explain texts and events beyond their apparent, plain-sense meaning. Khidr becomes a touchstone for this kind of interpretation.*

Moses (Musa) and Khidr 18:60–82

Then Musa said to his squire: I will not quit until I reach the confluence of the two seas, or else I will march on continually.

And when they reached the meeting of the seas, they found that they forgot to take their fish, which made its way to the sea through a hidden channel.

When they had proceeded further, he said to his squire: Bring us breakfast. What we have found in this journey of ours is exhaustion.

He replied: Did you notice that when we took refuge in the rock, I forgot the fish? It could only have been Satan that made me forget to remember it. In a marvelous fashion, it has made its way back to the sea.

He said: That is what we have been seeking! So they retraced their own tracks.

There they found one of our servants, to whom we had granted compassion and whom we had taught the special knowledge.

Musa said to him: May I follow you in order to learn the integrity of action you have been taught?

He replied: You will not be able to keep patience with me.

How can you be patient in what your experience has not encompassed?

He said: You will find me patient, God willing. I will not cross your command.

He replied: If you follow me, you must not ask me about anything until I mention the matter myself.

They set out. When they had boarded a ship, he gouged a hole in it. Musa said: You've gouged a hole in order to drown the passengers. You've committed a terrible crime!

He said: Did I not say you would not be able to keep patience with me?

Musa answered: Do not hold me to account for my forgetfulness and do not be harsh with me.

They set out again until they met a young boy. He killed him. Musa said: You've killed a person who was innocent of any killing. You've committed an atrocity!

He said: Did I not say you would not be able to be patient with me?

[Musa] said: If I ask you about anything else, cut me off from your company. You will be excused on my part.

They set out until they came to a town and asked its people for food, but they refused them hospitality. They came upon a wall on the point of collapsing. He repaired it. Musa said: If you had wanted, you could have taken payment.

He said: This is the parting of our ways. Now I'll give you the inner interpretation *(ta'wīl)* of what you couldn't bear with patience. As for the ship, it belonged to the poor who worked the sea. I wanted to cripple it, because just behind them was a king who was seizing by force every ship.

As for the boy, his parents were believers *(muslim)*. I had reason to fear that he would oppress them with abuse and disbelief.

We wanted their lord to substitute for him one who was more pure of heart and compassionate.

And as for the wall—there were a pair of orphans in town who had a treasure under it. Their father had been an upright man and your lord wished that they should retrieve the treasure upon reaching maturity, as a mercy from your lord. I did not act by my own command. This is the inner interpretation of what you could not bear with patience.

The second passage is the brief depiction of Moses' vision (or rather near vision) of the deity on Mount Sinai:

Moses on Mount Sinai 7:142–143

7:142 We designated for Musa thirty nights and we completed them with ten more; the appointed time of his lord was thus complete at forty nights. Musa said to his brother Harun: "Govern in my place among my people and act in the best interest; do not follow the way of those who would cause corruption."

7:143 When Moses arrived at our appointed time and his lord spoke to him, he said: "Lord, show me that I might gaze upon you." He said: "You will not see me. Look instead at the mountain. If it stays in place, you will see me." But when its lord manifested itself to the mountain, he caused it to shatter and Moses was struck down unconscious. When he awoke, he said: "Praise be to you! I have turned back to you in repentance and I am the first of the believers."

In the third passage, the divine voice pronounces: "Indeed I, I am your lord." Later exegetes interpreted this phrase in a manner similar to mystical interpretations of the biblical "I am that I am" (ehyeh asher ehyeh), *that is, as a divine name that turns back on itself, affirming that its essence is its existence, that it transcends any quiddity, definition, or name in the referential sense:*

Moses and the Fire: Sura 20:9–15

Has the account of Moses reached you? How he saw a fire and said to his people: "Stay behind, I make out a fire. Perhaps I can return from it with an ember or find at the fire some guidance. When he approached it, a voice called to him: "O Musa! Indeed I, I am your lord. Take off your sandals. You are in the sanctified valley of Ṭuwā. I am the one who selected you, so listen to what is revealed! I, I am Allah, there is no god but I. Worship me and perform the prayer in remembrance of me. The hour is coming. I almost hide it completely that each person might be requited for her labor.[14]

JOSEPH AS MASTER OF *TA'WĪL*

Another exemplar of the ability to see into the interior or hidden meanings of things is the Qur'anic prophet Joseph, whose mastery of the art of ta'wīl *led his brothers to throw him into a well. In the following passage, Joseph has a vision of the stars, sun, and moon bowing down to him in prayer, a vision his father Ya'qūb (Jacob) attributes to his knowledge of inner interpretation. The passage ends with Joseph, the interpreter of signs, becoming a sign for others who seek meaning. Verses 1–3, with their evocations of the mysterious letters* alif, lām, ra', *introduce the crucial topic of signs:*

Alif Lam Ra: These are signs (or verses, *āyāt*) of the book that makes clear.

We sent down an Arabic Qur'an, that you might perhaps be heedful.

We recounted to you the best of stories, in our inspiring in you the Qur'an, even if before that you were heedless.

When Joseph said to his father: O Father, I saw eleven stars and the sun and moon, I saw them bowing to me in prayer!

He said: Do not tell your vision to your brothers or they will contrive a plot against you; Satan to humankind is an enemy most clear.

In this way your lord chooses to teach the interpretation of events. He completes his bestowal upon you, and upon the family of Ya'qub, as he completed it upon your ancestors in earlier times, upon Ibrahim and Ishaq.

Apocalypse and Mysticism

Among the passages from the Qur'an that have been most admired—by Muslims and Western scholars alike—are the short, hymnic suras that evoke the yawm ad-dīn *(the day of judgment, moment of truth). In addition to the often noted beauty and power of the imagery, these suras contain the kind of gender dynamic noted above in connection with* sūrat al-qadr. *From assonance, phonological parallelism, and play on grammatical gender, sound figures and gender figures are created.*

These hymnic suras are quite different from other passages in the Qur'an (usually associated with the later Meccan and Medinan periods) in which the sense of reward and punishment, enticement and threat, is more prominent. In these short passages, the time of this radical "tearing of the veil" in which each person will confront his or her true reality and final destiny is left unspecified. In each case, there is a cosmic inversion. What seems secure and enduring (the earth, the mountains, the heavens, the seas, the grave) crumbles, melts, or is torn away, and what seems intangible (a mote's weight of kindness, a mote's weight of meanness) is revealed as ontologically absolute.

From the beginning of Sufi literature, there was a growing tendency to bring the mystical encounter close to, even parallel to, the eschatological encounter—without ever collapsing the two. The reality revealed in the tearing of the veil lies from one point of view in the future, in the "after," but in much of Sufism it also resides within or behind the present moment as an "eternal now."

From the Sura of the Tearing (Sūrat al-Infiṭār 82:1–6)

When the sky is torn
When the stars are scattered
When the seas boil over
When the tombs burst open
Then a person will know what she has given and what she has held back
O humankind, what has deluded you from your generous lord.

Sūrat al-qāri'a *(the sura of the calamity, striking, or smiting) is composed within a pyramid structure. The sura begins in a hymnic mode, with repetition of words and of similar sound units. In the center it stretches out into longer verses and more elaborate images, with striking similes for the ontological inversion that occurs on the final day (a day on which humankind will be like scattered moths). The sura then evokes the scales of justice in which human deeds are weighed. The ending of the sura returns to the hymnic mode and introduces a strange term:* hāwiya, *a term that can mean abyss or a woman bereft of her child. The term is transformed into a sound and gender figure through its placement at the culmination of a series of feminine constructions that are metrically, syntactically, and phonologically stressed.*[15]

The Sura of the Smiting (Sūrat al-Qāri'a)

The *qāri'a*
What is the *qāri'a*
What can let you know what the *qāri'a* is
A day humankind are like scattered moths
And mountains are like wool dyed and carded
Whoever's scales weigh heavy

His is a life that is pleasing
Whoever's scales weigh light
His mother is *hāwiya*
What can let you know what she is
Raging fire.

In the famous Sura of the Quaking (al-zalzala *or* al-zilzāl), *as opposed to the cosmic apocalypse where the sky is ripped apart, there is what might be called a chthonic apocalypse, with the earth opening up to yield her secrets. The bearing forth of these secrets is conveyed through a birth metaphor, with the earth* (al-arḍ) *in the feminine gender and governing a series of feminine grammatical constructions.*

The Sura of the Quaking (Sūrat al-Zalzala)

When the earth is shaken, quaking
And she yields up her burdens
And someone says "What is with her"
At that time she will tell her news
[How] her lord inspired [in] her
At that time people will straggle forth
  in scattered groups to see their deeds
Whoever does a mote's weight good will see it
Whoever does a mote's weight wrong will see it.

TAWḤĪD

All of the themes discussed in connection with the three archetypal moments are integrated throughout the Qur'an with the affirmation of unity; the ground of Qur'anic revelation is the affirmation of divine unity. The Sufis engaged in a sophisticated meditation on the various meanings of such unity, using a variety of terms for unity: aḥadiyya, waḥdaniyya, waḥadiyya, *all based on the Arabic root for "one":* a(w)/ḥ/d. *A related key term is* tawḥīd, *which refers to the activity of affirming divine unity.*[16] *The most famous Qur'anic passage of* tawḥīd *is among the short suras of the Qur'an. In this passage, Allah is affirmed as one, as not begetting, and as not begotten, and as* ṣamad, *an enigmatic term in classical Arabic, with connotations of perdurance and indestructibility.*[17]

Sura 112: Sincerity (Sūrat al-Ikhlās _or_ Tawḥīd)

Say he is Allahu *aḥad* (one)
Allahu the *ṣamad*
Not begetting, not begotten,
  And having for an equal *aḥad* (no one)

Another Qur'anic phrase asserting that there is no God but God/Allah is so central to Qur'anic discourse that it has a name of its own, the tahlīl. *To note the centrality of the phrase within Islam, it is sufficient to trace its complex embedding within the crucial ritual elements of Islam as a whole and Sufism in particular. For example, the* tahlīl *makes up the first section of the* shahāda, *the Islamic profession of faith: "There is no god but God and Muhammad is his Messenger." In turn, the* shahāda *makes up the central section of the call to prayer* (idh'ān) *that is chanted five times per day from the minarets around the world and that resonates across the cities, towns, and villages and through the lives of their Muslim inhabitants. The effectiveness of the* tahlīl *within the call-to-prayer chant is partially bound up with the rhythm and assonance of the phrase, a rhythm and assonance that capture in particularly condensed form the distinctive rhythmic and assonantal character of Qur'anic language:*

	lā	ilāha	illa	llāh
(there is)	*no*	*god*	*but*	*God*

It is not surprising then that the tahlīl *becomes the primary Sufi* dhikr, *a phrase repeated continually (aloud or mentally) as a form of devotion and meditation.*

These are only a few Qur'anic texts that have been considered exemplars of Islamic spirituality and that are central to Sufi thought and writings. The spirituality of these passages extends far beyond the Sufi world, however, into every aspect of Islamic culture. These texts are presented in this section for appreciation on their own. The reader will encounter them anew in their Sufi context throughout the volume, and other key texts from the Qur'an will be presented in the following chapters when the texts allude to them.

♦ ♦ ♦

THE MI'RAJ (SACRED COSMOLOGY AND MYSTICAL ORIENTATION)

INTRODUCTION

The Mi'raj, Muhammad's ascent through the seven heavens to the divine throne, was paradigmatic for Sufi understandings of their own mystical journeys.[18] *Even when Sufis are not alluding to the Mi'raj openly (as in the case of Abu Yazid's Mi'raj, Chapter 7 in this volume), Muhammad's ascent was a continual subtext, evoked by subtle allusions to inspiration, vision of the divine, and the gaze of the contemplator.*

The Mi'raj is not depicted within any specificity in the Qur'an. The major Qur'anic proof-text for the tradition is the first verse of Sura 19:

The Night-Journey Verse (17:1)

> Glory to the one who took his servant on a night journey from the sacred place of prayer to the furthest place of prayer upon which we have sent down our blessing, that we might show him some of our signs. He is the All-Hearing, the All-Seeing.

This verse was collated with the depiction of Muhammad's prophetic vision (53:1–18), and elements from that vision, such as the lote tree, were incorporated into the topography of the ascent. It was also collated with another famous passage of the Qur'an, the "opening of Muhammad's breast." The short Qur'anic sura cited below became the proof-text for the extraction of Muhammad's heart and its purification in the waters of zamzam *(the waters opened up for Hagar at Mecca as she desperately searched for water for her dying son Isma'il).*

Did We Not Open Your Breast (al-Inshirāḥ: Sura 94)

> Did we not open your breast
> And take from you your burden
> Which was breaking your back

Did we not raise high your name in remembrance
With every hardship there is ease
With every hardship there is ease
When you are free, stand tall
And turn to your lord in longing.

The depictions of the Mi'raj seem to expand as the Islamic tradition grows into a variety of areas, with more elaborate accounts of the levels of hell and the physical descriptions of the prophets residing in the seven heavens. The Sufis, who drew on the "lote tree" passage in a psychological examination of mystical experience, also appropriated the full Mi'raj cosmology as a paradigm for mystical ascent.

Presented here is the account of Muhammad's Mi'raj from the authoritative hadith collection known as the Ṣaḥīḥ Muslim *(the "Sound" Collection of Muslim ibn al-Ḥajjāj [d. 261/874]).*[19] *The account of Muslim (the word "Muslim" here is a proper name) is one of the more extensive early accounts.*

In the early hadith accounts, key elements of the Qur'anic passages (the lote tree of the furthest boundary, the shrouding of the lote tree, the inspiration of Muhammad, the opening of the prophet's breast) are found in various levels of the prophet's ascent through the seven heavens. The Mi'raj accounts incorporate these Qur'anic themes into other major topics not mentioned in the Qur'an. Muhammad is taken to Jerusalem by a magical beast named Burāq. *In Jerusalem, Muhammad enters the sanctified house or house of sanctity* (bayt al-muqaddas, bayt al-maqdis). *From there he ascends through the seven heavens. At the culmination of his ascent, in the seventh heaven, he sees the "enlivened house" or "house of life"* (al-bayt al-ma'mūr)*—a celestial analogue to the "sacred house"* (al-bayt al-ḥarām). *These three* bayts*—abodes or temples—resonate down the long history of Islamic literature.*

Either before or after the vision of the lote tree (depending on the account), Muhammad comes before the divine presence and is commanded to enjoin his community to perform the prescribed ritual prayer fifty times per day. At the instigation of Moses he engages in a series of negotiations, finally coming away with five prayers that will earn the benefit of fifty prayers.

The hadith accounts offer some fascinating variations on this larger theme. In one account, Muhammad is portrayed as ascending through the heavens immediately after the opening of his breast; in that account his night-journey to the masjid al-aqsā *(furthest place of prayer) and the* bayt al-muqaddas *is ignored. The shrouding of the lote tree, one of the deeper, archetypal images in the Qur'anic account of Muhammad's prophetic vision, is given various depictions in the Mi'raj accounts. In one account, four rivers (the Nile, the Euphrates, and two rivers of paradise) stream forth from beneath the trunk of the lote tree.*[20]

At times the Mir'aj accounts need some commentary to guide the nonspecialist reader; this commentary is placed in italics. Both the hadith (traditions of Muhammad's sayings) and the sīra *accounts embed the phrase "he said"* (qāla) *within the narrative. In order to avoid sets of quotation marks, these references to the original narrator are placed in parentheses in the translations below. These "he said" phrases are a sign of something distinctive and critical in early Islamic literature: the performative voice of authoritative knowledge and blessing. The chain* (isnād) *of authorities is a feature not only of the hadith, but of the accounts of early Sufi sayings as well. The "he said" phrase serves as a constant reminder of this performative sense of language; it is as if the original voice of Muhammad were being made present and performed as it was channeled down through the chain of transmitters. To which person in the chain of authorities does the "he" refer? Clearly it refers to each of them, as the actual content of each saying of Muhammad (the* matn*) echoes down through to the last speaker. Though the English reader may not be familiar, as would the educated Muslim, with the lives and characters of the various named authorities, it is meaningful to preserve some sense of the full hadith form, with both* isnād *and* matn. *In the hadith, as in Sufi writings that model themselves on that genre, the act of transmitting and performing tradition is as important as the content of what is transmitted.*

The Mi'raj in the Saḥīḥ-Muslim Hadith

Shaybān ibn Farrūkh informed us that Ḥammād ibn Salama informed us that Thābit Lubnanī related from Anas ibn Mālik that the Envoy of God, blessings and peace on him, said:

I was brought Buraq, a tall, white beast, larger than a donkey and smaller than a mule. In each stride, he would place his hooves as far as his eyes could see.[21] (He said:) I was mounted on him and he brought me to the house of sanctuary *(bayt al-maqdisi)*. (He said:) I tied him on the tie-ring of the prophets. (He said:) Then I entered the place of prayer and there performed two *rak'as* of prayer. When I left, Jibril (Gabriel), peace on him, approached me with a vessel of wine and a vessel of milk. I chose the milk. Jibril, peace and blessings on him, said: You have chosen the innate character *(fiṭra)*.[22]

Then he took us up *('araja binā)*[23] to [the first] heaven. Jibril requested admittance. He was asked: "Who are you?" He said "Jibril." Jibril was asked: "Who is with you?" He replied, "Muhammad." He was asked: "Was he sent for?" He replied: "He was sent for." The heaven was opened before us, and there stood Adam! He received me warmly and invoked blessings for me.

Then he took me up to the second heaven. Jibril requested admittance. He was asked: "Who are you?" He said "Jibril." Jibril was asked: "Who is with you?" He replied, "Muhammad." He was asked: "Was he sent for?" He replied: "He was sent for." The heaven was opened before us, and there stood my maternal relatives Jesus, the son of Mary ('Isā ibn Maryam), and John, the son of Zakaraya (Yaḥyā ibn Zakarayyā'), God's blessings on them both. They received me warmly and invoked blessings for me.

Then he took me up to the third heaven. Jibril requested admittance. He was asked: "Who are you?" He said "Jibril." Jibril was asked: "Who is with you?" He replied, "Muhammad." He was asked: "Was he sent for?" He replied: "He was sent for." The heaven was opened before us, and there, standing before me, was Joseph (Yusuf), endowed with half the world's beauty. He received me warmly and invoked blessings for me.

Then Jibril took me up to the fourth heaven. Jibril requested admittance. He was asked: "Who are you?" He said "Jibril." Jibril was asked: "Who is with you?" He replied, "Muhammad." He was asked: "Was he sent for?" He replied: "He was sent for." The heaven was opened before us, and there, standing before me, was Idris (Enoch).[24] He welcomed me and bid me well. Allah, Most High and Glorious, has said (19:57): "We took him up to a high station."

Then he took us up to the fifth heaven. Jibril requested admittance. He was asked: "Who are you?" He said "Jibril." Jibril was asked: "Who is with you?" He replied, "Muhammad." He was asked: "Was he sent for?" He replied: "He was sent for." The heaven was opened before us, and there, standing before me, was Aaron (Harun), peace and blessings on him. He received me warmly and invoked blessings for me.

Then he took us up to the sixth heaven. Jibril requested admittance. He was asked: "Who are you?" He said "Jibril." Jibril was asked: "Who is with you?" He replied, "Muhammad." He was asked: "Was he sent for?" He replied: "He was sent for." The heaven was opened before us, and there, standing before me, was Moses (Musa), peace and blessings on him. He received me warmly and invoked blessings for me.

Then he took us up to the seventh heaven. Jibril requested admittance. He was asked: "Who are you?" He said "Jibril." Jibril was asked: "Who is with you?" He replied, "Muhammad." He was asked: "Was he sent for?" He replied: "He was sent for." The heaven was opened before us, and there, before me, was Abraham, peace and blessings on him. He received me warmly and invoked blessings for me.

He was resting his back against the house of life *(al-bayt al-ma'mūr)* into which seventy thousand angels would disappear each day, not to return.

Then I was taken to the (53:14) "lote tree of the furthest boundary [*sidrat al-muntahā*]." Its leaves were like the ears of elephants and its fruits were as large as jugs of clay. (He said:) When by the command of its lord (53:16) "there enveloped the tree what enveloped it," it was transformed. None of the creatures of God could describe its beauty. (53:10) "Then Allah inspired in me what he inspired."

Allah gave me the obligation of fifty prayers every full day and night. When I descended to Musa (Moses), peace and blessings on him, he said: "What obligation did your lord place on your community *(umma)*?" I said: "Fifty prayers." He said: "Go back to your lord and ask him to lighten the burden. Your community is not capable of that. I myself tried the people of Israel *(banī isrā'īl)* and tested them." (He said:) So I went back up to my lord and said: "My lord, lighten the burden on my community." He took away five. I returned to Musa and said: "He took away five." He said: "Your community is still not capable of doing that. Go back up to your lord and ask him to lighten the burden."

(He said:) So I continued going back and forth between my lord, Most High and Blessed, and Musa, peace on him, until he said: "Muhammad, there are five prayers for every full day and night, and each prayer gains the credit of ten, making fifty. Whoever intends a good deed but does not perform it is credited with one good deed. For whoever performs it is credited with ten. Whoever intends an evil deed but does not perform it, receives no credit or discredit. Whoever performs it is discredited with one evil deed. (He said:) I descended again until I reached Musa, peace and blessings on him, and informed him of the issue. He said: "Return to your lord and ask him to lighten the burden." (The messenger of God, peace and blessings on him, said:) I replied: "I returned to my lord to the point that I am embarrassed."

In another version of the Mi'raj from Ṣaḥīḥ Muslim, *the ending is different, with the vision of the lote tree coming after the negotiations over the number of prayers.*

Ḥarmala ibn Yaḥyā at-Tujībī related to me that Ibn Wahb informed us that Yunus informed him on the authority of Ibn Shihāb on the authority of Anas ibn Mālik that Abu Dharr related that the Envoy of God, God's blessings and peace on him, said:

When I was in Mecca, the roof of my house was split open. Jibril, God's blessings and peace on him, came down and split my breast. Then he cleansed it with the water of *zamzam*. Then he brought a gold basin filled with wisdom and faith, which he emptied into my breast. Then he closed up my breast, grasped me by the hand, and took me up to [the first] heaven.

[Omitted here is an account of rise through the heavens and, on the authority of Ibn 'Abbās and Abu Habba al-Anṣārī, of the negotiations over the number of prayers that is almost identical to the versions given above].[25]

Moses said: "Return to your lord." I said: "I am embarrassed to return again." Then Jibril bore me off and took me to the lote tree of the furthest boundary. It was shrouded with colors that I could not recognize. (He said:) Then I was brought into the garden *(al-janna)*. It has domes of pearl and earth of musk.[26]

Yet another version in Ṣaḥīḥ Muslim *begins with the opening of Muhammad's chest, moves directly to the Mi'raj (with no account of the journey to Jerusalem), and places the test of wine and milk after the Mi'raj.*[27]

Muḥammad ibn al-Muthannā reported to us that Ibn Abū 'Adī, on the authority of Sa'īd on the authority of Qatāda on the authority of Anas ibn Mālik who might have said, on the authority of Mālik ibn Ṣa'ṣa'a, a man of his tribe, that the Prophet of God, peace and blessing on him, said:

While I was in my house, in a state halfway between waking and sleep, I heard someone say: "One of the three between the other two." I was taken and carried off. I was brought to a basin of gold in which there was the water of *zamzam*. My breast was opened as far as that. (Qatāda said: "I asked the one with me what he meant by 'that.' He replied: 'To the lower part of his abdomen.' ") My heart was taken out and washed in the water of *zamzam*. Then it was returned to its place and filled with faith and wisdom.

Then I was brought a white beast said to be Buraq. He was between a donkey and mule in size. In each stride, he would place his hooves as far as his eyes could see. I was mounted on him and borne away as far as the first heaven.

The account of the ascent through the seven heavens is substantially the same as the first account above. When the Prophet arrives before Abraham in the seventh heaven, the account continues:[28]

Then we sped off until we reached the seventh heaven and I was brought before Abraham. (The Prophet, peace and blessings on him, related in the hadith that) he saw four rivers flowing from beneath its trunk [i.e., the trunk of the lote tree],[29] two manifest rivers and two hidden rivers. I said to Jibril: "What rivers are these, Jibril?" He said: The two hidden rivers are two rivers of paradise. The two manifest rivers are the Nile and the Euphrates.

Then he was taken up to the house of life *(al-bayt al-ma'mūr)*. I said: "Jibril, what is this?" He said: "This is the house of life. Every day seventy thousand angels enter it. When they go out from it they never return."[30]

I was then brought two vessels, one of wine and the other of milk. They were shown to me and I chose the milk. I was told: "You have chosen well. Allah will choose your community through you, according to the innate disposition *(fiṭra)*." Then fifty prayers per day were given as a requirement to the community. And he continued relating the story until the end of the hadith.

The genre of literature known as the life of Muhammad (sīrat an-nabī, *or simply, the* sīra*) contains other, significant versions of the night journey and Mi'raj. In one of the earliest and most widely accepted versions, that of Ibn Isḥāq as retold by Ibn Hishām, the accounts of the Mi'raj are more detailed than those of the hadith of Muslim ibn Hajjāj, more directly related to the life of Muhammad, and present a clearer separation of the night journey from the Mi'raj. The miraculous mount Buraq, who carried Muhammad away, is presented in the* Ṣaḥīḥ Muslim *as male (or at least through the masculine grammatical constructions), and in Ibn Hishām as either male or female, depending on the account. In the* Ṣaḥīḥ Muslim, *Muhammad chooses between a vessel of wine and a vessel of milk; in the* sīra *of Ibn Hishām, two versions are given. In one version, the Prophet chooses between vessels of wine and milk; in the other he chooses between three vessels, one filled with wine, one with milk, and one with water.*

Larger, theological issues also separate the two accounts. Ibn Hishām presents early debates over the validity and possibility of the night journey. He also represents the Prophet's wife A'isha's position that the night journey and Mi'raj were purely spiritual events, with A'isha testifying that she was with Muhammad the whole time and that his body did not move. Pre-

sented below are those portions of the Ibn Hishām's account that are particularly important for Islamic mystical texts.

The Isrā' *and* Mi'raj
***The Account of Ibn Isḥāq as Recounted by Ibn Hishām in the* Sīra of the Rasūl Allāh *(The Life of the Messenger of Allah)*[31]**

THE NIGHT JOURNEY (*ISRĀ'*)

'Abdallah ibn Mas'ūd used to say—as it has come down to me—that Buraq was brought to the Envoy of God. She was a beast who used to carry prophets before his [Muhammad's] time. In each stride, she would place her hooves as far as her eyes could see. He was mounted on her. His companion[32] went out with him to see the signs between the heavens and the earth, until he came at last to the house of the sanctified *(bayt al-muqaddas)*. There he found Ibrāhīm and Musā and 'Isā in a group of prophets who had been assembled for him. After he performed the prayer with them, he was given three vessels; a vessel containing milk, a vessel containing wine, and a vessel containing water. (He said: So the Envoy of God, God's peace and blessings on him, said:) I heard a voice say, as these vessels were offered to me: "If he takes the water, he drowns and his community drowns. If he takes the wine, he goes astray and his community goes astray. If he takes the milk, he receives guidance and his community receives guidance." (He said:) So I took the vessel of milk and drank from it. Jibrīl then said to me: "You and your community have received guidance, Muhammad."

I have been told that al-Ḥasan said: The Envoy of God, God's peace and blessings on him, said: "While I was sleeping in the sanctuary *(ḥijr)*, Jibril came to me and roused me with his foot. I sat up but saw nothing, so I went back to sleep. He came and roused me with his foot a second time and I sat up and, seeing nothing, went back to sleep. He came and roused me with his foot a third time. I sat up, he took my arm, and I rose with him. He took me out to the door of the place of prayer *(masjid)* and there was a white beast, part mule and part donkey. The beast had two wings for thighs with which he would propel his lower legs, placing his hooves as far as his eye could see. He mounted me on himself and took me out. He did not pass me and I did not pass him.[33]

Al-Ḥasan said in his hadith: The Envoy of God, God's peace and blessings on him, went on, and with him Jibril, until he came at last to the house of the sanctified *(bayt al-muqaddas)* and found there Ibrahim, Musa, and 'Isa in a group of prophets. The Envoy of God, peace and blessings on him, led them in prayer and prayed with them. Then he was brought two vessels, in one of which was wine and in the other milk. (He said:) The Rasul Allah, God's peace and blessings on him, took the vessel of milk and drank from it, leaving aside the vessel of wine. (He said:) So Jibril said to him: "You have been given guidance through innate disposition *(fiṭra)* and your community has been given guidance, and wine has been forbidden to you."

At this point, Ibn Hishām recounts the skepticism of Muhammad's followers in Mecca and the controversy roused by his claim to have gone to the "house of sanctity" in Jerusalem in a single night's journey.[34] *This particular account ends with the belief in the night journey interpreted as a test of the faith of the new community:*

(Al-Ḥasan said:) "As for those who went back on Islam because of that [their skepticism about Muhammad's claim of a night journey], Allah sent down the verse (13:62): "We made the vision we showed you only as a test *(fitna)* for people and the cursed tree in the Qur'an and we frighten them but it only increases them in their most grievous error." This is the hadith of al-Ḥasan on the night journey of the Envoy of God, peace and blessings on him, with some additions by Qatāda.

Ibn Isḥāq said: One of the family of Abū Bakr reported to me that 'A'isha used to say: "The body of the Rasul Allah, God's peace and blessings on him, did not disappear, but Allah took his spirit away by night."

Ibn Isḥāq said: Ya'qūb ibn 'Ataba ibn al-Mughīra ibn al-Akhnas reported to me that when Mu'āwiya ibn abī Sufyān was asked about the night journey of the Envoy of God, peace and blessings on him, he said: "It was a true dream/vision *(ru'yā)* from Allah. Their statements ['A'isha and Mu'āwiya's] do not contradict the saying of al-Ḥasan, for the following verse, a saying of Allah Most High and Exalted, came down about that (13:62): "We made the vision we showed you only as a *fitna* for people." Nor does it contradict the saying of Allah Most High and Exalted in the statement about Ibrahim, God's peace and blessings on him, when he said to his son (37:10), "O my son, I have seen in my dream/vision that I was slaughtering you," and then went on. I have realized that the inspiration from Allah comes to the prophets both awake and asleep.[35]

THE MI'RAJ

The Hadith of Abū Sa'īd Al-Khudrī concerning the Mi'raj: Ibn Isḥāq said: Someone about whom I have no doubts told me of Abū Sa'īd al-Khudrī, God's peace and blessings on him, that he said: I heard the Envoy of Allah, God's peace and blessings on him, say:

When I was no longer occupied with what had occurred in the *bayt al-muqaddas*, I was given a ladder *(mi'rāj)* that was as fine as anything I have ever seen. It was the same as that ladder to which a dying person turns his eyes when his time is at hand. My friend *(ṣāḥibī)* led me up it and brought me all the way to one of the doors of heaven, said to be the door of the Guardians. An angel, said to be Isma'il, was in charge of them. Under his command were twelve thousand angels, with twelve thousand more angels under each one of them. (Al-Khudrī said that the Prophet, as he would tell this hadith, would say: No one knows the troops of your lord except him.) When he brought me in, Isma'il said: Who is that, O Jibril? "Muhammad," he replied. "Has he been sent for?" Isma'il asked. "Yes," replied Jibril. Upon hearing that, Isma'il wished me well.[36]

In the later chapters of this present volume, there will be continual allusions to the Mir'aj traditions, and an entire section (the Mi'raj of Abu Yazid al-Bistami) that is a direct appropriation of symbolic cosmos and quest of the original Mi'raj of Muhammad. When these allusions and direct references to Muhammad's Mi'raj occur, their role in Sufi spirituality will become more explicit. The Mi'raj accounts are presented here, at first, in their own right. As with the Qur'an, they contain a spirituality not limited to Sufi thought. The Mi'raj is a deeply ingrained aspect of Islamic popular culture, a continual theme or object of allusion in Islamic literature, and, in those periods and places where painting was encouraged, a central theme in art as well.

♦ ♦ ♦

THE BELOVED (POETIC DIMENSIONS OF ISLAMIC SPIRITUALITY)

Introduction

Islamic mysticism is indelibly marked with the poetic heritage of the Near East. Most important to the periods discussed in this book is the early Arabic poetry. The Sufis did not borrow the poetic themes of the lost beloved, the intoxication of wine, or the "perishing" out of love for the beloved to use as a vehicle for expressing ideas and sensibility developed independently from the poetry. Rather, the refinement of theme, mood, emotion, and diction within the poetry was from very early on in Sufism an integral aspect of the mystical sensibility.

It is frequently impossible to tell whether the anonymous verses on love and intoxication cited by writers such as Sarraj and Qushayri are originally part of the secular poetic tradition or were composed as part of a Sufi discourse. Or rather, notion of a purely secular poetry may be inappropriate within the Sufi context. Even the poems that are almost certainly of a pre-Islamic origin and that are viewed by many as the epitome of the Jahiliyya (age of ignorance) are more than tales of love, drinking, and tribal battle.

The way in which Sufis play on this tradition suggests that they are continuing and developing a poetic and lyrical tradition that has continued unbroken to the present day in most Islamic regions. The examples and discussion offered here are meant to offer a taste of that sensibility and a guide to how it is used throughout the Sufi passages in this volume.[37]

Central to Islamic spirituality is the poetry that grew out of the pre-Islamic Arabic nasīb, *the first part of the classical Arabic ode or Qasida. The nasīb begins with the remembrance of the lost beloved. Remembrance is incited in turn by certain key symbols: the ruins of the beloved's campsite* (aṭlāl); *the apparition* (khayāl, ṭayf) *of the lost beloved to the poet; the recalling of the secret* (sirr) *of the relationship between poet and beloved.*

The Mu'allaqa ("hanging ode,") of the poet Labid begins with a poetic meditation on the ruins of the poet's beloved, Nawár, ruins that are found in places named Mínan, Ghawl, and Rijám.[38] *The tent ruins spark a poetic reverie in which the desert suddenly becomes a garden containing lush vegetation and animals at peace. The reverie begins with a reference to the months gone by, the months of war or profane* (ḥalāl) *months and the months of peace or sacred* (ḥarām) *months during which all warfare was prohibited and the various tribes would come together for fairs, poetry festivals, and pilgrimage. The tent marks and torrent marks of Nawár's abandoned encampment appear, transform themselves into gardens, turn back to marks in the sand, and disappear. At the end of the reverie, the poet is once again faced with the barren stones at the desert campsite, asking them a question they cannot answer. The marks and rocks perdure, endlessly signifying something about the loss of the beloved, deferring all answers as to what precisely is signified.*

The tent marks in Mínan are worn away
where she encamped
and where she alighted,
Ghawl and Rijám now left to the wild,

And the torrent beds of Rayyán
naked tracings
worn thin, like inscriptions
carved in flattened stones.

Dung-stained ground
that tells the years passed
since human presence, months of peace
gone by, months of war,

Replenished by the rain stars
of spring and struck
by thunderclap downpour, or steady,
fine dropped, silken rains

From every kind of cloud
passing at night,
darkening the morning,
or rumbling in peals across the evening sky.

The white pondcress has shot upward,
and on the wadi slopes,
gazelles among their newborn,
and ostriches,

And the wide-of-eyes
silent above monthling fawns.
On the open terrain
yearlings cluster.

The rills and the runlets
uncovered marks like the script
of faded scrolls
restored with pens of reed,

Or tracings of a tattoo woman
   beneath the indigo powder,
sifted in spirals,
   the form begins to reappear.

      I stopped to question them.
   How is one to question
      deaf, immutable,
   inarticulate stones?[39]

These verses began with a reference to where the beloved had camped (muqāmuhā) *and where she had alighted* (maḥalluhā). *While the three campsites mentioned at the beginning of the poem are presented as the abandoned ruins or* aṭlal, *at the end of the verses cited above they are viewed as part of a larger pattern: as stations* (maqāmāt, manāzil) *of the beloved as she moves away from the poet with the women of her tribe. The transition to the wider theme is the motif of the* ẓa'n: *the remembrance of the beloved's departure with the other women of the tribe, their disappearance into the elaborate camel litters or "howdahs," the most colorful part of Bedouin society. In the following verses, Labid moves from the meditation on the ruins to remembrance of the departure. The poetic gaze follows the beloved and the other departing women of the tribe, gradually moving back further and further until the camel train is no longer distinguishable from "tamarisks and boulders on the slopes of Bíshah."*

Stripped bare now,
   what once held all that tribe—
they left in the early morning
   leaving a trench and some thatch.

      They stirred longing in you
   as they packed up their howdahs,
      disappearing into lairs of cotton,
   frames creaking,

Post-beams covered
   with twin-rodded curtains
of every kind of cloth brocade
   and a black, transparent, inner veil,

Strung out along the route
in groups, like oryx does of Túdih,
or Wájran gazelles, white fawns
below them, soft necks turning,

They faded into the distance
appearing in the shimmering haze
like tamarisks and boulders
on the slopes of Bíshah.[40]

At this point, the poetic voice tries to break out of the remembrance, asking what use there is in recalling Nawár. As if pushed along by a deeper current, however, the remembrance continues, overflowing into imagination as the poet recounts the stations of the beloved that he cannot have seen:

But why recall Nawár?
She's gone.
Her ties and bonds to you
are broken.

The Murrite lady
has lodged in Fayd,
then joined up with the Hijázi clans.
Who are you to aspire to reach her,

On the eastern slopes
of Twin Mountains or Muhájjar?
Lone butte has taken her in,
then Marblehead,

Then Tinderlands
if she heads toward Yemen—
I imagine her there—or at Thrall Mountain
or in the valley of Tilkhám.[41]

Thus this famous opening section of Labid's Mu'allaqa begins and ends with references to the stations and stages of the beloved's journey. The opening references to the stations are references to them as a poetic analogue of the sacred enclosure (himma). *In fact, the meditation at the abandoned campsite has been shown to have strong parallels with the practice of incubation at the shrine of a god or saint that was part of the Mediterranean world of late antiquity. A person who desired healing or inspiration would spend the night at the shrine of a god like Asclepius (the Hellenistic god of healing) or an early Christian saint like Thekla. Muhammad's vision and night-journey are related in early Arabic tradition to his vigil in the sacred enclosure in Mecca known as the* ḥijr. *The phantom of the god, goddess, or saint would appear to the pilgrim, often healing or revealing the secret of healing.*[42] *In a similar way, the phantom of the beloved will appear explicitly or implicitly to the poet who meditates within hallowed boundaries of the abandoned camp.*

At the end of the section from Labid cited above, the stations of the beloved's journey are recounted, one by one, with ritual solemnity. The Mu'allaqat and other pre-Islamic poems were recited at the festival of 'Ukāẓ, which itself was connected with the annual pre-Islamic pilgrimage or ḥajj. *The language of ritually solemn recitation of stations is associated with Arabic pilgrimages, and this connection is continually evoked when referring to the stations of the beloved's departure—as if those stations were a kind of reverse pilgrimage, with the seeker remaining stationary and the object of devotion or desire moving in stages away from the seeker. The Sufis continually combined the two notions of stages, pilgrimage stages toward Mecca and the stages of the beloved in her journey away from the poet. The result is a kind of mystical bewilderment, as in the verses cited by Qushayri:*

I continued to alight
  in your affection,
a way-stop for which
  hearts are bewildered.

In Labid's ode, there is no description of the beloved. The beloved is evoked, but the traces of the beloved's campsite lead the poetic voice into an idyll of imagined lush gardens and peaceful animals. A famous poem by Mukhabbal also moves to the idyll, but Mukhabbal does so more indirectly through the dissembling simile. The poem seems to be describing the beloved, but the similes dissemble; they create the expectation of a description of the beloved, but end up presenting a description of the beloved's symbolic analogue, the lost garden or meadow. As with Labid, while the beloved is evoked, what is actually depicted is an idyll of cool flowing water, lush vegetation, and wild animals at peace.

Mukhabbal begins with the phantom of the beloved and a particularly desolate depiction of the ruins of her campsite, before moving on to the dissembling similes and the idyll:

He remembered Rabáb.
  Her memory was sickness.
He was young again,
  unaware.

    When her phantom came round
  my eye stung
    along the tear lines
  and began to water,

Like pearls
  slipping
from a necklace
  poorly strung.

    I make out a dwelling there,
  hers,
    amid the pools of Sidán,
  traces unfaded,

Ashes, cold,
  banked and shielded
from the winds
  by blackened hearthstones,

    Ruins of a flood-break,
  stone walls
    around the base,
  broken in,

As if what the side winds
  and rains had left
there on the empty yards
  were a tattoo.

Doe-oryx pasture there,
following along toward water,
white-backs
and brown-backs mingling,

The fawns of oryx
and gazelle,
around her tracings there,
like kids and lambs.

Rabáb might have alighted there,
with an advance guard,
well-armed,
to ward off foes.

Graceful as a rush of papyrus,
beauty comes to her
before others,
and she matures more quickly.

She shows you a face
smooth as paper,
unwrinkled
and unblemished,

Like the pearl of pearls
distant Persians use
to light up the throne-hall
of a king,

Purchased at high price,
retrieved by a diver,
bone-thin,
like an arrow,

His chest smeared with oil,
bringing it out
from the billow-waved deep
of the swordfish.[43]

The dissembling nature of the beloved's image that Mukhabbal offers recurs in a famous poem by Ka'b ibn Zuhayr. Ka'b's poem is known as the Burda Qasida because the Prophet Muhammad is said to have given Ka'b his mantle (burda) *upon hearing it. Ka'b begins with a bitter commentary on the shifting states* (aḥwal) *of his beloved, Su'ād, comparing her to a* ghūl *who changes guises in every moment. This complaint can actually be read as a comment on the nature of the description of the beloved in the Qasida. When Ka'b says: "What is Su'ad but . . ." the reader might ask the same question of the beloveds of all the classical Qasidas. The poetic voice entrances the reader with the impression that the beloved has been described, but if the reader tries to seize on what she actually is like, like the* ghūl *she vanishes into a constantly changing series of images. With Ka'b for example, we start out with Su'ad, but end up with a draught of wine "Mixed with the hard cold of a winding, backsloped, / gorge-bottom stream, pure, / cooled in the morning by the north wind."*

Su'ad is gone,
   my heart stunned,
lost in her traces,
   shackled, unransomed.

      What was Su'ad
   the morning they went away
      but a faint song,
   languor in the eyes, kohl,

Revealing as she smiled
   side-teeth wet
as a first draught of wine
   or a second,

      Mixed with the hard cold
   of a winding, backsloped,
      gorge-bottom stream, pure,
   cooled in the morning by the north wind,

Filtered through the winds,
   then flooded
with rains of a night traveler,
   flowing white and over.

Misery she
who might have been a friend
had she kept her promise,
had a well-meant word been taken.

Some friend. In her blood
brew trouble and lies,
the withdrawal of vows,
the trade-in of lovers.

From form to form,
she turns and changes,
like a *ghūl*
slipping through her guises.

She makes a vow,
then holds it
like a linen sieve
holds water.

The theme of the beloved's constantly changing conditions or states (aḥwāl) *contains an ironic tension. The poet blames the beloved for the changes and claims he is cutting his bonds with her, but never succeeds in abandoning the beloved or her memory; the more he claims he has forgotten her, the more he protests too much. The Qasida eventually moves on beyond the* nasīb *into new sections of poetry, but the beloved comes back, often in haunting ways. Ultimately, when Ka'b compares his beloved Su'ad to a* ghūl, *he is evoking the theme of fate* (dahr), *often compared to a ghul, which continually changes form and shape, bewildering the human and wearing away all attempts at permanence.*

The "blaming" of the beloved, which is actually a displaced blaming of fate, is connected with the accusation of the betrayal of the secret (sirr) *held by lover and beloved. A pre-Islamic nasīb by 'Alqama begins with a reference to the secret:*

Is what you came to know,
given in trust,
kept secret? Is her bond to you
broken, now that she is far?

Does a grown man weeping
tears without end for those he loved,
the dawn of parting,
receive his fair reward?

By the time I knew,
they had set their leave,
all the camel stallions
standing bridled before dawn.[44]

The relationship of the Qur'an to classical poetry is complex. The Qur'an emphatically rejects the notion that it is sh'ir, formal poetry in the classical sense with a complex meter and inspired by jinn. The Qur'an is the word of the deity. In referring to the poets, the Qur'an says dryly, "Do you not see them in every dried out river-bed, wandering aimlessly?"[45] Yet the Prophet had his own circle of poets, one of whom composed an elegy upon the death of Muhammad that figures the remains of the Prophet's house and mosque in Medina as the ruins of the abandoned campsite of the beloved. Like the traces of Nawár's campsite in the Qasida of Labid, the traces of the Prophet's abode endure, even while everything else wastes away:

At Táybah there remain the Prophet's
relics and a luminous
Encounter place, while other relics fade
and waste away.

Indelible are the signs of that inviolate abode,
Where the Guide's pulpit stands on which he used to mount.

It stands so clear, the contours firm—and there
His precinct with a prayer-place and mosque.

There his chambers are, there
The lord's light found its repose,
to give him light and warmth—

Signs which will not be effaced as time goes by,
Finding renewal in each decay.

There I recognized the Prophet's traces
  and where I saw him last,
A grave in whose dust he, hidden, lies.[46]

In the classical Qasida, the nasīb remembrance of the beloved eventually yields to the second major movement of the ode, the journey or quest, in which the poet/hero is depicted in solitary encounter with the desert heat, the darkness of the desert night, fate, and human mortality. After this rite of passage, the poet/hero returns to the community, and the poem ends with a boast (fakhr) *in which the poet redefines his place within a new community. That new community is less idealistic than the original idyllic world of remembrance. The transition between the remembrance of the beloved and the journey, or between the journey and the boast, is frequently a wine song. It should be emphasized that the pre-Islamic wine song, although obviously extolling the virtues of wine, has a symbolic register far deeper than a simple drinking song. The wine is often viewed in a ritual fashion as in the following famous section from the ode of ʻAlqama in which the wine is formally unveiled:*

I could well see the drinkers,
  among them a ringing lyre,
men laid low
  by golden, foaming wine,

  The drink of a potentate,
aged by tavernkeepers
  for a special occasion.
It'll take you up and spin you around.

For the headache it's a cure.
  A jolt of it won't harm you.
No dizziness from it
  will mix in the brain,

  A vintage of ʻAnah, a slammer,
for a full year unexposed,
  kept in a clay-stoppered jug
with a waxen seal,

Glistening in its decanter,
 while a foreign-born page,
mouth covered with a cotton band,
 pours it,

 Flagon like a gazelle
 high on the cliff face,
 neck and spout sealed
 with a linen sieve.

Its keeper brings it out into the sun.
 It flashes white,
ringed by branches of sweet basil,
 fragrance brimming over.[47]

Sufis continually play on the ambiguity of the wine song. Is this the earthly wine they are speaking of, or the allegorical wine of mystical intoxication? Such a question can be answered by referring to commentaries on Sufi verse or by appealing to biography. Yet more often the Sufi writer will deliberately subvert any either-or question and answer. Some verses found in Sufi texts are identical to verses attributed to Abu Nuwas, the poet and free-living gallant famous for his ribald verses on wine and love-making. And one Sufi, Ibn al-Farid, became recognized as a "friend of God" through his experiences of mystical ecstasy (wajd), *which were themselves validated by the verses he would recite in his state of* wajd—*verses that stem directly from the classical poetic tradition and that could be read and were read by many as purely secular songs of love and wine.*[48] *In discussing the concept of* wajd *and the related notion of ecstatic existence* (wujūd), *in Chapter 3 in this volume, we will find the Sufi Qushayri quoting a wine song:*

They rained down into the goblets
 water from their pitchers
while pearls blossomed
 in an earth of gold.

The folk praised what they saw
 in wonder
a light from water
 on fire in the grapes,

A pure wine,
inherited by 'Ad from Iram,[49]
the ancient treasure of Khusraw[50]
from his father's father's father.

Following his typical method of returning to a concept introduced earlier (seemingly as an illustration), Qushayri then goes on to devote an entire section to the theme of drunkenness and sobriety, with liberal poetic citations.

Out of the pre-Islamic Qasida grew several forms of lyrical love poetry: the ghazal (literally "love talk") and, most important for Sufism, the poetry called 'Udhri (after a tribe known for its practitioners of this style). The most famous 'Udhri poet, Qays ibn al-Mulawwiḥ, became known by the epithet Majnūn Layla: "Mad for Layla." The term mad, majnūn, *literally means jinned, taken over by the jinn or genies. The jinn were associated with poetic inspiration (they were the pre-Islamic equivalent of the Muses and were believed to speak through the poet), madness, and love. In 'Udhri poetry, the unattainability of the beloved that was central to the pre-Islamic* nasīb *becomes heightened even further as the poet is driven mad and "perishes" out of love for the beloved. Both the love-madness and the perishing became key Sufi motifs. The motifs were combined by Sufis with the bewilderment of reason on contact with ultimate reality, and the annihilation of the human in mystical union. Thus Sarraj—in his discussion of the ecstatic utterances of Bistami and the bewilderment of identity caused by the annihilation of the ego-self in mystical union—is led to quote the Majnūn tradition.[51] Bistami's utterance "Glory to me" is understandable from the point of view of mystical union in which the deity hears, sees, walks, touches, and speaks through the emptied faculties of the Sufi whose ego-self has been annihilated. It is also understandable in terms of love-madness, when the beloved becomes the sole object of existence, as in the case of Majnūn and Layla:*

In this way Majnūn of the Banī 'Amir would say, when looking at a wild animal, "Layla," when looking at the mountains, "Layla," and when looking at other people, "Layla," to the point that when he was asked his name and condition, he said "Layla"!

In that regard he said:

I pass by the ruined abodes of Layla,
  kissing this wall and that.
It is not love of the ruins that inflames my heart
  but love of the one who inhabited the ruins.

Another said:

I search the secret of my heart for desire for you
  but find only myself and that I am you[52]
    and the inner essence greater.
If she finds that I am found raptured in her
  she speaks of herself when she speaks of me.

The lightning flash, in the classical Qasida, was sign of both the beloved's presence and absence. The emphemerality of the moment of union between lover and beloved, symbolized by the lightning, became the occasion for Sufi meditations on the ephemerality of the states (aḥwāl) *of Sufi ecstatic experience. Qushayri first quotes Junayd, who explicitly grounds the Sufi meditation on the fleeting moment in the poetic tradition.*[53]

Sudden gleams of light
  when they appear, apparitions,
revealing a secret,
  telling of union.

Qushayri then dedicates a full section to various forms of ephemerality. On the "flash," he quotes an anonymous poet:

O lightning flashing
  from which folds
of the sky
  do you shine?

These few short passages from the poetic heritage offer a glimpse of a highly refined symbolic world with some key vocabulary: the ruins (aṭlāl) *and traces* (rusūm) *that are effaced but somehow endure, that signify but cannot answer; the phantom or apparition* (khayāl—*a term that later comes to mean "imagination"); the stations* (maqāmāt) *and way-stops* (maḥallāt) *along the pilgrimage; the constantly changing conditions or states* (aḥwāl); *remembrance* (dhikr) *of the beloved* (al-mahbūb); *the secret* (sirr) *entrusted from lover to beloved; the sacred or "prohibited"* (ḥarām) *and profane or "allowed"* (ḥalāl); *the lightning flash of an ephemeral union; the love-mad* (majnūn) *lover who experiences bewilderment* (ḥayra) *in the shifting conditions of the beloved and who ends in ruin* (halāk). *All this vocabulary becomes an essential part of the Sufi mystical lexicon.*

This overview of the poetic heritage ends with the nasīb *of a poem by Dhu al-Rumma, who lived in the first century of Islam. Once again we find what appears to be a description of the beloved yielding in fact to a metamorphosis. The similes dissemble. They seem to describe the beloved, Máyya, but in fact she is transformed into the symbolic analogue, the garden—in this case the oasis garden. The true beloved, in both the poetic and the Sufi traditions, can never be revealed—to reveal her would be to violate the secret.*

Dhu ar-Rumma to the Encampments of Máyya

To the encampments of Máyya,
   both of you,
a well-meant word
   and distant greeting:

      May the rain-star Arcturus
   be over you still . . .
      and the rains of the Pleiades,
   pouring down and spreading,

Though it was you
   who stirred a lover's
disheartened desire,
   until the eye shed

      Tears, yes, that nearly,
   on knowing a campsite as Máyya's
      if not released,
   would have killed,

Though I was already nearing thirty
 and my friends had learned better
and good sense had begun
 to weigh down folly.

  When distance turns other lovers,
 the first premonition
  of loving Máyya
 will still be with me.

Nearness to her
 cannot impoverish desire
nor distance, wherever she might be,
 run it dry.

  The inner whisper
 of memory,
  reminiscence of Máyya
 is enough to bruise your heart.

Desires have their way,
 circulate freely,
but I can't see your share of my heart
 given away.

  Though in parting some love
 is effaced and disappears,
  yours in me is made over
 and compounded.

You came to mind
 when a doe ariel passed us,
right flank turned to the camel mounts,
 neck lowered,

  A doe of the sands, earth-hued,
 with a white blaze on the forehead
  and the afternoon sun
 clear upon her back.

She leaves her fawn
   on a dune, a grassy dune
in Múshrif, the glance of her year
   gleaming around him,

      Gazing at us as if we intended harm
   where we would meet him,
      approaching us,
   then backing away.

She is her like, in shoulder,
   neck, and eye,
but Máyya is more radiant than she, still—
   more beautiful.

      After sleep she is languor.
   The house exudes her fragrance.
      She adorns it
   when she appears in the morning,

Her anklets and ivory,
   as if entwined around a caltrop
stopping the flow
   in the bed of a wadi,

      With buttocks like a soft dune
   over which a rain shower falls
      matting the sand
   as it sprinkles down.

Her hair-fall
   over the lower curve of her back,
soft as the moringa's gossamer flowers,
   curled with pins and combed,

      With long cheek hollows
   where tears flow,
      and a lengthened curve at the breast-sash
   where it crosses and falls.

You see her ear-pendant
along the exposed ridge of her neck,
swaying out,
dangling over the abyss.

With a red thornberry tooth-twig,
fragrant as musk and Indian ambergris
brought in in the morning,
she reveals

Petals of a camomile
cooled by the night
to which the dew has risen at evening
from Ráma oasis,

Wafting in from all sides
with the earth scent of the garden,
redolent as a musk pod
falling open.

The white gleam of her teeth,
her immoderate laugh,
almost to the unhearing
speak secrets.[54]

As with the Qur'an and the Mi'raj, the translations are presented here without detailed discussion of their importance in Sufi literature. The tradition of love poetry in Islam is of fundamental importance to Islamic spirituality, in all its aspects, of which Sufism is only one. For that reason, these poems must be appreciated on their own, as poems, before they are seen in their later, Sufi context.

The poetic tradition is equally rich in Persian, Ottoman, Urdu, and other languages. It would require a full volume to give an introduction to all the poetic traditions of the Islamic world. Yet many of the central themes in most Islamic poetic traditions have already been covered in the Arabic examples, and these selections might also provide an introduction to the reader wishing to explore the intercultural world of poetry within Islam.

2

Early Sufi Qur'an Interpretation

♦ ♦ ♦

THE QUR'ANIC COMMENTARY ATTRIBUTED TO JA'FAR AS-SADIQ (THE SIXTH IMAM)

Introduction

Early Sufi Qur'anic interpretation offers a distinctive set of challenges and an equally distinctive depth of riches. The Qur'an is composed in a nonlinear and non-narrative fashion. Sufi exegesis, by following the Qur'an in order, reflects the "scattering" and nonlinear aspects of the original text. In addition, instead of marginal comments alongside the Qur'an or full treatises in which substantial Qur'anic passages are cited in full and discussed, the commentaries of early Sufis have come down to us in the form of discussions instigated by the mention of a key Qur'anic word that can then suddenly jump to a new Qur'anic term and a new discussion. For the educated Muslim, infused with the Qur'anic voice, such a technique is not unexpected. But any audience not so imbued with the Qur'anic text will need some explanations, and even with explanations may find the technique jarring at first. Finally, Sufi interpretation plays on some key Sufi technical terms, a play that demands explanation of the meaning of those terms within Sufi thought.

The first example of Sufi exegesis is in the form of a collection of sayings attributed to Ja'far aṣ-Ṣādiq (the trustworthy) (d. 148/765).[1] This collection brings up the intriguing issue of the relationship of early Sufism

(Islamic mysticism) to Shi'ism (the Islamic community that recognizes a series of leaders starting with 'Ali as their Imams or guides). According to Shi'ite belief, the prophet Muhammad entrusted the spiritual leadership (the imamate) of the Muslim community to his closest male heir, his cousin and son-in-law 'Ali, who had married his daughter Fatima. 'Ali, the first Imam, passed on the leadership to his first son, Hasan, the second Imam. Hasan passed it on to his brother Husayn, the third Imam. Husayn was killed fighting against the Caliph Yazid at the battle of Karbala', the central tragic event in Shi'ism. One of the few survivors of Husayn's family, his son 'Ali, became the fourth Imam, and 'Ali's son Muhammad Baqir, the fifth. Most Shi'ite groups are in agreement, then, that the first six Imams are:

1. *'Alī*
2. *Ḥasan ibn 'Alī*
3. *Ḥusayn ibn 'Alī*
4. *'Alī ibn Ḥusayn*
5. *Muḥammad ibn 'Alī ibn Ḥusayn, al-Bāqir*
6. *Ja'far ibn Muḥammad aṣ-Ṣādīq*

Ja'far is a central figure in Islamic tradition. Although Shi'ites and Sunnis accept the same basic principles of the shari'a, they differ on their view of the authority and leadership role of the Islamic community, and in aspects of Qur'anic interpretation. It was around Ja'far that the Shi'ite community formed itself as an explicit and articulate version of Islam. To Ja'far are attributed an enormous set of alchemical and astrological writings, and he is considered by tradition to have been the teacher of the famous alchemist Jabir ibn Hayyan, although modern scholars have cast doubt on the authenticity of the writings attributed to Ja'far. Theological writings are attributed to Ja'far, and he is said to have had a position between determinism and free will. The legal writings attributed to Ja'far are the basis for what is called the Ja'fari school of Islamic jurisprudence.

Ja'far's Sufi commentary comes down primarily through the collection of mystical commentaries made by Sulami. What is immediately striking is the lack of any particularly Shi'ite slant to the comments. These Sufi interpretations attributed to Ja'far would be a major influence in the development of mystical interpretations of the Qur'an. Did early Shi'ite views of ta'wil (symbolic interpretation) help found mystical commentary? Have the Shi'ite aspects of Ja'far's commentary been edited out by later Sufi compilers? This question becomes even more intriguing with the discovery of two manuscripts that partially overlap with the Sulami version of Ja'far's Qur'an commentary, but contain explicit Shi'ite references.[2] In addition, there is a single manuscript of the Sulami-Ja'far that contains another explicit Shi'ite commentary in which the family of the Prophet (Muhammad, Ali, Fatima, Hasan, and Husayn) are given cosmic and mystical roles.[3]

The translation below will use the Sulami-Ja'far, which is the only text so far to be edited, but it will also include the openly Shi'ite passage from the anomalous Sulami-Ja'far text to give a sense of what kind of Shi'ite mystical commentary may have also been included in the Ja'far text.

The Sulami-Ja'far commentary is striking for the vividness and self-confidence, at an apparently very early period, with which it offers a strong mystical interpretation of the Qur'an, focusing on the key themes of passing away (fanā') *and abiding* (baqā'). *Sometimes several interpretations of a given verse will be ascribed to Ja'far, each introduced by the phrase "Ja'far said" or "As-Sadiq said." Although the commentary is unified around the general theme of mystical union with the divine beloved, the style of the commentary varies. Some comments are short and cryptic, others are long and sustained. The selections below focus on the following themes: (1) Shi'ite interpretation of the "names" known by Adam as the key members of the family of Muhammad; (2) interpretation of the Qur'anic Moses stories as a paradigm for Sufi mystical experience; (3) interpretation of the Qur'anic accounts (53:1–18) of Muhammad's prophetic vision; (4) spirituality of ritual Islam, the Ka'ba, and the orientation of ritual prayer as symbolic of Abrahamic intimacy with the divine; (5) the Sufi stress on an interior interpretation of Qur'anic accounts of the afterlife; and (6) examples of early Sufi letter symbolism.*

The Shi'ite Passage from Ja'far: The Five Names

2:27: "Adam received from his lord the names."

[Ja'far said:] Before any of his creation existed, God was. He created five creatures from the light of his glory, and attributed to each one of them, one of his names. As the Glorified *(maḥmūd)*, he called his Prophet Muḥammad [which also means "the praised" or "the deserving-of-praise"]. Being the Sublime *('alī)* he called the Emir of believers 'Alī. Being the Creator *(fāṭir)* of the heavens and earth, he fashioned the name

Fāṭima. Because he had names that were called [in the Qur'an] the most beautiful *(ḥusnā)*, he fashioned two names [from the same Arabic root] for Ḥasan and Ḥusayn. Then he placed them to the right of the throne.[4]

Ja'far's Intepretation of Qur'anic Accounts of Moses

The Qur'anic Moses (Musa) is a prototype of the mystical knower ('ārif), *but the Qur'anic accounts of Moses stress more both the intimacy and the intensity of his encounter with the deity than the character of the knowledge he attains. Like Abraham (Ibrahim), who was known as the intimate companion* (khalīl) *of the divine, Moses is also renowned for the intimacy of his relations with the deity. In Sura 19:51–52 Moses is said to be brought near the divine presence as a confidant* (najiyyan). *There is a major tradition in Islam of intimate conversation* (munājāt) *as a form of private prayer and petition* (du'ā), *though such prayer is not as well known as the performed ritual prayer* (ṣalạ).[5] *This intimate relationship of human and divine becomes one of the central features of Sufi language. Some of the most moving passages of Sufi literature will be in the form of* munājāt.

Yet this intimacy coexists with graphic evocations of awe in the face of the transcendent. In the account of Moses' vision of the divine, the divine presence is so strong that Moses cannot look at it directly; instead he is told to look at the mountain which is destroyed as it encounters the presence of the deity. Moses' vision at Mt. Sinai (Ṭūr as-Sinīn, *or simply* aṭ-Ṭūr) *is compared to Muhammad's prophetic vision of the lote tree of the furthest limit (53:14). The commentary on the vision of Moses (or rather nonvision, since Moses never really sees the deity) is used to discuss the central Sufi concepts of* fanā' *(passing away or annihilation of the ego-self)*, baqā' *(the abiding of the person in union with the divine), and* balā' *(the trial or tribulation that is an essential aspect of Sufi spirituality).*

In the Qur'anic account of Moses and the fire, there is a Qur'anic equivalent (at least in Sufi interpretations) of the biblical "I am that I am" (ehyeh asher ehyeh): *"I, I am your lord"* (innī anā rabbuka).[6] *This duplication of the "I" is used by Sufis in a manner similar to Jewish and Christian exegetes of the "I am that I am" to deny any definable essence or quiddity of the divine. For many Sufis, it is divine self-revelation, more as act than as content, that is the only true knowledge of the divine. In his commentary, Ja'far supplies an explanatory dialogue in which the deity and Moses engage in a more explicit discussion, with the grammatical duplication (I, I am your lord) discussed in terms of the experience of awe and the moment of mystical annihilation in the divine.*

The final Qur'anic passage on Moses discussed in this excerpt from Ja'far involves the appearance of Moses before the Pharoah. After the magic of Moses overcomes that of the Pharoah's sorcerers, the sorcerers acknowledge the God of Moses, saying, "We believe in the lord of the two worlds"—usually interpreted as the lord of heaven and earth. The Pharoah threatens them with mutilation and crucifixion for turning their loyalty to the God of Moses and Aaron (Hārun). Their response, "No harm: to our lord is the return" becomes the occasion for a Ja'farian meditation on the torment, trial, or testing (balā') *that each Sufi must pass through on the path to union with the beloved, a theme that will be central to the passages from Junayd in Chapter 8 of this volume.*

The commentaries of Ja'far and of Tustari presuppose intimate knowledge of the Qur'an. A simple word or phrase from the Qur'an is given and the commentary follows. The reader is expected to know from that word or phrase the entire passage. In this chapter, the entire passage is given in each case, so that the reader will be able to consult it. To indicate that the full citations of the passage were not part of the original text attributed to Ja'far and Tustari, but are the translator's explanatory interpolations, such passages have been italicized.

JA'FAR'S COMMENTARY ON THE QUR'ANIC MOSES

7:142 We designated for Musa thirty nights and we completed them with ten more; the appointed time of his lord was thus complete at forty nights. Musa said to his brother Harun: "Govern in my place among my people and act in the best interest; do not follow the way of those who would cause corruption."
7:143 When Musa came at our appointed time and his lord spoke to him, he said: "Lord, show me that I might gaze upon you." He said: "You will not see me. Look at the mountain. If it stays in place, you will see me." But when its lord appeared to the mountain, he caused it to shatter and Moses was struck down unconscious. When he awoke, he said: "Glory to you! I have turned back to you in repentance and I am the first of the believers."

"When Musa came to our appointed time and his lord spoke to him." Ja'far said: The appointed time was the time for seeking a vision. Ja'far also said: Musa heard words coming forth from his humanity and attributed the words to him [the deity][7] and he spoke to him from the selfhood of Musa and his servanthood. Musa was hidden from his self and passed away from his attributes *(ṣifātihi)*. His lord spoke to him from the realities of his meanings. Musa heard his own attribute from his lord, while Muhammad heard from his lord the attribute of his lord and thus was the most praised *(aḥmad)* of the praised *(maḥmūdīn)*. Therefore the station of Muhammad was the lote tree of the furthest boundary while the station of Musa was aṭ-Ṭūr [Mt. Sinai]. When God spoke to Musa on Ṭūr, he annihilated its attributes so that no vegetation has ever appeared upon it and it is the abode of no one.

He said: "Lord, show me that I might gaze upon you!" Ja'far said: "He confided in his lord concerning the matter of seeing him because he saw the phantom of his[8] words upon his heart." He replied: "You will not see me," that is, you are not able to see me because you pass away. How can that which passes away *(fānin)* find a way to that which abides *(bāqin)?*

"Look at the mountain." Ja'far said: The mountain was struck by the knowledge of beholding, was split and shattered. The mountain was destroyed by the mere mention *(dhikr)* of beholding its lord and Musa was struck down upon seeing the mountain fall to pieces. How would it be, then, if one were to behold his lord with his own eyes, face to face! The lord's face-to-face vision in respect to the servant is the annihilation of the servant.[9] The servant's face-to-face vision of the lord and in the lord is enduring.[10]

He said: Three things are impossible for servants in regard to their lord: manifestation, contact, and insight. No eye can see him, no heart attain him, and no intellect intuit him. The origin of intuition is innate disposition; the root of connection is the interval of distance; the root of witness is apparition.[11]

Concerning his saying "You will not see me. Look instead at the mountain," Ja'far said: He occupied him with the mountain and then manifested himself. Were it not for Musa's preoccupation with the mountain, he would have been killed, struck unconscious, never to awake.

Concerning his saying "Glory to you! I have turned back to you in repentance," Ja'far said: He affirmed the transcendence of his lord, acknowledged toward him his own weakness, and disavowed his own intellect. "I have returned to you in repentance": I have returned to you from my self and no longer rely upon my knowledge. Knowledge is what you have taught me and intellect is what you have graced me with. "And I am the first of the believers": That is, surely you [Allah] cannot be seen in the world.[12]

20:9 Has the account of Musa reached you?
10 How he saw a fire and said to his people: "Stay behind, I make out a fire. Perhaps I can return from it with an ember or find at the fire some guidance."
11 When he approached it, he was called: "O Musa!
12 Indeed I, I am your lord. Take off your sandals. You are in the sanctified valley of Ṭuwā.
13 I am the one who selected you, so listen to what is revealed!
14 I am Allah, there is no god but I. Worship me and perform the prayer in remembrance of me."[13]

20:11–12 "When he came to it, a voice called out: O Musa, I, I am your lord." Ja'far said: Musa was asked "How did you know that the call was the call of the real?" He said: Because he annihilated me, then encompassed me, and it was as if all the hairs on my body were speaking from all sides about the call, and were themselves on their own power responding to the call! When the lights of awe encompassed me and the lights of majesty and *jabarūt* addressed me, I knew that I was being addressed on the part of the truth.[14] The beginning of the address, "Indeed, I" was followed by another "I." This repetition of the "I" indicated to me that no one but the real can refer to himself with two consecutive phrases. I was astonished and that was the way-station of passing away. So I said: You, you are that which has endured and will endure and Musa has no station with you nor does he dare to speak except that you make him endure in your enduring and give him your attribute so that you are the addresser and the addressee together. He replied: No one can bear my address but I and no one can respond but I. I am the speaker and the spoken-to and you are in-between, a phantom upon whom falls the way-station of speaking.

26:48–50
They said: we believed in the lord of the two worlds!
The lord of Mūsa and Hārun
He said: "You believed in him before I gave you permission.
He is your chief who taught you sorcery: you will surely know!
I will cut off your hands and legs, alternatively, and crucify you all together."
They said: "No harm. To our lord is our return."

"They said: 'No harm, To our lord is our return.' " Ja'far said: Whoever feels the trial *(balā')* in love is not a lover. Rather, whoever witnesses trial in it is not a lover. Rather, whoever does not take pleasure in the trial in love is not a lover. Do you not see that when the first signs of love came upon the sorcerers, their own destinies faded away and became of little concern through the submission of their spirits in the witness of their beloved, so that they said: "No harm"?

Ja'far's Interpretation of Muhammad's Prophetic Vision

While Moses looked at the Mountain, which was obliterated by the divine theophany, Muhammad is said in the Qur'an to have gazed upon "it" (the antecedent is never specified) in such a way that his eye neither swerved aside nor exceeded its appropriate function. Exactly what Muhammad saw (the deity, the angel Gabriel, etc.) and what the Qur'an means by saying "his eye neither swerved nor exceeded" are central themes of Sufi meditation on mystical experience and the possibility of vision or witness (shahāda) *of the divine. The interpretations attributed to Ja'far of this famous passage are also representative of another aspect of Islamic interpretation: the attribution to one person of several different interpretations. Thus Ja'far is said to have given at least three interpretations to the opening Qur'anic oath (53:1), "by the star when it falls* (hawā)."

What is central to the Qur'anic passage, and brought out further by Ja'far, is the play between hawā *(to fall, to set) and the homonym used later on to mean desire. The Qur'an announces that Muhammad does not speak out of desire* (hawā), *as do, it is implied, poets who are inspired by the jinn. Muhammad, as Ja'far goes on to make explicit, speaks out of the divine command* (amr) *and prohibition* (nuhā). *Not only does he proclaim his message out of the divine command, but he completes the Islamic way of life, the shari'a, by refining the commands and prohibitions that were central to all previous prophetic communities.*

As in all Sufi interpretations of these verses, the ambiguity over the object seen (him/it) becomes a centerpiece of linguistic play and mystical meditation. Because we are in the context of fanā' *(passing away) in which the Sufi passes away in mystical union with the divine, the standard grammatical distinction between self and other, human and divine, reflexive and nonreflexive, begins to break down. At these points the translations make use of the locution him(self) to indicate the ambiguity of the object pronoun and the breakdown of the reflexive/nonreflexive grammatical distinction at the point of mystical union.*

JA'FAR'S COMMENTARY ON MUHAMMAD'S VISION

Sūrat an-Najm (*The Sura of the Star*) *53:1–12*

By the star when it falls
Your companion has not gone astray nor is he deluded
He does not speak out of desire
It is nothing less than an inspiration inspired
Taught to him by one of great power
And strength that stretched out over
While on the highest horizon
Then it drew near and descended
At a distance of two bows' length or nearer
He revealed to his servant what he revealed
The heart did not lie in what it saw
Will you then dispute with him on his vision?

Sūrat an-Najm, *53:13–18*

He saw it descending another time
At the lote tree of the furthest limit
Therein was the garden of sanctuary
When there enveloped the tree what enveloped it
His gaze did not turn aside nor did it overreach
He had seen the signs of his lord, great signs.

53:1–12 "By the star when it falls" *(hawā)*. Ja'far said: This is the way-station of manifestation and veiling from the hearts of the knowers.

Concerning the saying of the Most High, "by the star when it falls," it is related of Ja'far ibn Muḥammad that he said: The star is Muḥammad, peace and blessings upon him. When he fell light diffused from him.[15]

He said: The star is the heart of Muḥammad. "When it falls," that is, when it cuts itself off from everything other than Allah.

"Your companion has not gone astray nor is he deluded." Ja'far said: He did not stray from his nearness even for the blink of an eye.

"He does not speak out of desire" *(hawā)*. Ja'far said: How could he speak out of desire, he who proclaims the coming forth of unity, and completes the shari'a with the proper command and prohibition? Rather he proclaimed only through command and was silent only through command. He was given the command as an approach to the real. He was given the prohibition as a warning and chiding.

"Then it drew near and descended." Ja'far said: In its nearness, how-it-was[16] was cut off from all understanding. Do you not see that God most high veiled Jibril when Jibril came near, and when his Lord came near to him?

He also said: Muḥammad, God's peace and blessings upon him, came near to the insight and the faith that was placed in his heart, and he descended in the quiet of his heart to what he had come near. All doubt and anxiety was removed from his heart.

"At a distance of two bows' length or nearer." Ja'far said: He brought him(self) near to him until he was two bows-length away. Nearness on the part of God Most High has no limit, while nearness on the part of the servant has limits.

"He revealed to him what he revealed." Ja'far said: Without intermediary between the two of them, secretly to his [Muhammad's] heart. No one knows him(self) without intermediary but him(self) except at the final end, when he gives intercession to his community.

Of his saying, "It drew near and descended," [Ja'far] as-Sadiq said: When the lover draws as near to his beloved as is possible, he is overcome by utter terror. Then the truth treats him with complete gentleness because nothing but complete gentleness can endure utter terror. That is the meaning of his saying, "He revealed to his servant what he revealed," that is: what was, was, and what happened, happened, and the lover said what a lover says to his beloved, treated him gently as the lover treats the beloved, and told him the secret a lover tells his beloved. They kept it secret and let no one in on it but the two of them. For that reason he said: "He revealed to his servant what he revealed." No one knows that revelation except the one who revealed it and the one to whom it was revealed.

"The heart did not lie in what it saw." Ja'far said: No one knows what he saw except the seer and the seen. The lover has come near to the beloved, as intimate and confidant to him. God Most High said: "We raise in degree whomsoever we will" (6:83).

"He had seen the signs of his lord, great signs." Ja'far said: He witnessed marks of love beyond what can be told.[17]

Ja'far on Abraham and the Ka'ba

Ja'far's short discussion on the Ka'ba, or as it is known in Arabic, the bayt *(dwelling), constructed according to the Qur'an by Abraham and his son Ishmael is less complex than the previous discussion. Yet it offers an impor-*

tant discussion of the spirituality of Islamic ritual prayer (ṣalā), *the physical motions and position* (rak'a) *of the prayer, its spatial orientation (the* qibla *or direction of the Ka'ba marked by the prayer niche), and the intimacy it provides with the divine, an intimacy associated throughout the Qur'an with Abraham, the intimate* (al-khalīl) *of God and builder of the Ka'ba.*

JA'FAR'S COMMENTARY ON ABRAHAM AND THE KA'BA

> *2:125 When we made the dwelling* (bayt) *a refuge for people and a sanctuary—so make the station of Ibrahim a place for prayer!—and we made a covenant with Ibrahim and Isma'il that they should purify the house for those who would circumambulate it, withdraw to it, or make the positions* (rak'as) *of prayer.*

"When we made the dwelling a refuge for people." It is reported of Ja'far ibn Muḥammad that he said: The dwelling here is Muhammad. Whoever believes in him and in the truth of his message enters into the fields of refuge and faith. "The station of Ibrahim": that is, the station of the *qibla* [the direction facing the Ka'ba or *bayt*]. He made your heart the station of knowing and your tongue the station of witness and your body the station of obedience. Whoever maintains it will have his prayer answered completely.

Ja'far and Sufi Understanding of the Qur'anic Afterlife

Contrary to some stereotypes about the Qur'anic afterlife, a nonphysical (though never antiphysical) notion of paradise does exist within the Qur'an, as is made clear in the following passage. The passage begins on a cosmic level (a garden whose breadth is the heavens and the earth) and then moves toward an intimate questioning of the human person, his hopes, angers, and motivations, with a central meditation on forgiveness and remembrance:

SURAT AL-IMRĀN *(THE SURA OF THE FAMILY OF IMRAN)* 3:133–136

And race to a forgiveness from your lord
and a garden whose breadth is the heavens and earth
made ready for the self-vigilant[18]

Who spend in ease and in adversity
and check their wrath and show forgiveness to others
Allah loves those who show kindness

And those who when they corrupt others or oppress themselves
remember Allah and ask forgiveness for their offense
—who forgives offenses but Allah?—
and do not persist knowingly in what they did

For them is a reward of forgiveness from their lord
and gardens with rivers flowing underneath
eternal there
fine is the recompense for those whose deeds are fine.

In the passages that follow here, Ja'far extends this aspect of Qur'anic spirituality by integrating it into the sophisticated Sufi psychology of the human heart. In many Sufi interpretations the temporal ("after") and spatial (heavens and hells) aspects of the afterlife are transformed into an interior reality, the heart-secret or destiny, that lies behind or within each person. Both the afterlife and the bounty of the compassionate deity given to humankind in this life, one example of which is included below, are interiorized within the Sufi symbolic interpretation. The selections conclude with a reference to the creation and "renewal of creation," which could be interpreted as a reference to creation and the final resurrection (qiyāma), *or as a reference to the original creation and keeping it in existence through bestowal of life and fertility. While not abandoning these possibilities, Ja'far's commentary stresses creation and renewal as a cycle of original coming-to-be, annihilation in mystical union* (fanā'), *and the final abiding* (baqā') *of the human in the divine and the divine in the human.*

The reader will note that the following passages take very small sections of the Qur'an and comment on them without referring to their larger Qur'anic context. This kind of commentary exists in a world where the larger context is presumed to be known by the audience. For the reader not immersed in the Qur'an, contextual questions will no doubt arise that would require lengthy Qur'anic quotations and explanations of them—something beyond the scope of this book. Yet the interpretations of Ja'far here can be appreciated on another level without a large contextualization apparatus. Although they might seem atomized in the way they are presented, certain key themes and images in Ja'far's commentary keep coming back and will set the stage for later Sufi developments.

JA'FAR'S COMMENTARY ON SELECTED AFTERLIFE VERSES

43:70–72

Enter the garden, you and your spouses, gladdened!
Around them plates of gold will be passed and cups of gold

Containing what each self craves and what pleases the eye
You are there, eternally!
That is the garden that you have inherited with what you have done.

"Containing what each self craves and what pleases the eye." Ja'far said: What the self craves and what pleases the eye are two distinct categories. All of what the garden contains, of bliss, gratification, and pleasures—next to what pleases the eye—is like a finger plunged into the sea. The gratifications of the garden have a limit and an end because they are created. The eye finds no pleasure in this enduring abode, but rather in the enduring one *(al-bāqī)*, the majestic, the most high. There is no limit in that, no attribute, no end.

55:11 "In it are fruit and date palms with unfolding calyxes." Ja'far said: The real made the hearts of his friends into gardens of his intimacy. He planted in them the trees of knowing, roots firm in the secrets of their hearts, branches standing in the presence of witness. In every time they gather the fruits of intimacy. This is what is meant by his saying "In it are fruit and date palms with unfolding calyxes," that is, of all kinds. Each one gathers from it a kind according to the capacity of his labor and what is unveiled for him of the manifestations of knowing and the traces of friendship with the divine.[19]

76:21: "And their lord quenched them with a drink that was pure." Ja'far said: He quenched them with unity in their hearts' secret. They were lost *(tāhū)* to everything other than him, not waking except upon the vision, the lifting of the veil between them and him, and the taking of the drink in what it was taken from. No state from him endures. He comes forth in joy, in presence, in seizure.[20]

Concerning "a drink that was pure," Ja'far said: He purified them with it of everything other than him, since no creature can be in any way pure of defilement.

82:13–14: "Surely the pious are bound for bounty and surely the corrupt are bound to hell-fire." Ja'far said: The bounty is insight and witness. The hell-fire consists of ego-selves; they contain kindled fires.

85:13: "He is the one who creates and renews his creation." Ja'far said: He creates and then annihilates everything that is other than him. Then he renews his creation and causes it to endure in his enduring.[21] Concerning the words "he is the one who creates and renews his creation," Ja'far aṣ-Ṣādiq also said: That is, he clothes the enemies in the garb of friends so they might be led along little by little. He clothes his friends in the garb of enemies that they might not admire themselves.[22] Then, at the moment of death, he renews his creation.

Ja'far's Letter Symbolism and Mystical Exegesis of the Opening of the Qur'an

The first sura of the Qur'an begins with the phrase "In the name of Allah, the Compassionate, the Caring." This phrase is also pronounced at the beginning of every sura of the Qur'an, though it is only with the first that the phrase is considered an integral part of the sura. The first section of the commentary focuses on this first Qur'anic verse, 1:1, taking each letter (short vowels excluded) of the phrase and discussing its symbolic meaning. For example, the first expression, "in the name of," in Arabic is bismi. *Thus the major letters,* B, S, *and* M,[23] *will each be attached to a key word based on one of the letters. In another example, Ja'far associates the letter* A, *the Arabic* alif, *which in Arabic is a straight vertical line, with a column, making a connection not through a key word that begins with* alif, *but through the shape of the letter. The column will become central in Sufi meditation on columns of light. These letter-symbols occur at the very beginning of Ja'far's commentary. Ja'far's commentary on the first words of the Qur'an is an example of the kind of letter symbolism that has been popular in the Islamic world to the present day.*[24] *The commentary also contains a fourfold hierarchy of interpretation that might bear interesting comparison with similar hierarchies in medieval Kabbalah and Christian mysticism.*

JA'FAR'S COMMENTARY ON THE BEGINNING OF THE QUR'AN

1: Introduction: It is related of Ja'far ibn Muḥammad that he said: The book of Allah has four aspects: The expression, the allusion, the subtleties, and the realities. The expression is for the masses, the allusion for the elite, the subtleties for the Godfriends, and the realities for the prophets.

> *1:1* bismi allahi r-raḥmāni r-raḥīm *(In the name of Allah, the Compassionate, the Caring)*

1:1: *bismi.* It is said of Ja'far ibn Muḥammad that he said: The *b* is his enduring *(baqā')* and the *s* is his names *(aSmā')* and the *M* is his dominion *(mulk)*. The faith of the believer—his remembrance is through his enduring. The service of the seeker—his remembrance is through his names. The knower passes away from the kingdom into its king.

1:1 He also said: *bism* has three letters: The *B*, *S*, and *M*. The *B* is the *bāb* (gate) of prophecy. The *S* the *sirr* (secret) of the Prophet to the elite of his community. The *M* is the kingdom *(mulk)* of the faith which includes the white and the black.

1:1 It is related that when Ja'far ibn Muḥammad was asked about the verse *bismi llāhi r-raḥmān ar-raḥīm* (In the name of Allah, the Compassionate, the Caring) he said: The *B* is the splendor *(bahā')* of Allah and the *S* is his brilliance *(sanā')* and the *M* is his glory *(majd)*. Allah is a God of every thing, the Compassionate to all his creatures, the Caring for his believers especially. Of Ja'far it is related that he said of the word "Allah" [in this verse] that it is the complete name because it has four letters: the *A*—and that is the column of unity;[25] the first *l* and that is the tablet *(lawḥ)* of understanding, the second *l* and that is the tablet *(lawḥ)* of prophecy, and the *h* is the furthest reach of allusion. Allah is a singular name, unique, that cannot be attributed to anything; rather all things are attributed to it. Its interpretation is the object of worship which is the God of creatures, yet beyond any perception of what-it-is[26] and any comprehension of how-it-is[27]— veiled from all gaze and imaging, covered by its majesty from all perception.

These excerpts are relatively brief, and sometimes cryptic. As the reader proceeds through this volume, however, the key Qur'anic passages and Ja'farian interpretations should become clearer as they are reflected in a wide variety of later Sufi literature. Also helping to clarify the Ja'farian exegesis is the second example of early Sufi Qur'an interpretation that follows here: the interpretation of Sahl at-Tustari.

♦ ♦ ♦

SAHL AT-TUSTARI (FROM THE INTERPRETATION OF THE MAJESTIC QUR'AN)

INTRODUCTION

The second selection of Sufi exegesis is taken from the Qur'anic commentary of Muḥammad Sahl ibn 'Abdullāh at-Tustarī.[28] Sahl was born in the town of Tustar, from which he takes his nickname, and died in the famous center of Arabic learning, Basra, in 283/986. Sahl did not write treatises of his own, but his sayings were collected by his pupil Muḥammad ibn Sālim (d. 297/909). As will become apparent throughout this volume, Sahl's influence on later Sufi writings is enormous. Sahl is given credit for the first major expression of a number of key Sufi themes: the pre-eternal covenant between humanity and deity, the eternal column of Muhammadian light, the view that only the deity has the right to say "I," and the notion that Satan will eventually be redeemed.[29] *Tustari is presented in the classical sources as having been influenced by the famous early Sufi master Dhu n-Nun al-Misri. In turn, he had a strong influence on such key figures as Junayd, Hallaj, and Muhammad ibn Salim, all of whom will be discussed later in this volume. Sahl's thought, though deeply grounded in the Qur'an and the shari'a, provoked criticism on the part of certain groups. Sahl died in exile in Basra.*

The selections below focus on two of Sahl's more original and influential contributions to Sufi thought: his theories of the pre-eternal convenant (mithāq) *and the Muhammadian light. These selections are translated in full, even though at times Sahl seems to digress into other issues, such as the rather enigmatic definition of* adab, *refined behavior, which he offers right in the middle of his exegesis of the pre-eternal covenant passage. Although such passages are puzzling, I have not deleted them because what seems digression by some contemporary standards was simply a part of a less linear form of thought in early Sufi writings.*

Tustari's understanding of the pre-eternal covenant is based on a single famous verse in Sura 7. In the previous verses (7:169–171), the Qur'an had been discussing the covenant of previous prophetic communities with their lord and the consequences of breaking that covenant. Then suddenly, in verse 7:172, the perspective shifts from the historical to the pre- and post-historical: "When your lord took from the sons of Adam, from their loins, their progeny (dhuriyya) *and had them witness over themselves. Am I not your lord? Indeed, we bear witness, they replied. That they might say on the day of resurrection, of this we were unaware!"*[30]

There is a difficulty in the Qur'anic verse in distinguishing the sons of Adam from their progency. If the verse is referring to all human beings in their latent, preexistent state, are not all humans both the sons of Adam and the progency of the sons of Adam? The difficult syntax of the Qur'anic verse is further complicated when brought into the framework of the pre-eternal convenant story of Tustari. Tustari takes "sons of Adam" as referring to the prophets, and their progeny as the rest of humankind over whom the prophets were placed as guides.

The verse regarding the progeny (dhuriyya) *of the sons of Adam becomes the foundation for Sufi "exemplarism," the view that at the end of time (the day of resurrection), or in the mystical experience, each person reverts back to that pure self which (as progeny of Adam and his sons) bore witness to its loyalty in its preexistence. A later example of the embedding of this idea in early Sufi thought can be found in one of the essays of Junayd (see Chapter 8 in this volume). The preexistent covenant of each person with his lord is balanced by a reference to the final day of resurrection, when each soul will see his eternal destiny. The logic of the Qur'anic phrase is that the preexistent covenant guarantees that the last judgment will not come as a total surprise. Yet the grammar is strange. The preeternal convenant seems to be intended as a warning, so that at the final judgment souls will not claim they were unaware of the consequences of their actions. But the text says: "That they might say on the day of resurrection, of this we were unaware!" One would expect: "lest" or "that they might not say on the day of resurrection, 'of this we were unaware.' " Some Qur'anic interpreters fill in the negative. But the lack of the negative might be an aspect of a certain sardonic voice that tends to recur in Qur'anic discussions of the day of resurrection or judgment. At any rate, Tustari's interpretation of this verse was to place the preexistent convenant at the heart of early Sufi notions of mystical union.*

Tustari's views on the "light of Muhammad" are of particular interest for their lyrical beauty and the sweep of the mystical conception. Although we might expect such "light mysticism" to emerge from a commentary on the famous "light verse" of the Qur'an, and though that verse is clearly behind much of Tustari's discussion, the articulation of his light mysticism occurs in the context of other Qur'anic citations, especially the commentary on the "vision" episodes (53:1–18). Yet it is the light verse that is the unspoken foundation of this majestic commentary, as it was to become the matrix of the long tradition of light mysticism within Islam.[31] *Before presenting selections from Tustari's commentary then, we begin with the Qur'anic light verse. Of special interest is the way in which the supremely lyrical depiction of divine light, with a continual movement from simile to simile, is framed by a more theoretical discourse on the nature of symbols, signs, and likeness.*

The "Light Verse" from the Sura of Light (24:35):

God is the light of the heavens and earth.
The light like the light of a lamp in a niche
The lamp enclosed in a cover of glass

The glass like a glistening star
Kindled from the oil of a blessed tree
An olive not of the East not of the West
Its oil glows forth nearly without the touch of fire
Light on light God guides to his light whomever he wills
Allah strikes symbols for humankind
Allah in all things is most knowing.

SELECTIONS FROM TUSTARI'S TAFSIR

(7:172) *When your lord took from the sons of Adam, from their loins, their progeny and had them witness over themselves.*[32]

Concerning this saying of the Most High, Sahl said that God Most High took the prophets from the loins of Adam, blessings and peace upon him. Then he took from the loin of each prophet his progeny *(dhuriyya)* in the form of seeds *(dhurr)* with intellects. He took from the prophets their covenant, as he said (33:7): *When we make a covenant with the prophets and with you [i.e., Muhammad] and with Noah.*[33] The covenant bound them to attain from God Most High his command and his prohibition.[34]

Then the Most High called them to affirm all together his lordship, through his word: "Am I not your lord?" He displayed his power until they said: "Yes, indeed." In their saying "yes, indeed," Allah brought together his design from his creatures and their original and final destiny.[35] The expression "yes, indeed" *(balā)* in their reply is related to the word *ibtilā'* [trial].[36] God Most High said (11:7): "His throne was upon water that he might try you."[37]

He had the prophets bear witness against them[38]—as is indicated in his saying: "He made them bear witness against themselves." Then he returned them to the loins of Adam, peace upon him. Then he sent the prophets to remind them of his compact and covenant.

On the day they made their avowal, he had already stored in his knowledge who would go back on it and who would remain loyal to it. The hour will not occur until every person upon whom the covenant was sworn emerges [into the world]. Then the hour will arrive. He [Ja'far] was asked: What are the signs of joy and wretchedness? He said that among the signs of wretchedness is the denial of the [divine] power *(qudra)* and among the signs of grace is that you should be open-hearted in faith, and that you should prosper in the heart and be preserved in obedience and be granted success in renunciation.

Among the most important kinds of refined relationship *(adab)* between him and God Most High are purity of heart and taking grace as nourishment. There is nothing more difficult than the preservation of *adab*. He was asked: What is *adab*? He said: Make barley your food, dates your sweets, salt your tanning agent, milk your grease, wool your clothing, mosques your houses, the sun your light, the moon your lamp, water your perfume, cleanliness your splendor, precaution your adornment, being-content (or he might have said "contentment") your work—self-vigilance your provisions; your meals nocturnal; your sleep diurnal; remembrance your speech; meditation your silence and your care; admonition your gaze, lord, refuge, and champion. In him, till death, be patient. He said that three of the signs of wretchedness are missing the prayer service while near mosque, missing the prayer service while in a city, and missing the pilgrimage *(ḥajj)* while in Mecca.[39]

Sahl said: Now as for the progeny, there are three kinds.

1. The first is Muhammad—God's blessings and peace upon him— because God Most High, when he wished to create Muhammad, God's blessings and peace upon him, manifested some of his light. When it attained the veil of majesty, it bowed down in prayer before Allah. Allah created from the *sajda* (position of prayer) a great column like a glass of light, as both his interior and exterior. In it is the *'ayn* (very being, essence, source, eye) of Muhammad, God's blessings and peace upon him. He stood in service before the lord of the two worlds for one thousand thousand years with the dispositions of faith, the beholding of faith, the unveiling of certitude, and the witness of the lord. Allah Most High favored him with such a witness a thousand thousand years before the beginning of creation. There is no one in the world whom Iblis—God's curse upon him—does not master and take captive, except for the prophets—God's blessings upon them—and the sincere ones *(ṣiddīqūn)* whose hearts have borne witness to their faith, in their stations, and who have known God's awareness of them in all their conditions. According to the measure of their witness, they recognize the trial. According to the measure of their recognition of the trial, they seek preservation from error. According to their poverty and need for him, they recognize harm and benefit and they grow in knowledge, understanding, and vision.

Then he said: Allah Most High did not make any of the prophets bear the service that he made our prophet Muhammad bear—God's blessings and peace upon him. Nor is there among the sons of Adam, God's blessings upon him, any station of service to God Most High before the sending of our Prophet—God's peace and blessings upon him—that our Prophet, blessings and peace upon him, had not already fulfilled.[40]

When asked about the meaning of the word of the Prophet—blessings and peace of Allah upon him—"I am not like any of you; my lord gives me to eat and drink"[41]—Sahl [at-Tustari] said: It is not that he had food or drink with him but rather he was recalling his uniqueness before God Most High. He would be *like* one who eats and drinks. If he had food and drink, he would have preferred [to give it] to his family and the people of the bench.[42]

2. The second is Adam, God bless him. Allah created him from light [of Muhammad?] (so said the Prophet—peace upon him)[43] and he created Muhammad, God bless him and grant him peace, that is, Muhammad's body, from the clay of Adam, peace upon him.

3. The third is the progeny of Adam. Allah Almighty and Majestic created the seekers from the light of Adam and created the guides from the light of Muhammad, God bless him and grant him peace.[44] The common people live in the compassion of the people of nearness and the people of nearness live in the compassion of the one who makes (or is made) near. Their light became available at their disposal and through their faith.

He said, Most High (7:176), "If we had wished, we would have raised him high." This saying refers to Bal'ām ibn Bā'ūrā'.[45] However (7:176), "he lingered on the earth and followed his desire," and turned away through following his desire. God Most High portioned out desire among his enemies, allotting each enemy his share. When one of his enemies inclines to desire, harm rises to his heart.

Know that the self contains a secret. He did not manifest that secret to any of his creatures except Pharaoh, who said (79:24): "I am your lord most high." He said: How can we find peace from desire? He replied, whoever imposes *adab* upon his self finds peace from it. Whoever overwhelms his self with *adab* worships with sincerity Allah Almighty and Majestic.

He said: And the self has seven heavenly veils and seven earthly veils. Whenever a self entombs itself in the earth, its heart rises up through heaven after heaven. When the self is entombed beneath the soil, the heart rises to the throne.

It has been related of Kahmas that he would pray one thousand *rak'a*s [sets of bodily motions and positions in prayer] every night and day and that he would say the *taslīm* invocation between each pair of *rak'a*s, and then say to himself: Rise, O refuge of every evil; I am not content with you.[46]

Of his word, Most High (7:180): "Allah's are the beautiful names. Call him by them": Sahl said that behind the names and the attributes are attributes that cannot be penetrated by understanding because the real is a raging fire. There is no way there. There is no choice but to plunge into it.[47]

Surat an-Najm (The Sura of the Star) *53:1–12*

By the star when it falls
Your companion has not gone astray nor is he deluded
He does not speak out of desire
It is nothing less than an inspiration inspired
Taught to him by one of great power
And strength that stretched out over
While on the highest horizon
Then it drew near and descended
At a distance of two bows' length or nearer
He inspired in his servant what he inspired
The heart did not lie in what it saw
Will you then dispute with him on his vision?

Surat an-Najm, 53:13–18

He saw it descending another time
At the lote tree of the furthest limit
Therein was the garden of sanctuary
When there enveloped the tree what enveloped it
His gaze did not turn aside nor did it overreach
He had seen the signs of his lord, great signs.

His saying, Most High (53:1–12), "By the star when it falls," means: By Muhammad, God bless him and bring him peace, when he returns from heaven.

Of his saying, Most High, "Your companion has not gone astray nor is he deluded," Sahl said: That is, he has not gone astray from the reality of unity in any way and he did not follow the satan in his condition.[48]

His saying "He does not speak out of desire" means that he does not pronounce any falsehood. Sahl said: His pronouncement was one of the veils of Allah Most High, so how could desire or the Shayṭan oppose him?

His saying, Most High, "Then it drew near and descended" means it came closer and closer. His saying, Most High, "The heart did not lie in what it saw," refers to his face-to-face witness of his lord with the insight of his heart. "Will you then dispute with him on his version?"—that is, from us and through us.[49] What he saw from us and through us is better than what he saw through himself.

Of the saying "He saw it descending another time," he said: This means in the beginning when God Most High and Most Praised created him—it is said—as light in the form of a column of light,[50] one thousand thousand years before the creation of creations, with the dispositions of faith unveiling hidden through the hidden. He stood before him in worshipfulness.

"At the lote tree of the furthest limit," that is the tree at which the knowledge of everyone ends. "When there enveloped the tree what enveloped it." This means that the lote tree of the light of Muhammad—God's blessing and peace upon him—in his worship, is like moths of gold. The real sends them out as a marvel from its secrets. All that serves to increase support for him when he is assailed by the oncomings.[51]

"His gaze did not turn aside nor did it overreach." He said: He did not incline to the signs of himself nor to the witnessing of himself. Rather he witnessed through his universality his lord most high, witnessing the attributes that were made manifest to him and that required constancy in that stage.

"He had seen the signs of his lord, great signs." This statement refers to the attributes that appeared from his signs. He saw them but in seeing them he did not abandon the object of his witness and was not cut off from the proximity of his object of worship. The vision only increased him in love, longing, and power. Allah gave him the power to bear the manifestation and the sublime illuminations. That was a special favor for him over the rest of the prophets. Do you not see how Musa was struck down upon the manifestation? In an experience of double that intensity, the Prophet, blessing and peace of Allah upon him, broke through in his face-to-face witness with the gaze of his heart. He was held firm through the power of his condition and the grandeur of his station and rank.[52]

3

Qushayri: Interpreting Mystical Expressions from the Treatise

INTRODUCTION

In refinement of style, ability to combine a searching discussion of the most difficult concepts with a lucid and readable exposition, and combination of precise analysis with theatrical anecdote, few works rival the famous Treatise *of Qushayri.*[1]

'Abd al-Karīm ibn Hawāzin al-Qushayrī (d. 465/1074) was born near Nishapur in the Khurasan area of what is present-day Iran. He received the full Islamic education of the time, memorizing the Qur'an, studying Islamic law (fiqh) *and Ash'arite theology, and becoming a disciple to the Sufi master Abū 'Alī ad-Daqqāq (d. 412/1021). His treatise on Sufism continued the movement toward a synoptic view of Sufi thought and practice exemplified by Sarraj (d. 378/988) and Sulami (d. 412/1021). Qushayri's* Treatise *became so popular that it is known simply as the* Qushayriyyan Treatise *or the* Treatise. *It is perhaps the most popular classical work on Sufism, admired for its subtlety, acuity, and clarity.*

Presented here is section three of the Treatise, *the section on key Sufi terms and concepts.*[2] *The intricate discursive texture of the section is immediately apparent. The analysis of each major concept is woven around the sayings of earlier Sufis. Qushayri is particularly fond of unattributed proverbs, introduced by phrases such as "they say," "some say" or "some-*

one said."[3] *When Qushayri does cite named shaykhs, his citations tend to cluster around a few figures; most frequently cited are Qushayri's teacher, ad-Daqqaq, and ad-Daqqaq's teacher, Sulami. The various proverbs and poetic verses are woven into a highly sophisticated analysis. A single term, such as* waqt *(moment), will be defined from various points of view, non-Sufi and Sufi, and as each short essay progresses, deeper understandings of the term gradually unfold. In many cases, a term will undergo a progression through various meanings in one essay, only to be viewed in the following essay from the opposite point of view. Thus, "witnessing"* (mushāhada, shuhūd) *is first treated as a lower state in which a person witnesses his actions as his own. In the very next essay, it becomes the highest state, in which a person witnesses nothing other than the deity. Such reversals can and do occur within a single essay as a term is viewed positively, then negatively, and then in a manner that transcends both or takes both aspects up into a new term.*

This perspectivalism keeps the essay in a continual state of dynamic tension; no single static definition stands on its own. The dialectical movement of perspectives is achieved in part through a careful harnessing of the living oral tradition, by placing various "voices" and "sayings" into conversation with one another. Anecdotes and sayings of Shibli are of special importance; Shibli's intensity (often passing over the boundary into madness) is a kind of horizon of language, a marker beyond which the words can only beckon, but not call. Such dialectical use of oral tradition had been employed by earlier writers such as Sarraj (see Chapter 6, in this volume). Within Qushayri's exquisitely wrought narrative framework, the dialectic is combined with a rigorous and precise conceptual analysis and a series of poetic echoes that sound the depth of the Middle East lyrical traditions.

Stylistic and emotive variation also surprises the reader. The endings of individual sections can range from Junayd's searing account of the mystical states of qabḍ *(constriction) and* basṭ *(expansion), to the comic episode of two Sufis who, carried away by the experience of ecstatic existentiality* (wujūd), *rip trees out by the roots and wrestle one another into submission in* wajd *combat. The closing episodes, often relating stories of strange behavior and miracles, condense and dramatize the previous, sophisticated discussion into a story indelibly fixed in the reader's imagination.*

There is more involved here than is suggested by the title of the section "explanation of expressions" (tafsīr alfāz). *The discussion of each term does include an acknowledgement of the common meaning of the term and its basic semantic field, as well as a discussion of the various ways it is defined and employed by different groups of Sufis. Also included is a probing analysis of the emotive and psychological ramifications of the concept, along with its moral and experiential dimensions; an analysis of the theological implications of the concept, with special attention to the classic tension between human free-agency and divine predetermination; and a careful relation of the term and concept to the dimensions of the lyric (through poetry citations) and the dramatic (through extended anecdotes).*

In addition to the multidimensional character of each essay in itself, the various essays are interconnected by both foreshadowing and retrospection. Frequently an essay will explain one term in terms of another not introduced until later; or a later discussion of a new term will cause the reader to re-evaluate the understanding of a term previously introduced. Of course, any "dictionary" must explain one term through other terms, but Qushayri's Treatise *intensifies the sense that the key Sufi terms and concepts create an interdependent web of meaning in which each term or nexus is made up of, and dependent on, all the other terms. In this way, the* Treatise *is not only an illuminating examination of key Sufi concepts, but also an illustration of the dynamic and multiperspectival character of Sufi discourse.*

♦ ♦ ♦

FROM QUSHAYRI'S TREATISE: THE INTERPRETATION OF SUFI EXPRESSIONS

The Moment (*Waqt*)

Qushayri 's exposition of the term waqt *(moment, instant) is an explosive opening to this section of the* Treatise, *with a searching discussion of the relationships among time, experience, and identity. In Sufism, the* waqt *is the period of the* ḥāl *(state, condition). There is constant progression through stages of intensity in both moments and states, aiming at a complete giving over of the self to each moment, as if that moment were the totality of one's existence.*[4] *A further element of the Sufi moment is the lack of self-will or choice* (ikhtiyār). *A moment and state come upon the Sufi spontaneously, independent of any intention or deliberate effort. However, in this section, as throughout the* Treatise, *Qushayri is especially careful to stress that such radical spontaneity is never seen as an excuse to evade ritual obli-*

gations, such as the five prescribed prayers, and is never seen in contradiction with them. It is not by accident that Qushayri begins his essay on the twenty-seven central Sufi concepts with the "moment." The moment, a time-out-of-time within time, bringing the eschatological afterworld into the present, is the basis on which the Sufi psychology of the "states" (aḥwāl) *will be constructed. Each moment is a universe of promise and danger, the latter aspect brought out in a proverb comparing time to a cutting sword.*

Realized masters employ the term "moment" *(waqt)* to refer to the relation between the anticipation of an event and the event's actual occurrence.[5] Conversely, the actual occurrence can be considered the moment of the anticipated occurrence. You say, for example: "I'll meet you at the beginning of the month." The meeting is an anticipation. The beginning of the month is its actual occurrence. Thus, the beginning of the month is the moment of the meeting.

I heard the teacher Abū 'Alī ad-Daqqāq, God's mercy upon him, say: "The moment is what you are in. If you are in the world, your moment is the world. If you are in the afterworld, your moment is the afterworld. If you are in happiness, your moment is happiness. If you are in sorrow, your moment is sorrow." By that he means that the moment is that which dominates a person.[6]

Some people mean by the moment the time in which a person happens to be. Some of the folk say that the moment is between two times, between the past and the present.

They call the Sufi "a son of his moment" *(ibn waqtihi)*, meaning that he is completely occupied with the religious obligation of his present state, carrying out what is demanded of him at the time. It is said that one who embraces poverty has concern neither for the moment past nor for the moment to come.[7] He is concerned only with the present moment in which he finds himself. They also say: "to be preoccupied with a past moment is to lose a second moment."[8]

By moment they can also mean that which happens to them through the dispositions of the real[9] that come upon them without any choice on their part. They say: "So and so is in the power of his moment," that is, he surrenders to whatever comes over him, without his own will, from the unknown. This meaning applies only for those things that are not under God's prophetically given command or injunction. To neglect or to consign to providence what has been commanded or to neglect the complete carrying out of the command is to be outside the faith.

They say: "The moment is a sword," that is, just as the sword is cutting, so the moment prevails in what the real brings to pass and completes. It is said: "The sword is gentle to the touch, but its edge cuts. Whoever handles it gently is unharmed. Whoever treats it roughly is cut." Similarly for the moment, whoever submits to its decree is saved, and whoever opposes it is thrown over and destroyed. In this regard they composed the following verse:

Like a sword—if you handle it gently
  its touch is gentle,
but its edges, if you treat it roughly
  are rough.

When the moment favors someone, the moment for him is just a moment. When the moment opposes someone, the moment for him is loathing.

I heard my teacher Abu 'Ali ad-Daqqaq say: "The moment is a file. It files you down without effacing you." He means that were it to efface you and make you pass away, you would be—in your passing away—liberated. However, the moment takes from you without entirely annihilating you.

He recited in this regard:

Every day that passes
  takes part of me,
leaves my heart a portion of loss,
  and passes away.

He also recited:

Just as the people of fire
  when their skin is well roasted
have prepared for their wretchedness
  new skin.

And with similar meaning:

No one truly dies
  who finds rest in dying.
To truly die
  is to live your death.

Astute is one who remains in the rule of his moment. If his moment is waking consciousness *(ṣaḥw)*, his performance is of the shari'a, and if his moment is effacement, the rule of reality prevails upon him.

THE STATION (*MAQĀM*)

This essay starts off by following the standard distinction between a station (maqām), *which is attained through a self-directed effort, and a state* (ḥāl), *which comes on a person independent of intention or will. Stations are initially defined as relatively stable, sequential stages that involve self-discipline and willed human activity. A Sufi must attain perfection in one station before moving on to the next. However, in both the essay on station and that on state, Qushayri goes on to a more sophisticated exploration of the relationship between intentional efforts and spontaneity that is characteristic of the most valued Sufi experience.*

The short essay on the station ends abruptly with an anecdote about the early Sufi al-Wasiti, who criticized as "pure Magianism"[10] *another Shaykh's injunction to his disciples to focus on how they carry out their acts and whether there is any deficiency in carrying them out.*

The station is the particular place along the path of refinement *(adab)* realized by the godservant through a kind of behavior and through a form of quest and self-discipline. A person's station is his standing in such matters and the practices in which he is engaged. An essential condition of the station is that you cannot rise from one station to another until you have fulfilled the provisions of the first. Whoever has not attained contentedness is not ready for the station of trust-in-God; whoever has not attained trust-in-God is not ready for the station of surrender; similarly, whoever has not attained repentance is not ready for contrition; and whoever has not attained watchfulness is not ready for renunciation.[11]

As opposed to *mAqām* (station), the *mUqām* [with a "u" after the "m"] is the act of being placed somewhere (like "entrance"—in the sense of the act of being brought in, and "exit" in the sense of the act of being brought out).[12] No one merits a station except through witnessing to his being placed in that station by God Most High, that God's command might be established upon sound foundations.

I heard my teacher Abu 'Ali ad-Daqqaq (God's mercy upon him) say:

> When al-Wāsiṭī entered Nishapur, he asked the disciples of Abū 'Uthmān what their Shaykh commanded them to do. They said:

"He enjoins upon us the adherence to acts of obedience and the constant vigilance against any falling short in such acts." He replied: "He enjoins upon you nothing other than Magianism. Did he not enjoin upon you a lack of attention to the acts themselves by ordering you to pay attention to the construction and carrying out of the acts?" Al-Wāsiṭī meant to put them on guard against any occasion for self-admiration. He did not mean to turn them aside into the regions of negligence or to authorize the transgression of any proper behavior.[13]

The State (Ḥāl)

In the essay on the state (ḥāl), *Qushayri begins with the common emphasis on the ephemerality of the states, as opposed to the relative stability of the stations. He then offers another perspective, according to which some states are not ephemeral, and those that are ephemeral are viewed as inferior. The example given is the state of* riḍā *(contentedness, acceptance), which is relatively stable. Much depends on the particularities of classification.*[14] *Qushayri in a dialectical move accepts the nonephemeral state, but as a taste or portion* (shirb) *of something that can then grow. Ephemeral experiences are not inferior states, but beacons of a yet higher consciousness that will gradually be realized as more continuous.*

The discussion deepens to an examination of the continual progressivity and movement within the consciousness of the seeker as he moves ever deeper along the infinite road to the real.[15] *Of special importance is Qushayri's use of the word* maʿnā *here. The word can mean "meaning," "essence," or "feeling." Qushayri uses it to refer to the "content" of the individual state (delight, constriction, longing, anxiety, terror). The word indicates more than a feeling and yet something more specific than consciousness. I have used the term "mode of consciousness."*

Among the folk, the state is a mode of consciousness that comes upon the heart without a person's intending it, attracting it, or trying to gain it—a feeling of delight or sorrow, constriction, longing, anxiety, terror, or want. States are bestowed; stations are attained. States come freely given while stations are gained with *majhūd* (the expending of effort).[16] The possessor of a station is secure in his station, while the possessor of a state can be taken up out of his state.

Dhū n-Nūn al-Miṣrī was asked about the knower. He said: "He was here but left!" Some shaykhs say: "States are like lightning flashes. If it continues, it is a notion."[17] They also say: "States reflect their name," that is, just as they alight upon the heart, they pass on with the moment.[18]

They recite:

If it did not change
   It would not be named a state
Everything that changes,
   passes.

Look at the shadow
   as it comes to its end,
It moves toward its decline
   when it grows long.

On the other hand, some of the folk have maintained the stability and perdurance of the states. They claim that if the experiences do not last or continue, they are shimmerings *(lawā'iḥ)* and flashes of intuition *(bawādih)*, and their possessor has not yet attained true states. Insofar as the attribute lasts, then they are properly called states. Abū 'Uthmān al-Ḥirī said: "For forty years Allah did not place me in a state that I disliked." He was referring to the continuation of contentedness which is numbered among the states.[19]

What must be said of all this is that they are correct who claim that the state is continuous. The particular mode of consciousness *(ma'nā)* is a taste or portion *(shirb)* in a person that can later grow into something more. But the possessor of such a continuous state has other states beyond those that have become a taste for him. These other states are ephemeral. When these ephemeral happenings become continuous for him like those previous states, then he rises up to another, higher and subtler state.[20] He never ceases to rise higher.

The Prophet, God's peace and blessings upon him, said:

"My heart becomes shrouded, so that I ask God Most High for pardon seventy times a day."[21] In regard to this hadith, I heard Abu 'Ali ad-Daqqaq, God's mercy upon him, say: "The Prophet (God's mercy and blessings upon him) was continually rising in his states. When he rose from one condition *(ḥāla)* to a higher one, he might glance at the condition he has risen beyond, and he would

> count it as a covering or shroud in relationship to what he had attained. His states were continually being intensified.

The providential graces of the real Most Glorious are infinite. For if the real Most High is deserving of majesty, and a truly realized attainment of it is impossible, then the servant will be perpetually rising from state to state.[22]

He can attain no mode of consciousness which does not have yet a higher mode within the decree of the All-Praised, which he is destined to attain. This is how the following saying is to be taken: "The good deeds of the pious are the bad deeds of the intimates of God."

When Junayd was asked about this, he recited:

Sudden gleams of light
  when they appear, apparitions,
revealing a secret,
  telling of union.

Constriction (*Qabḍ*) and Expansion (*Basṭ*)

In this essay, Qushayri plunges into the heart of Sufi psychology with a crucial distinction between states involving future expectations (such as hope and fear) and states involving immediate experience (such as constriction and expansion). Constriction is a gripping of the heart, an experience analogous to fear, but far more intense in that it is an experience of something immediate, in the present. Expansion is a dilation, a feeling of peace or well-being, again intensified down into the immediate present. Although expansion is originally viewed as the more desirable state, the essay moves—in a typically Qushayrian twist—to a sudden reversal of perspective in which the comfort of expansion is seen as a trap.

The essay ends with Junayd's comments on qabḍ *and* basṭ. *The comments of Junayd come as a shock. His writing is rough and staccato. The voice speaks from the point of "I am there." Coming at the end of Qushayri's "set up" of the concepts, Junayd's comments resonate down through centuries of Sufi thought and experience.*

Junayd's sayings require a change in standard translation vocabulary. The terms constriction *and* expansion, *while accurate as translations of their Arabic equivalents on the conceptual level within many texts, are unworkable within the short semantic bursts of Junayd. For this passage of Junayd, shorter, less Latinate terms are used: "Fear of God grips me. . . ." However the passage of Junayd is interpreted, it is unlikely that it merits the trait so frequently attributed to Junayd's writings, "sobriety."*

These two states [constriction and expansion] arise after the servant has risen beyond the condition of fear *(khawf)* and hope *(rajā')*. Constriction is to the master as fear is to the beginner. Expansion is to the master as hope is to the beginner. What is the precise distinction between constriction and fear, and between expansion and hope? Fear concerns something in the future only. One might fear, for example, the loss of something desired, or the onslaught of something unwanted. The same holds true for hope, whether the hope arises in contemplating something desired for the future or in awaiting the anticipated cessation of something unwanted or detested.

As for constriction and expansion, their mode of consciousness occurs in the present moment. The heart of the possessor of fear or hope is related to these two conditions through a deferring *(bi ājilihi)* of the expected. But the possessor of constriction and expansion is a captive of his moment in the "oncomings"[23] that prevail upon him in the immediate now *(fī 'ājilihi)*.[24] A person's attributes in constriction and expansion differ in accordance with his rankings in the states. There are oncomings that cause a constriction that still allows a place for other things in the person gripped by constriction; the constriction has not filled him completely. There are also people so constricted that they have no room for the oncoming of anything else, because all such room has been snatched away entirely in a single oncoming. That leaves no room for any other oncoming because the first oncoming has taken over the person completely. Thus the expression used by some: "I am full," that is, there is no more room left in me.

The same is true for a person experiencing expansion. He might have an expansion that contains all creatures, so that the most spectacular things do not move him. He experiences an expansion so great that no state can affect him. I heard the master Abu 'Ali ad-Daqqaq, God's mercy upon him, say:

> Some people came to visit 'Alī Abū Bakr al-Qaḥṭī.[25] He had a son who was occupying himself as boys will do. The visitors crossed the path of the boy, but he and his companions were so occupied they did not notice. His heart was moved to pity and commiseration for al-Qaḥṭī, and he said: "Poor Shaykh, how he must be tried by the misbehavior of such a son!" Then he approached al-Qaḥṭī and found him completely unaware of these amusements and goings-on. He marveled at him and said: "May I be ransom for

> one whom the rock-rooted mountains cannot move!" Al-Qaḥṭī replied: "We have been liberated in eternity from the bondage of things."

Among the more common occasions of constriction is an oncoming that overwhelms the heart as an intimation of fault or a sign that blame is deserved. Inevitably, constriction comes upon the heart. Another occasion of oncoming might be a sign of nearness or approach to favor and acceptance. Then expansion comes upon the heart.

In general, each person undergoes constriction in proportion to his expansion and expansion in proportion to his constriction. One can undergo constriction while its cause remains uncertain; he finds constriction in his heart without knowing its occasion or cause. The proper path for one undergoing such constriction is to submit to it until the moment passes. If he goes to the trouble of expelling it or tries to anticipate the [new] moment through his own choice before it comes upon him, his constriction will only increase. Or his action may be accounted as poor behavior. However, if he submits to the provision of the moment, then the constriction should shortly pass. The All-Praised said (2:245): "God constricts [the heart] and expands it."

Expansion can also occur all of a sudden, happening upon a person unexpectedly, without any recognizable cause. It shakes him up and disconcerts him. The proper path for anyone undergoing it is to stay still and to watch over his behavior. In such a moment there is a great danger. Anyone in such a moment should be on guard against a hidden snare. In this regard, the folk have said: "The door of expansion was opened before me and I slipped and became veiled from my station." For this reason they say: "Stay on the prayer carpet *(bisāṭ)*, beware of expansion *(inbisāṭ)*." The realized masters have numbered the states of constriction and expansion among those from which one should ask refuge. In relation to what is above these states—the perishing of the godservant and his advancement in reality—they are poverty and harm.

I heard the Shaykh Abū 'Abd ar-Raḥmān as-Sulamī say: I heard al-Ḥusayn ibn Yaḥyā say: I heard Ja'far ibn Muḥammad say: I heard al-Junayd say:

> Fear of God grips me. Hope unfolds me. Reality draws me together. The real sets me apart. When he seizes me with fear, he annihilates me from myself. When he unfolds me with hope, he returns me to myself. When he recollects me in reality, he makes me present. When he sets me apart through the real, he makes

me witness the other-than-me, then veils me from himself. He is exalted beyond all of that, transforming me rather than holding me secure, desolating me rather than granting me his intimacy. Through my being-present I taste the flavor of my existence *(wujūd).* Would that he had annihilated me from myself and compensated me, or had absented me from myself and revived me.[26]

AWE *(HAYBA)* AND INTIMACY *(UNS)*

Beyond constriction and expansion, Qushayri moves to awe and intimacy. Rudolf Otto, in his influential definition of the holy as the mysterium tremendum *(dread-inspiring mystery), attributed to the human experience of the holy the simultaneous modes of intense desire and intense fear.*[27] *For the early Sufis, the* mysterium tremendum *is based on a somewhat different pair of modes of consciousness: the experience of intense intimacy and intense dread or awe. Intimacy* (uns) *and awe* (hayba) *are two of the fundamental modes of Qur'anic discourse and classical poetry, and Sufis have developed these modes into a highly sophisticated experiential psychology. Qushayri quite naturally turns to the classical poetic tradition for proof-texts on the experience of intimacy. After saying that awe is associated with "absence" and intimacy with "wakefulness," Qushayri goes on, in dialectical fashion, to challenge the distinction he has set up. Both the "intimate" and the awe-struck (and therefore "absent") in his examples are, in one manner or another, unconscious of themselves and their surroundings. This fusion of intimacy and awe is a key aspect of Qur'anic literary power.*[28]

The section ends with several occurrences of the term wujūd, *one of the more definitively untranslatable terms in Sufism, combining as it does the senses of ecstasy, discovery, and existence. For the moment the phrase "ecstatic existentiality" is used as a gloss for the term. In the very next section, Qushayri will provide an analysis of the semantic field of this key Sufi term.*

These two states [awe and intimacy] are above constriction and expansion, just as constriction is above the rank of fear and expansion is above the level of hope. For awe is higher than constriction and intimacy is more perfect than expansion. The reality of *hayba* (awe) is *ghayba* (absence); every *hā'ib* (person in a state of awe) is *ghā'ib* (absent, disappeared).

The awe-struck are ranked in awe according to their distinction in absence; some are higher than others. Intimacy, on the other hand, requires a proper wakefulness *(ṣaḥw)*. Every intimate is awake. Each is distinguished according to his distinction in the initial taste *(shirb)*. Therefore they say: "The lowest way-station of intimacy is this: that if a person were thrown into a blazing fire, his intimacy would not be troubled."

Junayd, God grant him compassion, said:

> I heard Sarī say: "The godservant reaches the point that were his face to be struck with a sword, he would not feel it." There was something in my heart [opposing this] until it became clear to me that this is the case.

My father reported that Muqātil al-'Akkī said:

> I paid a visit to Shiblī. He was plucking out the hair of his eyebrows with a pair of tweezers. I said: "My master, you do this to yourself but the pain comes back to my heart!" He said: "Woe to you. Reality is apparent to me, and I am not able to bear it. It's like this: I cause pain to myself, that I might feel it and that it might be veiled from me. But I do not find the pain, and it is not veiled from me, and I cannot bear it!"[29]

The realized masters consider the states of awe and intimacy, majestic as they are, to be deficient because they entail variability in the godservant. The states of the people of firm-rootedness *(tamkīn)* are beyond any variation. They are obliterated in the ecstatic existentiality of the essence *('ayn)*. They have no awe and no intimacy, no knowledge and no sensation.

The story related of Abū Sa'īd al-Kharrāz is well known. He said:

> I was once lost in the wasteland, and said:
>
> I wander lost and from the desert
> I know not who I am
> beyond what people say about me
> and about my kind.
>
> I wander lost among the jinn
> of the land, and the people.
> If I find no one,
> With myself alone I wander lost.

He then said: I heard a voice call me, saying:

O you who view causes
  as your highest part of existence
and rejoice in the loss of the world
  and its company

Were you really
  one of the people of true existing
You would be absent from the worlds,
  from the throne, and from the footstool[30]

You would be without state
  with Allah, standing
Protected from calling to mind
  jinn and human company.[31]

The servant can only rise from this state [of awe or intimacy] in ecstatic existentiality.

Making-Ecstatic *(Tawājud)*, Ecstasy/Finding *(Wajd)*, and Ecstatic Existentiality *(Wujūd)*

This is one of the essays most bound up with Arabic word play, etymology, and morphology. At the center of the verbal play are the three consonants w/j/d. *It is also a key essay in the sense that it brings into clear and explicit focus the worlds of meaning that are evoked by these terms when used in Sufi discourse. Thus it serves as an introduction to the Sufi concept of ecstasy or mystical rapture, as well as to the Sufi method of using verbal play.*

Most Arabic words are based on three consonants (called the "radical"). From one radical (such as w/j/d), *a morphological system, with permutations of the vowels, prefixes, and suffixes, generates a large number of words whose relationship to the radical and whose meanings vis-à-vis the radical can be in part deduced from the form of the word. Thus the native Arabic speaker would immediately recognize the* w/j/d *radical within the words* wajd *(ecstasy),* wujūd *(existence),* wajada *(to find), and* tawājud *(making-ecstatic), and would immediately comprehend the way the Sufis* are using the underlying radical to place these meanings into relationship with one another and at times fuse them into a single term..

We note immediately the difference in metaphor between the Latinate term ecstasy (ek stasis) as "standing outside of oneself" or "rapture" (from raptus), as "being taken" or "seized up" out of oneself, and the Arabic term wajd. Wajd combines the meaning of "intense feeling" with the notion of "finding." Though we might translate the term as ecstasy or rapture, as Qushayri shows here explicitly, and as Junayd implies continually (see Chapter 8 in this volume), the Sufis always kept in mind the term's specific meanings of finding and intensity of feeling carried within the term's tri-consonantal root w/j/d.

In addition to intense experience and finding, the lexical field of wajd also includes "existence" (wujūd). As the essay comes to its conclusion, it becomes clear that the Sufi notion of existence is experiential.[32] To exist is not simply to have being or phenomenal reality. On the contrary, as Qushayri shows, many saw existence as achieved only insofar as one's ego-self, one's normal identity and center of being, is annihilated. Existence occurs in the ecstasy and in the discovery that occurs through "passing away." The full lexical field of w/j/d—ecstasy, finding, existence—corresponds as closely as any Sufi term to what is currently called the mystical experience, though in its own distinctive conceptual configuration. After a more abstract discussion, where various meanings of the root w/j/d are placed in tension with one another, Qushayri follows with a poetic version a more poetic set of distinctions: "I heard the master Abu 'Ali ad-Daqqaq say: 'Tawḥīd entails the encompassing of the servant. Ecstasy (wajd) entails the immersion of the servant. Wujūd entails the extinction of the servant. It is like one who witnesses the sea, then sails upon the sea, then drowns in the sea.' "

Before Qushayri can approach these issues at such a degree of analytic precision and poetic depth, he must treat the question of tawājud, yet another term based on the Arabic w/j/d radical. Tawājud is based on a morphological form that can take on several senses: attempting to do something, affecting something, doing something in a studious or deliberate manner.[33] In the case of tawājud, all of these meanings apply. The term is translated below by the phrase "making-ecstatic" (in the intransitive sense). One who makes ecstatic is attempting to achieve ecstasy through his own initiative or, more negatively, is affecting ecstasy.

The same issue is involved in all states: On the one hand, they occur during the process of a life of devotion and are, in some sense, the consequence of acts of devotion and practices of contemplation. On the other *hand, the Sufis emphasized continually the fact that states are bestowed freely, come spontaneously, and are not earned or gained through any particular efforts.*

Making-Ecstatic (tawājud)

Making-ecstatic is the petitioning of ecstasy through a kind of self-will. Its possessor does not have the completeness of *wajd*; if he did, he would already be ecstatic *(wājid)*. Most words in the morphology of *tawājud* indicate the [attempted or deliberate] manifestation of an attribute.[34] Thus the poet said:

> I made as if I were squint-eyed[35]
> though my eye was not deformed.
> Then my eye no longer saw,
> though I still had two good eyes.

Some say: Making-ecstatic is not condoned for anyone because of the self-conscious effort *(takalluf)* it entails and the manner in which it distances its practitioner from realization.

Others say that it is condoned for those dervishes who remove everything from themselves, who have observed closely the ecstatic mode of consciousness.[36] They base their reasoning upon the saying of the Messenger, God's peace and blessings upon him: Weep, and if you cannot weep, make like you are weeping *(tabā kū)*. Then there is the well-known story [in favor of making-ecstatic] concerning Abū Muḥammad al-Jurayrī, who said:

> I was at the home of Junayd, where Ibn Masrūq and others were present. There was a musician present. Ibn Masrūq and the others rose, but Junayd stayed put. I said: "My master, Do you feel nothing in the audition?"[37] Junayd replied (27:88): "You see the mountains and think they are fixed, but they pass like clouds!" Then he said: "And you, Abū Muḥammad, do you feel nothing in the audition?" I said: "Master, if I am present in a place where there is an audition, and there is somebody who is reticent, I hold my ecstasy within myself. Then when I am alone, I let it loose. Thus I make-ecstatic *(tawājadtu)*."

In this story, he [Abū Muḥammad] employed the expression "making-ecstatic," and Junayd did not contradict it.

I heard the master Abu 'Ali ad-Daqqaq, God's mercy upon him, say: When Abū Muḥammad heeded the refined behavior *(adab)* of the notables in the state of audition, Allah preserved his moment for him through the blessings of *adab*, so that he said: "I held my ecstasy in myself. When I was alone, I let it out and made-ecstatic," that is, once the moment *(waqt)* has come down and prevailed, you cannot let out your ecstasy when you wish. When he was sincere in respecting the dignity of the shaykhs, Allah preserved his moment until he could let out his ecstasy once he was alone.

Ecstasy (wajd)

As suggested by the above remarks, making-ecstatic *(tawājud)* is the beginning of ecstasy, after which comes ecstasy *(wajd)* proper. Ecstasy is what happens upon your heart and comes upon it without any intention or self-conscious effort. In this regard, the shaykhs say: Ecstasy is a happening though ecstasies are the fruits of devotions *(awrād)*. The more your devotions increase, the more graces *(laṭā'if)* you receive from Allah.

I heard master Abu 'Ali ad-Daqqaq, God have mercy upon him, say: "The oncomings are in proportion to the devotions. Whoever has no *wird* (devotion) in his exterior being will have no oncoming *(wārid)* in his secret being *(sarā'iruhu)*."[38] No ecstasy that contains anything of its possessor is truly an ecstasy. Just as the good works taken on by the godservant in his exterior activities result in the sweetness of obedient acts, so the interior rules that he encounters result in ecstasies. Sweets are the fruits of activities, ecstasies are the results of encounters.[39]

Ecstatic Existentiality (wujūd)

As for ecstatic existentiality *(wujūd)*, it occurs after one rises beyond *wajd*. There is [for the godservant] no existential ecstatic experience *(wujūd)* of the real except after the extinction of the mortal.[40] The mortal human cannot endure the appearance of the sovereignty of the real.

In this regard, Abū l-Ḥusayn an-Nūrī said: "For twenty years I was between *wajd* (ecstasy/finding) and *faqd* (loss). When I found my lord, I lost my heart, and when I found my heart, I lost my lord."

In the same regard, Junayd said: "His knowledge of oneness *(tawḥid)* is distinct from his *wujūd*, and his *wujūd* is distinct from his knowledge." In this regard, they recite:

My existence *(wujūd)* is
  absence from existing,

through what I was shown
  and witnessed.

Tawḥīd is a beginning and *wujūd* is an end, and ecstasy is an intermediary between the beginning and the end.

I heard the master Abu 'Ali ad-Daqqaq say: "*Tawḥīd* entails the encompassing of the servant. Ecstasy *(wajd)* entails the immersion of the servant. *Wujūd* entails the extinction of the servant. It is like one who witnesses the sea, then sails upon the sea, then drowns in the sea. The order of the matter is: quest, then witnessing, then *wujūd*, then *khamūd* (extinction). The possessor of *wujūd* embraces both waking and effacement. His waking state is his abiding through the real, and his state of effacement is his passing away through the real. These two states succeed one another continuously. If waking through the real prevails upon him, then into him it [the real] rushes and through him it speaks."[41] He said, peace upon him, in reporting from the real: "In me he hears and through me he sees."[42]

I heard the shaykh Abū 'Abd ar-Raḥmān as-Sulamī say: I heard Manṣūr ibn 'Abdullāh say:

> A man stood in front of the circle of Shibli and asked him: "Do the marks of proper ecstatic existentiality *(wujūd)* appear upon the ecstatics *(wājidīn)*?" He said: "Yes, a light is radiated similar to the light of longing. Its vestiges make an apparition upon the body-temples,"[43] as Ibn al-Mu'tazz said:

They rained down into the goblets
  water from their pitchers
while pearls blossomed
  in an earth of gold.

The folk praised what they saw
  in wonder
a light from water
  on fire in the grapes,

A pure wine,
  inherited by 'Ad from Iram,
the ancient treasure of Khusraw
  from his father's father's father.[44]

About Abū Bakr ad-Duqqī the following tale was told:

> Jahm ar-Raqqī in his excitement in his state of audition had taken hold of a tree with his hand and ripped it out by the roots. The two (ad-Duqqī and Jahm ar-Raqqī) met in a gathering to which they were both invited. Duqqī was blind. Jahm ar-Raqqī stood and whirled in a state of fervent excitement. Duqqī said: "If he comes near me, I'll show him." Raqqī was weak as he came by. When he drew near to Duqqī, they said: "That's him." Duqqī seized Jahm by the leg and held him up, immobile. Raqqī said: "O Shaykh, I repent, I repent." He then released him.[45]

The Imam and Teacher, God make his beauty last, said: The excitement of Jahm was grounded in the real. Duqqī's grasping of his leg was grounded in the real. When Jahm realized that Duqqī's state was beyond his own he regained the proper balance and submitted. For anyone grounded in the real, none of this is difficult. When effacement comes to dominate a person, however, he has no knowledge, no reason, no understanding, and no sense.

I heard the shaykh Abū 'Abd al-Raḥmān as-Sulamī, God grant him mercy, recall through his chain of authorities *(isnād)*:

> Abū 'Iqāl al-Maghribī stayed in Mecca for four years without eating or drinking, until he died. A dervish came in to visit Abū 'Iqāl and said to him: "Peace upon you." Abū 'Iqāl said to him: "And upon you, peace." The man said: "I am so and so." Abū 'Iqāl replied: "How are you and how is your condition?" The man said: I again said to him "Peace be with you." He replied "And with you, peace," as if he did not see me at all. I repeated the greeting more than once until I realized that the man was absent. Then I left him and departed from his house.[46]

I heard Muḥammad ibn al-Ḥusayn say: I heard 'Amr ibn Muḥammad ibn Aḥmad say: I heard the wife of my father 'Abdullāh al-Turughbadhī say:

> When the days of famine had come and people were dying of hunger, Abū 'Abdallāh al-Turughbadhī entered his house and saw in it a *ruṭl* of wheat. He said: "People are starving and there is wheat in my house?" His mind became disordered and he did not come to consciousness after that except for the times of prayer.

> He would perform his obligation and return to his state. He continued on like that until he died.

This story indicates that the man was protected in his proper behavior in fulfilling the shari'a whenever he underwent the onslaught of the rule of *ḥaqīqa* (reality). That is the way of the people of reality.[47]

Union (*Jam'*) and Separation (*Farq*)

In this essay Qushayri begins with a clear distinction between separation and union. Separation entails acts of devotion carried out by the human agent. Union is the result of the deity acting through the human. Qushayri makes a critical point when he states that both separation and union are necessary. Without separation there is no worship. Without union there can be no true knowing (ma'rifa). *Later in the essay, Qushayri offers some anecdotes exploring the grammatical implications of interpreting according to union or separation: The Arabic verbal form does not distinguish between first person ("I made") and second person ("You made") unless the short vowels are written in. Such an ambiguity is perfect for exploring the topic. It is unclear whether the final category (union of union) is meant as a separate essay or part of the "union and separation" essay. Union of union is the annihilation of all consciousness of others through immersion in the divine. That is followed by a particularly rare state of mystical empowerment that Qushayri calls "second separation."*

The expressions "union" and "separation" are frequently employed among them. The master Abu 'Ali ad-Daqqaq used to say: "Separation is what is attributed to you. Union is what is stripped from you." He meant that what is acquired by the servant[48] through acts of worship and what conforms to the states of the mortal is separation. What is from the real—by way of origination of meanings and conferring[49] of grace and kindness—is union. These remarks concern the lowest states in union and separation because they concern the witnessing of acts. When the real allows a person to witness his acts of obedience and disobedience, that person is a servant characterized by separation. When the real, All-Praised, allows a person to witness what the real has entrusted to him of its own acts, All-Praised, that person is a servant under the sign of union.[50] The confirmation of creation fits into the category of separation. The confirmation of the real is an attribute of union.

The servant must have both union and separation. Whoever has no separation has no worshipfulness. Whoever has no union has no experience of knowing *(ma'rifa)*. His words (1:5) "You, we worship" are an allusion to separation, and the words (1:5) "In you, we seek refuge" are an allusion to union.[51]

When a servant addresses the real, Most Praised, in the language of intimate conversation, either in petition, pleading, avowal, gratitude, falling to the ground (in remorse)[52] or supplication, that person stands in the position of separation. When a person hearkens through the heart-secret and listens through his heart as the real addresses him, in calling him, speaking intimately with him, bestowing recognition upon him, and bestowing apparitions upon his heart that he might see him,[53] that person is under the sign of union.

I heard the master Abu 'Ali ad-Daqqaq, God have mercy on him, say:

> A singer recited the following verse in front of the master Abū Sahl aṣ-Ṣu'lūkī, God have mercy upon him: "I/you *(ja'altu/ ja'alta)*[54] made gazing at you my promenade." Abū l-Qāsim an-Naṣrābādhī, God have mercy on him, was present. Master Abū Sahl said: "[It should be read] 'you made' with a final 'a' *(ja'alta)*." Naṣrābādhī said: "No, it should be read 'I made' with a final 'u' *(ja'altu)*. " The master Abū Sahl said: "Is not the essence of union more perfect?" Naṣrābādhī was silent.

I have also heard that the shaykh Abū 'Abd ar-Raḥmān as-Sulamī related this story in a similar fashion.

The meaning of the story is that whoever says "I made" [*ja'altu*, with a final "u"] is relating information about the state of his ego-self *(nafs)*, as if the servant were saying "this [action] is from me." When one says "you made" [*ja'alta*, with a final "a"], it is as if he were disavowing that the action occurred through his own intentional effort, and were addressing his master, saying: "It is you who has chosen me for this, not I through my own intentional effort." The first interpretation risks the danger of presumption. The second exhibits the disavowal of power and the affirmation of divine favor and might. There is a distinction to be made between one who says "Through my own effort I worship you" and one who says "Through your favor and grace I witness you." Then there is: [55]

Union of Union (*Jam' al-Jam'*)

Beyond union and separation is union of union. People differ in this regard according to the distinctions among their states and ranks. When a person affirms his self and affirms creation but witnesses it all as existing through the real, that is union. But if he is snatched from all regard of creation, uprooted from his own self, utterly removed from perceiving any "other" through the sovereign power of reality when it appears and seizes him, that is union of union.

Separation is the witnessing of others-than-God, Most Glorious and Sublime. Union is witnessing the others through God. Union of union is the utter perishing and passing away of all perception of any other-than-God, Most Glorious and Sublime, through the onslaughts of reality.

And beyond union of union, there is a sublime condition that the people call second separation *(al-farq ath-thanī)*. It concerns the servant being brought back to waking consciousness *(ṣaḥw)* at the times for the performance of ritually prescribed duties so that these duties might be performed in their proper moments. This return is God's and through God Most High. It does not belong to the servant nor is it of him.

In such a condition, the servant observes himself within the free disposition *(taṣrīf)* of the real, Most Praised. He witnesses the one who originates through his divine power *(qudra)* his very identity and essence, who carries out through divine knowledge and will *(mashi'a)* his acts and the states that come over him.

Some use the expression "union and separation" to refer to the free disposition of the real over all creatures. The real unites them all by turning them and exercising its free disposition over them, insofar as it originates their identities and their attributes. Then it separates them into their various kinds. Some it makes happy, some it distances and makes wretched, some it guides, some it leads astray and blinds, some it veils, some it attracts, some it brings into intimate union with itself, some it makes despair of its mercy, some it honors with success, some it uproots from their desire through their realization of it, some it awakens, some it effaces, some it brings near to itself, some it makes absent, some it brings close and makes present, some it gives to drink and makes drunk, some it gives wretchedness and alienates, treats cruelly, and abandons. The varieties of its acts cannot be counted, and details of its acts cannot be explained or recounted.[56]

Concerning union and separation, they recite the following verses of Junayd, God have mercy on him:

I realized your presence in the secret of my heart
and my tongue spoke to you intimately.
We came together in modes of consciousness
We parted in modes.
Although glorifying you may have absented you
from the glance of my vision
Still, ecstasy has brought you
into my viscera, near.

They recite:

When your majesty appears before me
I go out into a state from which there is no return.
I was brought together, then separated from myself through it.
In intimate union, the individual is a party of two.

Passing Away (*Fanā'*) and Abiding (*Baqā'*)

This essay on the central concepts of passing away and abiding begins cautiously, with special emphasis on the moral aspects of mystical union. Qushayri plays on the tension between the struggle for moral improvement and purification, on the one hand, and the acknowledgment, on the other hand, that ultimately all improvement and even all acts are bestowed through the free disposition of the all-powerful deity. Rather than resulting in any sort of fatalism, the tension between human initiative and divine predetermination raises the stakes and heightens the urgency of cultivating the virtues.

Passing away is seen in a largely subjective sense, that is, the passing away of the subject's awareness of himself, other creatures, or anything other than the deity. A homespun analogy for such passing away is the story of the common man who enters the presence of a powerful potentate and is so overcome with awe that, on leaving, he cannot remember anything about it. The Qur'anic story of the female entourage of Pharoah's wife cutting their hands at the sudden sight of the beauty of Joseph offers another illustration of "passing away" as self-forgetfulness. Only the final reference to a passing away into the existence of the real hints at a more radical, objective perspective.

By passing away, the folk indicate the shedding of blameworthy characteristics. By abiding, they indicate the maintenance of praiseworthy characteristics. The servant is never free from one or the other of these two categories, without exception. When a person passes away from his blameworthy characteristics, the praiseworthy characteristics appear in him. When the blameworthy qualities prevail over him, he is veiled from the praiseworthy attributes.

Know that the servant is characterized by these three things: acts *(af'āl)*, character traits *(akhlāq)*, and states *(aḥwāl)*. Acts are the exercise of the free disposition of his will. Character traits are his innate temperament, though that temperament can change through the cultivation of certain habitual practices. States are what come upon a servant newly created, but their purity follows the purity of the acts. The states are like the character traits in this regard because when character traits come down upon his heart, and he rejects through his efforts the baser traits, then Allah grants him an improvement in character, just as when he persists in purifying his actions by expending every effort, then Allah grants him a purification of his states, or rather a fulfillment of his states.

Whoever abandons acts that in the language of the shari'a are blameworthy is said to have passed away from his carnal desires. When he passes away from his carnal desires, he endures in his intention and sincerity in worshipfulness. Whoever in his heart renounces his world is said to have passed away from his appetitive nature.[57] When he passes away from his appetites, he endures in the sincerity of his contrition. Whoever cultivates his traits of character will reject from his heart envy, hate, stinginess, avarice, anger, pride, and other vanities of the self. He is said to have passed away from bad character. When he passes away from bad character, he endures in chivalry and sincerity. Whoever witnesses the pervasion of divine power in the free disposition of divine decrees is said to have passed away from taking into account the effects upon him of creatures. When he passes away from imagining effects of any others, he endures through the attributes of the real. Whoever is seized by the sovereign power of reality, to the point that he no longer witnesses any vision, vestige, trace, or ruin of the others, is said to have passed away from creatures and to endure through the real.[58]

The servant's passing away from his blameworthy acts and baser character traits occurs through the abolition of such acts. His passing away from himself and from creatures occurs through the cessation of his perception of himself and of creatures. What he has passed away from could not truly have existed in the first place. Someone might object that he passed away from his self and from creatures and that both his self and creatures truly exist. However, he has no knowledge of self or creatures, no perception, no information, so that even if self and creatures exist, he is utterly unaware of them, not perceiving them in any way.

Think of a man who enters the presence of a powerful and shame-inspiring potentate. He is overwhelmed with awe and distracted from himself, from the others in the assembly, and perhaps even from the shame-inspiring ruler himself. On leaving he is asked who was in the assembly, what the big man was like, and what it was like to be before him, and he is unable to give any information.

Allah Most High said (12:31): "When they saw him, they were struck by his majesty and cut their hands." Upon encountering Joseph (Yusuf) in that first moment, they experienced no pain when they cut their hands—and they were the weakest of people. They said: "This one is no human," but he was human. They said: "This one is a glorious angel," but he was not an angel. This is how a creature can disregard his own states on meeting another creature. What do you think would happen to a person when the veil is parted and he witnesses the real, Most Praised? If he were to disregard himself and those of his own species, would that be such a marvel?

Whoever passes away from his ignorance endures through his knowledge. Whoever passes away from his carnal desire endures through his contrition. Whoever passes away from his appetitive nature endures through his renunciation. Whoever passes away from his wish endures through the will of the Most High. The same can be said for all the attributes. When the servant passes away from the attribute through which his memory operates, then he rises from that through passing away from the vision of his own passing away. It was to this that that poet referred:

A people wanders
  lost in the wasteland.
A people wanders
  lost on the plain of love.
They passed away, passed away,
  then passed away again,
Then abided in abiding
  of nearness to their lord.

The first passing away is the passing away of the self and its attributes to endure through the attributes of the real. Then there is the passing away from the attributes of the real through witnessing of the real. Then there is a person's passing away from witnessing his own passing away through his perishing in the ecstatic existentiality *(wujūd)* of the real.

ABSENCE (*GHAYBA*) AND PRESENCE (*ḤUḌŪR*)

As categories, absence and presence are parallel to the categories of passing away, but they reflect them in a different register, a different set of circumstances and issues. A number of examples of absence are given; those who are absent when they faint from contemplation of the eternal fire; those who through contemplation or madness are absent from some of their closest colleagues. The essay ends with perhaps the most famous legend of its kind, the story of the man sent by Dhu n-Nun al-Misri to find Abu Yazid al-Bistami and report back about him.

Absence is the absence of the heart from the knowledge of the states that are occurring in creatures, due to the preoccupation of the perception with what is coming upon it. Then the heart can become absent from its perception of itself and its other, when reminders of reward or punishment come over it.

In this regard, it is related that Rabīʻa ibn Khaytham was on his way to visit Ibn Masʻūd, God be pleased with him, when he passed by the shop of a blacksmith. When he glanced into the oven and saw the blowing iron, he fainted and did not come to until the next day. When he awoke and was asked what had happened, he said: "I remembered the situation of the people of fire in the fire."[59] This is an absence that goes beyond its own boundary and becomes a fainting. It is related that when ʻAlī ibn al-Ḥusayn was performing his ritual prayer, a fire broke out in his house. He did not turn from his prayer. When asked about it, he said: "The great fire diverted me from this fire."

Absence can entail a person being absent from his own sense faculties because of what is disclosed to him from the real, Most High and All-Praised. People vary in degrees of absence according to their stages. There is a famous story about how Abū Ḥafṣ an-Naysābūrī the blacksmith came to give up his craft. He was at his smith shop when someone recited a verse from the Qur'an. There came upon the heart of Abū Ḥafṣ an "oncoming" that made him disregard his own senses, so that he put his hand into the fire and took out—in his bare hand—the glowing iron. One of his apprentices saw what was happening and said: "Master, what's this!" Abū Ḥafṣ considered what had come over him, gave up his craft, and left his shop.

Once Junayd was sitting in the company of his wife. Shibli came in to visit, and his wife wished to veil herself. Junayd said to her: "Shibli is not aware of you. Stay seated." Junayd continued speaking to Shibli until Shibli began to weep. At that point, Junayd said to his wife: "Veil yourself. Shibli has awakened from his absence."

In Nishapur, I heard Abū Naṣr al-Mu'adhdhin, who was an upright man, say:

> I used to recite the Qur'an for the circle of the master Abu 'Ali ad-Daqqaq in Nishapur, during his stay there. He would often talk about the *ḥajj* and his words had an effect on my heart. That year I set out on the *ḥajj*, abandoning my craft and my workshop. The master Abu 'Ali ad-Daqqaq happened to be making the *ḥajj* that same year. Now during his stay in Nishapur, I had served him and recited the Qur'an regularly in his circle. When I saw him in the desert, he had forgotten the ablution bottle he had had in his hand. I retrieved it, and when I brought it to him, he said: "God requite you well for bringing me this." Then he looked at me for a long time, as if he had never seen me. Finally he said to me: "I've seen you once somewhere. Who are you?" I said: "Mercy in God! I was a member of your circle for some time. Because of you, I left my house and possessions and traversed the desert. Now you say to me: 'I've seen you once somewhere!' "

As for presence, a person might be present to the real because when he is absent from creatures, he is present to the real—that is, it is as if he were present. His heart is seized by remembrance of the real so that he is present with his heart before the real. His presence to the real is in proportion to his absence from creatures. If his absence is total, his presence will be total.

If someone says: "So and so is present," he means that he is present with his heart before his lord, not heedless or inattentive of him, constant in his remembrance of him. Then, in his presence, according to his rank, the veil is parted for him for whatever the real, most praiseworthy and most high, has chosen him.

It can also be said in regard to the return of the servant to his senses, to the states of his self, and to the states of creatures, that he is present—that is, he has returned from his absence. This is presence to creation. The former kind of presence is presence to the real.

People's states can differ in the degree of absence. For some, the absence does not endure. For others, the absence is continual. It is related that:

> Dhū n-Nūn al-Miṣrī sent a man from his circle to Abu Yazid to report back to him about Abu Yazid's circumstance. The man

came to Bistam, asked directions for the house of Abu Yazid, and went to visit him there. Abu Yazid said: "What do you want?" The man said: "I want Abu Yazid." He replied: "Who is Abu Yazid? Where is Abu Yazid? I am seeking Abu Yazid myself." The man departed, saying to himself: "He's mad." When the man returned to Dhu n-Nun and reported what he had seen, Dhu n-Nun wept and said: "My brother Abu Yazid has gone the way of those departed to God."

WAKING (*ṢAḤW*) AND DRUNKENNESS (*SUKR*)

In this essay, Qushayri shifts into a series of essays grounded in vocabulary and themes common to the Arabic lyrical poetic tradition. The essay opens, as is frequent in Qushayri, with a seeming redundancy or synonymy. In this case, drunkenness is described as absence, a state depicted in the previous essay. Gradually, however, distinctions and oppositions are developed. The creative tension between earthly wine and the wine of mystical intoxication is especially notable. The constant references to faithfulness to the shari'a, and particularly to the "protection" (that is, from violating sacred law in a state of intoxication), make it clear that the Sufis are not advocating violating the Islamic prohibition on drinking. Yet, on the rhetorical level and in the choice of particular verses, they deliberately leave the identity of the wine and the beloved unspecified. In this essay, for example, one of the sets of verses quoted is taken from a poem by the notorious Abu Nuwas, one of the most famous, and most ribald, secular wine poets in the Arabic tradition. The essay on drunkenness and waking ends with an evocation of the divine manifestation before Moses (see Chapters 1 and 2 in this volume), to which Qushayri comes back time after time, seeing it as a fundamental paradigm of mystical experience in which the self of the mystic is annihilated. Here he uses a technical term, the "sign" (shāhid), *that will not be fully explained until a later essay. The sign is whatever the mystic sees or is preoccupied with, and thus serves to determine his particular reality at that moment.*

Waking is the return to the senses after absence. Drunkenness is absence due to a strong "oncoming." Drunkenness can be greater than absence in one respect. A person who is drunk can be "feeling good" *(mabsūṭ)*[60] without being in a state of complete drunkenness and without his heart losing all awareness of things. The first state is that of a would-be drunk *(mutasākir)* whose oncoming has not completely taken him over, so that he still has access to his senses.[61] However, the drunkenness can intensify to the point that it exceeds absence. Through an intensification of drunkenness, the drunk can exceed in absence even one who is in the state of absence or the one who is absent can be more completely absent than the drunk—if the latter is a would-be drunk and has not achieved complete drunkenness.

Absence can occur to worshipers because of the effects engendered by desire and dread, fear and hope. Drunkenness, on the other hand, is only for the ecstatics *(aṣḥāb al-mawājīd).* If the attribute of beauty is unveiled to the servant, he attains drunkenness, his spirit is transported *(ṭarī ba)*, and his heart is wander-lost. In this regard, they recite:

Your waking through my words to you
  is complete union.
Your drunkenness from my gaze
  permits drinking for you.

The wine-pourer is never wearied,
  the drinker never full
from drinking to the dregs the gazes
  one whose wine intoxicates the inner heart.

They recite:

The round of a cup
  has made the people drunk
but my drunkenness is in
  the one who passes the cup around.

They recite:

I have two drunkennesses
  my drinking companions have but one.
In that, I've been singled out
  among them, alone.

They recite:

Two drunkennesses, one of desire,
  the other of wine—
When a young man wakes
  are the two within him?

Know that waking is in proportion to drunkenness. Whoever is drunk in the real is awake in the real. Whoever's drunkenness is clouded with good fortune, his waking is accompanied by good fortune. Whoever is sound in his state is protected in his drunkenness. Drunkenness and waking indicate a certain degree of separation. When an emblem of the sovereign power of reality appears, then the attribute of the servant is destruction and vanquishment. In regard to this, they recite:

When the morning arose
  on the star of a strong wine,
drunkenness and soberness
  were the same to me.

He said, Most High (7:143): "But when its lord manifested itself to the mountain, he caused it to shatter and Moses was struck down unconscious." The one, despite his status as a messenger of God and the greatness of his power, "was struck down unconscious." The other, despite its solidity and strength, shattered and fell to pieces.

The servant in the state of his drunkenness is under the sign of the state. The servant in the state of his waking is under the sign of knowledge. Except that—in the state of his drunkenness he is protected, but not through his own intentional efforts, while in the state of his waking, he protects himself through his own free disposition. Waking and drunkenness come after taste and drink.

TASTE (*DHAWQ*) AND DRINK (*SHURB*)

Qushayri moves more deeply into the vocabulary and themes of classical poetry, speaking of the mystical experience in terms of drunkenness. He speaks of drunkenness in the vocabulary and sensibility of classical poetry. In classical tradition, wine is drunk to help the poet forget the beloved, but often, in a subtle switch, the wine ends up making him remember her all the more. Here Qushayri develops another hierarchy, a hierarchy of drinking. The highest point of intoxication becomes, dialectically, the point of most lucid and sober wakefulness.

Two frequently used terms among them are taste and drink. Through these terms they expressed what they find or experience *(yajidūn)* of the fruits of self-manifestation, the results of unveilings, and the sudden thoughts and emotions of "oncomings."[62] First there is taste, then drink, then quenching. The purity of their conduct secures for them the taste of meanings. The purity of their encounters secures drink for them. The continuity of their intimacies necessitates quenching.[63] The master of taste is a would-be intoxicate, the master of drink is drunk, and the master of quenching is lucidly awake *(ṣāḥin)*. When a person's love is strengthened, his drink becomes endless. When this trait persists in him, the drink no longer makes him drunk, but he achieves awakening into the real, passing away from every portion of delight *(ḥaẓẓ)*, unaffected by what comes down upon him, unable to be moved from where he is.

Whoever's heart-secret is pure is unpolluted by wine. When wine has become his nourishment, he cannot be patient in its lack and cannot endure without it. They recite:

> The cup of wine for us
> is mother's milk.
> If we don't taste it
> we no longer live.

They recite:

> I marveled at one who said
> I remembered my lord.
> Do I forget so that I must remember
> what I forgot?

> Cup after cup I drank
> of love.
> The wine was not depleted.
> I was not quenched.

It is said that Yaḥyā ibn Mu'ādh wrote to Abu Yazid al-Bistami: "Here is one who has drunk from the cup of love, after which there is no thirst." Abu Yazid wrote back to him: "I marvel at the weakness of your state! Here is one who has drank up the seas of creation. His mouth is wide open, wanting more."

Know that the wine-cups of nearness appear from the unknown, and do not circulate except among freed[64] heart-secrets and spirits emancipated from the slavery of things.

Effacement (*Maḥw*) and Confirmation (*Ithbāt*)

The suppleness and dynamism of early Sufi psychology are given new expression in this essay. According to the anecdote with which it begins, the Sufi notion of "moment," the foundation of Sufi psychology, is itself dependent on a continual interplay of effacement and confirmation. Without a continual, personal, and intense involvement in such an interplay, there can be no moment.

Qushayri offers a three-tiered pattern of effacements: effacements of the ritual lapse (ghafla), *of mental negligence, and of defects of the heart. He parallels that with three tiers of confirmation: good conduct, encounters (of purer mental states), and intimacies.*

He then goes on to affirm that it is the real (al-ḥaqq) *that is the agent of effacement and confirmation (not the ego-agency of the individual). At this point, the essay grows denser, with paradoxes entailed by complete effacement of the ego-self* (nafs) *that was the cause of the blameworthy traits* (ḥisāl) *that had to be effaced in the first place.*

Effacement is the lifting of the traits of habit. Confirmation is the upholding of the decrees of worship. Whoever rejects blameworthy states and substitutes for them those that are praiseworthy—that person is a master of effacement and confirmation. I heard Abu 'Ali ad-Daqqaq, God have mercy on him, say: "A certain shaykh said to someone: 'What do you efface and what do you confirm?' The man was silent. So he [the shaykh] commented: 'Did you not know that the moment consists in effacement and confirmation? Whoever has no effacement and no confirmation is idle and negligent.' "

Effacement can be divided into three categories: (1) the effacement of any lapse in performance of exterior duties; (2) the effacement of any negligence in the inner mind; and (3) the effacement of any defect in the inner heart. In the effacement of lapse is the confirmation of good conduct *(mu'āmalāt)*. In the effacement of negligence is the confirmation of the encounters *(munāzalāt)*, and in the effacement of defect is the affirmation of the intimacies *(muwāṣalāt)*. This is effacement and confirmation in the sense of worshipfulness *('ibāda)*.

As for the reality *(ḥaqīqa)* of effacement and confirmation: The two emerge from the power of divine decree.[65] Effacement is what the real veils and purifies.[66] Confirmation is what it manifests and discloses. Effacement and confirmation are exclusive to the divine will.[67] God Most High said (13:39): "Allah effaces what he wills and confirms [what he wills]." It is said: "He effaces from the hearts of the knowers the remembrance of any other than God Most High, and he affirms upon the tongues of the seekers the remembrance of God." The acts of effacement and confirmation by the real in each person are in accordance with that person's state.

Whoever is effaced from witnessing by the real, Most Praised, is confirmed by the real in his reality. Whoever is effaced by the real from confirmation is returned to the witnessing of others and affirmed in the ravines of distinction.[68] A man said to Shibli, God have mercy on him: "How is it I see you upset? Are you not with him, and is he not with you?"[69] Shibli said: "If I were with him, I would be I, but I am effaced in what is he."

Obliteration is beyond effacement. Effacement leaves a trace, but obliteration does not. The highest aspiration *(himma)* of the folk is that the real obliterate them from their sign,[70] without returning them to themselves after he has obliterated them from themselves.

Veil (*Sitr*) and Self-Manifestation (*Tajallī*)

In this short essay, Qushayri evokes the theme of the destructive brilliance of unmediated divine light. The common condition of humankind is to seek divine light and to seek the removal of the veils that deprive humankind of that light. But for the advanced Sufis, the "select," divine light becomes overwhelming in its brilliance; it blinds, stuns, and can even burn up the quester. The advanced Sufis are wander-lost in such brilliance and find relief in being veiled. Once again, in the midst of such ethereal discussions, Qushayri cites a home-spun anecdote, this time concerning a dervish who is so overcome by the brilliance of the dust from his beloved's footsteps that the beloved is afraid of what would happen to him were she to accept him into her presence.

The master of the veil is in the characteristic of his witnessing. The master of self-manifestation is characterized always by his self-humbling. For the common people, the veil is a punishment. For the select, it is a mercy. For if it did not veil them from what it disclosed to them, they would perish from the sovereign power of reality. Just as he disclosed it to them, he veiled them from it. I heard Manṣūr al-Maghribī say:

> A dervish appeared among one of the bedouin tribes. A young man offered him hospitality. While the young man was serving the dervish, he suddenly fell unconcious. The dervish asked about

> the young man's swoon, and they said: "He has fallen for his paternal cousin. As she was moving about in her tent, the young man caught a glimpse of the dust raised by the train of her gown and fainted." The dervish went to the door of the tent and said: "Your custom is to offer the stranger a certain esteemed position and prerogatives of hospitality. I have come to intercede with you on behalf of the young man. Show your favor for the love he holds for you." She said: "God be praised! You are a man of sound heart. He cannot bear to witness the dust of the train of my gown. How could he possibly bear keeping company with me?"

For common folk of this party, life is in self-manifestation, suffering *(balā')* is in being veiled. The select, however, are between wander-loss and life because when there is a self-manifestation to them, they wander lost *(ṭāshū)*, and when they are veiled, they return to well-being and life.

Someone said: "The real, Most High, said to Musa, peace upon him (20:17), 'What is that in your right hand, O Musa?' in order to veil him by distracting him from the overwhelming effect upon him of the unveiling that occurred through his sudden hearing [of the divine voice]."

The Prophet said, peace and blessings upon him, "My heart is shrouded over, so that I ask God's pardon seventy times a day."[71] The asking of pardon is the asking for a veil because pardon is a veil [according to the etymology of the Arabic radical *gh/f/r*] as in the expression *ghafara ath-thawb* (the clothing covers) and *mighfar* (hair covering), and the like. It is as if he were requesting a veil for his heart when experiencing the onslaught of reality since there creation does not endure upon the *wujūd* (existence of, experiencing of) the real. In the hadith report, "If his face were unveiled, the sublimities of his face would burn up everything reached by his gaze."[72]

Attendance (*al-Muḥāḍara*), Unveiling (*al-Mukāshafa*), and Witness (*al-Mushāhada*)

Here three gradations of experience are elaborated. Attendance occurs when a person is engaging in constant remembrance of the divine beloved, but is still behind a veil. It needs proof to maintain itself. Unveiling moves from the realm of proof to that of exposition. The most intense experience is that of witnessing, which occurs only through the loss of the self. The second part of the essay argues that true witnessing occurs only through the experience of the passing away or annihilation of the ego-self in mystical union. To make this point, Qushayri first acknowledges that the notion of witness usually implies two parties (a party seeing and a party seen), and that the Arabic verbal form, mushāhada, for witness can often suggest a mutuality and duality. He ends, however, with a strong affirmation of witness at the moment where duality is overcome, with poetic analogy to the way the light of morning extinguishes the multiple lights of the stars.

Attendance comes at the beginning, then unveiling, then witness. Attendance refers to the presence of the heart, which can occur through continued proof *(burhān)*. At first you find yourself behind the veil, even if you are present through the domination of the power of remembrance.

After that comes unveiling, which is a presence occurring through the attribute of explanation *(bayān)*. It has no need for meditating upon proofs or seeking the path, for taking refuge from the causes of doubt or being veiled from the attribute of the unknown.

Then there is witness, which is the presence of the real without any doubt. When the heaven of the heart-servant is clear of the clouds of the veiling, then the sun of witnessing shines down from the star-mansions of nobility. The truth of witnessing was expressed by Junayd, God's mercy upon him, when he said: "The *wujūd* (finding, experience, ecstasy, existence) of the real occurs though the loss of your self."

The "master of attendance" is bound to his signs, the "master of unveiling" is released in his attributes, the "master of witness" throws off his essence.[73] The master of attendance is guided by his intellect, the master of unveiling is brought near through traditional knowledge, and the master of witnessing is effaced by his recognition.

No one can outdo the explanation of the reality of witness given by 'Amr ibn 'Uthmān al-Makkī, God have mercy upon him. The gist of what he said is that the lights of manifestations come upon the heart in continual succession, without any veil coming between them, without interruption. It is as if lightning could become continual, and through successive, continual flashes—were such a thing possible—the night could turn into the light of day. They recite:

Through your radiant countenance
  my night shines brightly
while among the rest of humankind
  darkness makes its way.

The people are shrouded
in darkness
while we remain
in the light of day.

Nuri said: "Witness is not proper for the servant as long as there remains a single blood-vein in him."[74] They say: "When the morning light appears, the lamp is no longer needed."[75] Some folk are of the false opinion that witness indicates a party within a distinction because the Arabic morphological form of *mufā'ala* [on which the word of witness is based][76] implies two parties. Whoever holds this position is mistaken. For the appearance of the real, Most Praised, is the disappearance of the creature.[77] In addition, the form *mufā'ala* does not necessarily imply reciprocal action between two parties, for example in the case of "travel" or "line a boot" and the like.[78]

They recite:

When morning appears
its light extinguishes
the light of the lights
of the stars.

It gives people a swallow
from a cup
that were they suffering from a blazing fire
one gulp would put it out immediately.

GLIMMERINGS (*LAWĀ'IḤ*), RISINGS (*ṬAWĀLI'*), AND FLASHES (*LAWĀMI'*)

In the next section, Qushayri combines his psychological insights with lyrical meditations on the appearance and fading of light. On the one hand, these meditations evoke the love-poetry tradition.[79] On the other hand, they evoke the Qur'anic hymnic passages on day and night, as well as the famous Qur'anic passage in which human beings are pictured as groping their way through the dark with the aid of occasional, brief flashes of light (2:20): "Almost blinded by the flash of lightning, they grope forward in the light. Darkness returns and they stand still. Were God to wish it, he could take away their hearing and their sight; over every single thing God has the power." This long essay is followed by a short discussion of two modes of experience, "pangs" and "onslaughts."

The master [Qushayri], may God be pleased with him, said:[80] The difference in meaning among these expressions is not great, it is one of fine shades. They are among the attributes of those who are beginning the ascent of the heart. The radiance of the sun of recognition is not yet continuous for them. The real, Most Worthy of Praise and Most High, has given their heart sustenance in every instant, as he said (19:62): "There (i.e., in the gardens of Eden, *jannāti 'adani*) morning and evening they have their sustenance." Whenever the brightness of their heart's heaven is darkened by the clouds of fortune, well-omened gleams of unveiling appear to them, along with the flashes of coming-near. During the time that they are veiled, they observe sudden glimmerings that take them by surprise. As the poet said about them:

> O lightning flashing
> from which folds
> of the sky
> do you shine?

First come the glimmerings, then the flashes, then the risings. The glimmerings are like lightning; hardly do they appear before they are veiled, as the poet said:

> For a full year we were apart,
> and when again we met
> his greeting to me
> was already a good-bye.

And they also recite:

> Oh, that one who visits
> and visits not
> as if he were
> in search of fire,
>
> He passes by the door of the abode,
> in haste
> What would it have harmed him
> to come in?

The flashes are clearer than the glimmerings, and they do not fade away so quickly. Flashes might remain two or three moments. Even so, as they say:

The weeping eye
  cannot satisfy the gaze.

Or as they say:

The eye does not reach
  the water of his face
without, before it can drink its fill,
  choking before the watcher.[81]

When it flashes, it separates you from yourself and unites you with it.[82] Hardly does the light of its day disclose itself than it is fallen upon by the army of the night. Such people, who reside between revival and death, lament, insofar as they reside between unveiling and veiling. As they say:

The night envelops you
  in its flowing robe,
then morning wraps us
  in a mantle of gold.

The risings are more abiding in moment, stronger in sovereign power, more enduring, more opposite to darkness, and more contrary to suspicion. However, they are poised on the precipice of falling. They do not reach the heights of apogee nor do they long abide. The times of their arrival are the impending of their passing on, and in their states of falling, they trail a long trail.

The senses of these terms—glimmerings, flashes, and risings—differ in their determinations. One kind, on fading away, leaves behind no trace, like a rising star which, when it falls, leaves behind a darkness that seems to have always been. Another kind leaves a trace. When its imprint fades, its pain remains. When its lights fade, its traces remain. After its onslaughts are calmed, its possessor lives in the light of its blessings, and until it should gleam again, infuses his moment with hope in the expectation of its return, and lives in what he had experienced *(wajada)* at the time it was there.

PANGS (*BAWĀDIH*) AND ONSLAUGHTS (*HUJŪM*)

Pangs are what take the heart by surprise and unawares, resulting in either joy or grief. Onslaughts are what come over your heart through the power of the moment, without any deliberate activity on your part. They differ in kind according to the strength or weakness of the oncoming. Some people are changed by pangs and are under the sway of onslaughts. Others are beyond having their state and strength taken by surprise. These are the masters of the moment. In this regard it has been said:

The twists and turns of time
  cannot find them out,
and over the lofty circumstances
  they hold a bridle.

TRANSFORMATION (*TALWĪN*) AND FIXITY (*TAMKĪN*)

In the following essay, Qushayri gives a classically dialectic analysis. His topic is the Sufi tension between the dynamic vision of a constant change and transformation, on the one hand, and the goal of achieving a fixed and stable reality on the other. He begins with the position that only beginners experience constant transformation from state to state, but that the goal is a condition of fixity. He then explains that the tradition is divided over the possibility of fixity and the interpretation of hadiths appealed to in the debate. Then he speaks of a continual progression from one state of fixity to another, ending with a reference to the state of complete effacement in which there is neither transformation nor fixity, station nor state.

Transformation *(talwīn)* is an attribute of the lords of the states. Fixity *(tamkīn)* is an attribute of the people of realities. As long as the servant is on the path, he is a possessor of transformation because he is still rising from state to state, changing from one attribute to another, leaving one rest-stop, arriving at a meadow pasture. When he arrives, he attains fixity. They recite:

I continued to alight
  in your affection,
a way-stop for which
  hearts are bewildered.

A certain shaykh said: "The journey of the seekers ends with victory over their selves. When they are victorious over their selves, they have arrived." The master [Qushayri], peace upon him, said: "He means the retreat of the control of the mortal human and seizing of control by sovereign reality. If a servant can remain in such a condition, he possesses fixity."

The shaykh Abu 'Ali ad-Daqqaq, God have mercy on him, used to say:

> Moses, peace upon him, was a possessor of transformation. When he returned from hearing the discourse, he required a veil for his face because his state had affected him. Our Prophet, peace and blessings of Allah upon him, was the master of fixity. He returned as he had set out. What he witnessed that night did not affect him.[83]

In support of that position, he cited the story of Yusuf (Joseph), peace upon him. When the women saw Joseph, they cut their hands as they were taken by surprise at the sight of him. But the wife of the sovereign was more perfect in the test that Joseph offered. Not a hair on her was changed that day because in the story of Joseph, peace upon him, she was the master of fixity.[84]

The master [Qushayri] said: "Know that there are two reasons for the change a servant can experience through what comes upon him. The change is due either to the strength of the oncoming or to the weakness of the person upon which it comes. Tranquility in a person is also due to one of two causes: either the strength of the person possessing tranquility or the weakness of what comes upon him."

I heard the master Abu 'Ali ad-Daqqaq, God have mercy upon him, say:

> The basic premises of the folk concerning the possibility of continued fixity are of two kinds. According to the first, there is no way to achieve continued fixity because of what the Prophet, peace and blessings of God upon him, said: "If you had remained in the experience you had with me, the angels would have shaken your hand" and "I have a moment in which no one can contain me but my lord, most glorious and sublime." He was reporting upon a special moment.
>
> According to the second premise, persistence through the states is in fact possible, because the people of realities have risen above the characteristic of being affected by happenings. And the content of the report "the angels would have shaken your hand"

> does not indicate any impossibility in the matter. The angels' shaking of hands is less than what has been promised to the beginners in the word of the Prophet, peace and blessings upon him, "The angels will lower their wings for the seeker of knowledge to show their pleasure with what he is doing."[85] As for his saying "I have a moment . . . ," he made that statement according to the understanding of the hearer. In all his moments he was grounded in reality.

The first thing that needs to be said is that the servant, as long as he continues his ascent, is a master of transformation. He is properly characterized by continual waxing and waning of states. However, when he arrives at the real through the retreat of the self from its control over him, then the real, Most Praised, fixes him. It no longer returns him to the defects of the self. He becomes fixed in his state according to his position and what he deserves.

Now the possibilites bestowed in each breath by the real, Most Praised, are limitless.[86] A person experiences constant augmentation and transforms himself, or rather undergoes transformation. At the root of his state he is fixed, but in each case he is fixed in a condition higher than the previous one, only to rise to another even higher than that. There is no limit to the possibilities bestowed upon each species by the real, Most Praised.

Now as for one who is rooted out from his own mark *(shāhid),*[87] who has given up his sense capabilities entirely—at this point, the mortal has a limit. When he becomes vacant of himself as a whole, from his self, his sense, and all created aspects, and this absence remains in him, then he is effaced. He can no longer have fixity or transformation, station or state.

And while he is characterized in this way, he should be neither honored nor given responsibility, O God, without that honor and responsibility reverting back to what happened to him without any action of his own. In the opinion of creatures, he has disposition over his own actions, but in reality, he is the object of [another's] disposition.

Allah Most High said (18:18): "You think they are awake when they are sleeping, while we turn them right and left." In Allah is success.

NEARNESS *(QURB)* AND DISTANCE *(BU'D)*

In his treatment of nearness and distance, Qushayri offers a particularly intricate combination of perspectives. He begins with some tentative definitions, and then cites the hadith of free devotions in which the divine voice speaks of the godservant who through the practice of both obligatory and free devotions draws near to God. The divine voice states: "I become the hearing with which he hears, the seeing with which he sees." The hadith of free devotions grounds the rest of the essay in a meditation of the relationship of self-consciousness (occurring in close nearness) to loss of consciousness (occurring in closer nearness and union).

Qur'anic texts are then cited, including the famous verse in which God (speaking with the Qur'anic "we" form) speaks of divine nearness to every human being: (50:16): "We are nearer to him than his jugular vein." The divine nearness is then correlated to the divine "watchfulness," over every human. The divine watchfulness is a central theme of the Qur'an, bound up with the divine attributes: the All-Seeing (al-baṣir), and the All-Hearing (as-samī'), both of which are part of the hadith of free devotions, as well as the All-Knowing and al-Khabīr *(the one skilled in seeking out the inner secrets of every being).*

Qushayri then moves quickly through several contexts: (1) poems on the watcher or spy who constantly surveys the inner thoughts of lovers; (2) the famous poetic paradoxes that the lover is tortured by both his nearness to the beloved and his distance from her, so that the lover complains: "Your nearness is like your farness;"[88] *(3) a Sufi tradition about a shaykh and his students discussing divine watchfulness; and in a sudden switch (4) the transition from the intense self-awareness through the awareness of the watcher, to the state "beyond self-conscious notice." He ends with (5) a meditation on the divine core or identity (dhāt), the aspect of reality beyond all differentiated consciousness, separation, and nearness, and a return to a final three-tiered ranking of those who achieve nearness.*

The first rank of nearness is entailed by acts of obedience to him and by persistence through the moments in performing acts of worship for him.[89]

Distance is the defilement of resisting him and the alienation from acts of obedience to him. The first rank of distance is distance from success *(tawfīq)*. Then comes distance from complete fulfillment *(taḥqīq)*. Distance from success is distance from fulfillment. He said, peace and blessings upon him, relating what he had heard from the real, Most Praised:

> Those who come near to me do so with nothing so much as the performance of what I have enjoined upon them. The servant then continues to draw near to me through free acts of devotion *(nawāfil)* until he loves me, and I love him. When I love him, I become

for him the hearing and the seeing. Through me he sees and through me he hears.[90]

The nearness of the servant is first of all through his faith and his assent, then through his performance and complete fulfillment of acts of charity. The nearness of the real, Most Praised, is the recognition with which he distinguishes a person today, the witnessing and immediate vision *('ayān)* with which he will honor him in the afterlife, and the varieties of kindness and security he grants in the meantime.

The nearness of the real, All-Praised, is open to all capable people through knowledge and power, to the believer through grace and triumph, and to the Godfriends *(awliyā')* by being selected out for intimacy.

Allah Most High said (50:16): "We are nearer to him [the human being] than his jugular vein." God Most High also said (57:4): "We are nearer to him than you." And he said (58:7): "There are never three intimate conversation partners, except that he is the fourth."

Whoever realizes the nearness of the real, Glorified and Most High, the least of that realization is constant watchfulness over him.[91] He has over him a watcher of self-vigilance, then a watcher of observance and loyalty, then a watcher of shame.

They recite:

As if a spy from you
   were watching my inclinations,
and another were watching
   my gaze and tongue.

      Whenever my eyes saw,
   after you, any sight
      displeasing to you, I thought:
   They've seen me.

And whenever from my mouth,
   there emerged, in front of you,
a word meant for another than you,
   I thought: They've heard me,

And whenever through the secret of my heart
there passed, after you, a thought
for another than you,
they pull up on my reins.

These brothers sincere—I wearied
of their speech
and seized back from them
my gaze and tongue.

Renunciation could not console me
for their loss
until I experienced you *(wajadtuka)*
witnessed in every place.

There was a shaykh who singled out one of his disciples with permission to approach him. When the others asked him about that, he tossed a bird to each one of them and said: "Slaughter it where no one sees." Everyone went and slaughtered his bird in a private place, except for that one person who came back without having slaughtered his bird. The shaykh asked him about it, and he said: "You commanded me to slaughter it where no one sees, but there is no place that the real, Most Praised, does not see." The shaykh said [to his other pupils]: "This is why I place him before you. The discourse of creation prevails upon you, while your colleague is never unmindful of the real."

The vision of nearness is a veil over nearness. Whenever a person sees a place or even a breath as his own he falls into a snare of deception.[92] For this reason, they say: "God exiles you from his nearness," that is, from your seeing his nearness. The taking into account of his nearness is one of the marks of inattentiveness to him. The real, All-Praised, is beyond every self-conscious notice. The placements of reality entail astonishment and effacement.

In something close to that sense, they say:

My ordeal in you is that
I take no heed of my ordeal.
Your nearness is like your farness.
When is the moment of my rest?

The master Abu 'Ali ad-Daqqaq is fond of reciting:

Your affection is exile.
  Your love is hate.
To be near you is distance,
  your peace, war.

Abū l-Ḥusayn an-Nūrī saw a disciple of Abū Hamza. He said to him: "You are one of the followers of Abu Hamza who gives advice about nearness. When you meet him, say: 'Abū l-Ḥusayn an-Nūrī offers you salutations and says to you: The nearness of nearness is what we are in, the distance of distance.' "

As for the nearness to the identity *(dhāt)*—Allah, the king, the real, is exalted beyond it. He is transcendent to all boundaries, areas, ends, and measures. No created being attains union with him. No originated being preceded by him can separate from him. His *ṣamadiyya*[93] is too sublime for any union or separation. There is a quality of nearness that is impossible: the coming near of the essences.[94] There is a quality of nearness that is necessary: the nearness through knowledge and vision. There is a quality of nearness that is possible; he singles out those of his servants he wishes for it. This is the nearness of favor through graciousness *(luṭf)*.

Divine Law (*Sharī'a*) and Reality (*Ḥaqīqa*)

This short essay asserts the necessity of both the sharī'a and the ḥaqīqa. Shari'a is the divine law as it has been extrapolated from the Qur'an and traditions of the Prophet. Reality (ḥaqīqa) *is what is witnessed by the mystic.*[95]

Divine law is an order through the requiring of worship.
Reality is a witnessing of lordship.
No divine law unsupported by *ḥaqiqa* is acceptable.
No reality unbound by divine law is acceptable.
Divine law is performed through the efforts of creatures.
Reality is a report from the disposition of the real.
Divine law is that you worship it.
Reality is that you witness it.
Divine law is the performance of what is commanded.
Reality is the witness of what has been decreed and preordained,

hidden and made manifest.

I heard the master Abu 'Ali ad-Daqqaq, God's mercy upon him, say:

His saying (1:5) "You we worship" shows a mindfulness of divine law and (1:5) "In you we seek refuge" is an affirmation of reality.

Know that the divine law is reality insofar as it is required by his command, and that reality, as well, is divine law insofar as recognitions of him, All-Praised, have been required through his command.

Breath (*Nafas*)

Breath is traditionally associated with meditation and with spirit. In this short essay, Qushayri's hierarchy begins with the moments, moves to the states, and culminates in the breaths. Qushayri alludes here to a central Sufi goal: the renewal in each breath of the human recognition of unity, a recognition that in Qushayri's Sufi terms takes place most authentically within the mystical experience.

The breath is the inspiriting of the hearts with the subtle essences *(laṭā'if)* of the unknown. The master of the breaths is more refined and purer than the master of the stations. The master of the moment is a beginner, the master of the breaths an end, and the master of the states is in between. The states are intermediaries, and the breaths are the culmination of the ascent. The moments belong to the masters of the heart, the states to the lords of the spirits, and the breaths to the people of the inner secrets of the heart *(sarā'ir)*.

They said: "The best act of worship is to count your breaths with Allah, Most Praised and Most High."[96] They said: "God created the hearts and made them mines of recognition. He created the heart-secrets and made them the places of the affirmation of unity *(tawḥīd)*. Every breath that arrives upon the carpet of need without the guidance of recognition and the sign of *tawḥīd* is dead, and its master will be called to account for it."

Inclinations (*Khawāṭir*)

A perennial theme of Sufi psychology is the analysis of various forms of thought. The passing of ideas, notions, desires, and images through the mind was viewed as an essential aspect of humanity, but also an avenue of danger, particularly when this movement of thought was associated with the nafs, *the ego-self or concupiscent self. The* nafs *in turn was associated with the "whispering" of "Satan." Satans* (shayāṭīn) *in pre-Islamic Arabic were viewed as semi-spirits roughly comparable to the jinn, though with a more consistently dangerous posture toward humankind. The Qur'an speaks of "the satan"* (ash-shayṭān) *and relates the figure to the satan* (hā satān) *of Job.*[97] *In the Qur'anic account, Iblis (interpreted by some as an angel, others as a jinn) refuses to obey the divine command to prostrate himself before Adam and is therefore expelled from the divine presence. But his complete punishment is deferred and he is given permission to serve as a tempter to humankind. The insinuations or "whisperings"* (waswasa) *of the satan become a prime object of Sufi scrutiny. The key text in the Qur'an on the satanic whispering is Sura 114, the last sura of the Qur'an:*

Sura 114: Sūrat an-Nās (The Sura of the People):

Say I take refuge with the lord of humankind
The king of humankind
The God of humankind
From the evil of the slinking whisperer (al-waswās)
Who whispers in the breasts of humankind
From jinn and humankind.

Qushayri's examination of the flow of thought is based on the Sufi concept of the khawāṭir. Khawāṭir *could be translated as "passing thoughts," in that the* khawāṭir *"come upon" a person or "come to mind" without conscious intention. But they are much more likely to influence behavior than a passing thought. Here they are translated as "inclinations," but it should be emphasized that the Sufi term implies both a feeling and a thought.* Khawāṭir *are those modalities of thought and feeling that "come upon" the Sufi, whether from the ego-self's "murmurings"* (hawājis), *from the satanic whisperings* (wasāwis), *from an angelic source, or from the deity in mystical consciousness.*[98]

Inclinations consist of speech that comes upon the conscience or inner mind *(ḍamīr)*. The source of these thoughts can be either an angel or a satan. It can be the speech of the self, or it can come from the real, Most Praised. If it is from an angel, it is an inspiration. If it is from the self, it is said to consist of murmurings. If it is from the satan, it consists of whisperings *(waswās)*. If it is from the direction of Allah, Most Praised, who sends it into the heart, it is a true thought *(khāṭir ḥaqq)*. All of these varieties are included in the category of discourse.

When it is from an angel, one can determine its validity through its agreement with traditional knowledge. In this regard they say: "An inclination unsupported by the testimony of an exterior act of worship is false. When it is from the satan, it will in most cases call for acts of disobedience. When it is from the self, it will in most cases call for the following of carnal desire *(shahwa)* or a feeling of pride *(kibr)*, or whatever is from the particular characteristics of the self."

The shaykhs are in agreement that no one who eats forbidden food can distinguish between inspiration and whispering. I heard the shaykh Abu 'Ali ad-Daqqaq (God grant him mercy) say:

> Whoever's source of nourishment is secure will be unable to distinguish between inspiration and whispering. Whoever has quieted the notions of the self through the sincerity of struggle—his heart will declare itself through the rule of its hardships.

The shaykhs agree that the ego-self is never truthful and the heart never lies. Some of the shaykhs say: The self is never truthful, the heart never lies, and even if you expended your last effort to make your spirit address you, it would not speak.

Junayd makes the following distinction between the murmurings of the self and the whisperings of the satan:

> The self, when it asks anything of you, persists. It continues to come back at you, time and time again—even if it might bide its time for awhile—until it attains its goal and accomplishes its aim, O God, as long as the sincere struggle endures. Thus it comes back time after time with its request.
>
> But the satan, when it calls you to lapse, and you resist it by rejecting what it proposes, goes on to whisper about another lapse. It considers all resistance the same. It wishes to call you continually to some lapse or other, and it has no investment in any particular lapse as opposed to any other.

It has been said that "every inclination from an angel may or may not be accepted by the one to whom it occurs, but as for the inclination from the real, Most Praised, there can be no resistance to it on the part of the servant."

The shaykhs also discussed the possibility of a second inclination, and whether—if both are from the real, Most Praised—the second is stronger than the first. Junayd said: "The first thought is stronger because when it endures, its possessor returns to contemplation. This is through a condition of traditional knowledge.[99] Abandoning the first thought weakens the second." But Ibn 'Atā' said: "The second is stronger because it builds upon the power of the first." Abū 'Abdullāh ibn Khafīf, one of the more recent masters, said: "Both are equal because both are from the real. There is no advantage of one over the other." The first does not endure with existence of the second because traces cannot endure.[100]

KNOWLEDGE OF CERTAINTY (*'ILM AL-YAQĪN*), ESSENCE OF CERTAINTY (*'AYN AL-YAQĪN*), REALITY OF CERTAINTY (*ḤAQQ AL-YAQĪN*)

Qushayri moves on to three short essays. He first discusses the various forms of certainty (yaqīn) *that can be attained, from certainty based on proof, to that based on exposition, to the highest form of certainty based on immediate vision. He then discusses the "oncoming"* (wārid), *comparing and contrasting it with the "inclination"* (khātir). *Like the inclination, the oncoming occurs to a person without conscious intent, but it is a more general category than the inclination, including states of emotion without a verbal or cognitive element, while the inclination always has a verbal element. Then Qushayri turns to the double-edged notion of the "sign" or "mark"* (shāhid), *with the principle that whatever appears to a person's heart is that person's mark as both a sign of what that person is and will become, and a witness of what that person is experiencing.*

In common usage, certainty is knowledge whose possessor is not influenced by any doubt. The term "certainty" is not employed in the description of the real, Most Praised, because of the lack of any acquaintance. Knowledge of certainty is certainty, just as the essence of certainty and the reality of certainty are certainty itself. According to the requirements of their usage, knowledge of certainty emerges through proof, essence of certainty occurs through exposition, and reality of certainty occurs through the attribute of immediate vision. Knowledge of certainty belongs to the masters of intellect, essence of certainty to the masters of traditional sciences, and reality of certainty to the masters of recognition. A more detailed exposition is not possible here. Precise determination would return to the points mentioned above. They are given here in summary form as a kind of hint.

Oncoming (*Wārid*)

In their discourse they frequently employ the expression "the oncoming." Oncomings are praiseworthy inclinations *(khawāṭir)* that come upon the heart independent of any intention on the part of the servant. What is outside the category of inclinations can also be considered an oncoming. There is an oncoming from the real and an oncoming from knowledge. Oncomings form a more general category than inclinations. Inclinations are exclusively verbal, or else they include a verbal element. Oncomings include: an oncoming of happiness, an oncoming of sorrow, an oncoming of constriction, an oncoming of expansion, and so on, through the other modes of consciousness.

Mark (*Shāhid*) [101]

The expression "the mark" occurs frequently in their discourse: "So and so with the mark of knowledge, so and so with the mark of ecstasy *(wajd)*, so and so with the mark of the state." By the expression "the mark," they mean what is present before the heart of a human being. Its remembrance prevails upon him. He sees it as if it were before his eyes, even if it is not there. When something seizes control of a person's heart with its remembrance, it is that person's mark. If knowledge prevails upon him, he has the mark of knowledge. If it is ecstasy that prevails upon him, he has the mark of ecstasy.

The meaning of the mark is "the present." Whatever is present to your heart is your mark. Shibli was asked about witnessing *(mushāhada)*. He said: "Who are we to witness the real? The real is a *shāhid* (mark/witness) for us." By "the mark of the real," he referred to the heart being taken over by the remembrance of the real, the prevailing of that remembrance upon it, and its perpetual presence to it.

Now someone has taken upon himself the task of giving the etymology of the word. He said: The term *shāhid* is derived from *shahāda* (testimony, witness, attestation). Suppose someone gazes upon a person who is very beautiful. If his mortal nature falls away from him, and his seeing of that person does not distract him from the state that he is in, if being with that person does not affect him in any way, then that person becomes the *shāhid* (mark/witness) of the passing away of his ego-self. However, if anyone is affected by such a sight, then it becomes the *shāhid* to the remaining of his ego-self and his operating under the provisions of the mortal. Thus it is either a *shāhid* for him and/or a *shāhid* against him.

In this regard he said (peace and blessing upon him): "I saw my lord on the night of the Mi'raj in the most beautiful of forms." By this he meant that the most beautiful form which he saw that night did not distract him from the vision of the Most High. Rather, he saw the author of the image in the image and the constructor in what was constructed. He was referring to intellectual vision, not sensual perception.

EGO-SELF (NAFS)

Qushayri's Treatise *ends with essays on the ego-self, spirit, and heart-secret. The term "self"* (nafs) *is used in Arabic to mark reflexive grammatical constructions, such as "he saw himself." In Sufism, it comes to mean the ego-self, the locus of self-centered life, as opposed to the spirit, which is the locus of more authentic life. Qushayri offers a succinct dual definition of ego-self and spirit: "The ego-self can be considered a subtle being, placed within the corporeal substrate as the locus of blameworthy traits, just as the spirit is a subtle being, placed within the substrate as the locus of praiseworthy traits." Later he will suggest that the heart* (qalb) *is another locus of praiseworthy traits.*

In his essay on spirit, Qushayri goes on to explore the relationship between the spirit and the life-force of a person. He concludes his Treatise *with the heart-secret* (sirr), *the locus of the intimate relation between the human and the real. The term* sirr *is particularly subtle because at times it is used to refer to the secret or mystery, and at times to the locus or faculty associated with that secret or mystery. The heart in general is the faculty and locus of mystical knowing* (ma'rifa), *and the* sirr *is the most interior faculty of the heart. The heart-secret must remain inviolable; to disclose the secret is an act of betrayal in both psychological and poetic terms.*

However, among the folk, employment of the term *nafs* does not intend the being of a thing, nor the material substrate.[102] Rather, they intend by *nafs* the defective attributes of the servant, his blameworthy character traits and actions.

The defective attributes of the servant are themselves divisible into two categories. The first category relates to what (of blame) is acquired by the servant,[103] such as his disobedience and his offenses. The second category consists of his baser traits of character. These are blameworthy in themselves. When the servant treats them and when he struggles against them, these traits are extinguished through a continued struggle that takes on the force of habit. The first category in the determinations of the ego-self includes both what is explicitly prohibited by sacred law or judged wrong by the more rigorous standards of complete integrity.[104]

The second category of the ego-self consists of inferior and dishonorable traits of character. This is the general definition. Specific examples include pride, anger, hatred, envy, lax morals, weakness, and other blameworthy traits. The strongest determination of the ego-self and the most difficult to overcome is the delusion that it contains something good or that it deserves some status.[105] This is considered a secret form of idolatry.[106]

The treatment of character traits that consists in abandoning and breaking the self is more complete than simply enduring hunger, thirst, vigil, and other austerities of struggle, which can lead to a loss of strength, even though such austerities can be a part of the more general abandoning of the self.

The ego-self can be considered a subtle being, placed within the corporeal substrate as the locus of blameworthy traits, just as the spirit is a subtle being, placed within the substrate as the locus of praiseworthy traits. The being of the spirit and the bodies that are of a subtle form are like the being of the angels and satans as characterized by subtleness. Sight can properly be called the locus of vision, and the ear the locus of hearing, the nose the locus of smell, the mouth the locus of taste. However, the hearer, seer, smeller, and taster is the totality, which is the human being. Similarly, the locus of praiseworthy traits is the heart and the spirit, and the locus of blameworthy traits is the self. The self is a part of the whole, and the heart is a part of the whole. The determination and the name apply then to the whole.

Spirit (*Rūḥ*)

Concerning spirits, there are different opinions among the realized masters among the people of *sunna*.

Some say they constitute life.

Some say they are essences placed in the bodily forms.

A fine point: Allah brought about the norm that life is created in the bodily form as long as the spirits remain in the body.[107] The human person lives through life, but the spirits that are placed within the bodily forms can rise up out of them during sleep and become separated from the bodies, only to return to them later.

The human person is spirit and body, because Allah, Most Praised and Most High, has made each subservient to the other within the whole.[108] Resurrection will be as a whole [body and spirit], as will the rewards and punishments.

Spirits are created. Whoever maintains their beginningless eternity commits a grave error.

The reports indicate that spirits are subtle essences.

HEART-SECRET/SECRET (*SIRR*)

The heart-secret is considered a subtle essence in the bodily mold, similar to the spirit.[109]

They base this definition upon its being the locus *(maḥall)* of witness, just as the spirits are the locus of love, and the heart is the locus of recognitions.

They say: The heart-secret is what you cannot look upon, and the secret of the secret is known only to the real.

Following their particular usage and their basic premise, the folk hold that the heart-secret is more subtle than the spirit, and the spirit is more subtle than the heart.

They say: The heart-secrets have been formed from the bondage of the others, from traces and ruins.[110]

The term "secret" is employed for what is protected and concealed between the servant and the real in the states. In reference to this, someone said: Our secrets are virgin, undeflowered by anyone's guess.

They say: "The breasts of the free are the graves of secrets."

They say: "If the button of my cloak recognized my secret, I would throw it away."

Thus ends the section "Interpreting Mystical Expressions" from Qushayri's Treatise. *The composition is circular, in the sense that once one has finished the* Treatise, *it is possible to go back and begin again, this time at an entirely new level of understanding. The words that were used in early essays and were undefined at the time have been defined in subsequent essays. Thus the reader returns to the earlier essays with a new range of understanding. At the same time, some of the later essays will have deepened and extended the subjects of the earlier essays.*

Qushayri's Treatise *offers continually deepening definition of the key terms of Sufism. In the first place, it should help prepare readers for later chapters in this volume. As readers encounter these difficult terms and concepts in later chapters of this book, they may wish to return to Qushayri to read again his essays on those issues. As one proceeds further in this volume and then returns to Qushayri, his essays will reveal yet another horizon of meaning.*

4

Rabi'a: Her Words and Life in 'Attar's Memorial of the Friends of God

(TRANSLATED BY PAUL LOSENSKY WITH MICHAEL SELLS)[1]

Introduction

One day some friends-of-God saw Rabi'a running along with fire in one hand and water in the other. "Lady of the next world, where are you going and what does this mean?"

Rabi'a replied: "I am going to burn paradise and douse hell-fire, so that both veils may be lifted from those on the quest and they will become sincere of purpose. God's servants will learn to see him without hope for reward or fear of punishment. As it is now, if you took away hope for reward and fear of punishment, no one would worship or obey."[2]

The most famous Sufi woman, Rābi'a al-'Adawiyya (d. 185/801), also known as Rābi'a of Baṣra, is mentioned only briefly in the earliest accounts of Sufi saints. The fullest account of her life and sayings appears in the Persian text Memorial of the Friends of God *by the Sufi writer and poet of Nishapur, Farīdu d-Dīn 'Aṭṭār (d. ca. 627/1230). The* Memorial *consists of accounts of the lives and sayings of seventy-five Sufi masters. Because the accounts show a consistent hagiographic framework, and because in the case of Rabi'a we have few other sources against which to measure 'Attar's accounts of Rabi'a, the historicity of many Rabi'a legends, and even of Rabi'a herself, has been an object of scholarly questioning.*[3] *Questions remain concerning to what extent 'Attar's account reflected an already strong oral tradition about Rabi'a, and to what extent her important place in Sufi understanding is due to 'Attar's representation of her. The concern in this section, as with the sections on Bistami, Hallaj, and Junayd, is not to try to resolve questions of biography and historicity, but to explore the meaning of the figure's biography and sayings for the Sufi tradition.*

'Attar begins with an immediate and dramatic highlighting of the gender issue. Some might ask how a woman could be included in the ranks of Sufi masters, called, at the time, the "ranks of men" (ṣaff rijāl) *according to 'Attar. This question generates responses from a number of historical, social, and mystical perspectives. 'Attar appeals to historical precedent: the formative role of 'A'isha, a wife of the prophet Muhammad, in later Islamic tradition. 'A'isha, because of her massive influence on hadith, was called "the author of two thirds of the faith." He also appeals to the tradition according to which Maryam, the mother of 'Isa (Jesus), will be the first among the "ranks of men" at the final resurrection. He then makes a more abstract appeal to the principle that the deity regards only a person's inner intention, not the outward form. He ends with a justification based on a mystical notion of unity. The* qawm *(folk, Sufis) are "one," and in oneness* (tawḥīd), *there are no individuals, and thus what room is there for man or woman, you and I, just as in prophecy there is no room for class distinctions of "noble" and "common."*

Throughout the discussion of gender, an ironic twist is given to the stereotype of the "weak woman." Rabi'a refers to herself and is referred to as weak-woman (ḍa'īfa). *She also is called a "weak* pīr-zāne," *which can be translated as a "weak old woman," but which also can imply, within the contexts set up by the anecdotes, a certain role as master or teacher (the Persian* pīr *is the equivalent to the Arabic* shaykh). *Throughout 'Attar's account, this "weak" creature is shown commanding and criticizing the leading secular and religious leaders of her time, referring to the feared angels of judgment (Munkir and Nakir who tear the soul from the human and throw it to its fate) as "those two young gentlemen," and most interestingly, criticizing the Almighty itself for sending such angels to ask her about her faith. Perhaps most illustrative of the character of this weak creature is the story in which three great shaykhs come to visit her. Each is afraid to speak, saying, "You say something." Finally, they do speak, and in typical fashion, Rabi'a exposes and demolishes the spiritual pretensions hidden within their words.*[4]

In addition to a play on weakness and strength, the gender issue also generates a supple investigation of issues of veiling and unveiling, private and public. 'Attar's opening chapter on Rabi'a begins by referring to her, among other things, as "veiled by sincerity." Her status as a freedwoman, a former slave, allows her prerogatives—such as refusing marriage—unavailable to most women. Indeed, in one account, when someone proposes marriage to her, she refers the question to her master, the divine beloved (who in this metaphor is figured as masculine), thus sending the issue of gender into a wicked spin; to marry her is in some sense to marry her master, because of the implication of mystical union.

A large number of anecdotes consist of verbal jousts among Rabi'a and several famous early Sufis, including Ḥasan of Baṣra and Ibrāhīm Adham. In comparison with her, these great men of the age are shown as still held down by affectation and egoism.[5] *Of special interest in these stories is her relationship with the deity. Her absolute devotion is often related directly to her intimate and unaffected conversations, in which she calls on the deity with confidence and even with familiarity. Here Rabi'a's role as a former slave, mendicant, and yet personal confidant of the deity bears comparison with the biblical Hagar, a slave who was rejected and exiled by Abraham after the birth of Isaac, but to whom the deity spoke directly in the desert—one of the few cases in which the deity directly speaks to human beings in the Hebrew Bible.*

In one story, when Rabi'a is lost in the desert, she sends away a group of men who offer to help her, and then engages in an intimate dialogue with the deity. The more profound dimensions of the private-versus-public theme are revealed here. If she is alone in the desert, how does the narrator come to know of the conversation? If her telling of the conversation to someone else is implicitly assumed, it seems to be in tension with the emphasis on the confidentiality of her relationship with the divine. A similar tension exists in the earlier story in which her owner sees her entreating God one night, with a lamp suspended without a cord above her head, illuminating the entire house. Again, a private, intimate moment is made public. Once the owner sees this, he calls Rabi'a in and gives her freedom. Exemplifying this contradiction of private made public are the intimate entreaties or supplications (munājāt) *attributed to Rabi'a, several of which are listed at the end of the account.*

The familiarities Rabi'a takes with the deity are dramatically illustrated in the story of the Ka'ba coming to meet her when she is lost in the desert on her way to making the ḥajj, *and her casual statement that she is interested in the lord of the Ka'ba, so what could the Ka'ba itself have to offer her. At one point she says to the deity: "You come to me, right here!"—a highly unusual way for a Sufi to address the deity. The deity responds by reminding her what happened when Musa asked for a vision: One atom's worth of divine manifestation fell on the mountain and it shattered into forty pieces. Here we have a powerful dynamic between the dialogical and the visual. Rabi'a has a very intimate, oral, and aural relationship with the deity through her* munājat. *She speaks at times with utter devotion; at other times with surprising casualness—taking literally and to its logical extreme her references to the deity and the deity's references to her as "friend" or "beloved"* (dost). *This intimacy is held in balance with the cosmic sense of awe, evoked particularly in the visual imagery of the annihilation of the mountain in the Moses-vision story.*

The stories revolve around a cluster of basic themes of mystical practice: tawakkul *(the absolute trust-in-God);* riḍā *(complete acceptance of the lot willed for one by the deity to the point of refusing prayer as petition, since one's own will has been merged with that of the divine will);*[6] faqr *(absolute poverty, including—as was seen in the earlier essay by as-Sarrāj—the paradoxical poverty that is so great one gives up one's own possession of the state of poverty itself). The central Islamic doctrine of affirmation of unity* (tawḥīd) *is given its Sufi moral and relational emphasis: Unity for Rabi'a means that there is only one object of desire, of interest, of concern—the divine beloved—and in such an absolute relational* tawḥīd, *Rabi'a declared even love for Muhammad or hatred for Satan to be distractions. This unified center of her being leads to a life of of utter intensity, dramatized throughout the anecdotes as a living as if each moment were the last moment of her life.*

At the center of this cluster of interrelated themes is ṣidq *(sincerity). It is her sincerity that is the touchstone in Rabi'a's encounters with the other religious leaders, the* buzurgān *(great men, important personages) of her time. The sincerity is dramatized in the story from the biographer Aflaki cited above on Rabi'a's announced intent to burn paradise and douse hellfire so that no one will serve the deity except out of sincere love, stripped of desire for reward and fear of punishment. 'Attar offers a number of stories with a similar message.*

◆ ◆ ◆

RĀBI'A AL-'ADAWĪYA[7]

1. Veiled with a special veil, veiled with the veil of sincerity, burned up in love and longing, enamored of proximity and immolation, lost in love-union,[8] deputy of Maryam the pure, accepted among men, Rābi'a 'Adawīya—the mercy of God Most High upon her.

If anyone asks why her memorial is placed among the ranks of men, we reply that the chief of the prophets—peace and blessing upon him—declares: *God does not regard your forms.* It is not a matter of form, but of right intention. If it is right to derive two-thirds of religion from 'A'isha Ṣādiqah—God be pleased with her—then it is also right to derive benefit from one of his maidservants. When a woman is a man on the path of the lord Most High, she cannot be called woman.[9]

2. Thus it is that 'Abbāsah Ṭūsī said, "When on the morrow on the plain of resurrection they call out, 'O men,' the first person to step into the ranks of men will be Maryam." When Ḥasan Baṣrī would not hold a meeting unless a certain person were present, then certainly that person's memorial can be entered in the ranks of men.[10] Indeed, when it comes to the truth [*ḥaqīqat*], where this folk is, there is no one—all are unity. In unity, how can your existence or mine remain, much less "man" or "woman"? As Abū 'Alī Fārmadī, God's mercy upon him, says, "Prophecy is the essence of might and sublimity. Noble or common do not enter into it." Thus, being God's friend is also exactly like this. This is especially so for Rabi'a, who in her age had no equal in proper behavior or mystical knowledge. She was esteemed by the great people of the age and was a decisive proof for those who lived in her time.

3. It is related that on the night she was born, there was no lamp in her father's house, nor a drop of oil to anoint her navel, nor so much as a piece of cloth to swaddle her in. Her father had three daughters, and Rabi'a was the fourth. And so they called her Rabi'a, meaning "the fourth one."

So his wife said to him, "Go to neighbor so-and-so and ask for a lamp's worth of oil."

Rabi'a's father had sworn not to ask any creature for anything. He got up, went to that neighbor's door, and returned, saying, "They were asleep."

He fell asleep grieving. He saw the Prophet—peace and blessing upon him—in a dream. He said, "Don't be sad. This daughter is a noble lady who will intercede before him for seventy thousand of my community."[11] He went on to say, "Go to 'Isa Rādān, the emir of Basra, and say, 'This last Friday, you forgot how you call upon my blessings a hundred times each night and four hundred times on Friday. In atonement, give me four hundred gold dinars.' "

When he awoke in tears in the morning, Rabi'a's father wrote this dream down on a piece of paper and took it to the palace of 'Isá Rādān. He gave it to someone to deliver. When the Emir examined it, he commanded that ten thousand dirhams be given in alms, in gratitude that the Prophet—peace and blessing upon him—had remembered him. And he ordered that four hundred dinars be given to Rabi'a's father and said, "Tell him, 'I want you to come in, so I may pay my respects to you. But I do not consider it right that one like you, delivering the message of the Prophet—peace and blessing upon him—should come to visit me. I myself will come and sweep the dust on your doorstep with my beard. By God, if you ever happen to need anything, let me know.' "

So Rabi'a's father took that gold and spent it.

4. When Rabi'a grew older, her mother and father died. A great famine occurred in Basra. The sisters were separated, and Rabi'a fell into the hands of a wicked man who sold her for a few dirhams. That master ordered her to work long and hard.

One day on the street, she fled from the indignity. She fell and broke her hand. She put her face on the ground and said, "I am a stranger without mother or father. I am a captive and my hand is broken. None of this saddens me. All I need is for you to be pleased with me, to know whether you are pleased with me or not."

She heard a voice say, "Do not be sad. Tomorrow a grandeur will be yours such that the closest of the heavenly company will take pride in you."

5. So Rabi'a went to the house. She fasted continuously and prayed all night, remaining on her feet until daybreak. One night, her master started from sleep. He heard a voice. He looked and saw Rabi'a prostrate in prayer, saying, "O my God, you know that the desire of my heart is in accord with your command and that the light of my eye is in service to your court. If the matter were in my hands, I would not rest a moment from serving you. But you have put me in the hands of this creature. Because of this, I came late to serve you."

Her master looked and saw a lantern hanging suspended over Rabi'a's head without a chain and the whole room filled with light. He arose, saying to himself, "She cannot be kept in servitude." So he said to Rabi'a, "I free you. If you wish to stay here, we are entirely at your service. If not, go wherever you have a mind to." Rabi'a asked leave to go, departed, and immersed herself in devotions.

They say she used to perform one thousand *rak'as* of prayer a day. From time to time, she went to Hasan Basri's meetings. One group says that she fell into being a musician, repented again, and dwelled in a ruin. Afterward, she retired to a meditation cell and worshiped there awhile.

6. Later, she resolved to make the *ḥajj* and went into the desert. She had a donkey upon which she loaded her belongings. But in the middle of the desert, it died. The people in the caravan said, "We'll carry your things." She said, "I have not come this far by putting my trust [*tavakkul*] in you. Go on ahead."

The caravan departed. Rabi'a said, "My God, do kings treat a helpless woman this way? You invited me to your house, then killed my donkey in the middle of the journey, and left me alone in the desert."

The donkey immediately got up. Rabi'a loaded it and went on. The narrator of this report said that sometime later he saw that little donkey being sold.

7. While Rabi'a was on her way to Mecca, she was left helpless in the desert for several days. She said, "My God, I am sore at heart. Where will I go? I am a clod of earth, and that house is a rock. I must have you."

The real Most High addressed her heart without intermediary: "O Rabi'a, you wash in the blood of eighteen thousand worlds. Don't you see that when Moses—peace be upon him—desired a vision, we cast a few motes of self-manifestation upon the mountain and it shattered into forty pieces!"

8. It is related that she was going to Mecca another time. In the middle of the desert, she saw that the Ka'ba had come out to welcome her. Rabi'a said, "I need the lord of the house. What am I to do with the house? Its power means nothing to me. What delight is there in the Ka'ba's beauty? What I need to welcome me is the one who said '*Whoever approaches me by a hand's span, I will approach by an arm's span.*'[12] Why should I look at the Ka'ba?"

9. It is related that Ibrāhīm Adham—God have mercy upon him—traveled fourteen years to reach Mecca. He said, "Others have crossed this desert with their feet. I will cross it with my eyes!" He would perform two *rak'as* of prayer and take one step. When he reached Mecca, he did not see the house. He said, "What's happened? Could something be wrong with my eyes?"

A voice said, "There's nothing wrong with your eyes! The Ka'ba has gone to welcome a weak woman who is on her way here." Ibrahim roared with jealousy, "Who could this be?" As soon as he saw Rabi'a coming, walking with a cane, the Ka'ba was back in place.

Ibrahim said, "O Rabi'a, what a commotion and fuss you've stirred up in the world!"

She said, "It's you who've stirred up this commotion, tarrying for fourteen years to reach the house!"

Ibrahim said, "Yes, indeed, for fourteen years I traversed the desert in prayer [*namāz*]!"

Rabi'a said, "You traversed it in prayer, I in longing [*niyāz*]."

10. Then she performed the *ḥajj* and wept bitterly, saying, "O my God, you promised good things both for performing the ḥajj and for enduring catastrophe. Now, if my *ḥajj* is not acceptable, this is a great catastrophe. Where is the reward for my catastrophe?"

11. Then she came to Basra, staying until the following year. She said, "If last year the Ka'ba came to welcome me, this year I will go to welcome the Ka'ba." When the time came, so shaykh Abū'Alī Fārmadī relates, she set out into the desert and crawled for seven years until she arrived at 'Araf āt.[13] A voice called out, "O claimant, what quest has led you here? If you want me to manifest myself just once, you will melt on the spot!"

She said, "O lord of might, Rabi'a does not have the means to attain that station. I only wish for a drop of poverty."

The voice called out, "O Rabi'a, poverty is the drought year of our wrath, which we have placed in people's path. When no more than a hair's width remains before they arrive in the presence of union with us, then the matter is turned about and union is changed into separation. You are still within the seventy veils of your life. Until you come out from under all of these, take a step on our path, and pass these seventy stations, you cannot speak of our poverty. If not, behold!"

Rabi'a looked and saw a sea of blood suspended in the air. A voice called out, "This is the blood of our lovers who came seeking union with us. They alighted at the first way-station, so no trace or sign of them appears anywhere in the two worlds."

Rabi'a said, "O lord of power, show me one characteristic of their estate." Immediately they appeared, making apologies to her. A voice spoke, "Their first station is to crawl for seven years to come on our path to pay homage to a clod of earth. When they near that clod, they themselves cause the road to be closed before them."

Rabi'a was afflicted and said, "O Lord, you do not allow me into your house. Nor will you let me stay in my house in Basra. Either leave me in my house in Basra, or bring me to your house in Mecca. At first, I did not bow to the house—I wanted you. Now I am not even worthy of your house."[14]

She said this and returned. She came back to Basra and retired to a place of meditation.

12. It is related that two religious dignitaries came to pay their respects to her. They were hungry and said to one another, "We'll eat any food that she brings, for it will be ritually pure [*ḥalāl*]." Rabi'a had two loaves of bread and set them before her guests. Suddenly a beggar cried out. Rabi'a took the bread from them and gave it to the beggar.

They were dumbfounded, but immediately a serving girl came, carrying an armful of warm bread, and said, "The lady of the house has sent these." Rabi'a counted: There were eighteen loaves. "You've made a mistake," she said, "Take them back."

"There's no mistake," the girl said.

"You've made a mistake. Take them back."

She took them back and told the story to her mistress. She added two more loaves and sent them back. Rabi'a counted: There were twenty. She took them and set them before her guests. They ate them and marveled. So they said to her, "What's the secret behind this?"

She said, "When you came, I knew that you were hungry. I said to myself, 'How can I put two loaves before two great men?' When the beggar came, I gave them to him and prayed, saying, 'O my God, you have said, "For each thing given, I will return ten-fold." Certain of this, I have given away two loaves to please you, so that you would give back ten-fold.' When she brought eighteen, I knew that there'd been some filching or that they'd not been meant for me. I sent them back to make up twenty altogether."

13. It is related that one night she was praying in her cell. She fell asleep. A reed[15] pierced her eye, but in such a way that in her total rapture and absorption, her utter devotion, she was unaware of it. A thief entered and

picked up her chadur. As he was about to carry it off, he could not see the way. He put it back and realized how to get out. He picked the chadur back up and again could not see the way. Seven times this happened. A voice came from the corner of the cell: "Man, don't trouble yourself! For several years now, she has entrusted herself to us. Iblis doesn't have the gall to come around her. How could a thief have the gall to come around her chadur? Don't trouble yourself, imposter. If one friend is sleeping, another is awake."

14. It is related that one day, when Rabi'a had not eaten for several days, her serving girl was preparing a soup from lard. She needed onions and said, "I'll get some from the neighbors."

"It's been forty years," Rabi'a said, "since I made a covenant with the Lord mighty and glorious not to ask for anything from any other than him. Say, 'Onions we'll do without.' "

Immediately, a bird swooped down from the sky and dropped several onions, already peeled, into her pot. Rabi'a said, "I'm not safe from being tricked." She gave up the soup and ate plain bread.

15. It is related that one day Rabi'a had gone up on a mountain. Wild goats and gazelles[16] gathered around, gazing upon her. Suddenly, Hasan Basri appeared. All the animals shied away. When Hasan saw that, he was preplexed and said, "Rabi'a, why do they shy away from me when they were so intimate with you?"

Rabi'a said, "What did you eat today?"

"Soup."

"You ate their lard. How would they not shy away from you?"

16. It is related that one time Rabi'a happened to pass by Hasan's house. He was sitting on the roof of his meditation cell, weeping so much that water was dripping from the rain spouts. Several drops landed on Rabi'a. She searched to find out where this water was coming from. When she realized what was happening, she said, "Hasan, if this weeping is from the foolish whims of the self [*nafs*], hold back your tears, lest a sea well up within you, such a sea that when you seek your heart there, you will not find it 'Except before a most powerful king [54:55].' "[17]

17. These words were hard for Hasan to take, but he said nothing. One day he saw Rabi'a on the banks of the Euphrates. Hasan threw his prayer

rug on the water and said, "Rabi'a, come here! Let's perform two *rak'as* of prayer."

Rabi'a said, "Master, if you're going to display the goods of the afterworld in the market of this world, you must do what others of your species are incapable of doing."[18]

Then Rabi'a threw her prayer rug into the air and said, "Hasan, come here, where you will be hidden from the people's gaze."[19]

Then she wished to win him over again. She said, "Master, what you did, a fish can do, and what I did, a fly can do. The real business is beyond both."

18. It is related that Hasan Basri said, "I was with Rabi'a for one full day and night. We discussed the way and the truth [*ṭarīqat va ḥaqīqat*] in such a way that the thought 'I am a man' never crossed my mind, nor did 'I am a woman' ever cross hers. In the end when I arose, I considered myself a pauper and her a devotee."

19. It is related that one evening Hasan went with some friends to visit Rabi'a. Rabi'a had no lantern, and they needed one. Rabi'a blew on her fingertips—they blazed like a lantern until daybreak.

If someone asks, "What was this like?" we answer, "Just like the hand of Moses, peace upon him."[20]

If they should say, "He was a prophet," we would respond, "Whoever follows a prophet has a portion of those wonders [*karāmāt*]. If the prophet performs miracles [*mu'jiza*], the friend of God performs wonders by the blessings of following the prophet. As the prophet declares, 'Whoever returns a farthing of what is forbidden has attained a degree of prophecy,' that is, anyone who gives back to the enemy Satan a penny of what is forbidden achieves a degree of prophecy."

He also said, "The true dream is a quarter share of prophecy."

20. It is related that Rabi'a once sent Hasan three things: a piece of wax, a needle, and a hair. She said, "Like the wax, give light to the world as you yourself burn. Like the needle, be naked and work continually. When you have achieved these two things, be like the hair, so your work will not be in vain."

21. It is related that Hasan said to Rabi'a, "Would you like to take a husband?"

She said, "The marriage knot can only tie one who exists. Where is existence here? I am not my own—I am his and under his command. You must ask permission from him."

"O Rabi'a," he said, "by what means did you attain this degree?"

"By losing in him everything I'd attained."

"How do you know him?"

"You know the how. We know the no-how."[21]

22. It is related that one day Hasan came to her cell and said, "Say a word to me about that knowledge that, untaught and unheard, came down to your heart without the intermediary of any creature."

She said, "I spun some skeins of yarn to sell and earn a bit of food. I sold it for two pieces of silver. I took one in one hand and one in the other. I was afraid that if I took both in one hand, they would join forces and lead me from the path. My victory today was this."

23. They said to Rabi'a, "Hasan says that if he is deprived of the vision of the real for one moment in paradise, he will weep and moan so much that all the people of paradise will take pity on him."

She said, "This is a good thing to say. But if in this world he neglects remembering the real for one moment, and the very same anguish and weeping and lamentation appears, then it is a sign that the same thing will happen in the afterworld. Otherwise, it will not be so."

24. They said, "Why don't you take a husband?"

She said, "I am dismayed with care over three things. If you free me of these cares, I'll take a husband. First, at the moment of death, will my faith be sound or not? Second, will they put the book of my deeds in my right hand or not?[22] Third, which group will I be in on that hour when they lead a group to the right to paradise and a group to the left to hell?"

They said, "We don't know."

She said, "With such anguish before me, how can I be concerned with taking a husband?"

25. They said, "Where do you come from?"

She said, "From that world."

"Where are you going?"

"To that world."

"What are you doing in this world?"

"Grieving."

"Why?"

"I eat the bread of this world and do the work of that."

"Such a sweet tongue!" they said. "You are fit to be an abbess."

"I am abbess of myself. Whatever is within me, I do not bring out. Whatever is outside me, I do not let in. If anyone enters and leaves, it has nothing to do with me. I watch over my heart, not mud and clay."

26. They said, "Do you love the presence of majesty?"

She said, "I do."

They said, "Do you hate Satan?"

She said, "Out of love of the compassionate, I have no occasion for hatred toward Satan. I saw the Prophet in a dream. He said, 'Rabi'a, do you love me?' I said, 'O Prophet of God, who is there that doesn't love you? But love of the real has so pervaded me that there is no place in my heart for love or hatred of another.' "

27. They asked her about love. She said, "Love came down from eternity [*azal*] and passed over to eternity [*abad*]. It found no one in eighteen thousand worlds to take a single drink of it. It arrived at last to the real, and of him this expression remains: He loves them and they love him."

They said, "Do you see the one you worship?"

She said, "If I did not see, I would not worship."

28. It is related that Rabi'a was always weeping. "Why do you weep so much?" they said.

She said, "I'm afraid of being cut off, for I've grown accustomed to him. No voice must cry out at the moment of death, 'You are not worthy of us!' "[23]

29. They asked, "When is a servant of God contented?"

She said, "When he is as thankful for tribulation as he is for bliss."

They asked, "If a sinner repents, does he accept him or not?"

She said, "How can he repent, unless the Lord gives him repentance and accepts him? Until he gives him repentance, he cannot repent."

30. She said, "O Sons of Adam, from the eye, there is no way-station to the real. From the tongue, there is no path to him. Hearing is the highway of complainers. Hand and foot dwell in perplexity. The matter falls to the heart. Strive to acquire a wakeful heart. When the heart is awake, it has no need for a friend. In other words, the wakeful heart is one that has lost itself

in the real. When someone is lost, what is he to do with a friend? Extinction in God [*fanā*] is here."

31. She said, "Asking for mercy with the tongue is the business of liars."

She said, "When we repent ourselves, we need the repentance of another."

She said, "If patience were a man, he would be generous."

She said, "The fruit of gnosis is turning to the mighty and glorious Lord."

She said, "The gnostic is one who asks the real for a heart. When he gives him a heart, he immediately gives it back to the mighty and glorious lord, so it will be protected in his grasp and hidden from creatures in his veil."

32. Ṣāliḥ Murrī, God's mercy upon him, often used to say, "Whoever knocks at a door will have it opened in the end."

Once Rabi'a was present. She said, "How long will you say, 'He will open it again'? When did he close it that he will open it again?"

Ṣāliḥ said, "Amazing! An ignorant man and a wise weak woman."

33. One day Rabi'a saw a man saying, "O sorrow!"

She said, "Say it this way: O without sorrow! For if you *were* sorrowful, you wouldn't have the gall to breathe."

34. It is related that once someone had tied a bandage on his head. She said, "Why have you tied the bandage on your head?"

He said, "My head hurts."

She said, "How old are you?"

"Thirty."

"In these thirty years, have you been mostly healthy or sick?"

"Healthy."

"Have you ever, in these thirty years, tied on the bandage of gratitude? Now because you have a single headache, you tie on the bandage of complaint."

35. It is related that she gave someone four dinars, saying "Get a blanket for me."

"Black or white?"

She immediately took back the dinars, threw them in the Tigris, and said, "Because of an unpurchased blanket, division has come into view: Must it be black or white?"

36. It is related that in the springtime she entered a house and did not come out. Her serving girl said, "O mistress, come outside and see the effects of the creation!"

She said, "You come in for once and see the creator! Witnessing the creator has preoccupied me from gazing on the creation."

37. Once a group came to visit Rabi'a. They saw her cutting up a piece of meat with her teeth. They said, "Don't you have a knife?"

She said, "For fear of being cut off, I've never had a knife."

38. It is related that once she did not break her fast for seven days and nights without sleep. On the eighth night, hunger overcame her. Her soul [*nafs*] cried out, "How long will you torment me?" Suddenly, someone knocked at the door, bringing a bowl of food. She took it and set it down to bring the lantern. The cat came in and spilled the food.

She said, "I will go and bring a jug of water and break my fast." When she left, the lantern went out. When she was about to drink the water, the jug fell from her hand and broke. Rabi'a let out a sigh that might have burned down the house. She said, "O my God, why is it that you are making me so helpless?"

She heard a voice say, "Beware, O Rabi'a! If you wish, I will bestow the bliss of the world upon you, but I will remove the grief for me from your heart. The bliss of the world and grief for me cannot be joined in one heart. O Rabi'a, you desire one thing, and we another. Our desire and yours cannot be joined in one heart."

She said, "When I heard this address, I so detached my heart from the world and cut short my hopes that for thirty years now I have performed each prayer as though it were my last and I were praying the prayer of farewell. I made myself so independent of creatures, so cut off, that when day broke, for fear that creatures would preoccupy me, I prayed, 'O Lord, so preoccupy me with yourself that no one will preoccupy me from you.' "

39. It is related that she lamented continually. People said, "There's no apparent reason for it. What's the cause of her lament?"

She said, "I have a sickness within my breast that physicians have proved unable to cure. The salve for our wound is union with him. I excuse myself for this lamentation with the possibility of reaching my goal tomorrow in the hereafter. Although I am not among those racked with pain, still I liken myself to them. Anything less than this is impossible."

40. It is related that a group of important people came to Rabi'a. Rabi'a asked one of them, "Why do you worship the Lord?"

He said, "The seven levels of hell have a majestic power, and everyone must pass through them, distressed by fear and dread."

Another said, "The degrees of paradise contain an excellent way-station, wherein much repose is promised."

Rabi'a said, "It is an evil servant who worships his Lord out of fear or out of desire for reward."

So they said, "Why do you worship the Lord? Have you no desire?" She said, " 'The neighbor, then the house.'[24] Isn't it everything to me that I have been commanded to worship him? If there were no heaven or hell, then it wouldn't be necessary to worship him! Wouldn't he deserve to be worshiped without intermediary?"

41. It is related that an important man came to visit her. He saw her clothes in tatters. He said, "There are many people who would look after you if you would just give the word."

Rabi'a said, "I am ashamed to ask for things of this world from someone who has them on loan."

That important man said, "Behold the lofty aspiration of this weak woman! He has brought her to such a height that she refuses to occupy her time with making requests."

42. It is related that a group came to Rabi'a to put her to the test. They said, "All the virtues have been dispersed among men. The crown of nobility [*muruvvat*] has been placed upon the heads of men, and the belt of magnanimity has been tied around their waists. Prophecy has never descended upon any woman. What can you boast of?"

Rabi'a said, "Everything you said is true. But egoism, egotism, self-worship, and (79:24) 'I am your highest lord' have not welled up in any woman.[25] And no woman has ever been a pederast."

43. It is related that one day Rabi'a fell ill. She was asked about the cause of her illness. She said, "I looked into the garden, and my Lord reproved me. An inclination for paradise appeared on the horizon of my heart, and the friend punished me. This illness is because of that."

44. Hasan Basri visited her in her sickness. He said, "I saw a rich gentleman of Basra with a pouch of gold sitting and weeping on the doorstep of her cell. I said, 'Why are you weeping?' He said, 'Because of this devoted ascetic, dear to our age. Without her blessing, humankind will perish. I've brought something to take care of her, but I'm afraid she won't accept it. Intercede for me, and perhaps she will.' "

Hasan said, "I entered and delivered the message. Rabi'a looked at me from the corner of her eye and said, 'If he provides for someone who insults him, will he withhold daily bread from one whose soul seethes with love for him?[26] As long as I've known him, I've turned my back on created things. How can I accept someone's money, not knowing whether it's lawful or not? Once I sewed up my torn shirt by the light of the Sultan's lantern. A turn of fate had sealed my heart. Until I tore it up again, my heart was not opened. Beg my pardon from the gentleman, so he won't put my heart in bondage.' "

45. 'Abd al-Waḥīd ibn 'Amir says, "With Sufyān Thawrī, we paid a sick-call on Rabi'a. We couldn't speak for awe of her. They said to Sufyān, 'Say something.' He said, 'O Rabi'a, pray, so the real Most High will ease your pain.' Rabi'a said, 'O Sufyān, don't you know that the real Most High has willed my pain?' He said, 'Yes.' She said, 'You know this and still you tell me to request what is at odds with his will. It is not proper to be at odds with the friend.'

"Then Sufyān said, 'Rabi'a, is there something you desire?' She said, 'Sufyān, you are a man of the people of knowledge. How can you talk this way? By the majesty of the Lord, for twelve years I have desired fresh dates, and you know there's no shortage of fresh dates in Basra. I still haven't eaten any. I am a servant, and what business does a servant have with desire? If I wish for something and my Lord does not, this is infidelity.'

"Then Sufyān said, 'I can say nothing with regard to your situation. Say something with regard to mine.' She said, 'You are a good man, but isn't it the case that you love this world?' He said, 'How so?' She said, 'By reciting *ḥadiths*,' meaning that this too is a sort of pomp. Sufyān said, 'I have been lax.' I, 'Abd al-Wāḥid ibn'Amir, said, 'O Lord, be pleased with me!' Rabi'a said, 'Aren't you ashamed to seek the good pleasure of someone with whom you are not pleased?' "

46. Mālik Dīnār said, "I went to visit Rabi'a. I saw she had a broken pitcher that she used for ablutions and drinking water. Her reed mat was old and worn, and she had a brick to rest her head on. This hurt me to the core,

and I said, 'Rabi'a, I have wealthy friends. If you permit, I'll ask them for something for you.'

"She said, 'You've made an error. Do not I and they have the same provider?'

"I said, 'Of course.'

"She said, 'Has he forgotten the poor [*darvīshān*] because of their poverty? Does he aid the wealthy because of their wealth?'

"I said, 'No.'

"She said, 'Since he knows my condition, why should I remind him? He wills it so. We in turn will whatever he wills.' "

47. It is related that Hasan Baṣrī, Mālik Dīnār, and Shaqīq Balkhī, God Most High have mercy upon them, went to visit Rabi'a, God have mercy upon her. The conversation turned to the question of sincerity. Hasan said, "No one is sincere in his claim who is not patient under the blows of his master."

Rabi'a said, "This talk stinks of egoism."

Shaqīq said, "No one is sincere in his claim who is not grateful for the blows of his master."

Rabi'a said, "We need something better than this."

Mālik Dīnār said, "No one is sincere in his claim who does not delight in the blows of his master."

Rabi'a said, "We need something better than this."

They said, "Now you speak."

Rabi'a said, "No one is sincere in his claim who does not forget the wound of the blow in the vision of his master. There's nothing strange in this. The women of Egypt did not perceive the wound of the blow while they viewed Joseph, peace be upon him. Why should it be strange if someone is like this while viewing the creator?"

48. It is related that one of the religious dignitaries of Basra came to visit Rabi'a, sat at her bedside, and began condemning the world. Rabi'a said, "You love the world dearly. If you didn't, you wouldn't remember it so much. The buyer's the one who disparages the goods. Were you free of the world, you'd not remember it for good or ill. You'll recall that 'whoever loves a thing, remembers it all the more.' "[27]

49. It is related that Hasan said, "I was with Rabi'a at the afternoon prayer. She was about to cook something. The meat was in the pot when we started talking. She said, 'This talk is better than putting the pot on to cook.' She left the pot as it was while we performed the evening prayer. She brought

dry bread and a jug of water so we could break our fast. She went over to the pot to pick it up. The pot was boiling through the power of the real Most High. Then she poured the food in a bowl, brought it over, and we ate some of the meat. It was a dish the likes of which we had never tasted. She said, 'Such a dish agrees with someone who's risen from prayer.' "

50. Sufyān Thawrī said, "One night I was with Rabi'a. She went to the mihrab and prayed until daybreak. I was praying in the other corner. At dawn she said, 'In thanks for our success, today we will fast.' "

She has the following devotional prayers.

The Devotions of Rabi'a Adawiya

51. "O Lord, if you send me to hell on the morrow of the resurrection, I will reveal a secret such that hell will flee from me, not to return for a thousand years."

52. "O my God, whatever share of this world you have given me, give it to your enemies, and whatever share of the next world you have given me, give it to your friends. You are enough for us."

53. "O Lord, if I worship you out of fear of hell, burn me in hell. If I worship you in the hope of paradise, forbid it to me. And if I worship you for your own sake, do not deprive me of your eternal beauty."

54. "O Lord, if tomorrow you put me in hell, I will cry out, 'You have befriended me. Is this how one treats friends?' " A voice called out, "Rabi'a, do not think ill of us. Be assured that we will bring you into the circle of our friends, so you may converse with us."

55. "O my God, my work and my desire, in all this world, is recollection of you and in the afterworld, meeting with you. This is what is mine—you do as you will."

56. And nightly she would say, "O Lord, make my heart present or accept my prayers without my heart."

57. When her death approached, important people were at her bedside. She said, "For the sake of God's prophets, arise and leave the room." They arose, went out, and closed the door. They heard a voice (89:27–29): "O soul now in peace, return to your Lord, well pleased and well pleasing."[28]

Some time passed, and no voice was heard. When they entered, she had died. The religious dignitaries said, "Rabi'a came to this world and left for the afterworld, never having been arrogant with the real Most High, never wanting anything, never saying, 'Make me thus' or 'Do such-and-such.' "

58. It is related that she was seen in a dream. She was asked, "Tell us about Munkir and Nakir."[29]

She said, "When those young gentlemen came to me and said, 'Who is your Lord?' I said, 'Go back to the real and say, "Out of so many thousand creatures, you didn't forget an old woman? Out of all the world, I have only you. Do I ever forget you, so that you need to send someone to ask, 'Who is your Lord?' "

59. It is related that Muḥammad ibn Aslam Ṭūsī and Na'im Ṭarsūsī, God's mercy on them both, who gave water to thirty thousand people in the desert, were both present at Rabi'a's grave. They said, "You—who boasted that you would not bow your head to anyone in the two worlds—what state have you attained?"

A voice replied, "May what I have seen be to my good health!"

5

Muhasibi: Moral Psychology

Introduction

Al-Muḥāsibi (d. 243/857) was born in Basra and spent most of his life in Baghdad.[1] *He developed the most rigorous and influential moral psychology within the Islamic mystical tradition. His masterwork,* The Book on the Observance of the Rights of God (kitāb ar-ri'āya li ḥuqūq Allāh) *contains a fully developed analysis of the various forms of human egoism, and a method of examining them, being wary of them, without falling into preoccupation with them. Although aspects of Muhasibi's thought were attacked by the influential thinker Ibn Ḥanbal, Muhasibi's moral psychology exerted enormous influence on later Sufism and on Islamic thought more widely.*[2]

Muhasibi's major contribution is to be found in his Book on the Observance of the Rights of God.[3] *The book is in the form of a dialogue between one of Muhasibi's students and the master. The student poses short questions, with the master offering elaborate answers. Muhasibi's prose is rough and unpoetic. It is as if the author had decided that his main topic—the rights of God and the manner in which human egoism interferes with them—was a topic so unpalatable that any artifice would allow the reader to escape from the grim conclusions. The nickname "Muḥāsibī" is derived from the concept of* muḥāsiba, *that is, a continual calling-into-account or examination of conscience that Muhasibi believes every human needs to engage in. Whereas Qushayri examined the stations and moments* (awqāt) *of mystical experience and the inclinations that occur to the mystic, Muhasibi examines or calls into account—with equal precision and subtlety—the stations and moments of egoism and the various forms it can take.*

Muhasibi's style consists of abrupt changes in grammatical person (from first and second person, to a more abstract third person), as well as a circling, repetitious return to key themes. With each repetition, Muhasibi adds something new—a testimony from the Qur'an or the tradition of the Prophet, or a roughhewn example from everyday life. It is as if the author were trying to hem the reader in and block off the ego's natural and well-developed habits of escaping such scrutiny.

The major forms of egoism examined by Muhasibi include the following: (1) egoistic self-display or conceit (riyā'), *what we might call in contemporary terms "narcissism"; (2) pride* (kibr), *defined by Muhasibi as the human godservant putting himself in the place of the master or lord,*[4] *what we might call in contemporary terms the impulse toward megalomania in which a person sees himself as the center of reality; (3) vanity* ('ujb), *through which a person deludes himself into an exaggeration of the worth and value of his acts and a forgetting of his faults; and (4) self-delusion proper* (ghirra), *through which a person imagines that his own refusal to change his destructive behavior is justified by his hope in divine compassion. Each of these major modes of egoism is related to the others, and each generates submodes, such as competitiveness, rivalry, acquisitiveness, and self-vaunting.*[5] *Each of the submodes has a modality for each of its relations to the principle modes; thus there is a competitiveness grounded in conceit, and different forms of competitiveness grounded in vanity and pride. Each of the modes and submodes has a particular antidote within the life of devotion. The virtue of sincerity (ikhlāṣ), for example, is the antidote for conceit. Finally, each antidote is grounded in meditation on the one deity, the revelation of the Qur'an, the traditions of the Prophet, and human reason when it stays within the framework of divine revelation.*

Muhasibi provides concise definitions for the various forms of egoism, as in the following question and answer:[6]

I said, Please tell me about vanity *('ujb)*—what it is, where it resides, and how it can be rejected and warded off.

He said: You have asked about a profound flaw that, within many servants of God, blinds them to their sins and embroiders over their flaws and failings. Vanity blinds the heart until the vain person sees himself as doing good when he is doing wrong, as succeeding when he is perishing, as hitting the mark when he is going astray. The person who falls into vanity does not hesitate to become mired in self-delusion *(ghirra)*. He makes small of the sins of his that he knows and recalls while forgetting many of them as well. He becomes blind to most of his sins so that he overrates his actions, deludes himself about them, loses his fear of doing wrong, and increases his self-delusion concerning God Most High. The vain person even goes so far as to lie about God Most High while thinking he is being true, to stray into error while thinking he is well guided. Through vanity, one perishes in error by waxing self-important, becoming arrogant, and turning pretentious. In conceit are other forms of moral destruction for the community as well.

In another work, the Book of Counsels, *Muhasibi offers a set of concise definitions for each aspect of egoism and each method of overcoming it. His definition of narcissistic vanity complements the definition in the* Book of the Observance, *but adds another perspective:*[7]

I said: What is this vanity *('ijāb)* which you fear on my account?

He said: Attention to yourself in any act, and the exaggeration of your own role in it—forgetting that it was God Most High who graced you with it and gave you success. It is praising oneself for any good deed. Exaggerating one's role in a deed is vanity. God Most High said (9:25): "On the day of [the battle of Ḥunayn], since you admired with vanity your own might, but it was of no use . . ."[8]

I said: How is vanity warded off and removed from the heart?

He said: When you know that it was Allah Most High who set you into action in the deed, who granted it to you or made it a grace from him to you. He singled you out for that deed, without you having done anything to deserve it. When you know that it was from God Most High, then you will show gratitude for the grace to the one who gave it.

I said: What is the result of that?

He said: Ability to act and an increased ability to act.

While Rabi'a vividly denounces the fear of divine punishment and the desire for divine reward as motivations, Muhasibi embraces them. He makes them ciphers for the opposition between those whose consciousness is rooted in the world and those whose consciousness is rooted in the afterlife (akhira)—*or, rather, the "finality," since what Muhasibi stresses is the final moment in which all one's life and deeds will be judged as worthy of compassion or deserving wrath. Of course the issue of whether the pure motivation should eschew concern with divine reward or punishment is a perennial issue in mysticism. There is no necessary contradiction between Muhasibi and Rabi'a on this score. They are focused on different stages of development. Muhasibi views divine reward and punishment as motives for purifying the human act of all other egoistic concerns. Muhasibi is a master of ordinary human psychology. Rabi'a is grounded in a notion of pure action—for the love of the beloved alone—eschewing all reward and punishment, even by the beloved. We might say she is a master of extraordinary human psychology achieved only within mystical union* (fanā') *where the self is annihilated.*

When Muhasibi makes the opposition between the world and the finality, he is not making the worldly/spiritual opposition of a thousand clichés about religion. In fact, his most scathing moral exposés are directed toward those who by all normal accounts are living a religious life. Rather than directing his analytical rigor toward those who amass fortunes or power, he directs it toward those whose acts of prayer, of generosity, of self-denial, are mixed with egoism.

Although Muhasibi offers concise definitions for each mode of egoism and each antidote to it, in his Book on the Observance *he is seldom content with the basic definitions he offers. After the above translated definition of vanity, for example, he goes on to ground his definition in the Qur'an and in the traditions of the prophets, and then goes on to expand on it with numerous examples.*[9]

Of all Muhasibi's discussions of egoism, none is as extensive or as intricate as his treatment of self-display or conceit (ar-riyā'), *and none more theologically significant than his definition of sincerity* (ikhlāṣ) *as the antidote to conceit.*[10] *Sincerity in the Qur'an is the worshiping of only one God, and the rejection of associating* (shirk) *any other deity with that one God. By offering an ethical understanding of sincerity, Muhasibi anchored Sufi ethics within the central monotheistic principle of the Qur'an and, conversely, exposed the ethical implications of the affirmation of one deity.*

The longer passages that follow are taken from the Book on the Observance. *But before following Muhasibi on his intricate path through the world of ego, the deceptions of the self, and "the enemy" (Satan), and the antidotes for these deceptions (antidotes such as contemplation of mortality, death, and the finality), it seems best to begin with his concise definition of conceit and sincerity from the* Book of Counsels. *In it, he defines sincerity as purity-of-intention, that is, the purity of any act from all other concerns except the divine will. The sincere act is performed out of a consciousness totally rooted in the one God, without any mixture of consciousness of the praise of other humans or the blame of other humans.*[11]

I said: God grant you compassion, what is the characteristic of sincerity?

He said: The disentanglement of the self from a relationship of transaction with the lord Most High,[12] and the observance of the reward of God Most High, without any desire for praise or any aversion to blame.

I said: Why is sincerity called sincerity?

He said: Because it removes all deficiency from the act.

I said: Tell me more.

He said: Because sincerity removes from the act all flaws. As the Arabs say: "So-and-so wore himself out from love for so-and-so," that is, nothing was mixed in with his love. Similarly, with sincerity, no conceit mixes with the act, nor is there mixed in with the act any concern with reputation, vanity, love of praise, or aversion to blame, because sincerity has purified the act of all pollutions.[13]

I said: What is the root of conceit?

He said: Love of the world.

I said: How is that? Detail for me what you mean and clarify your argument for it.

He said: When one loves the world, desires to remain within it, desires to have an honorable record within it, desires the dissemination of his fame, desires to be well remembered and praised, and desires that children and descendants follow his path so that his desires can be achieved through them [that is the root of conceit].

I said: What is the meaning of conceit?

He said: Love of human praise for the good act.

I said: What is the sign of one who is conceited?

He said: Three traits: that he is zealous in front of others, that he is lazy when no one is watching, and that he desires to be praised in all his acts.[14]

Each section translated below is preceded by the title that has been abstracted from the question-and-answer format of the text. For the purposes of an overview, the following more thematic set of topic headings is provided:

1. *Confirmation* (tathabbut) *and inclinations* (khaṭarāt)

2. *Preparedness for death and cutting short the expectation that death will be postponed*

3. *The power of sincerity*

4. *Wariness*

5. *What conceited self-display* (riyā') *entails*

6. *On how a person can be certain an act is sincere*

♦ ♦ ♦

FROM MUHASIBI'S BOOK ON THE OBSERVANCE OF THE RIGHTS OF GOD

In the first passage presented here, Muhasibi presents the foundation of his moral psychology. The key concept and term is the khaṭir—*the thought, notion, or inclination that "strikes a person" or "comes to mind." In the Qushayri selection on "inclinations" (Chapter 3 in this volume), the complex concept of inclination was integrated into a poetics and psychology of extraordinary experience. Muhasibi was more concerned with the inclinations* (khatarāt) *of everyday experience. How can we know their source? Which should we follow?*

Muhasibi suggests three basic sources of inclinations: the ego-self (nafs), *the enemy (Satan or Iblis), and the deity, as mediated through divine revelation and human reason. Muhasibi is most famous for his analysis of the inclinations of the ego-self and the enemy, but it is crucial to remember that he believed the deity also was the source of the inclination. The god-servant grounded in tradition can actually hear the voice of the divine within her heart. Such a person achieves confirmation* (tathabbut) *when she examines the inclination and confirms that it is grounded in revelation and tradition, refusing any hasty action that might be propelled by egoism or the enemy.*

At the basis of his discussion of inclinations that come from the whispering of Satan is the last Qur'anic sura (114):

Say, I take refuge in the lord of humankind
King of humankind, God of humankind
From the evil of the whispering snub-nose
Who whispers in the breasts of humankind
From jinn and humankind.

Much of Muhasibi's text is a psychological examination of the way in which human beings can "take refuge" from the inclinations of the "whispering snub-nose" (Satan) and the inclinations of the ego-self.[15]

On the Care for the Rights of God Most High during the Various Inclinations That Impact upon the Belief of the Heart

I said: How does one care for the rights of Allah Most High when inclinations occur? And what are the indications of such care? And what are the inclinations, anyway?

He said: One cares for them with confirmation. The indication of that is through knowledge of the motivations of the inclinations—whether they motivate the heart toward good or evil.

I said: Where do the inclinations come from and what are their kinds? That is, are they of one kind or several?

He said: Their origin is either from the desire of the ego-self, from reason after its illumination by Allah Most High, or from the enemy. Thus there are three modes of inclination.

As for illumination of the Compassionate—and there are many traditions on this—it is related of the Prophet, peace and blessings upon him, that he said: "When Allah wills the good for someone, he instigates counsel in that person's heart." It is related from an-Nawās ibn Sam'ān that the Prophet, God's peace and blessing upon him, made the following analogy: "It is like a road on which are veils, with voices calling from the lower and higher parts of the road; the voice from the higher part is the counsel of Allah Most High in the heart of every Muslim."

This is confirmed through the saying of the Prophet, peace and blessings upon him, "Allah warns his servant and his memory comes to his mind." There is an inclination that comes to his mind—when the inclination first occurs—and which moves him in his heart. There is another kind of inclination which Allah orders the angel to make occur to the mind of the godservant, in order to warn him and to awaken him. It was this kind of inclination that 'Abdallāh ibn Mas'ūd meant with his saying, "a flash from the angel." It is said in some traditions from 'Abdullah that the "flash from the angel" means Allah, Most High and Blessed.

As for the second form of inclination,[16] it is an enticement, something that comes from the self. In this respect God Most High represented the word of his prophet Isra'il [Isaac] (12:83): "You have let your self entice you into something. Patience is becoming."[17] The Most High also said in the story of the two sons of Adam (5:30) that "his self permitted him the killing of his brother so he killed him."[18] God Most High also spoke (12:53) of "the self that dominates with wrong."[19]

As for the third kind of inclination, it is an embroidery, incitement, and whispering insinuation fròm Satán. In this regard, Allah Most High ordered his Prophet, peace and blessings upon him, to take refuge with him from the inclinations from Satan. The Most High said (7:200): "If you encounter an insinuation from Satan, seek refuge in God who is, indeed, The All-Hearing, The All-Knowing."[20] And he said, Most High (114:5): "Who whispers in the hearts of humans?" And he said, Most High, in describing Adam and Eve, peace upon them both (7:19): "Satan whispered to them." And he said, Most High (6:43) "And Satan embroidered for them what they were doing."

It is incumbent upon the servant of God to find confirmation in a knowledge that will indicate the source of the inclination. If he does not confirm with his reason and make his knowledge his guide, he will not be able to distinguish between that which harms him and that which benefits him. One of the ulama said: If you wish that reason win out over desire, do not rush into an eager act without looking into the consequence.

I said: What is confirmation *(tathabbut)*?

He said: Holding in check the ego-self during any action and refusal to rush into an action, that is, patience before the action.[21]

I said: If the ego-self agitates toward precipitous action, what is going to hold it in check?

He said: One should remind it of the watchfulness of God over it, and frighten it with the coming of his vengeance. If it refuses to hold itself in check, he should reproach it with the words: Allah Most High sees you. Don't rush forward. Stand still, for you will be stood one day upon your action. And one should not cease seeking help in God Most High, that he might strengthen his weakness and conquer for him his desire. Whoever intensifies his consciousness of God's standing him upon his action tomorrow will find it easier to stand and confirm before entering into action, out of fear and shame at the prospect of God standing him upon his action in the morrow.

With reason, knowledge, and confirmation, one can perceive the harm and error within the inclinations that motivate the heart. Otherwise one is never secure from accepting inclinations—from the insinuations of the satan and from the enticements of the ego-selves—thinking they are from the Compassionate, Most Praised. Or one might reject an inclination of counsel *(tanbīh)* for the good, thinking it an enticement of the ego-self or an embellishment of the satan. No one can distinguish among these things except through knowledge and confirmation by reason.

It is like a person in deep darkness on a dangerous path, filled with ruts and holes, during a heavy rain. His eyesight is of no use without a lamp, and the lamp is of no avail if he does not have eyesight. Neither eyesight nor lamp is of any avail if he does not look to where he is walking to confirm his steps. If he is looking at the sky or turns his gaze away, even though the lamp is lit, he is like one without sight or lamp. If he looks where he is going but does not have a lamp, he is still like someone without eyesight.

The healthy sight is like reason. The lamp is like knowledge. And watching where he is going is like confirmation—confirmation through reason—the seeking of illumination in knowledge and exposing whatever inclination he experiences to the Book and tradition. That is all there is to taking time before action, as long as one understands how much wariness is willed of him. And if an inclination offers any opposition, he recognizes it in the blink of an eye because of the knowledge rooted in his heart, awakened as he is by wariness. So when he encounters that thing that disguises itself *(yaltabisa)* and is ambiguous, he takes his time until he knows. If he doesn't have knowledge, he is obliged to wait however long it takes, until he knows whether God Most High would be pleased or displeased with his acceptance of the motivation that occurs to his heart. He does not rush into action hastily without that knowledge.

On Preparedness for Death and Restraint of Expectation

Muhasibi's relentless meditation on death serves as a primary antidote to all the forms of egoism. Indeed, as Muhasibi's meditation proceeds, it could be said that egoism is, fundamentally, a forgetfulness of mortality. Muhasibi uses the "preparedness" for death as the sword that can cut the bonds of egoism. It has been remarked that Muhasibi's writing combines the most sophisticated psychology with the most naive devotional perspectives.[22] *Thus, while Muhasibi is ready to inspect every aspect of egoistic impulse, he reduces eschatology to a schematized version of threat and reward. Death is to be feared not on its own account, but rather for the "accounting" that it entails, a judgment of absolute finality in which a person receives unlimited compassion or unmitigated wrath. In other words, Muhasibi uses eschatology in a particularly condensed way to focus the attention on that moment when a person's every thought and deed will be inspected with absolute totality, and to draw the reader into the sense of awe and terror that a person will feel at the moment of such inspection. To draw the reader and the seeker into such a feeling, Muhasibi moves on to the concept of "shortened expectations." Human beings tend toward a length of expectation, toward the assumption that death and its moment of accounting will be indefinitely postponed or deferred. This implicit denial of mortality leads the human into egoism. To be prepared for death is to have cut such expectations, to live on the edge of mortality and the final reckoning it brings.*[23]

I said: Tell me about preparedness *(isti'dād)*. What is it?

He said: Preparedness is of two kinds. The first kind is obligatory. Those who are sorry at the moment of their death will rue the fact that they allowed it to pass them by. This preparedness is the godservant's sincere repentance of sins and errors. If he were told "you will die this very hour" he would not find any sin still in need of repentance for which he would have to account. If he should find a sin still in need of repentance, he would not be ready to meet his lord.

No one is consulted about the extraction of his spirit from his body. Death comes upon us all of a sudden. If death should come to a person while sin is still with him, he will not be secure from the wrath of God Most High. How can anyone who remains fixed in what angers God be prepared to meet the Most High?

He cannot be secure from death catching him unready—and death is coming, for sure.

Those who fear what is displeasing to God Most High hasten to repent before death can overtake them, before death can beat them to their spirits and block their repentance and contrition before their lord—leaving them in a state of regret where regret is no longer accepted and excuses will not be heard.

Therefore they hasten to repent, take precautions, and ask compassion from being taken in a state of neglect by sudden death. This kind of preparedness is made obligatory by God Most High for all his creatures.

As for the second kind of preparedness, it is an exertion of the heart and body beyond what is obligatory. It is a person's giving up of what he possesses of the world, except that which has been put in his care. If it were said, "You will die tomorrow," he would not increase his activity. God

Most High values in his creatures this form of preparedness more than [the first] because its validity cannot be flawed, its bounty cannot be requited, and its grandeur can have no equal.

Nothing will motivate you toward preparedness for death and toward an end to procrastination more than restraint of expectation *(qaṣr al-aml)*.

I said: How can restraint of expectation be achieved?

He said: With fear of the appointed destiny which death in a state of neglect will bring. For the spirit of the godservant is something borrowed and does not know when the owner will send for its return. When one fears the appointed destiny, he cuts his expectation in the world and he awaits in it his appointed time. And he awaits the coming of death.

I said: How does he attain fear of the appointed destiny?

He said: Through profound knowledge *(ma'rifa)* of the uncertainty of the appointed time—and knowledge that the Appointer-of-the-time does not dispute with him, consult him, or inform him when he wishes to take his spirit from him, taking into account as a lesson those who died before him.

I said: How does one attain that knowledge and understand its lesson?

He said: By continual remembrance and contemplation of the uncertainty of the appointed time and coming of death—when it shall overcome him and the entire matter is ended—and the remembrance of those who were taken by sudden death.

I said: What is this uncertainty of the appointed time like that I should meditate on it in order to gain a more profound knowledge?

He said: You need only know that death has no hour known to the servant that he might fear that particular time but be secure at other times. It doesn't come upon mortals in winter as opposed to summer, or take possession of mortals in summer as opposed to winter, or in any particular month of the year so that one could be safe the rest of the months, or at night, leaving one secure at day, or by day, leaving one secure at night, or in the morning, leaving one secure in the evening, or in the evening, leaving one secure in the morning, or in any particular time of day as opposed to any other time. Nor does it come in any particular stage of life, taking a twenty-year-old but leaving those younger, or taking a thirty-year-old but leaving the twenty-year-old alone. Nor does it have a particular cause: such as fever, or interior illness, or decrepitude, or drowning, or other causes of harm.[24] So it becomes clear for the wise and knowledgeable in the order of God Most High that since death has no known time, one can never be secure from it at any given time. If it does not come down at any particular period of life, one cannot be secure from it in childhood or maturity, in youth or old age. Since it has no particular cause, one cannot be secure from it in health or in illness, in city or in desert, on land or on sea.

The godservant remembers death by emptying the heart of everything except for his consciousness that death has no specific known time or cause or stage of life and his awareness of what death will bring to the human being—of torment or compassion of God Most High. This awareness continues as he takes into account those who went before him (those who were above him or below him or equal to him in station).

When all this occurs, his knowledge of death and of the suddenness of death becomes profound. He is powerfully aware that he will be descending to death as those who walked the path before him descended to it, for sure.

When his knowledge of this condition is deepened, then his expectation is shortened. When his expectation is diminished, he keeps his heart in a state of wariness about death. When his heart is wary, he is on the watch for death. When he is watchful for death, he hastens to be prepared for it and races to complete good works before the angel of death can reach his spirit.

In this regard it is related of 'Ali ibn Talib, God's favor upon him, that he said: "Whoever is on the watch for death hastens to good works."

It is also related that 'Ali, God bring him true compassion, said: "Two things bring ruin: Desire and length of expectation. Desire blocks access to the real *(al-ḥaqq)*, while length of expectation brings forgetfulness of the finality *(akhira)*."[25]

It is as if there were two people you knew who had been away for some time. You knew that one of them was coming back quickly—that very day, or night, or the next day. You knew that the other was not arriving for a month or a year. You would prepare yourself for the one who was coming quickly. If he had asked you to do something, you would rush to make sure it was done, so that you would not be taken by surprise before you could carry it out, thus earning his disfavor and chastisement. You would prepare for him a reception of respect and gentility. If there were any wrongs or harms on your part against him, you would hasten to think and plan how to apologize to him to alleviate any bad feelings or blame he might have toward you, and to make sure your stature was not diminished in his estimation.

An indication of this is what is related of Ka'b ibn Malik, God grant him favor, when he stayed behind during the battle of Tabuk. When it was reported that the Prophet, God's peace and blessings upon him, was on his way back from the battle, Ka'b began to think about—and ask anyone in his clan who might have advice to give—how he might apologize and escape from the Prophet's bad feelings toward him.

Such is the case when a person's heart is overpowered with the consciousness that death is coming upon him quickly. He knows that upon his death he will hear the certain announcement of his ruin or salvation. He acts with dispatch until Allah Most High favors him or blames him in regard to his actions and in regard to the purity of his heart and body from disobedience. All this he does so that he might meet his lord in a state of purity.[26]

Thus, the family of a person who is away prepares for his arrival by sweeping the house and tents and getting dressed up, so that he will know that they hold him in high regard and have prepared themselves for his arrival.

In the same way, one who has shortened expectation has purified himself, prepared himself, beautified himself so that God Most High might know that he holds in high regard the meeting of his lord. He puts on his best clothes and purifies himself for the meeting, so that his lord might not bear him any ill will, might accept him and hold him in his favor.

As for what will incite the godservant to remember the fearfully swift coming of death—it is (as I informed you) nothing other than the passing of moments which cannot ever be a source of security.

In this regard it is related that Luqman, peace upon him, said to his son: "My son, there is a certain something that you do not know when it is coming to you. Prepare for it or else it will take you by surprise."

Luqman also said to his son: "Son, do not put off repentance. The coming of the angel of death is all of a sudden."[27]

It is related of a certain man that while he slept he was continually shifting from his right side to his left. When he got up in the morning, he was asked about it. He said: "I was anticipating from which side the angel of death would come."

Someone said to Rabī' ibn Haytham: "How did you wake?" He said: "We woke up as poor sinners, eating our bread and waiting our appointed times."

A man said to Sa'īd ibn Abī s-Sā'ib: "How have you woken?" He said: "I've woken in anticipation of a death without preparation."

Chapter on the Knowledge of the Power of Sincerity

The following brief section is an example of how much Muhasibi can convey in a brief passage. Here he divides people according to their rank in sincerity, from those whose determination or resolution (ʻazm) *allows them to simply reject an egoistic inclination, to the more complex case of those who delude themselves into thinking that, by delaying and struggling with the egoistic inclination, they are somehow gaining credit for their struggle. While the discussion is presented in terms of following the shariʻa and rejecting impulses to neglect it, the pyschological acuity of Muhasibi's analysis can be applied to any situation. Particularly important is his dissection of the self-deluding nature of procrastination and his analysis of the way in which egoism can affect the intentionality of an act, causing the act to fail.*[28]

I said: When I have disdained and rejected the occasion, what is the indication that sincerity is dominant in my heart over the discord and will of the ego-self?

He said: Do you not know that the quest for God Most High and the quest for creatures are equal motivations in the heart? But if a person disdains [the realm of creatures], then the will for God Most High and the disdain [for anything else] come together as two motives, while the struggle of the ego-self is only one. Thus the two will win out over the one.

I said: Are those who reject conceit in a single station of promptness and slowness, of accomplishment and deficiency?

He said: No, the number of stations are four. There is the person who rejects conceit quickly, through the power of determination. There is one who is delayed in struggling.

There is one who rejects the [conceitful] thought. The enemy sees him in such a condition, not craving anything that would cause his act to fail. When the enemy wishes to gain from him something that would detract from the accomplishment and perfection of his prayer and the like, he suggests to him that if he quarrels with him in trying to make him reject the action, and struggles with him, this will make him purer in sincerity and more successful. So the servant enters into a quarrel and struggle over the rejection [of conceit]. This only brings about more deficiency, however, because he becomes preoccupied with his struggle from his prayer. He was not ordered to struggle. He did not affirm his belief through this struggle.[29]

Rather he was told [by the enemy] to disobey and he disobeyed, not accepting what he was called to do.

All his struggle amounts to nothing other than distraction from prayer and from the devotion he had attained, preoccupying his heart with something he does not truly regret.[30]

As for the person in the second station, he is one who accepts giving-the-lie to the occasion [of conceit] without need or struggle.

And the third—he continues in his state of disdain and rejection [of the occasion of temptation], knowing that was his portion of giving-the-lie-to-falsehood, struggle, and quarrel, and proceeds to go on doing what he was doing, without accepting any distraction and without any thought occurring that would distract him from what he was about.[31]

As for the fourth—he is one who knows even before the call of conceit can occur to him that it wills nothing other than to make him lose the grace of his lord, out of jealousy toward him. This knowledge has already come into his heart before the call of temptation. Thus, even if his heart is already fully occupied with the Most High, he increases his occupation. Even if he has been assiduous in his acts of devotion, he now races even more quickly to remembrance, meditation, and occupation with God Most High, out of spite for the temptation. The increase of his advantage in regard to the occasion of temptation makes of it a lesson in remembrance of his lord.

Description of Wariness from the Enemy Iblis

It is perhaps not surprising that Muhasibi would consider "wariness" (ḥadhar) *a crucial aspect in the effort to achieve sincerity and avoid conceit. A person must be in a state of continual vigilance against the subtle and incessant inclinations toward one form of egoism or another. Yet, in the passage below, Muhasibi makes a crucial distinction between wariness, on the one hand, and expectation and preoccupation on the other. To be expecting the egoistic inclination, to become preoccupied with one's own egoism, is to fall prey to it all the more. For Muhasibi, a person's attention must remain fixed on the one source of all sincerity, the one deity. Through constant awareness and consciousness of the one God, a person is able to be instantly awakened (as a wary sleeper can wake himself at an unusual time) at any egoistic inclination, awakened to its danger, and therefore able to reject it. If a person spends his time dwelling on the ego-self and the enemy (Satan), the two sources of egoism, he loses that crucial connection to the one God, which is the source of sincerity.*[32]

I said: What is wariness *(ḥadhar)*: Is it the expectation and preparation for the occasion that will arrive? Or are we to be wary of the unexpected?

He said: The believers in wariness through the command of God have divided into three positions, only one of which is correct.

One position maintains that God orders us to struggle against one we do not see. God puts the fear of him into us and teaches us that his victory over us is our ruin. There is nothing that has more power over our hearts and to which our hearts should cling more strongly than wariness and expectation of the precise occasions of his temptation. Distraction from [wariness] of him entails forgetfulness and forgetfulness entails the acceptance of inclination without intuition *(ma'rifa)*—and that leads to ruin. This group believes we should keep our hearts in a state of anticipation for Satan, awaiting each inclination from him. They anticipate the inclination with aversion that it might come when they are neglectful and they should fall into ruin without being aware of it.

Another group maintains that the first position is wrong because of its preoccupation with anticipating Satan. They say it is not for us to believe in that. Satan wishes us to make our hearts desolate of the remembrance of God Most High and the memory of the finality. Satan wishes us to populate our hearts with remembrance of him [Satan] and the observation of his inclinations.[33] Instead, we should make our hearts persist in remembrance of the finality *(akhira)*. Minding what occasions [of temptation] might occur does not keep us from remembrance of the finality. At the same time we should not forget the one concerning whom we were commanded to be wary, or else he will come upon us in a state of neglect and ruin our remembrance.

The result is that with this group, the remembrance of Allah Most High and remembrance of the whispering insinuations of Satan become two equal contraries in the heart. Every time they remember the finality, they remember the enemy out of concern for an occasion of his temptation, so that their hearts fall away from the remembrance of God Most High and fixate themselves on what might ruin their actions when they are displayed before their lord Most High.

The third group, who represent the people of knowledge and those most secure in the truth, state that both of the first two positions are wrong. The first position makes the heart desolate of the remembrance of the finality. The worship of the first group is the clinging of the heart to the remembrance of Satan. They have wrongly allowed the remembrance of Satan to occupy their hearts more than the remembrance of God Most

High.[34] Our hearts were commanded to be wary of any neglect of remembrance [of God] and acts of devotion. If our hearts give up remembrance, then the enemy can attain what he wants. If an inclination comes upon a heart empty of remembrance, the heart is on the point of accepting it already because it does not have the light of the finality and the power of preoccupation with God Most High. "You, then, are weaker in rejecting inclinations and your hearts are emptier of the finality than others. You were not ordered to anticipate him or to continue in remembering him."

The second group shares some of the position of the first group insofar as they have made the remembrance of God Most High and the remembrance of Satan equal within the heart. It is as if they had been ordered to remember God Most High and to remember Satan, to be preoccupied with God Most High and with Satan.[35] I have not heard of anyone—strong or weak—who followed and believed in that. God Most High ordered his servants to be obedient to him and entrusted them with preoccupation with him from all of his creatures, including Iblis, of whose temptations he ordered his servants to be wary. Thus the friends of God Most High and his purest servants are completely occupied with remembrance of their lord and remembrance of what he has entrusted them and caused them to love. They make their hearts cling to wariness of that which he commanded them to be wary, without anticipating it or being preoccupied with remembering it. Wariness makes the heart cling to the concern for salvation from the enemy and fear of the ruin he brings. To be preoccupied with God Most High to the point of abandoning any remembrance of the enemy or preoccupation with him does not at all interfere with the agitation of mindfulness and wakefulness upon any inclination the enemy might occasion.

This is the case in something even more total than preoccupation with Allah Most High, that is, the case of the complete cessation of reason during sleep, such that one is not even aware of the world. If a person goes to sleep with wariness to wake, he can wake up at a time other than that at which he would normally wake, because of the wariness clinging to his heart. One preoccupied with Allah Most High does not lose his reason. Thus his wariness is even more able to wake him and make him mindful of the enemy, despite his preoccupation with his lord and abandonment of all mindfulness of the enemy and preoccupation with him. One who wakes from sleep [at an unusual time due to his wariness] does so without a constant remembrance in his heart. How can he remember when he is sleeping, out of contact with his reason? Wariness wakes him.

Such is one who does all his works for Allah Most High, preoccupied with remembering him. Through his occupation with God Most High, he is oblivious of any remembrance of Satan. If any occasion from him presents itself, the wariness in his heart makes him mindful of it, and his mindfulness enables him to be aware of the inclination, instigating opposition to it and alarm at his ruin that lies within it. One who is asleep, on the other hand, has no mindfulness in his heart and no occasion to wake him [yet even so, wariness succeeds in waking him].

If an [egoistic] inclination occurs, the seeker is mindful of and more able to reject it, because it has occurred to a heart preoccupied with Allah Most High, overwhelmed by the light of a preoccupation that has killed desire, strengthened reason, chided away intemperance, and accompanied him with the light of knowledge. Thus he easily rejects the inclination.

One who makes his heart cling to preoccupation with God Most High is like one who makes a dam and barrier; when the water comes, it is rejected by that dam and barrier without effort and worry. The well is purified from the run-off of polluting waters, while he remains unexhausted and unburdened with cleaning.

In this way, whoever is preoccupied with Allah Most High easily rejects the inclination, because his heart is occupied with his lord Most High, with his lord's light and power of determination.

This group follows more the Qur'an and the Sunna and those who do good works. In repelling inclinations they are stronger. From deception and failure they are further. They make their hearts cling to wariness without occupying themselves with the enemy. They have no fear of the enemy's power in relation to their lord Most High whom they obey alone, on whom they rely alone, following his command. They do not cease their occupation with their lord Most High and they do not cease turning away from any preoccupation with Satan or any remembrance of him.

They are untiringly occupied with their lord, and because of their wariness, whenever there is an occasion for an inclination, they are awake. With the power of their preoccupation with Allah they can easily reject any inclination that is an occasion for ruin. They are secure and they attain their goal. They follow and they stand firm.

Chapter on What Conceit Entails of Blameworthy Character Traits and their Description

For Muhasibi, there is no end to the intricacies and insinuations of conceited self-display. It can enter as an inclination while a person is considering an act, or just before an act, or during an act. It can occur without any regretful consciousness of the lack of sincerity, or it can occur with a regret about the lack of sincerity, but without the impetus to change—a regret that is only a regret about not being perfect, not true horror of lack of sincerity.[36] *It can enter as an inclination after an act, a desire, post facto, that people know of its virtue.*

In addition to the manifold ways it can ruin an act by mixing with the intentionality of the act, conceited self-display can engender a host of other egoistic faults. Some of these same faults can be engendered by other cardinal forms of egoism, such as pride, but in the passage presented below Muhasibi examines them only insofar as they are directly grounded in conceit.[37]

I said: Tell me which traits, blameworthy before God Most High, are entailed by conceit.

He said: Those traits that are entailed by conceit alone, not anything else, include a variety of flaws, such as pride in action and knowledge and arrogance in faith and in the world.

Now arrogance can also come from pride *(kibr)*. The arrogance related to conceit, however, is a particular anxiety a person has that he not be lorded over, along with a love of lording it over others. It also includes acquisitiveness *(takāthur)* in wealth and other things of the world, in knowledge and action.

And [it includes] enviousness regarding knowledge and action without any real competitiveness, but out of worry that the one he envies might gain in station and in praise what he has not gained. Thus he refuses the right of one who commands him or is of an equal station with him, out of fear that somebody be said to know more than he.

This flaw can also come from pride, but out of revulsion that it might be said: "So and so defeated him" or "He made a mistake."

I said: What is powerlust *(ri'āsa)*?

He said: The love of aggrandizement and exercising power over creatures and looking down upon them—that not a single word of his be rejected, that not a single person equal him in knowledge, that no one be put before him. When such a one is admonished, he becomes stubborn and refuses advice. When he admonishes, he causes resistance and his advice is not accepted. He remains stubborn even when he knows he is in the wrong. When people let him know he is wrong and admonish him, he refuses to admit fault, out of fear that his powerlust will be put in jeopardy.

I said: What is competitiveness *(mubāha)*, how does it operate, and what does it entail, and what is the root of its harm?

He said: It occurs with knowledge and action.

As for knowledge, it is a persistence in seeking it, and guarding it, and being obsessed with it—and this occurs with many scholars of hadith, and the jumping in with the answer whether it is he who is asked or someone else. In this manner he desires to be right in order to aggrandize himself, to show that he is above someone else, and to let someone else know that he is more learned than him. He races to recall the hadith so that his companion will see he is the more learned. If his companion recalls a hadith, he lets him know that he knew it anyway, out of competitiveness to put himself over his companion.

As for competitiveness in actions—competitiveness can occur between people in remembering God Most High, or in fighting in the path of God Most High or in praying or in any act of devotion.

Thus, if anyone else performs the prayer, he immediately jumps up to pray out of worry that the other person might be put above him. He detests the prayer of the one praying with him out of love for his own favor to be shown. If there is a group praying together, he prolongs his prayer so that his companion will become embarrassed and discomfited, and will leave the prayer. In this way, he will be raised above his companion. He will have bested him in stature among those who know what happened. He will make his companion feel small as he is raised above him and displays his superiority over him.

Similarly in battle, he rushes ahead of his companion, wishing to be shown in charge and given preference. He charges into battle with all he has to best his companion and display his superiority over him. If by chance he is killed in such a condition, his reward is lost and he is not secure from God's wrath toward him.

As for competitiveness in the world—it can occur with endowing the construction of buildings. So he spends what, if he were alone, he would not spend. But when he is with a neighbor, relative, friend, colleague in work, and the like, then he spends more than he would have spent on his own account out of concern for the building. Out of competitiveness he spends many times the normal amount so that no one will best him, but he will best anyone else.

Similarly, he redoubles his efforts in seeking the possessions of the world, so that no one will best him in the honor of property ownership, and that he might be remembered for his wealth. So it is in his occupation, or in the furniture of his house, and the like.

I said: What is vaunting *(tafākhur)*?

He said: Vaunting can comprise many aspects of competitiveness, but it has features that distinguish it, such as its implication in knowledge. When a person vaunts knowledge, he becomes presumptuous, saying, for example: "How much did you hear?[38] Did you get anything right? What do you say about such and such?" He says such things to another, implying that he has not done well and has not heard well, "has not heard what I heard, and has not occupied the station I occupy."[39]

Similarly, there is the vaunting of worldly items that goes along with competitiveness. "You're a pauper, with nothing, how much did you earn?" "How much property do you have?" "When did you come by your property?" "I own more than you." "My master is wealthier than you."

Similarly, in action: "You weren't a hero in war. You didn't fight in battle. You were a battle coward and a failure."

Similarly, in scholarly debate and competition: "How many traditions have you memorized? Who were your teachers? How much have you attained from the scholars? So and so preferred me to you." He says such things to another even when the other is not listening to him, vaunting it over him, driven by his conceit into vaunting it over his fellow, driven into presumptuousness and injuriousness.

Acquisitiveness *(takāthur)* can include vaunting and go beyond it in some aspects. Thus one says: "I heard such and such a tradition. I fought in such and such battle. I made such and such pilgrimages. I learned from the masters such and such. I haven't eaten for such and such a time. Who am I to be sleeping at dawn?"[40]

And if he is clever in acquisitiveness and vaunting—wishing to be praised and held aloft rather than blamed, then he is not open about what he is doing. He hides what he is doing to better obtain competitiveness and vaunting and acquisition. He is not open about what he is doing lest they consider him competitive, egotistical, self-vaunting, and acquisitive.

All these traits are overlapping, but each of them has something that distinguishes it from the other. For this reason the scripture and the tradition distinguished among them. God Most High said (19:59): "Flaunting and vaunting among you and acquisitiveness in property and children. . . ."

The Prophet, God's peace and blessings upon him, said "Whoever seeks the world with acquisitiveness and vaunting," adding at the end of the hadith "faults"—and thus he distinguished among them.

I said: What is envy?

He said: It is caused by conceit and the like. What is from conceit consists of envy and rivalry on the part of someone out of worry that someone else attain a higher stature or more praise from people. So he loves to take away from such people any enjoyment, that they might not be seen as superior to him by their companions. It is related of 'Umar, God's peace and blessing upon him, that he said to Abu Umayya: "May God not keep me—or you—around until such a time as people envy one another over knowledge as they envy one another over women!"

I said: How can one reject the truth, knowing that it is the truth?

He said: Out of dislike that anyone come near to him in being right, or best him. Thus the people of the Book have fallen apart out of covetousness and envy.

I said: What is rivalry *(ḥubb al-ghalaba)*?

He said: Rivalry comes from conceit and other causes. That which is caused by conceit is a person's dislike of being bested in any competition and having the victor placed above him, and himself losing stature in the eyes of the person who knows the result. He loves to win, to be honored, praised, respected, and preferred.

How many a godservant has fought and competed with someone in knowledge until he won? The loser had been respected and honored, but once he is defeated, those who used to respect him disparage him and turn their respect and honor to the victor.

So one wishes the other person to be wrong, and oneself to be right. If the other is right, he is pained. Such is the insinuation of Iblis among people: that they err in the belief of God Most High, and go wrong. If they are right, he is pained. Such a person does not try to understand what his opponent in argument is saying; his concern is refutation and dissension.

This is how God Most High has described the unbelievers (25:41): "Those who disbelieve and refuse to hear this Qur'an, yet declare it invalid, they shall one day perhaps be overthrown."

I said: And how is it possible for someone to abandon learning and cease seeking it when he needs it so?

He said: That can come from conceit or something else. That which comes from conceit is a distaste for asking about something and having someone say: "So and so is less than so and so." So he gives up seeking the real and asking about the forbidden [and the lawful], even though he knows he needs to ask. Then he deludes himself into thinking that he withholds his question out of shame, but it is really out of conceit. If the issue is shame, he should more properly be ashamed before Allah Most High. He claims before people that he seeks the truth. He does this so that they might not know his situation and intuit his ignorance, but he shows no shame before Allah Most High, even though he knows that Allah knows he has given up learning and seeking the truth.

All these traits branch out from vanity *('ujb)* and pride *(kibr)* and the like. We have discussed here only those aspects of them that are incited by conceit *(riyā')*—the effect of rejection and blame in these cases comes from the direction of conceit.

It is related of Ḥudhayfa, God be pleased with him, concerning the Prophet, God's peace and blessings upon him, that he said: "Do not seek knowledge to vie with the scholars in it, or to dispute with the ignorant, or to draw the regard of people to you."

Ka'b said: "A time comes when people envy one another in knowledge as they envy one another over women. That is their fortune from it [their knowledge]."

To What Extent the Godservant Can Be Certain That He Is Sincere in an Act and to What Extent He Cannot Be Certain

In this final passage, Muhasibi exhibits once more a balance between intense analytical scrutiny of conceit, on the one hand, and a fixation or preoccupation with it, on the other hand. A person needs always to be wary, but wariness should not lead to a lack of confidence or a paralyzing sense of self-consciousness. It is true that a person can never be sure that conceit has not mixed in with his act (yukhāliṭu 'amalahu), *causing it to fail morally. However, if one has begun an action with good intention* (niyya), *and has followed the practice of confirmation (see the first passage above), then such a balance between wariness and confidence can be achieved. Below, Muhasibi outlines how an intense wariness can still allow for a life of hope.*[41]

I said: Is it possible for anyone to be certain that he has sincerely carried out a given act for Allah alone—when he is uncertain if any conceit might have mixed in with it, or when fear and doubt take control of him?

He said: Before he begins an act, he should not enter into the act until he knows that Allah wills it and no other wills it. He ought not to enter into an act while being unsure what agent wills the act. It is his responsibility to be certain that Allah Most High wills it, and if not, he should not enter upon it.

When he knows that he is sincere and that only Allah Most High wills it, he enters upon the act. And after a few moments—it could be no more than the blink of an eye—which is enough for the creature to fall prey to forgetfulness and inauthenticity, fear takes him over.[42] He does not know if perhaps an inclination might have occurred to his heart, an inclination of conceit, vanity, arrogance, and the like. He might have accepted the inclination and then forgotten that it came from conceit. Thus he remains in a state of worry and fear.

I said: If he is in such a state of doubt, how can he achieve hope over doubt? How can he hope for the good favor of Allah Most High?

He said: As for the doubt by which he would not know whether he entered upon the act with sincerity or not—there can be no such doubt, since he knew that he entered upon the act on the will of God Most High alone.

But as for the doubt he has when fearful that Allah might have reckoned against him his acceptance of an inclination which he has forgotten about and does not intuit—yes indeed, there can be fear concerning his act, and nervousness, and anxiety on that account.

I said: Therefore he has equal amounts of fear and hope concerning whether he carried out the act for God Most High or for an other-than-God. Thus his hope in God Most High will be weak. How can he enjoy his obedience to Allah and enjoy its sweetness in such circumstances?

He said: In fact, hope is dominant and greater, because he was certain that he entered upon the act with sincerity for God alone, but he is not certain that he fell to any conceit in it.

So the sincerity is certain, and there is doubt about the conceit. His fear about the possibility of conceit mixing into act is among the things that he hopes that God will purify him of—in his worry over those things he does not know. So his hope is increased [because it includes hope Allah will purify him of any conceit he might have fallen for and forgotten]. And if no conceit entered into his act, his worry about it has made his act greater and increased his devotion.

The more he is anxious [about conceit], the more he enjoys his obedience and the greater his hope in Allah Most High. He entered upon the act with certainty of its sincerity, and then he sealed it with anxiety and fear concerning the knowledge of God Most High.[43] In this way his hope is made greater and he is able to enjoy his obedience to his lord Most High.

In his Book on the Observance, *Muhasibi's moral psychology is presented within an almost purely psychological dimension. Eschatology, the finality, the reward and punishment, are almost exclusively invoked as aspects of the effort to escape the subtle traps of egoism. There is no particularly Sufi world depicted; the moral psychology is as an aspect of universal human disposition and within the general framework of the Qur'an and the traditions of the Prophet. Within two centuries, the rigorous self-examination exemplified in Muhasibi's psychology will become a central aspect of a distinctively Sufi world. That Sufi world would include delineations of stations of attainment, states of consciousness, technical vocabulary, and gradually developing institutions built around the life of a particular group of Muslims (Sufis) who wished to engage in distinctive forms of free devotions, within distinctive guidelines. One of the earliest examples of such a development is Sarraj's essay on the "seven stations," the next chapter in this volume.*

6

Sarraj: The Seven Stations from The Book of Flashes (Kitāb al-Luma')

Introduction

The first systematic exposition of Sufism as a way of life and thought was The Book of Flashes (Kitāb al-Luma') *by Abū Naṣr as-Sarrāj (d. 378/988). Sarraj was from the city of Tus in the Iranian region of Khurasan, a central region in the development of early Sufism. Sarraj's work became the model for a series of major studies by Sulami, Kalabadhi, Qushayri, Abu Nu'aym al-Isfahani, Abu Hamid al-Ghazali, and 'Attar, to name only the most famous. Major topics discussed by Sarraj include: the stations and states; the grounding of Sufi claims in the Qur'an; the companions of the Prophet as exemplars of Sufi life, with sections on Abu Bakr, 'Umar, 'Uthman, and 'Abu Talib; proper behavior* (adab); *audition* (samā'); *ecstasy* (wajd); *marvels and miracles; Sufi terms and expressions; ecstatic utterances; and theological errors.*

Presented here is Sarraj's discussion of the seven Maqāmat *or stations along the Sufi path.*[1] *In each of his seven sections, Sarraj employs the same dialectical method. He begins with the conventional understanding of a given station (such as poverty), then treats a second version practiced by "the select"* (al-khāṣṣ), *and ends with a culminating version practiced by the realized "knower"* (al-'ārif). *Sarraj uses the words of other Sufis to make his point, carefully arranging them within his dialectical format. Though the three-stage dialectic can seem forced at times, it enables Sarraj to place a wide variety of Sufi proverbs, many of them contradictory to one another, within a compelling context.*

When compared with the refined and honed style of a later treatise such as Qushayri's Risāla, *Sarraj's prose is rough. Yet it exhibits a sustained and consistent critical thinking. The voices of various Sufis—Nuri, Sahl at-Tustari, Muhasibi, Dhu n-Nun, Muhammad ibn Salim, his son Ahmad ibn Salim, Junayd, and Shibli, to mention only the more important—resound throughout Sarraj's exposition. The continual appearances of these various Sufis can be disconcerting to the reader not versed in Sufi lineage and history; however, what is most important in many cases is how the saying is used, rather than any information on the biography of the alleged author.*[2] *Even more so than with Qushayri, Shibli stands out in Sarraj's presentation in a particularly telling manner, his holy rage, screams, and frantic language pushing expression and behavior as well to the limit.*

Representative of Sarraj's method is his essay on the station of poverty (faqr). *Sarraj begins by citing the traditions of the Prophet and other sages in praise of the virtue of poverty, with an elegant twist in which poverty is portrayed as the ornament and rich robe of one who has renounced all possessions.*

Sarraj then divides poverty into three categories, that of the seeker or novice, that of the select, and that of the select of the select, that is, those who have mystical knowledge, the 'ārifin, *and the finders/ecstatics* (wājidin). *This language of the select and the select of the select has led some to charge Sufism with being elitist. As with all mystical traditions, there is a tension in Sufism in this regard. On the one hand, early Sufis do not call themselves "Sufis," but rather simply "the folk" or the "commonfolk." Anyone can join, anyone can participate. On the other hand, there is a rigorous set of standards in the areas of self-discipline, psychological self-awareness, intuitive or mystical understanding, and emotional and poetic sensitivity. In this area, for Sufis like Sarraj, some are more advanced than others, and the stages of advancement can be outlined. But in presenting these stages or stations, we should bear in mind that they are themselves in tension with the "states" or "conditions," many of which were detailed in the essay by Qushayri (Chapter 3 in this volume), that come suddenly and unexpectedly upon the individual and cannot be placed in any simple sequence.*

The first category of poverty is the poverty of those who have renounced all possessions and who ask nothing from any creature. The second category is the poverty of those who renounce everything but who, if given something insistently, do not make an argument about refusing it. Those in this category of poverty do not make a show of their poverty and hide all traces of their tribulation. If they possess something, "they do not possess it," that is, even those things that someone in the first category might make a show of rejecting, they can technically possess without having the least attachment to them. In some sense, they no longer possess their own poverty. The third category is more difficult to characterize (the categories become more complex and difficult as one advances through them). Part of it refers to accepting something from an intimate friend as a "free gift." Part of it consists in the "absence of everything that is and the entering into things for others, not for oneself." With the achievement of this life "for others," without consciousness of the self or the self's own poverty or achievement of poverty, one enters into the next station, that of patience.

This summary cannot do justice to the subtleties of Sarraj's essay on poverty, nor to the way in which he builds his argument from the oral tradition and sayings of various Sufis. It is meant only as an introductory comment on the psychological acuity of the seven essays, which might otherwise be obscured by the stylized form and the sudden shifts from one speaker to the next.

The stations begin from the most everyday, even mundane considerations; the watchfulness in observing Islamic law, for example, on which foods are proper (ḥalāl) *to eat—a rigorism dramatized by the figures of Muḥāsibi and Bishr al-Ḥāfī, whose hands (beyond the conscious intent of the two individuals) would literally refuse to reach for any food whose ritual and social purity was in doubt—making them, a commentator says dryly, poor dinner guests. It is important to reemphasize here that such concern with the everyday experiences of the world is not viewed as a lower level of spirituality; it is the ground and basis of the spiritual. Nor is it in opposition to the mystical; rather, embodiment and spirit,* sharīʿa *(the Islamic way of life as prescribed in Islamic law) and* maʿrifa *(mystical knowledge), are correlative and interdependent. Finally, it is the mode by which Sufi spirituality is enlarged from the microcosm to the macrocosm, and the medium through which the most elemental aspect of daily life becomes a vital and dramatic aspect of a cosmic drama.*

The structure of the seven essays becomes more complex and difficult with each essay. And despite the stylized format and apparently simple analytical framework of the three categories, the seven essays are actually a complex integration of various Sufi statements—many of them difficult and laconic aphorisms—that were frequently being taken out of context in Sarraj's time and becoming the object of controversy. Thus apparently bizarre and antinomian statements are recontextualized in Sarraj's account and become meaningful moments within a Sufi way of life, and apparently contradictory sets of sayings take on a creative tension rather than a confusion when placed in dialectical relationship to one another.

If there is a guide who can take us back to those extraordinary early years of Sufism, introduce us to the major actors, ease our way into their debates and conversations, and provide us with a theologically and psychologically sensitive interpretive framework, that guide would be Abu Nasr as-Sarraj in his Book of Flashes.

♦ ♦ ♦

THE STATION OF REPENTANCE *(TAWBA)*

Abū Ya'qūb Yūsuf ibn Ḥamdān as-Sūsī (God grant him compassion) said: "The first station of those devoted completely to God Most High is repentance."

When as-Sūsī was asked about repentance, he replied: "Repentance is the return from everything that knowledge condemns toward what knowledge praises." When Sahl ibn 'Abdullāh was asked about repentance, he responded, "It is to never forget your fault." When Junayd was asked about repentance, he said, "It is forgetting your fault."

The Shaykh (God grant him compassion)[3] said: The response of as-Sūsī (God grant him compassion) concerning repentance was in reference to the repentance of the novice, the venturers, the seekers, the questers, those who are sometimes in the right and sometimes in the wrong. The same is the case for what Sahl ibn 'Abdullāh [at-Tustarī] (God grant him compassion) said.

However, the response of Junayd (God grant him compassion)—that repentance is forgetting your fault—concerns the repentance of those who have achieved realization. They do not remember their faults; their hearts are overwhelmed with God's majesty and with his continual remembrance.

Similarly, Ruwaym ibn Aḥmad (God grant him compassion), when asked about repentance, said: "It is the repentance from repentance." Likewise, Dhū n-Nūn, when asked about repentance, said: "The masses repent of their faults. The select repent of their neglect."[4]

As for the pronouncement of the people of knowing, the *wājidīn*, and the select of the select, concerning the meaning of repentance—Abū l-Ḥasan an-Nūrī (God grant him compassion) said when asked about repentance: "It is turning away from everything except God Most High."

Someone else alluded to that when he said: "The faults of those near to God are the virtues of the pious"— that was Dhū n-Nūn. He also said:

> What is sincerity for the seeker or novice is self-display for the knowers *('ārifīn)*. When the knower has become firm and self-realized in that through which he draws near to God Most High and Transcendent—in the moment of his quest, in his beginning stage, upon his undertaking of offerings and pious deeds—when he has been encompassed by the lights of guidance, when providence has touched him, when he has been encircled by divine care, when his heart is witness to the majesty of his master, when he contemplates what God has fashioned and the eternity of his goodness, then he turns away from noticing, relying upon, and attending to his pious deeds and acts and offerings, as he did as a seeker and a beginner.

How great are the differences among the repentant! One turns away from faults and bad acts; a second turns away from slips and oversights; a third turns his attention away from his good and pious deeds.

Repentance demands watchfulness.

♦ ♦ ♦

THE STATION OF WATCHFULNESS *(WARA')*

The Shaykh (God grant him compassion) said: "The station of watchfulness is a noble station."

The Prophet (God's peace and blessings upon him) said: "The foundation of your faith is watchfulness."[5] The people of watchfulness are of three ranks.

The first rank consists of those who are scrupulous in avoiding those things that are uncertain, that is, whatever lies between the prohibited *(ḥarām)* and the permitted *(ḥalāl)*, which has not received the name of absolute prohibition or absolute permission. Such uncertain items are the objects of watchfulness.

In this regard, Ibn Sīrān (God grant him compassion) said: "There is nothing easier for me than watchfulness: If something causes doubt in me, I leave it."

The second rank consists of those who are scrupulous concerning anything that the heart stands back from, from anything that contrives in the breast when grasped. This can be known only by the masters of the heart and by those who have achieved realization. In this regard, the Prophet (God's peace and blessings upon him) said: "Sin is what contrives in your breast."[6]

Abū Sa'īd al-Kharrāz (God grant him compassion) said: "Watchfulness is remaining free from even a mote's weight of wrong among creatures, so that no one can associate with you any wrong, claim of wrong, or desire for wrong."

In this regard, it has been related of al-Ḥārith al-Muḥāsibī (God grant him compassion) that he would not extend his hand to any uncertain food. Ja'far al-Khuldī (God grant him compassion) said: "There was at the end of one of his middle fingers a vein that would begin pulsing if he extended his hand toward any uncertain food."

They say of Bishr al-Ḥāfī (God grant him compassion) that he was brought to a gathering and seated in front of a repast, but when he tried to extend his hand toward the food, it would not move. He tried again, and yet a third time, and still his hand would not move forward. An acquaintance of his said: "His hand will not extend to food that is prohibited or the status of which is uncertain. The host of that gathering could have done without inviting such a man to his house!"

That point is reinforced by a story of Sahl ibn 'Abdullāh [at-Tustarī].

I heard Aḥmad ibn Muḥammad ibn Sālim say one time in Basra: "Sahl ibn 'Abdullāh [at-Tustarī] was asked about the permitted. He said: 'The permitted is that which occasions no disobedience to God.' "

Abū Naṣr (God grant him compassion) said: "That which occasions no disobedience to God cannot be ascertained by anyone except through the counsel of the heart.

"If someone should say: 'Can you find any basis in knowledge to hold onto?' the answer will be: 'Yes, the saying of the Prophet (God grant him compassion) to Wābiṣa: "Ask your heart, even if the masters of law render an opinion for you."[7] And who said as well, "Sin is that which devises in your breast." Do you not see that he referred it back to what the heart evokes?' "

As for the third rank in watchfulness—it consists of the knowers *('ārifūn)* and the finders/ecstatics *(wājidūn)*, just as Abū Sulaymān ad-Dārānī (God grant him compassion) said: "Everything that distracts you from God is suspicious."

The watchfulness in which God is not forgotten is the watchfulness about which Shiblī (God grant him compassion) was asked. Someone said to him: "O Abū Bakr, what is watchfulness?" He said: "That you are scrupulous lest your heart be scattered from God Most High and Transcendent for the blink of an eye."

The first rank is the watchfulness of the common people. The second is the watchfulness of the select. The third is the watchfulness of the select of the select.

Watchfulness demands renunciation.

♦ ♦ ♦

THE STATION OF RENUNCIATION *(ZUHD)*

The Shaykh (God grant him compassion) said: Renunciation is a noble station. It is the foundation for the conditions of contentedness and for the more lofty ranks. It is the first step of those in quest of God Most High and Transcendent, those devoted to God, and those content in God, those who trust God. Whoever cannot control his foundation through renunciation is not suitable for anything beyond it, because love of the world is the beginning of all sins and renunciation of the world is the beginning of all goods and all acts of obedience.

It is said that whoever is given the name of renunciation of the world is thereby named with one thousand names of praise, and whoever is given the name of desire for the world is thereby named with one thousand names of blame. And that is what God's messenger chose for himself through the choice of God for him.[8]

Renunciation concerns what is permitted and is at hand. As for that which is prohibited and that which is uncertain—giving it up is obligatory.

There are three ranks of renouncers. The first rank consists of beginners, those whose hands are free of possession and whose hearts are free of what their hands are free of. In this regard, Junayd (God grant him compassion) was asked about renunciation and said: "That the hands are free of possession and the hearts are free of craving."

Sarī as-Saqaṭī (God grant him compassion) was asked about renunciation and said: "That the heart be free of what the hands are free."

The second rank consists of those who have realized renunciation. A description of them can be found in the response of Ruwaym ibn Aḥmad (God grant him compassion) when he was asked about renunciation. He said: "It is the giving up of all goods or benefits for the self from whatever exists in the world." This is the renunciation of those who have achieved realization, because even in renunciation of the world there are goods for the self: the tranquillity, honor, praise, and status among the people that comes with renunciation. Whoever renounces in his heart goods such as these has realized renunciation.

The third rank consists of those who know with utter certainty that if the entire world were given to them as a possession, and if possessing it caused no reckoning in the afterlife and no diminution in what God has in store for them, and if they were to renounce it for God, their renunciation would concern something that from the time of its creation received not a single divine regard. And if the world weighed even the weight of a gnat's wing in God's estimation, no unbeliever in the world could take a single drink from it.

So they renounce and repent of their renunciation. Shiblī (God grant him compassion) was asked about renunciation and said: "Renunciation is neglect, because the world is nothing and renunciation of nothing is neglect."

Yaḥyā ibn Mu'ādh (God grant him compassion) said: "The world is like a bride and whoever seeks it is like her handmaid. The renouncer blackens her face, tears out her hair, and rends her clothes. The knower, however, is preoccupied with God and does not turn toward her at all."

Renunciation demands the embrace of poverty and choosing of poverty.

♦ ♦ ♦

THE STATION OF POVERTY *(FAQR)* AND THE CHARACTERISTIC OF THE POOR

The Shaykh (God grant him compassion), said: Poverty is a noble station. In his book, God Most High has recalled and described the poor (2:273): "The poor are those who have been brought together in the path of God." The Prophet said, peace and blessing upon him: "Poverty is more becoming for the faithful servant than a fine bridle on the cheek of a stallion."[9]

Ibrāhīm ibn Aḥmad al-Khawwāṣ (God's compassion upon him) said: "Poverty is the cloak of those who are noble, the clothing of those who have been given a mission, the jalaba of the righteous, the crown of the vigilant, the adornment of the believers, the booty of the knowers, the warning of the seekers, the fortress of the obedient, the prison of sinners. It is something that covers over wrong deeds, exalts good deeds, raises one through the ranks, transports one to the goal, and makes the mighty content; it is a bestowal of God to his friends among the pious.[10] Poverty is the emblem of the righteous and the persistence of the vigilant."

There are three ranks among the poor. The first rank includes those who do not own anything, who do not seek anything from anyone, outwardly or inwardly, who do not expect anything from anybody, and who, if they are offered anything, refuse it. This station is the station of the near.

In this regard it was related of Sahl ibn 'Alī ibn Iṣbahānī that he used to say: "Shame on those who name our friends 'the poor.' Of all God's creatures they are the most free of want."

Similarly, Abū 'Abdullāh ibn al-Jallā' was asked about the reality of poverty. He said: "Dash your two sleeves against the wall and say: 'My lord is God!' "

Abū 'Alī al-Rūdhabārī said: "Abū Bakr az-Zaqāq said to me: 'O Abū 'Alī, Why do the poor refrain from taking what would be adequate for them in a time of need?'

I replied: 'Because the Provider has freed them from need for anyone's giving.'

He said, 'Yes, but something else has occurred to me.'

'Go on,' I said, 'Tell me. What is it that occurred to you?'

He said: 'Because they are a people whom existence cannot benefit if they lack God, and whom existential lack cannot harm insofar as God is their existence.' "

I heard Abū Bakr al-Wajīhī say I heard Abū 'Ali say this.

And I heard Abū Bakr aṭ-Ṭūsī say: "For a long time I asked about the significance of the preference of our friends for this poverty over everything else, but no one offered me a convincing answer until I asked Naṣr ibn al-Ḥamāmī. He said to me, 'Because it is the first way-station in the affirmation of unity.' That response convinced me."

The second rank consists of those who do not own anything, who do not ask of anyone, who do not make requests, who do not busy themselves about anything, who do not make hints, but who, if they are given something without asking for it, accept it. It has been related from Junayd, God grant him compassion, that he said: "The mark of the truly poor is that he does not ask, does not argue, and if someone argues, desists. "

It has been related of Sahl ibn 'Abdullāh [at-Tustarī] God grant him peace, that he said when he was asked about the truly poor: "One who does not ask, does not refuse, and does not hoard."

Abū 'Abdullāh al-Jallā' (God's compassion upon him), when asked about the reality of poverty, responded: "It is that you possess nothing, and that if you possess something you still do not possess it, and insofar as you do not possess it, you do not possess it."

Ibrāhīm al-Khawwāṣ (God's compassion upon him) was asked about the mark of the truly poor. He said, "It is the refraining from complaint and hiding the trace of tribulation."[11]

In this regard it had been said: "This is his station, the station of the true."

The third rank consists of those who do not own anything. If one of them is in need, he opens himself to a brother that he knows will rejoice in his confidence in him. The atonement gift for a request is the free gift.[12] This is in accordance with what al-Jarīrī, God's compassion upon him, said when asked a question about the reality of poverty: "To refrain from requesting what is not lest one lose what is."

Ruwaym, God's compassion upon him, was asked about poverty and said: "It is the absence of everything that is and the entering into things for others, not for oneself." This station is the station of the truly poor.

Poverty demands patience.

♦ ♦ ♦

THE STATION OF PATIENCE (*ṢABR*)

The Shaykh, God grant him compassion, said: Patience is a noble station. God recalled and praised in his book those who are patient, saying (39:10): "The patient will be paid their due without measure."

Junayd was asked about patience and said: "The bearing of the burden for the sake of God Most High until the times of hardship have passed."

Ibrāhīm al-Khawwāṣ (God grant him compassion) said: "Most creatures flee from the burdens of patience and take refuge in demands and means, depending upon them as if they were lords."

A man stood before Shiblī (God's compassion upon him) and said to him: "Which act of patience is hardest for one who is patient?"

Shiblī said: "Patience in God."

"No," the man said.

Shiblī said: "Patience for God."

The man said "No."

Shiblī said: "The patience with God."

"No," he said.

Shiblī grew angry and said: "Damn you, what then?"

The man said: "Patience without God Most High."

Shiblī let out a scream that nearly tore apart his spirit.

In Basra I once asked Ibn Sālim about patience. He said: "There are three kinds of patient people: the would-be patient, the patient, and the truly patient. The would-be patient person is patient in God Most High. At times he is patient in hardship, at times he fails."

In this regard, al-Qannād (God grant him compassion) was asked about patience. He said: "The maintaining of obligation in turning from the forbidden and in persisting in what has been ordained. One who is patient is patient in God and for God. He is not anxious; anxiety has no power over him and complaint can expect nothing from him."

It has been related from Dhū n-Nūn (God grant him compassion) that he said: "I made a visit to someone who was ill and while he was speaking to me, he let out a moan. I said to him: 'He who is not patient with its blow is not true in his love.'[13] He replied: 'He is not true in his love who does not take pleasure in its blow.' "

When Shiblī (God grant him compassion) was brought into the asylum and put in chains, some of his friends came to visit him. He said to them: "Who are you?" They said: "We are people who love you." He began to throw stones at them. When they fled, he cried: "Liars! You claim to love me but you are not patient with my blow!"

As for the truly patient—he is one whose patience is in God and for God and through God. Were all possible trials to afflict him, he would not weaken or waver in regard to obligation and reality, nor in regard to the trace and natural disposition.[14]

Shiblī used to cite the following verses as an example when he was asked about patience:

Tears that traced a line along the cheek
read by one unversed in reading.
The sound of the lover in love-ache
and fear of parting, bequeaths harm.
He vied with patience in patience, and patience
sought help in him. The lover cried to patience,
patience!

The argument for such patience in traditional knowledge has been related in the report that Zakariyyā (God grant him compassion), when the saw was brought down upon his head, let out a single moan. God Most High revealed to him that "if another moan rises up to me from you, the heavens and earths will be turned upside down upon one another."

Patience demands trust.

♦ ♦ ♦

THE STATION OF TRUST *(TAWAKKUL)*

The Shaykh (God's compassion upon him) said: Trust is a noble station. God Most High enjoined trust and made it similar to faith through his word (5:23): "Trust in God if you are believers." He also said (14:12): "In God should the trustful trust." In another place he said (14:11): "In God should the believers trust." He singled out the trust of the trustful from the trust of the believers, and then mentioned the trust of the select of the select, saying (65:3): "For whoever trusts in God, God is his sufficiency."[15] He directed them to nothing outside himself. The lord of the messengers and the leader *(imām)* of the trustful said (25:58): "Trust in the living, the undying . . . who is sufficiently [aware of the faults of his servants]"; and (26:217–218): "Trust in the majestic one, the caring, who sees you when you rise."

They are of three ranks. As for the trust of the believers, the condition for trust is as Abū Turāb an-Nakhshabī (God's compassion upon him) said when he was asked about trust: "Trust is the casting off of the body in worship and the attachment of the heart to lordship and the assurance *(iṭma'iniyya)* of sufficiency. If one is given something, he gives thanks; if he is denied, he is patient, accepting, in agreement with destiny."

In this regard Dhū n-Nūn was asked about trust and replied: "To trust is to divest oneself of plans, of power and of might."

Abū Bakr az-Zaqāq (God grant him compassion) was asked about trust and replied: "The living for a single day and the silencing of care for tomorrow."

Ruwaym (God's compassion upon him) was asked about trust and said: "Confidence in the promise."

Sahl ibn 'Abdullāh (God grant him compassion) was asked about trust and said: "The giving of oneself up to God in whatever God wishes."

As for the trust of the select, Abū l-'Abbās ibn 'Aṭā' said in this regard: "Whoever trusts in God through something other than God does not arrive at trust in God, through God, for God, with no other motive or cause for his trust whatsoever."

Abū Ya'qūb an-Nahrajūrī (God grant him compassion) said: "The death of the self upon the disappearance of its share in the motives of the world and of the afterlife."

Abū Bakr al-Wāsiṭī said: "The root of trust is privation and poverty; that one does not distinguish trust in his faith; and that one does not turn in his heart-secret to his trust even for a single moment during his life."

Sahl ibn 'Abdullāh (God's compassion upon him) was asked about trust as well and replied: "Trust is all face. It has no back-of-the-head. It belongs only to the people of the tombs who indicate the reality of the trust of the trustful." These are the select.

As for the trust of the select of the select, it is as Shiblī (God grant him compassion) said when he was asked about trust: "That you should belong to God as if you did not exist and that God Most High should belong to you as if he never ceased to exist."

In this regard someone said: "The reality of trust is such that no creature attains it completely because complete completion belongs to no one but God Almighty."

Abū 'Abdullāh ibn al-Jalā' was asked about trust and said: "The bending toward God alone."

Al-Junayd (God's compassion upon him) was asked about trust and said: "The heart's relying upon God Most High in all its conditions."

It has been related of Abī Sulaymān ad-Dārāni (God's compassion upon him) that he said to Aḥmad ibn Abī l-Ḥawārī (God's compassion upon him): "Aḥmad, the paths of the afterlife are many and your shaykh is a knower in many of them except this blessed trust, of which I have not smelled a single whiff, and I have no organ to scent its scent."

Someone said: "Whoever wishes to attain the truth of trust, let him dig for himself a grave, entomb himself in it, and forget the world and its inhabitants. The reality of complete trust is not attained by any creature."

Trust demands acceptance.

♦ ♦ ♦

THE STATION OF ACCEPTANCE *(RIḌĀ)* AND THE CHARACTERISTIC OF ITS PEOPLE

Riḍā is another term that is resistant to translation into English. It means acceptance, but it also means the quality of taking pleasure in something or someone. Thus the word is used in connection with divine good-pleasure and good-favor in regard to the godservant. It also refers to a human being's acceptance and good-pleasure in whatever is decreed for that person in his or her life. Acceptance is depicted as "stillness in the face of the divine decree (qaḍā')." *That stillness is a lack of resistance to what the deity has forewilled for a person. Acceptance is not a passive virtue; for the Sufis, a person's active accepting and good-pleasure in his life will lead to an em-*

powerment to act effectively in fulfilling the divine will, which in Qur'anic spirituality centers on justice and resisting the unjust.

The Shaykh (God grant him compassion) said: Acceptance is a noble station. God Most High mentioned acceptance in his Book, saying (5:119): "God was accepting of them and they of him," and saying (9:72) "Acceptance from God is greater." He thereby mentioned that the acceptance by God Most High of his servants is greater than their acceptance of him and prior to it.[16]

Acceptance is the greatest gate of God and is the paradise of the world. It consists of this: that the heart of the servant be stilled under the decision of God Most High, Almighty.

Junayd (God grant him compassion) was asked about acceptance and said: "Acceptance is the removal of choice." Al-Qannād was asked about acceptance and said: "Stillness of the heart in the face of the Decree."[17]

Dhū n-Nūn (God's compassion upon him) was asked about acceptance and said: "The delight of the heart with the passing of the Decree."

Ibn 'Aṭā' (God grant him compassion) said: "Acceptance is the heart's regard for the eternal choice of God for the servant, because he knows that he has chosen the best for him and accepts it and abandons discontent."

Abū Bakr al-Wāsitī (God grant him compassion) said: "Use acceptance to your utmost. Do not let acceptance use you, so that you become veiled by its pleasure and by the viewing of its reality."[18]

The people of acceptance are ranged among three conditions of acceptance. There are those who work toward the silencing of anxiety until they achieve equanimity in God in whatever misfortunes, comforts, deprivations, or bounties are allotted to them by divine decree.

There are those who give up seeing their acceptance of God Most High in favor of seeing God's acceptance of them, according to the divine word: "May God be accepting of them and they of him." They do not affirm for themselves any priority in acceptance, even if they have attained the ability to view misfortune, prosperity, deprivation, and bounty as all the same for them.

There are those who surpass that and give up seeing God's acceptance of them and their acceptance of God in favor of the acceptance that God has preordained for his creatures. In this regard Abū Sulaymān ad-Dārānī (God grant him compassion) said: "The acts of the creature are nothing to cause acceptance or displeasure, but rather he accepts a people and employs in them the action of the people of acceptance and he is displeased with others and employs in them the action of the people of displeasure."

Acceptance is the last of the stations. It demands—beyond the conditions of the masters of the heart—the attainment of mysteries, the training of the heart-secrets for pure remembrance, and the realities of the conditions.

[As-Sarrāj then moves directly into a discussion of the conditions: "The first condition of the masters of the heart is the condition of self-observance. . . ."[19]]

7

Bistami

♦ ♦ ♦

SARRAJ ON BISTAMI'S MYSTICAL UTTERANCES FROM THE BOOK OF FLASHES *(KITĀB AL-LUMA')*

Introduction

Abū Yazīd al-Bisṭamī is widely considered one of the main figures in establishing Sufism as an integral dimension of Islamic thought and life. He is considered within the tradition to be one of the originators of the concept of passing away (fanā') *in mystical union with the deity. Yet we have little certain information about his life. He is said to have been born in the city of Bistam and to have led a rigorous life of ascetism and devotions. To Bistami are attributed a number of ecstatic utterances* (shaṭḥiyāt)*. One of these utterances, "Glory to me!" has remained a central controversy within Islam down to the present day. Is such an utterance blasphemy, insanity, or is it, as Bistami's many defenders would have it, simply the deity speaking through the tongue of Bistami, who has passed away in mystical union?*

Bistami's controversial sayings have given him the reputation of a free-thinking radical, particularly in many Western accounts of Sufism. Yet the Bistami we know varies depending on the source who presents him. In this chapter, there are three sections devoted to Bistami. In the first section, taken from the writings of as-Sarraj, Bistami is the likely (but not certain) author of a number of enigmatic sayings, which are involved in debates among several other influential early Sufis—Sahl at-Tustari, Junayd, Muhammad ibn Salim and his son Ahmad, and Sarraj himself. In the second section, taken from the Sufi biographies of Sulami and Qushayri, Bistami comes across as a multifaceted character with a deep concern for maintaining the shar'ia and for engaging in free devotions beyond the obligatory. In the third section, Bistami is presented as having dreamed that he ascended through the seven heavens in an ascent clearly patterned on the Mi'raj of Muhammad.

One of the more critically advanced and intellectually rich accounts of Bistami is one of the earliest: the section from Abū Naṣr as-Sarrāj's The Book of Flashes *on ecstatic utterances* (shaṭḥiyāt, shaṭaḥāt).[1] *This section reflects the features of* The Book of Flashes *discussed earlier, particularly the use of various Sufi voices within a dialectical framework. In this case, however, it uses that method to contextualize what for Sarraj were sayings of Bistami, or attributed to Bistami, that had been taken out of context and inappropriately criticized.*

In the account of Sarraj's ecstatic utterances, four Sufi figures are of particular importance: (1) Sahl at-Tustarī, who is cited by Sarraj as an example of a respected Sufi who said things in his own time that were controversial; (2–3) Muḥammad ibn Sālim and his son Aḥmad, followers of Tustari who founded a school that became known as the Sālimiyya; and (4) Junayd, another central figure in early Sufism (see Chapter 8 in this volume), whose remarks on Bistami are the occasion for Sarraj's discussion. Thus we have a highly intricate text, which consists of Sarraj's interpretations of Junayd's interpretations of Bistami's ecstatic sayings, in view of the criticism of Bistami by the Salimiyya and other unnamed "faultfinders."

The essay consists of five sections, the first of which is an introduction to the issue of Bistami's utterances. In it, Sarraj refers to a commentary that Junayd supposedly had made on the shaṭḥiyāt *of Bistami. Sarraj states that the written commentary was unavailable to him, and he therefore had to rely on other comments of Junayd on Bistami that had come down to him. He then cites a comment of Junayd's that he will later expand into his own central, hermeneutic principle; the utterances of Bistami represent various "stationings"* (mawāṭīn) *and moments* (awqāt) *of Bistami. In addition to the substance of Junayd's remarks (which are sometimes in alignment with those of Sarraj, sometimes in tension with them), Sarraj is also evoking the reputation of Junayd as a Sufi thinker of high esteem even among critics of other Sufis.*

In the four sections that follow, Sarraj engages in a four-step procedure: First he cites one of Bistami's shaṭḥiyāt. *Second, he cites the commentary on it by Junayd in defense of Bistami. Third, he brings up aspects of the controversy that he does not feel Junayd's comments engage. Finally, Sarraj offers his own interpretation of Bistami's utterances, with a stronger defense of them than he seems to have felt Junayd gave. Translated here are all the sections from Sarraj dedicated to the* shaṭḥiyāt *of Bistami. Sarraj also wrote on the* shaṭḥiyāt *of several other early Sufis as well as on other controversial Sufi topics. The Bistami sections have been chosen because of the centrality of Bistami to the tradition and to the controversies over* shaṭḥiyāt*, and because they contain some of Sarraj's most intricate and probing writing.*

CHAPTER 123 OF *THE BOOK OF FLASHES:* THE *SHAṬḤIYĀT* THAT HAVE BEEN PASSED DOWN FROM ABU YAZID (OF WHICH JUNAYD HAS EXPLICATED A PART)

1. The Shaykh [i.e., Sarraj],[2] may Allah grant him compassion, said that Junayd had explicated some small part of the *shaṭḥiyāt* of Abu Yazid; a sage can infer from the small to the greater. However, I have not been able to find a formal written commentary of Junayd (God grant him compassion) for the words of Abu Yazid,[3] so I will leave that aside and speak of other responses that I have from Junayd.

2. Junayd said: The accounts passed down from Abu Yazid are various and the raconteurs differ in what they heard. That might be—God knows best—because of the difference in the moments *(awqāt)* that had come upon him and the difference in stationings *(mawāṭin)* alternating in what was bestowed specially upon him. Each person recounts of Abu Yazid the words that he is able to verify of him and the particular stationing of him that he has heard about.[4]

3. Junayd said: The speech of Abu Yazid, because of his power, depth, and the semantic reach, forms a ladle for the sea that he alone inhabited, that was given to him only.

4. Junayd said: Then I saw that the furthest limit of his condition *(ḥāl)*—that is, Abu Yazid's—is a condition few can understand from him and few can express upon hearing. No one can bear it except one who knows its inner meanings and plumbs its well.[5] Whoever lacks such a constitution will, upon hearing it, reject it entirely.

5. Junayd said: I saw that in their depiction of him, the accounts of Abu Yazid suggested that he had drowned in the rapture he found and that he disappeared from the reality of the real never to return to it.[6] He was drowned at times in the inner meanings, each one different from the other.

6. Junayd said: As for what he described of the beginnings of his condition, it is solid, precise, and complete. The points he made in affirmation of unity *(tawḥīd)* are sound, but they are only beginnings in regard to what is being sought.

7. These words I wish to recall are not the kind that are written down in bound volumes, because they are not of the sciences disseminated among the ulama. However, I saw that people were delving more and more into their inner meanings. One was making Abu Yazid a pretext for his own falsehood,[7] another believed that anyone who could have said these things must be an infidel, and all were in error in the conclusions they were drawing. Allah alone guarantees success in truth.

Chapter 124:
The Chapter on the Recalling of What Was Passed Down from Abu Yazid (God Most High Grant Him Compassion)

The first of the four ecstatic utterances (shaṭḥiyāt) *involves a passage on mystical union:*

> *Once, he took me up, placed me before him, and said to me: "O Abu Yazid, my creation would love to seek you."*
>
> *I said: "Adorn me with your unity, clothe me with your subjectivity, and take me up to your oneness, until when your creation sees me they say 'We have seen you' and you will be* that, *and I will not be there."* [8]

Sarraj first cites Junayd's comment to the effect that such a statement revealed that Bistami was near to the real, but had not yet achieved it. Not only is this perhaps a faint praise on the part of Junayd, it is also, in Sarraj's view, a weak defense of Bistami; it does not address what the faultfinder would criticize in the statement. Because Sarraj does not give us the faultfinder's criticism, we can only infer it from Sarraj's defense.

Sarraj's defense of this utterance works on several levels. He evokes the poetic tradition of the secret conversation between lover and beloved that is not meant to be heard, let alone interpreted, by another, as a model for the intimate conversations (munājāt) *between the divine and the human. He explains Abu Yazid's comment that "I was no longer there" by speaking of those who are "singled out" for union with the divine, who pass away in union with the divine, and who pass away from the experience of their own passing away. Then he cites a version of the hadith of free devotions:*

> *My servant continues to draw near to me through free acts of devotion until I love him. When I love him, I am the eye with which he sees, the hearing with which he hears, the tongue with which he speaks, the hand with which he grasps.*

All aspects of Sarraj's defense are unified around the theme of mystical union; thus, Bistami's statement must have been criticized by the faultfinders as an improper claim of union with the deity.

1. People are saying about Abu Yazid—and I do not know whether it is true or not—that he said:

> Once, he took me up, placed me before him, and said to me: O Abu Yazid, my creation would love to seek you.
>
> I said: "Adorn me with your unity, clothe me with your subjectivity, and take me up to your oneness, until when your creation sees me they say 'We have seen you' and you will be *that,* and I will not be there."

2. If this is correct about him, then Junayd (God grant him compassion) said in his commentary concerning these words of Abu Yazid:

> These are the words of one who has not been clothed with the realities of the experience of *tafrīd* (singularity) in the completeness of the true *tawḥīd*, a clothing that would have freed him of the need for what he requested. His request indicates that he was near to what was there, but one who is near to a place is not in it in capacity and in actual command. His saying "clothe me" and "adorn me" and "take me up" indicates the reality of what he experienced according to his ability and his place. He attained precedence only insofar as his perception allowed.

3. I said: Junayd's interpretations were descriptions of Abu Yazid's condition in what he had spoken and clarifications of his place in what he had

alluded to. But Junayd did not clarify that which the faultfinder and quarrelmonger use as a pretext for criticizing anyone who would utter the kind of statement Abu Yazid uttered.[9]

As for both the import and purport (in Allah is success in truth) of his saying "Once, he took me up and placed me before him and made me witness and made my heart present to that"—the saying is based on the fact that all creatures are before Allah Most High. Not a single breath of theirs eludes him, nor a single thought. But they range widely in their presences before that[10] and their witness of it, and they are of various degrees in their attributes, concerning any dimness in the form of distracting preoccupations and obstructive thoughts that might veil them off from such a presence.

It has been related in the hadith that the Prophet (God's blessings and peace upon him) said, when he wished to enter into the prayer: "I stood before the almighty king."

4. As for his saying, "He said to me" and "I said to him"—by that he alludes to the intimate conversations of the secret of the heart and to the purity of remembrance that occurs with the heart's vision of the almighty king's watchful regard day and night. So weigh what I have elucidated for you, for each part of it is similar to the next. When a godservant becomes certain of the nearness of his master to him, and when he is present with his heart in watchfulness over his thoughts, then every thought that occurs to his heart is as if the real were addressing him, and everything he thinks of in the inner secret of his heart is as if he were addressing Allah Most High. Thoughts and motions of the inner heart, and whatever occurs, all have their origin with Allah and their end in Allah. And this is the correct meaning. Allah grants success in finding the right.

Someone said:

The aspirations stood forth before him.
  He remained my intimate companion.
Then I rejoiced, lost,
  in joy.

They stood forth before him
  as if I were conversing with him
in the secret of my heart
  and the secret of his heart, concealed.

Someone else said:

He said to me when I reached him
All this I have known.
Were he to weep the rest of his life
tears of blood I would not forgive him.[11]

He means that intimate conversations [of the secret of the heart] and the like are frequent in poetry and elsewhere.[12]

5. As for his saying, "Adorn me with your unity, clothe me with your subjectivity, and take me up to your oneness"—he means by that the increase and the transposition from his condition to the future condition of those who have realized the detachment of *tawḥīd* and those who are singled out for Allah with the reality of singularity *(tafrīd).* [13]

It has been related of the Envoy of God that he said: "Those who single themselves out *(al-mufarridūn)* have precedence." It has been recalled that someone asked: "O Rasul Allah—and who are 'those who single themselves out?' " He said: "Those who praise Allah in good times and bad."

6. As for his saying "Adorn me with your unity, clothe me with your subjectivity, and take me up to your oneness, until when your creation sees me they say 'we have seen you' and you will be *that,* and I will not be there"—this and the like describe his passing away, his passing away from passing away, and the taking over of his self by the real in unity—with no creature before it and no created being.

This all derives from the saying of the Most High: "My servant continues to draw near to me through free acts of devotion until I love him. When I love him, I am the eye with which he sees, the hearing with which he hears, the tongue with which he speaks, the hand with which he grasps"—as it has come down in the hadith.[14]

Someone has described his experience with his lover—a reference to his experience with a creature like himself—to the point of claiming:

I am my beloved, my beloved is I
If you see me, you see us both,
two spirits in one flesh,
clothed by Allah in a single body.[15]

7. Now if a creature can experience in this way a fellow creature, what would you make of something beyond that? A report has reached me of a certain sage who said: "Two lovers have not attained the reality of love until one says to the other: "I." It would prolong our discussion for me to give an in-depth explanation of that issue. What I have already recalled is enough. In Allah alone is success.

Chapter 125: Another Chapter on the Interpretation of an Account That Has Been Passed on concerning Abu Yazid May Allah Have Compassion on Him

The second utterance entails a trope in which Abu Yazid flies through various metaphysical realms to the "tree of unity." He then looks and sees that it was all "a cheat." This utterance was to become the basis for the elaborate mir'aj account attributed to Bistami, translated in section 3 of this chapter, in which Abu Yazid rises through the seven heavens to the divine throne.

Junayd continues his interpretation of Bistami as not having reached the goal of the mystical seeker, but still being somewhere along the path. In this case, however, Junayd seems to be making some other, enigmatic allusions.

The first part of Sarraj's discussion focuses on the image of flying, its meaning and possible metaphorical usage. The argument then deepens to the issue of wajd *(ecstasy) and its relationship to mystical union.*

1. The Shaykh said: I said—and it has been reported of him—that Abu Yazid said:

> As soon as I arrived at his oneness, I became a bird whose body was of unity and whose wings were of everlastingness.[16] So I continued to fly through the ether of howness *(kayfiyya)* for ten years until I came to the air of something like that one thousand thousand times. I did not cease flying until I came to the field of pre-eternity and saw there the tree of unity.

Then he described its roots, trunk, boughs, branches, and fruits. Then he said, "Then I looked and knew that it was all a cheat."

2. Junayd said: As for his saying "As soon as I had arrived at his oneness," that refers to his first glimpse of affirmation of unity *(tawḥīd)*. He described what he glimpsed of that, and described his end in the condition of its attainment and his abiding in the finitude of its establishment. All that is one stretch along the path of those who are called to attain the reality of the science of *tawḥīd* by visible signs of its meaning, conspicuous to those who seek it and who are sent forth in regard to the visions they have glimpsed. If all that is the case, this [stretch along the path] is not the most advanced inner essence that those who are called are capable of, nor is it a sifting down into the grave toward which they are advancing. Rather, that is grounded upon the sign of eternity and a trace of immortality upon those who find rapture in it.

3. Junayd also said: As for Abu Yazid's expression "one thousand thousand times"—it has no specific meaning. That desired characterization is grander than what he depicted and what he said. He characterized it as best he could. Then he described what was there, and that is not yet the reality sought nor the end requested, but it is only one stretch along the path.

Such is the interpretation of Junayd. It is enough for one who understands. Allah alone grants success in truth.

4. Junayd spoke of the condition of Abu Yazid reflected in his ecstatic utterances *(shaṭḥiyāt)*. He did not pronounce upon his ecstatic state *(wajd)*. He did not recall the saying of Abu Yazid that offers the faultfinder an inroad for attack: "I became a bird and did not cease to fly."

How can it be that a man becomes a bird and flies? The meaning he was alluding to is the loftiness of aspirations *(himam)* and the flight of the heart, a usage that can be found in the language of the Arabs. One says: "I almost flew out of joy," and "My heart flew," and "My mind was about to fly away."

Yaḥyā ibn Mu'ādh (God's compassion upon him) said: "The renunciate walks while the knower *('ārif)* flies." By that he means that the knower in his quest for what he seeks is faster than the renunciate. That might be. Allah Most High said [17:13]— "And for every person—we have bound around his neck his bird of omen."[17]

In regard to the interpretation of these words [concerning the bird of omen bound around the neck], it has been related from Sa'īd ibn Jubayr (God grant him compassion): "We attached to him the happiness and unhappiness preordained for him."

And the poet said:

How many a day like the day they went away
made by tears of separation a day of rain,
had you seen me you would have seen the day of parting
a body in place, heart flying.

5a. As for his expression attributing his wings and body to oneness and everlastingness, he meant by it his stripping himself of his own might and powers in his flight, that is, in his quest for the goal, characterizing his action and motion in his quest for the one, the everlasting, in an unusual expression. Such expressions can be found in the speech of the ecstatics and the love-lost. When the secret of the heart of the ecstatic *(wājid)* is overcome by the remembrance of the one in whom he has found rapture *(wajada bihi)*, he depicts all his conditions with the attributes of his beloved. In this way Majnūn of the Banī 'Amir would say, when looking at a wild animal, "Layla," when looking at the mountains, "Layla," and when looking at other people, "Layla," to the point that when he was asked his name and condition, he said "Layla."

In that regard he said:

I pass by the ruined abodes of Layla
kissing this wall and that.
It is not love of the ruins that inflames my heart
but love of the one who inhabited the ruins.

5b. Another said:

I search the secret of my heart for desire for you
but find only myself and that I am you[18]
and the inner essence greater.
If she finds that I am found raptured in her
she speaks of herself when she speaks of me.

There are many similar sayings. An approved speaker on the meaning of what they said in describing their ecstatic state—in a created being and in vain desire as a hint of the meaning intended in their mention of such things—makes explicit discussion superfluous.[19] Allah alone grants success.

6. Now as for the meaning of his saying "ten years" and "one thousand thousand times" and "the field of pre-eternity" and the "ether of howness *(kayfiyya),*"[20] Junayd (God grant him compassion) said that he described a part of the path. Junayd's statement is sufficient and needs no further discussion or repetition from us on the same subject.

As for his saying, "I looked and knew that it was all a cheat," its meaning—and God knows best—is that the turning to and preoccupation with creation[21] and dominion is a cheat next to the existence of the realities of *tafrīd* and the purity of *tawḥīd.* Therefore Junayd (God grant him compassion) said, "I do not see[22] that Abu Yazid, despite the grandeur of his allusions, has gone beyond the beginning and middle. I have not heard from him any pronouncement that would point to a meaning that would show the end." This applies to his mention of the body, the wings, the air, and the field.[23] He said, "I knew that it was all a cheat" because among the people of the end, the turning to anything other than God is a cheat. Lest anyone should deny that, the Master of the First and the Last, God's blessings and peace upon him, said "The truest word spoken by the Arabs is the saying of Labid:

Everything other than God
how true it is, is vanity."[24]

Chapter 126: Another Chapter on the Explanation of Words Related from Abu Yazid May Allah, the Exalted, Have Compassion on Him

The third essay begins with a dense aphorism in which Bistami states that he arrived from nothing in nothing through nothing, passed the domain "of perdition which is the domain of affirmation of unity (tawḥīd)," *and finally ended in "the vanishing of creatures from the knower and of knower from creatures." The commentary again turns on the central Sufi concept of the passing away of passing away* (fanā' al-fanā') *in which the Sufi passes away from consciousness of passing away.*

1. The Shaykh said: It has also been recalled from Abu Yazid that he said: I came upon the domain of nothingness *(laysiyya).* For ten years I continued flying in it until I arrived from nothing in nothing through nothing.[25] Then I came upon perdition, which is the domain of *tawḥīd.* I continued to fly

through nothing in perdition until I was lost in the loss of being lost. I was lost to the extent that I was lost from perdition in nothing, nothing in the loss of perdition. Then I came upon *tawḥīd* in the vanishing of creatures from the knower and the vanishing of the knower from creatures.

2. Junayd said: All this and what is like it is of the science of signs in the vanishing of the searching for the sign.[26] Here there are meanings of passing away *(fanā')* in the vanishing of passing away from passing away. His [Abu Yazid's] saying "I came upon the domain of nothingness until I arrived from nothing in nothing through nothing" signifies the first descent into the reality of passing away and the disappearance *(dhihāb)* of everything seen and unseen. In the first occurrence of passing away is the obliteration of the vestiges *(āthār)* of all things.

His saying "nothing through nothing" indicates the disappearance of all other than him, and his own disappearance from disappearance. "Nothing in nothing" means that nothing is perceived or found to exist. The traces have been effaced, the names have been cut off, the beholdings have vanished, and things have been swallowed up from view. Nothing can be found to exist, nothing is perceived as lacking, there is no name by which anything can be known. All that has disappeared along with the disappearance from it.

This is what some Sufis *(qawm)* call passing away *(fanā')*. Then passing away vanishes from passing away and is lost in its passing away, and this is the perdition which was in nothing through it and through it in nothing. This is the reality of the nonexistence *(faqd)* of everything and the nonexistence of the self after that, and the nonexistence of nonexistence in nonexistence, and the becoming dust in obliteration, and the disappearance from disappearance. This is something that has no duration nor any ascertainable moment.

3. Junayd said: His mention of ten years refers to his moment and is without meaning. In such a condition, moments vanish and if the moment has vanished from someone along with its content, then ten years or a hundred or more are all one in meaning.

Junayd said: As it came down to me, Abu Yazid said: "I came upon *tawḥīd* in the vanishing of creatures from the knower and in the vanishing of the knower from creatures." He continued: "When I came upon *tawḥīd*, there was realized in me the vanishing of all creatures from Allah Most High and the aloneness of Allah in his majesty from his creation."

Then Junayd said: These expressions of Abu Yazid are known for the couching of the intended meaning within the vehicle of meaning.

4. This is what has come down to me from Junayd (God's compassion upon him) of the interpretation of these words of Abu Yazid. Junayd's interpretation is obscure for the uninitiated.[27] That interpretation and others like it are obscure only for those who have not delved into the deep of knowledge, who have not looked at the traditions and description of the greatness and majesty of Allah Most High preserved in the books of the ulama. From that one can then infer to what is not preserved in the books of what has been uniquely bestowed upon the hearts of his friends, his chosen, his select.

On the other hand, the more discerning of the ulama in Allah know this: that everyone who witnesses his increase—in the particular condition that he has chosen from among the conditions of those devoted to Allah Most High—is increasing in his condition with Allah Most High and Transcendent in every breath and in every blink of an eye. In every breath the condition to which he is bound increases.[28] In every breath he is transformed from condition to condition, without end, until his position of homeland rests in its proper and desired site.[29] Thus every condition to which he is transformed causes him to pass away from the previous condition. This is the meaning of his saying "passing away" and "passing away from passing away," and "disappearance" and "disappearance from disappearance," and "I was lost," and "I was lost in the loss of being lost." Though the expressions are diverse, the meanings are in accord and harmonious with one another.

5. An elucidation of this matter can be found in what has been handed down from 'Abdullah ibn 'Abbās concerning the word of God (41:11): "Then he established himself in the heaven and it was smoke. So he said to it and to the earth: 'Come! willingly or unwillingly.' They said: 'Willingly have we come!' "

Ibn 'Abbās said: The angels asked, "O lord, if they had not come to you, what were you going to do with them?"

He answered: "I was going to unleash upon them one of my beasts to devour them in a single mouthful."

They said: "Lord, where is that beast?"

He answered: "In one of my meadows."

They said: "Lord, where is that meadow?"

He said: "In the hidden depth of my knowledge."

Do you not see that in the beast and the mouthful is the disappearance of the heavens and the earth, and in the meadow is the disappearance of disappearance, and in the disappearance is a warning for the hearts of the knowers? When one witnesses that in his heart, how is he to witness his self, and dominion, and everything created by Allah Most High?

It is said in some books that Allah announced to Jahannam: "If you do not carry out what I command, I will burn you up in a great bolt of fire!"

One of the knowers was asked: What is the meaning of his saying "I will burn you up in a great bolt of fire"?

He answered, "He would disclose to its foot a mote of his love, in comparison to which Jahannam would be like a mere baker's oven or even less."[30]

6. His saying "Nothing in nothing through nothing" points to the nothingness of what is experienced, since all things in their essences[31] and their existences are phantoms compared to what Allah Most High has. Even though they are marked in their inner realities for being brought into existence, nevertheless they are marked for privation and obliteration.

The people of the realities are of various ranks in their witness (2:245): "Allah constricts and Allah unfolds and to him you will be returned."

Chapter 127: Another Chapter on the Explanation of Expressions That Have Been Related from Abu Yazid (God Grant Him Compassion) and That Prompted Ibn Salim to Accuse Him of Heresy, Along with a Remembrance of the Controversy Between Ibn Salim and Myself Concerning That

The final saying is one of the more famous of the shaṭḥiyāt: subḥanī, subḥānī *(Glory to me, Glory to me). The word* subḥan *is applied uniquely to the deity, usually in the form* subḥanahu *(Glory to him). Sarraj begins immediately by countering the criticism of Ibn Salim against Bistami's famous saying: "Glory to me!" Sarraj's commentary first focuses on his perennial concern, context: How does one know when Bistami is saying "Glory to me" that he is not quoting the divine word? When a statement is taken out of its context, it can be radically misrepresented. This contextual argument might seem conservative, but in fact it cannot rest very easily on its own. There is no statement in the Qur'an or in the more recognized sacred hadith* (ḥadīth qudsī) *in which the deity says* subḥānī. *The verb* "subḥāna" *is used in the third person and second person in the canonical sacred texts, but not in the first person. Any educated Muslim would have known that it was unlikely that Bistami was reciting a verse from the Qur'an (as in the example Sarraj uses) when he made the famous utterance.*

The contextual argument then moves (as it must) to Sarraj's favorite argument, that of parallel experience: When a person speaks out of a state of wajd *(ecstasy), no one who is not in the same state* (ḥāl) *or moment* (waqt) *can understand what that person is saying. Implicit in the conjunction between the literary context and the experiential context is the famous "union hadith," which Sarraj had cited already in the defense of an earlier utterance: "When I love my servant . . . I become the hearer with which he hears, the seeing with which he sees . . . and the tongue with which he speaks." In this hadith, the deity states that he becomes the tongue with which the human speaks; thus Bistami could have been "quoting" divine speech—not from the sacred scriptures, but rather from an experience of mystical union in which the divine speaks through Bistami.*

The intricate and solid organization of the sections allows the reader to place the statements of Bistami and Junayd into critical encounter with one another, on their own, and then to see them in the light of Sarraj's illuminating critical framework and comments on particular issues. The issues are profound, the statements (particularly those by Junayd) are often, at the same time, polemical, critically acute, and metaphorically overdetermined—at once incisive and enigmatic. It is with relief, then, that the reader encounters Sarraj's frustration with the ambiguous nature of Junayd's language and Sarraj's citation of the view (playing upon his own experiential argument) that only those who had experienced what Junayd was talking about could decipher his cryptic symbolism. This "defense" of Junayd's opaqueness is an exquisite repayment to Junayd for his "defense" of Bistami, which often suggested that Bistami spoke opaquely.

The last part of the essay brings in a number of other controversial sayings of Bistami, such as his saying over a Jewish cemetery "forgiven" and over a Muslim cemetery "deluded." Most noteworthy, perhaps, is Sarraj's final appeal to Khadir (Khidr), the mysterious figure in the Qur'an (above, Chapter 1) whose actions seemed outrageous to his follower, Moses, (as they would have seemed to any rational person) until their true meaning was revealed.

Finally, in passing, Sarraj notes in an angry response to the Salimiyya that "the learned of our regions take blessings (yatabarrakūna) *at the tomb of Abu Yazid (God grant him compassion) down to the present day," and that earlier shaykhs used "to pay visit to him* (yazūrūnahu) *and take blessings from his devotions." This is a historically important statement. According to later purifiers of Islam, such as Ibn Taymiyya and the later Wahhabi sect, which now dominates the Kingdom of Saudi Arabia, the customs of "taking blessings" at the tomb of a holy person, or making visits to such a person or tomb (what can be called* baraka *Islam), was pure* bid'a, *"innovation," a late corruption of early Islam. Yet here is clear evidence that at the time of Sarraj, such popular veneration of saints and their tombs, which is still widely practiced throughout the Islamic world despite the most vehement efforts of would-be reformers, was viewed as perfectly compatible with Islam. Sarraj would even go so far as to appeal to them in his defense of the otherwise controversial Bistami, with the belief—clearly present in Sarraj's time—that such customs went back all the way to the time of Bistami.*

1. The Shaykh (God grant him compassion) said: I heard Ibn Sālim saying one day in his assembly:

> Pharaoh would not have said what Abu Yazid (God's compassion upon him) said. Pharaoh said (79:24): "I am your highest lord." "The lord" is a name that can be applied to the creature. We say "so and so is lord of a home, lord of property, and lord of a house." However Abu Yazid (God grant him compassion) said: *"subḥānī subḥānī* [glory to me, glory to me!]." Glorification and glory-to-me *(subbūḥ wa subḥānī)* form one of the names of Allah Most High. Such a name should not be applied to any other than Allah.

I said to him, "In your own mind you are right in attributing these words to Abu Yazid (God grant him compassion) and you are right in saying that his belief in saying them was similar to what Pharaoh believed in saying "I am your highest lord."

Ibn Salim responded, "He did indeed say that, and I am right in saying—whatever he meant by it—that his saying contains unbelief."

I said, "When you are not in a position to testify to what he believed in saying what he did, your charge of unbelief is invalid." His words might have had an introduction, which he followed by saying *subḥānī subḥānī* as a way of citing Allah's words *subḥānī subḥānī.* If we heard a man saying "There is no god but I, worship me!" (20:14; 21:25) there would not be any doubt in our hearts. We would know that he was reciting the Qur'an or that he was depicting Allah, be he exalted, in the same terms as Allah depicted himself. If that is the situation, as we have described it, then your charge of unbelief against a man famous for austerity, worship, knowledge, and understanding is of the highest absurdity. Now I set out for the city of

Bistam and asked some relatives of Abu Yazid (God's compassion upon him) about this report. They disclaimed it, saying "We know nothing of it." And unless it is current on the lips of the people or recorded by them in books, I have not bothered recalling it.[32]

2. And I have also heard Ibn Salim reporting in his assembly that Abu Yazid said: "I pitched my tent in the environs of the throne *('arsh)* or at the throne." He went on to say that such words were infidelity and that only the unfaithful would say such a thing. He also said that one time Abu Yazid (God grant him compassion) passed by a Jewish cemetery and said "forgiven!" and passed by a Muslim cemetery and said "deluded."

And despite his stature, Ibn Salim would go too far in his attack on Abu Yazid (God grant him compassion) and would even accuse him of infidelity in saying these things.

I said to him "God forgive you!" The learned of our regions take blessings *(yatabarrakūna)* at the tomb of Abu Yazid (God's compassion upon him) down to the present day. And they report about the earlier shaykhs that they used to pay visit to him *(yazūrūnahu)* and take blessings from his devotions *(du'āyahu)*. They considered him one of the most exalted of worshipers and renouncers and people of wisdom *(ma'rifa)* in Allah. They recall that he surpassed the people of his age in conscientiousness and striving *(ijtihād)* and the uninterrupted remembrance of Allah Most High.

Some people have even related that they saw him engaged in remembrance *(dhikr)* of Allah Most High until he urinated blood from awe of the Most High and from the continuance of his exalting of Allah Most High and Transcendent. So how are we to believe him guilty of infidelity because of some report about him, when we did not know what he intended in what he said[33] and we have not ascertained his state *(ḥālihi)* in the moment *(waqt)* in which he spoke? Then can we judge him concerning what has reached us about him except after experiencing a state like his state and a moment like his moment and an ecstatic experience *(wajd)* like his *wajd*?

Did not Allah Most High say (49:12) "O you who believe, avoid too much opinion—some opinion is sin." Those are the words that occurred with Ibn Salim in his assembly concerning the reports he related about Abu Yazid, God grant him compassion, or words of the same meaning or near to that meaning.

3. Now as for his saying, "I pitched my tent in the environs of the throne or at the throne"—if it is true that he said that—it is a known fact that all of humankind, creation itself, and each and every thing that Allah has created

are under the throne and in front of the throne. His saying "I pitched my tent in front of the throne" means "I faced my tent toward the lord of the throne." There is not a single footspace in the entire world that is not in front of the throne, so there is no inroad in that for the faultfinder to launch his attack.

4a. But as for his saying as he passed a Jewish cemetery "forgiven!"—that is, "as if they were forgiven"—it is as if he had gazed into the unhappiness and the Judaism Allah had ordained for them without any deed on their part having been committed in pre-eternity, and saw that Allah ordained resentment against them as part of their lot.[34] So how could they have been made agents of any deed other than the deed of the people who are resented? Therefore he spoke as if they were forgiven, but they are not forgiven in respect to what the pen has set down, what the book has pronounced, and the words Allah has attributed to them: (9:30) "Ezra is the son of God" and (5:18) "We are God's sons and favorites." Allah Most High is just in all that he has decreed, judicious in all that he has traced; (21:23) "He will not be asked to account for what he is doing; rather it is they who will be asked."

4b. And as for his saying, as he passed by a Muslim cemetery, "deluded!"—if it is true that he said that—it is as if he had observed the habits of the majority of Muslims who look to their deeds and who desire to gain salvation through their own interpretive endeavor *(ijtihād)*. Few are they who can free themselves from that! Therefore he called them deluded because all the acts of humankind—if placed alongside a single grace bestowed by Allah upon humankind, through which he guided them to him and adorned their hearts with faith and with the *ma'rifa* of his unity *(wahdāniyya)*—would be exposed as futile and would dwindle away. In all of creation there is not a single movement and not a single breath that does not originate from Allah Most High and end in Allah Most High and Transcendent. Whoever thinks anyone is saved other than through the favor of Allah and the profusion of his compassion is deluded, lost. Do you not know that the lord of the prophets and the Imam of the godfearing said: "There is among us no one who will be saved by his own deed," and when asked, "Not even you?" responded, "Not even I, unless the compassion of Allah envelops me."

5. The learned faultfinding and rush to attack and judgment—all on the basis of a report or a statement whose moment *(waqt)* is inaccessible to understanding, against a man whose bodily members are controlled and di-

rected with knowledge and *adab*—is a mistake for a learned person, a lapse for a sage, and a manifest error for one of intelligence. The maxim of a sage may be distorted against him. His maxim may have become current and been exposed to one who did not attain its meanings and whose understanding did not reach the intentions of its speaker. Thus it circulates on the tongues of people with a meaning contrary to its meaning, provoking criticism of the sage from those who do not perceive his goal and obscure his intended meaning without any perspective upon his situation and without asking for any clarification. The depths of knowledge are fathomed only by the depths of understanding.

6. A maxim *(ḥikma)* can suffer two kinds of distortion. One kind is distortion of the letters of the words, and that is the easier to correct. The second kind is distortion in meaning. That occurs when the sage *(ḥakīm)* speaks his word out of a particular moment and a condition to which the one listening has not attained. The latter is then led to distort its meaning and express it in a way incompatible with [the original] condition and moment and station. So he will fall into error and be led to ruin.

I heard Abū ʻAmr ibn ʻAlwān say: I heard Junayd say: "When I was a youth I frequented a certain circle in which I heard people say what I did not understand. However, my heart was safeguarded from renouncing them. Thus I attained to the position I have now."

7. What I have recalled here is reinforced by my experience in the circle of Ibn Salim in Basra after the controversy between us over the words of Abu Yazid. One day Ibn Salim related of Abu Yazid that he said: "Remembrance *(dhikr)* of Allah Most High with the tongue is raving. Remembrance of Allah Most High with the heart is *waswasa* (the whispering associated with Satan)."[35]

When asked about that, Ibn Salim said that it was as if Sahl had wished to affirm the one remembered rather than the remembrance.

In another assembly he reported of Sahl ibn ʻAbdullah (at-Tustari) that he said: "My master does not sleep and I do not sleep." So I said to one of Ibn Salim's specially chosen companions [in the third person, highly formal form]:

> If the Shaykh were not more inclined toward Sahl ibn ʻAbdullah than he is toward Abu Yazid, he would have accused him of error in what was reported of him, just as he accused Abu Yazid in front of you of error and infidelity in the words that were reported of

> him. For in what was related from Sahl, who was his Imam and the Imam of people in his estimation, there were propositions open to the faultfinder to criticize, should he so wish. And it is well known that, in what was related of Sahl ibn 'Abdullah, there is a something beyond that which the faultfinder makes an occasion for attack. Similarly, it could be that the words related from Abu Yazid contain a dimension beyond that which caused him to be accused of heresy.

He had no response and nothing to say to that.

This is close to the meaning of what was said.[36]

In Allah is success.

8. Someone said: Had not Allah chosen Moses for infallibility, prophetic support, and had he not embraced him with prophetic illumination, speech, and the role of messenger, so that he was given success and kept back from renouncing Khadir when he killed a person, an action prohibited by Allah and one of the greatest sins, Moses would not have wished to say to Khadir (18:74–75): "You have killed an innocent who had killed no one. You have committed an outrage!"

Nor, when Khadir replied: "Didn't I tell you that you would not be able to remain patient with me?" would Moses have wished to say: "If I ask you about anything again, do not allow me to accompany you further. You have my apologies," after he watched him kill, an action Allah has forbidden and for which he has ordered retaliation.

It was incumbent upon Moses to seek retribution against him, to abandon him, and to consider unlawful his circle and his companionship. However he was kept from doing that by the care of Allah for him, his selection of him, his withstraining of him, and his granting him the success which he made his companion. This is the habit of every Godfriend and every sincere one until the day of resurrection, even though none of them can ever attain the rank of prophecy. Allah alone leads us successfully to the proper course.

9. It is also related of Abu Yazid that he would never rest against a wall unless it were the wall of a mosque or retreat. It is also said that he was never seen breaking fast except on the days of the festival of fast-breaking until he met God.[37] There are many other similar reports about him.

♦ ♦ ♦

THE OTHER BISTAMI: THE BIOGRAPHIES OF SULAMI AND QUSHAYRI

Introduction

The portrait of Bistami that comes to us through his biographers Sulami (d. 412/1021) and Qushayri (d. 465/1074) inverts the method Sarraj utilizes in his portrait of Bistami and balances the portrait. Sarraj discussed the more controversial ecstatic utterances of Bistami, put them within a complex interpretive framework, and emphasized the hermeneutic principle that one cannot judge an utterance unless one not only knows its complete context, but also experiences the moment (waqt) *or condition* (ḥāl) *out of which it was spoken. Finally, Sarraj questions whether Bistami actually said the words attributed to him, stating that he, Sarraj, even traveled to the city of Bistam to ask its residents if they had recorded in their oral tradition such sayings of their most famous native son.*

As opposed to Sarraj's text, Sulami's and Qushayri's biographies are lists of sayings attributed to Bistami, without any interpretive gloss on the part of the biographers. The two biographers begin by establishing the isnād, *the listed chain of authorities, for each saying, placing the sayings within the isnad format found in the hadith or sayings of Muhammad. They were concerned with codifying and legitimizing a science of Sufism* ('ilm at-taṣawwuf) *as a discipline that could be transmitted formally in the religious school* (madrasa) *system. Sulami makes explicit the connection with hadith science by beginning, after the reference to Bistami's death, with a hadith of the Prophet in which Bistami is part of the isnad. Sulami and Qushayri present the sayings without commentary, and the sayings they present raise a set of issues quite different from those raised by ecstatic utterances in Sarraj.*

In both biographies, there is a tension between a mystical shari'a-rigorism, on the one hand, and a validation of mystical knowing (ma'rifa) *over worship* ('ibāda) *on the other. (The sayings are listed by number in the text below; references to any saying in this introduction will include the number of the saying as it appears in the text below.)*

The mystical sensibility to the shari'a is most vividly recalled in the Sulami account (no. 9) of Bistami leading a group of worshipers in prayer.

Bistami senses something wrong. He has a conversation with a man in the group who then gets up and leaves. When asked about it later, the man says that Bistami asked him if he had made the ritual ablutions mandatory before prayer. The man said he had made the sand-ablution (tayammum) *and Bistami responded that sand-ablutions, which are meant to allow for the exigencies of travel in the desert where water is unavailable for ablutions, were not permitted in town. What is remarkable about this episode is not simply that Bistami applied strictly the shari'a regulations about ablutions before prayer, but that he was so steeped in the shari'a that he was able to sense that someone in the prayer group had not performed the proper ablutions. Qushayri (no. 9) places this sensibility in terms of the "observance of boundaries"* (ḥifẓ al-ḥudūd), *that is, the complex topography of boundaries of sacred space and time that is articulated by the shari'a. He also expresses this sensibility in sayings (Sulami 3, Qushayri 4, 10) on* adab, *the proper behavior and sensitivity in relations with the divine.*

In balance with this mystical shari'a-mindedness is a series of sayings that posit a hierarchy. Those who only follow the strictures of proper worship are in a category below those who follow the path of knowing (ma'rifa). *What is this knowing? Knowing is strongly distinguished (Sulami 10, Qushayri 3) from knowledge* ('ilm), *which is the information accumulated within the tradition through the ulama, the religious, intellectual establishment. Beyond the knowledge of the ulama and beyond observance of the shari'a, the path of knowing entails free devotions (devotions beyond those enjoined in the shari'a) and asceticism (Sulami 25, 28, Qushayri 2). Interestingly, the sayings show that Bistami worried, not about being considered an antinomian free-thinker, but rather about being considered overly ascetic.*[38] *Throughout the two collections of sayings, Bistami is shown building a justification for the ascetic life as a taming of the craving of appetite* (shahwā: *Sulami 11).*

The sayings also take up the difficult issue of celibacy. Unlike Christianity, whose founder was portrayed as celibate and whose mysticism was largely grounded in monastic and cenobitic celibate life, early Islam never embraced celibacy as an ideal; indeed there is little room for it in the spirituality of pre-Sufi Islam. Muhammad, viewed as a human messenger of God, followed the custom of his time and had several wives, in addition to participating in a number of politically motivated marriages.

Once having justified the appropriateness of a celibate and ascetic life (Qushayri 5—where he asks to be freed from the need for food and women), Bistami is quick to point out the danger of reliance on asceticism, and the paradoxical manner in which asceticism can increase the attachments it is supposed to eliminate; as in Sulami 29: "The concern of the knower is the object of his hope; the concern of the renunciate is what he eats." The final position is expressed in Sulami 31: The mystical knower ('ārif) *will renounce everything that distracts him from the one God. Asceticism is not and should not be a goal; it may be part of the process of giving up all distractions from the one God, the only goal and pursuit of the knower.*

The sayings of Bistami in Sulami and Qushayri focus on social and moral questions, such as the homily on reconciliation (Sulami 24). Yet within the formal framework of isnad and sayings, and among the various sayings on strict observance of the shari'a and proper behavior in relations with the divine, are some powerful theological discussions. In Sulami 22, Bistami makes his famous remark—compatible with the key union hadith of free devotions—that he had erred in thinking he was "remembering him, recognizing him, loving him, and seeking him," when in fact it was the divine beloved working these acts through him. In Sulami 26–27, Bistami offers a stinging comment from the apophatic perspective; those who refer most often to deity are those furthest away from deity. In Sulami 12, he affirms the authentic love associated with sayings of Rabi'a, that is, a love of the divine beloved beyond all concern for paradise and punishment.

The biographies by Sulami and Qushayri have been placed together here because they reflect a similar method and a similar image of Bistami. It is obvious that Qushayri is modeling his biography on that of Sulami, and the beginnings of the two biographies are almost identical. There are, however, some subtle differences between the two accounts; for example, in Qushayri 6, Qushayri cites a saying of Bistami on the authority of Sulami that does not appear in Sulami's text. Together the two biographies show us a complex Bistami, one who is capable of radical theological critiques, balanced social and moral reflection, and psychologically sensitive homiletic advice. However we evaluate the historicity of Bistami, the figure of Bistami in Sufi tradition has little to do with common portrayals of him as an intoxicate antinomian incompatible with Islamic thought.[39]

THE SAYINGS OF ABU YAZID AL-BISTAMI

From Abū 'Abd ar-Raḥmān as-Sulamī (412/1021) Tabaqāt al-Awliyā' [*Ranks of the Friends of God*][40]

Among them [the friends of God] is Abū Yazīd Ṭayfūr ibn 'Isā ibn Sarūshān. His grandfather, Sarushan, was a Magian who converted to Islam. There were three brothers: Adam, Tayfur, and 'Ali.

Each of them was a renunciate and a worshiper and a possessor of mystical states *(arbāb aḥwāl)*. Abu Yazid was of the people of Bistām.

1. He died in the year 261 [H], according to what I [Sulami] heard. I heard 'Abdullāh ibn 'Alī say: I heard Ṭayfūr ibn 'Isā the Younger say: I heard 'Ammī al-Bisṭāmi say: I heard my father say: "Abu Yazid died in 261."[41]

However, I also heard Al-Ḥusayn ibn Yaḥyā say: "Abu Yazid died in the year 234 [H]." Allah knows best.

2. In Baghdad, Abū l-Ḥasan Manṣūr ibn 'Abd Allāh ad-Dīmarti related to us that Abū 'Amr, 'Uthmān ibn Jaḥda Darāhama al-Kāzarūnī said: Abū l-Fatḥ, Aḥmad ibn al-Ḥusayn ibn Muḥammad ibn Sahl, al-Miṣrī, known as ibn al-Ḥimsi, the preacher in Basra, said: 'Ali ibn Ja'far al-Baghdādī said: Abū Mūsā Ad-Daybulī said: Abu Yazid al-Bistami said: Abu 'Abd ar-Rahmān as-Suddī related on the authority of 'Amr ibn Qays al-Mulā'i, on the authority of 'Aṭiyya al-'Awfi, on the authority of Abu Sa'id al-Khudrī that the Envoy of God, God's blessings and peace upon him, said:

> It is a mark of weakness of certitude that you would have people be content with resenting Allah Almighty, that you would praise them according to Allah's bestowal, or that you should blame them because of what Allah has not given. The bestowal of Allah is not divided according to the greed of the greedy nor repulsed by the aversion of the averse. Allah, in his wisdom and glory, places the spirit and prosperity in contentment and certainty, and places care and sorrow in difficulty and wrath.[42]

3. I heard al-Ḥasan ibn 'Alī ibn Ḥanawiyya ad-Dāmighānī say: I heard al-Ḥasan ibn 'Alawiyya say: Abu Yazid said:

> One night I sat in my *mihrāb* (prayer niche). When I stretched out my leg a voice called out: "Whoever sits with kings must show proper behavior."

4. With the same isnad:

> Abu Yazid was asked about the ranking of the knower *('ārif)*. He said: "There is no rank there. Rather, the greatest benefit of the knower is the existence of the one known."[43]

5. With the same isnad, Abu Yazid said:

> The worshiper worships through the condition *(ḥāl)* and the knower, the attainer, worships in the condition.

6. With the same isnad:
Abu Yazid was asked: "What should be one's support in worship?"
He replied: " 'O God,' if you know him."

7. With the same isnad, Abu Yazid said:
The least thing incumbent upon the knower is that he be granted that over which he has already been placed in charge.[44]

8. With the same isnad, Abu Yazid said:
Whoever calls the group to the trial of the real should place upon himself the occasions of worship.[45]

9. I heard Manṣūr ibn 'Abdullah say: I heard Abū 'Imrān, Mūsā ibn 'Isā known as 'Ammī, say: I heard my father say:

Once Abu Yazid recited the call to prayer. When he wished to lead the performance of the prayer, he looked at the row of worshipers and saw a man who showed the traces of travel. Abu Yazid approached him and said something to him. The man rose and left the mosque.

One of those present asked the man about it. He said: "I had been traveling and performed the ablution with sand. Abu Yazid said to me: 'The ablution with sand is not appropriate in town.' I remembered that was the case and left."[46]

10. With the same isnad, Abu Yazid said:[47]
I engaged in the struggle for thirty years and found nothing more difficult than knowledge and the following of knowledge. Had it not been for the disagreement of the ulama, I would have continued in this way. The disagreement of the ulama is a mercy except in the pure affirmation of unity *(tawḥīd)*.

11. With the same isnad, Abu Yazid said:
No one knows himself who is accompanied by the craving of appetite.[48]

12. With the same isnad, Abu Yazid said:
Paradise is of no concern to the people of love, and the people of love are loved through their love.

13. I heard Abū 'Amr Muḥammad ibn Aḥmad ibn Ḥamdān say: I found in the handwriting of my father: I heard Abu 'Uthmān, Sa'īd ibn Ismā'īl say: Abu Yazid said:

Whoever listens to speech in order to converse with people, Allah will nourish him with the understanding to converse with people. Whoever listens in order to engage with Allah through them in his act, Allah will nourish him with the understanding to engage in intimate conversation with his lord Almighty.

14. With the same isnad, Abu Yazid said:
Allah has looked upon the hearts of his friends. Those who are unable to bear pure knowing, he has occupied with worship.

15. With the same isnad, Abu Yazid said:
The infidelity of the people of inner resolve is sounder than the faith of the people of tradition.[49]

16. With the same isnad, Abu Yazid was asked:
"How is knowing attained?" He replied: "By losing whatever you have and by relying upon whatever he has."

17. I heard Abu Naṣr al-Harawī say: [I heard Ya'qūb ibn Isḥāq say: I heard Ibrāhīm al-Harawī say] I heard Abu Yazid say:

This is my joy in you while I fear you. What will be my joy when I feel safe in you?

18. With the same isnad, Abu Yazid said:
O lord, let me understand you. I cannot understand from you except through you.

19. With the same isnad, Abu Yazid said:
I recognized Allah through Allah and I recognized what was below Allah through the light of Allah Almighty.[50]

20. I heard Manṣūr ibn 'Abdullāh say: I heard Ya'qūb ibn Isḥāq say: I heard Ibrāhīm al-Harawī say: I heard Abu Yazid al-Bistami—

He was asked: "What is the mark of the knower?"

He said: "He does not slacken in his remembrance of him, and he does not tire from the reality of him, and he does not keep company with any other than him."[51]

21. With the same isnad, Abu Yazid said:
God Most High enjoined upon worshipers his command and his prohibition, and they obeyed. He bestowed upon them his robe of honor and they were distracted from him by robes of honor. I do not wish from Allah anything other than Allah.[52]

22. With the same isnad, Abu Yazid said:
I erred in the beginning in four things. I thought that I was remembering him, recognizing him, loving him, and seeking him. Finally I realized that his remembrance preceded my remembrance; his act of recognition preceded my act of recognition; his love was older than my love; he sought me first so that I could then seek him.[53]

23. I heard Abū Faraj 'Abd al-Waḥīd ibn Bakr al-Warthānī say: al-Ḥasan ibn Ibrāhīm ad-Dāmighāni said: Mūsā ibn 'Isā said: I heard my father say: I heard Abu Yazid say:
My God, you have created your creation without their knowledge and have adorned them with faith without their will. If you don't help them, who will?

24. I heard Abū l-Ḥasan, 'Alī ibn Muḥammad, al-Qazwīnī aṣ-Ṣūfī, say: I heard Abu ṭ-Ṭayyab al-'Akkī say: I heard Ibn al-Anbārī say: One of the students of Abu Yazid said: Abu Yazid al-Bistami said to me:
If a person is your companion and abuses your intimacy, go to see him with the best behavior, that your life might be sweetened. If you are met with grace, begin with gratitude to Allah Almighty, for he is the one who turns people's hearts to you. If you are tried, turn to him immediately to bring about reconciliation, for he alone, not any creature, is the one with power to reveal it.

25. I heard 'Abd al-Wāḥid ibn Bakr say: I heard al-Qannād say: Abū Mūsā ad-Daybulī said: I heard Abu Yazid al-Bistami say:
Allah has provided his worshipers with sweets, and on account of the joy they take in them, he has forbidden them the realities of nearness.

26. With the same isnad, Abu Yazid said:
The furthest of creatures from Almighty God are those who refer to him the most!

27. I heard Aḥmad ibn 'Alī say: I heard al-Ḥasan ibn 'Alawī say: Abu Yazid said:

Knowing anything about the essence of the real is ignorance; knowledge of the reality of knowing is perplexity; referring is idolatry on the part of one who refers.[54]

28. I heard al-Ḥusayn al-Fārisī say: I heard al-Ḥasan ibn 'Alawī say: Abu Yazid was asked: "How have you experienced *(wajadta)* this knowing?" He replied: "With a hungry belly and a body naked."[55]

29. With the same isnad, Abu Yazid said:
The concern of the knower is the object of his hope; the concern of the renunciate is what he eats.

30. With the same isnad, Abu Yazid said:
Blessed is one whose concern is one, whose heart is not occupied with what his eyes have seen and his ears have heard.

31. With the same isnad, Abu Yazid said:
Whoever knows Allah will be an ascetic in everything that distracts him from him.[56]

32. With the same isnad,
Abu Yazid was asked about the tradition *(sunna)* and the obligation *(farīḍa)*. He said: "Tradition is the leaving behind of the world and obligation is keeping company with the master. Tradition, all of it, points to the leaving behind of the world, while the Book, all of it, points to keeping company with the master. Whoever has learned the tradition and the obligation has been perfected."[57]

33. With the same isnad, Abu Yazid said:
Bliss is everlasting; gratitude for bliss should be everlasting as well.

QUSHAYRI'S BIOGRAPHY OF BISTAMI

Al-Qushayri (465/1074), from The Risala among the Shaykhs of This Path Is Abu Yazid Tayfur ibn 'Isa al-Bistami[58]

1. His grandfather was a Magian who accepted Islam. Abu Yazid was one of three brothers, Adam, Tayfur, and 'Ali, each of whom was a renunciate and servant of God. Abu Yazid was the most illustrious of them all in his

mystical condition *(ḥāl)*. Some say he died in the year 261 [H]; others say he died in 234 [H].

2. I heard Muḥammad ibn al-Ḥusayn say: I heard Abū l-Ḥasan al-Fārisī say: I heard al-Ḥasan ibn ʿAlī say:

> Abu Yazid was asked: "Where did you find *(wajadta)* this knowing?" He replied: "In a hungry belly and a body naked."

3. I heard Muḥammad ibn al-Ḥusayn, Allah grant him mercy, say: I heard Manṣūr ibn ʿAbdullah say: I heard ʿAmmī al-Bisṭāmī say: I heard my father say: I heard Abu Yazid say:

> I engaged in the struggle for thirty years and found nothing more difficult than knowledge and the following of knowledge. Had it not been for the disagreement of the ulama, I would have continued in this way. The disagreement of the ulama is a mercy except in the pure affirmation of unity.[59]

It is also said that Abu Yazid did not leave this world until he had memorized the entire Qur'an.

4. Abū Ḥātim as-Sijistānī informed us that Abū Naṣr as-Sarrāj informed us, saying: I heard Ṭayfur al-Bisṭāmī say: I heard the one known as ʿAmmī al-Bisṭāmī say: I heard my father say:

> Abu Yazid said: "Come along with us as we go see that man who had proclaimed himself as possessing godfriendship *(wilāya)*." He was a man much sought after and renowned for renunciation. So we went to see him. When he came out of his house and entered the mosque, he spat in the direction of Mecca. Abu Yazid turned away without saluting him, saying: "He cannot be trusted in one of the proper behaviors of the messenger of Allah Most High. How then can he be trusted in what he claims?"[60]

5. With the same isnad, Abu Yazid is reported to have said:

> I resolved to ask Allah Most High to free me of the burden of food and the burden of women. Then I said to myself: "How can I ask Allah for something that the God-sent never asked for?"[61] I did not ask. Then Allah, praised beyond praise, freed me from the burden of women until I no longer took note whether it was a woman I encountered or a wall.

6. I heard Shaykh Abū 'Abd ar-Raḥmān as-Sulamī, Allah have mercy on him, say: I heard al-Ḥasan ibn 'Alī say: I heard 'Ammī al-Bisṭāmī say:

I heard my father say I asked Abu Yazid about his beginning and his renunciation.

He said: "Renunciation has no station."

I asked: "Why?"

He said: "Because I spent three days in renunciation. When the fourth day came, I left it behind. The first day I renounced this world and what it contains. The second day I renounced the world to come and what it contains. The third day I renounced everything other than God. When the fourth day arrived, nothing remained for me other than God. I understood. I heard a voice saying: 'Abu Yazid, you will not be able to endure being with us.'

"I said: 'This is what I want.'

"I heard a voice saying: 'You've found. You've found!' "[62]

7. Abu Yazid was asked

"What is the hardest thing you encountered on the path to Allah?"

He said: "I can't describe it."

He was asked: "What is the easiest thing your self encountered from you?"

He said: "As far as that, yes: I called it to some of the acts of obedience and it did not respond, so I forbade it water for a year."[63]

8. Abu Yazid also said:

For thirty years as I performed the prayer, the belief I held within myself in each prayer performed was as if I were a Magian wishing to cut my belt.[64]

9. I heard Muḥammad ibn al-Ḥusayn (Allah's mercy upon him) say: I heard 'Abd Allah ibn 'Alī say: I heard Mūsā ibn 'Isā say: My father said I heard Abu Yazid say:

If you see a man who has been given such divine favors *(karamāt)* that he rises into the air, do not be deceived. Watch and see how you find him with the command and prohibition, the guarding of the boundaries *(ḥifẓ al-ḥudūd)* and the carrying out of the shari'a.

10. 'Ammī al-Bisṭāmī related from his father that he said:

Abu Yazid went out one night to the retreat-house *(rabbāṭ)* in order to remember Allah, most praised, near the walls of the retreat. He remained there until morning without pronouncing the remembrance. I asked him about it. He said: "I remembered a word that came to my mouth in the condition of my youth and was ashamed to mention his name, Praised beyond Praise."

♦ ♦ ♦

THE MI'RAJ OF BISTAMI

INTRODUCTION

The story of the Mi'raj (heavenly ascent) of Abū Yazīd al-Bisṭāmī can be found in a number of accounts, including the biography of Bistami in 'Attar's Memorial of the Friends of God. *One of the earlier accounts is found in a text entitled the* Quest for God (al-qaṣd ilā llāh), *which is attributed to Abū l-Qāsim al-Junayd, but which was more likely composed considerably after Junayd's death.*

The ninth chapter of this work contains the account of Bistami's Mi'raj. One can immediately discern its connection to the mystical utterance of Bistami discussed by Sarraj (see Chapter 6 in this volume) in which Bistami discusses flying like a bird through realms and realms. The symbolic cosmology is based, of course, on the Mi'raj account of Muhammad. However, there is more involved in this text than a Sufi appropriation of the account of Muhammad's Mi'raj. The early Mi'raj accounts of Muhammad are themselves part of a rich and complex Near Eastern tradition of heavenly ascents, a tradition that includes the Enoch texts, most notably, the Enoch tradition and the account of the heavenly ascent of Moses). The parallels between Bistami's Mi'raj and the Jewish Merkavah (divine chariot) mystical tradition are particularly striking.[65]

Such parallels do not show that the Bistami Mi'raj was dependent on any particular Merkavah source, nor that the Merkavah tradition was dependent on the Mi'raj accounts. What the parallels reflect, rather, is the role of a partially shared symbolic cosmology of the heavenly ascent as one of the major meeting points—and arenas for interreligious and intrareligious contention—in the late antique and medieval Near East.[66] *With the tradition of Bistami's Mi'raj, the Sufis place the mystical ascent within this arena, echoing, reversing, and appropriating key themes or images of earlier accounts of heavenly ascent.*

The central drama of Bistami's ascent through the heavens is the rivalry between the human Abu Yazid and the angelic guardians of each heaven. This rivalry had been reflected in the Qur'anic story of the angels' protest over the creation of Adam (2:30), "a creature who will spill blood and corrupt the earth." The rivalry for control of the heavenly spheres was reflected as well in a multireligious and multidisciplinary context: in Bistami's Mi'raj, the ascensions of Enoch, in the Hermetic spheres of the Harranians, and in the cosmology of the philosophers such as Ibn Sina. In some cases prophets ruled the spheres. In some cases, as with the Harranians, angels or spirit-beings (ruḥāniyyāt) *ruled. With the philosophers, pure intellects* ('uqūl) *governed the spheres. The guardians of the spheres could be friendly or unfriendly. The human could pass through the spheres by knowing a password, by inner sincerity, or through some other test or trial. What is at stake in these symbolic worlds is the goal of the mystical path: to become more purely intellectual, more angelic, or more deeply human.*[67]

With Bistami, a voice rises out of his inner heart-secret refusing the temptations (rewards of paradise) offered by the angels. In refusing the rewards of paradise, Bistami follows the example of Rabi'a, but in this Mi'raj story the setting is transformed from debates among religious scholars in Basra or at Mecca to refusal of angels' temptations in each of the seven heavens. With each refusal to stop at a heavenly station, Bistami affirms the inherent dynamism of Sufi thought, the refusal to stop at any given station of mystical attainment. With each Bistami refusal, the glorious angel is reduced to the like of a mosquito in the eyes of the heavenly voyager.

In many heavenly ascent texts, the arrival at the divine throne is filled with ambiguity and identity confusion. Is the figure on the throne a deity, an angel, a prophet, Satan, or an idol? A frequent motif is the danger of reflections. The human heavenly voyager might see his image reflected in the polished tiles of the divine throne, and a mistake in interpreting the reflections can cause disaster. The voyager is in particular danger of confusing the polished reflecting tiles with water and thinking he is drowning. In the Merkavah texts, the trials of the human tend also toward trial by fire, a purification in which the human is burned up and transformed. With Bistami, it is light imagery that takes over from fire and that unifies the various heavens.

At the culmination of Bistami's ascent, there is the experience of mystical union, depicted as a "melting like lead," after which Bistami achieves a state of nearness to the deity:

And when Allah Most High and Glorious knew the sincerity of my will in quest for him, he called out "to me, to me!" and said O my chosen one (ṣafī), *come near to me and look upon the plains of my splendor and the domains of my brightness. Sit upon the carpet of my holiness until you see the subtleties of my artisanship I-ness. You are my chosen one, my beloved, and the best of my creatures.*

Upon hearing that it was as if I were melting like melting lead. Then he gave me a drink from the spring of graciousness (luṭf) *with the cup of intimacy. Then he brought me to a state that I am unable to describe. Then he brought me closer and closer to him until I was nearer to him than the spirit is to the body.*

THE NINTH CHAPTER OF *AL-QAṢD ILĀ ALLAH*: ON THE VISION OF ABU YAZID IN QUEST FOR ALLAH MOST HIGH WITH AN ELUCIDATION OF HIS QUEST[68]

Abū l-Qāsim al-'Arif, may Allah be pleased with him, said: Know, O you tribes in quest of Allah Most High and Glorious, that Abu Yazid has had states and stations which the hearts of the neglectful and the common people would not be able to bear. He also has secrets with Allah which would astonish the heedless if they could come to know them. In a book containing the virtues of Abu Yazid I have seen things concerning his states and moments and words that would wear out the tongue to describe and depict. Whoever wishes to know Abu Yazid's completeness and rank should regard Abu Yazid's dream and vision, which is sounder in content and more verifiable than is the waking state of others. This is what has been related from the retainer of Abu Yazid,[69] that he said: I heard Abu Yazid al-Bistami, may Allah be pleased with him, say:

I saw myself in the dream as if I had risen to the heavens in quest of Allah, seeking union with Allah Most High that I might abide with him forever. I was tried in a trial that the heavens and earth and everything in them could not stand. He spread out before me gifts of every kind and showed me dominion over every heaven. Throughout, I kept my gaze lowered from these things. I knew he was testing me with them. Through all of this I kept saying: O my dear one, my goal is other than what you are showing me.

He said: I said to him, may Allah have compassion on you! Describe for me some of what he showed you of the dominion over every heaven!

The First Heaven

He said: I saw myself in the dream, as if I had risen to the heavens. When I came to the lowest heaven, I was in the presence of a green bird. It spread out one of its wings and bore me away, taking me as far as some legions of angels who were standing with their feet aflame amidst the stars, praising Allah morning and evening. I saluted them and they returned my salutation. The bird set me down among them and departed. I remained among them and continued to recite Allah's praises and to glorify Allah Most High *(ta'ālā)* in their tongue, while they were saying: This is an Adamite, not a Luminary, who comes among us and speaks to us. He said: I was inspired with words and said: In the name of Allah who is able to release me from all need for you! Then he continued to show me dominion that would wear out the tongue to describe and depict. I knew that he was testing me with it in that. I was saying: My goal is other than what you are showing me. I did not turn toward it out of respect for his sanctity.

The Second Heaven

Then I saw myself as if I had risen to the second heaven. Droves of angels came upon me, gazing at me like people gazing upon a prince who is entering their city. Then the chief of the angels approached me. His name was Lawīdh. He said: O Abu Yazid, your lord offers you salutations and says: You have loved me and I have loved you. He took me as far as a green garden. In it was a flowing river surrounded by flying angels. Every day they would fly to the earth one thousand times to look upon the friends of God, faces radiant as the sun, who had known me according to the *ma'rifa* of the earth, that is, on the earth. Then they approached me, greeted me, and took me down to the shore of that river. Upon its banks were trees of light with numerous boughs hanging out into the air. Upon each bough was the nest of a bird, that is, of one of the angels. And in every nest was an angel bowing down in prayer. Throughout all that, I was saying: O my dear one, my goal is other than what you are showing me. Be for me, dear one, a protector of protectors and a companion of companions. Then there surged up in the secret of my heart something like the thirst of the flame of longing, so that the angels with their trees were reduced to a gnat alongside my aspiration. They were all gazing at me, amazed and astonished at the grandeur of what they saw in me. When Allah Most High knew the sincerity of my will in the quest for him and my self-divestment of everyone beside him, behold, there was an angel extending his hand, drawing me toward him.

The Third Heaven

Then I saw myself as if I had risen to the third heaven. All the angels with all their qualities and attributes had approached me and greeted me. Suddenly from among them an angel stood with four faces:[70] a face turned toward the heaven that wept tears without cease; a face turned toward the earth that cried out: O servants of Allah, the day of cessation![71] the day of seizure! the day of reckoning!; a face whose right side was turned toward angels reciting Allah's praises; and a face whose left side sent forth an army into the quarters of the heavens to chant throughout them the praises of Allah. I saluted him and he returned my salutation. Then he said: Who are you to be preferred over us? I said: a servant whom Allah Most High *(ta'ālā)* has granted a share of his favor. He said: Do you wish to look upon the marvels of Allah? I said "Of course!" He spread out one of his wings and behold: On each of his feathers there was a lamp whose light would darken the sun. Then he said: Come up *(ta'āli)*, O Abu Yazid, and take shade in the shade of my wing where you can recite the praises of Allah until death. Then I said to him: Allah is able to release me from all need for you. Then there surged up from the secret of my heart the bright light of my *ma'rifa*, the brightness of which clouded over theirs, that is, the brightness of the lamps, and the angel was reduced to a gnat alongside my completeness. He continued to show me dominion that would wear out the tongue to describe. Through all that, I knew that he was testing me. I did not turn toward that out of respect for his sanctity. Throughout I was saying: O my dear one! My goal is not what you are showing me. When Allah knew the sincerity of my will in quest for him, behold there was an angel extending his hand and raising me up.

The Fourth Heaven

Then I saw myself as if I had risen to the fourth heaven. There were all the angels with their attributes, figures, and qualities. They approached me, greeted me, and gazed at me like a people gazing at their prince the moment he enters their country. They raised their voices in praise and affirmation of divine unity because of the grandeur they saw in my cutting myself off for him and my refusal to turn to them. An angel greeted me who was said to be named Nayā'īl. He extended his hand and sat me upon a throne *(kursī)* placed upon the shore of a roaring sea whose beginning and end could not be seen. I was inspired with his recitation of praise and found myself pronouncing in his tongue. Still, I did not turn to him. He continued to show me dominion that would wear out the tongue to describe. Through all that, I knew that he was testing me with it. I did not turn to him out of respect for his sanctity. I kept saying: O my dear one! My goal is other than that which you are showing me. When Allah Most High knew the sincerity of my aloneness for him in the quest toward him, behold, there was an angel extending his hand and raising me up to him.

The Fifth Heaven

Then I saw myself as if I had risen to the fifth heaven. There I was in the presence of angels who stood in the fifth heaven with their heads in the sixth, which dropped down light that would make the heavens flash. They all saluted me in various languages and I returned the salutations to them in every language in which they had saluted me. They were amazed at that. They said: O Abu Yazid, come up *(ta'āli)* to recite Allah's praises and unity and we will set aside for you whatever you wish. I did not turn to them out of respect for my lord. At that point, there surged up, in the secret of my heart, springs of longing, and the light of the angels became, in the light that radiated from me, like a lamp placed on the sun. He continued to show me dominion that would wear out the tongue to describe. Through all that, I knew that he was testing me. I kept saying: O my dear one! My goal is other than that which you are showing me. When Allah Most High *(ta'ālā)* knew the sincerity of my will in quest for him, behold there was an angel raising me up to himself.[72]

The Sixth Heaven

Then I saw myself as if I had ascended to the sixth heaven and stood before the angels of longing. They approached me, greeted me, and boasted over me of their longing, so I boasted over them with something of the secret of my heart. He continued to show me dominion that would wear out the tongue to describe. Throughout all that, I knew that he was testing me in these things and I did not turn to them.[73] When Allah Most High saw the sincerity of my will in my quest for him, behold an angel was extending his arm and raising me up to himself.

The Seventh Heaven

Then I saw myself as if I had risen to the seventh heaven. There were a hundred thousand legions of angels greeting me, each legion like the two heavy ones[74] one thousand thousand times. With every angel was a standard of light and under every standard were one thousand thousand angels, the height of each angel a journey of five hundred years.[75] At their front was an angel named Baryā'īl. They saluted me in their language and I returned the salutation in their language. They were amazed at that. Then behold, a crier was crying out: O Abu Yazid, stop, stop, you have arrived at the end! I did not turn toward his words. He continued to show me dominion that would wear out the tongue to describe. Through all that, I knew that he was testing me in it. I kept saying: O my dear one! My goal is other than that which you are showing me. When Allah knew the sincerity of my will in quest for him, he turned me into a bird, each wing feather of which was greater than the distance from East to West one thousand thousand times. I continued flying through the *Malakūt* and roaming through the *Jabarūt*.[76] I cut across kingdom after kingdom, veils after veils, domains after domains, seas after seas, curtains after curtains, until I stood before the angel of the throne *(kursī)*, who received me.

He had a column of light as he greeted me. He said: Take the column. As soon as I took it, the heavens and everything in them were sheltered in the shade of my *ma'rifa* and were illuminated in the light of my longing. All the angels were reduced to a gnat alongside the completeness of my aspiration in quest for him. Through all that, I knew he was testing me with it and I did not turn to it out of respect for the sanctity of my lord, Allah Most High.

I continued to fly and roam kingdom after kingdom, veil after veil, domain after domain, sea after sea, curtain after curtain, until I ended up at a throne. I was received by angels with eyes as numerous as the stars of the heavens. From each eye there was flashing a light that would illumine the viewer. Those lights became lamps. From the interior of the lamps I heard chants of praise and divine unity.

I continued to fly like that until I ended up at a sea of light with crashing waves. Alongside it the light of the sun was darkened. There on the sea was a ship of light. Alongside its light the lights of those seas were darkened.

I continued to cross sea after sea until I ended up at the greatest sea on which was the royal throne *('arsh)* of the Compassionate. I continued to recite his praises until I saw that all that there was—from the throne to the earth, of Cherubim *(karūbiyyīn)*, angels, and the bearers of the royal throne and others created by Allah Most High and Glorious in the heavens and the earth—was smaller, from the perspective of the flight of the secret of my heart in quest for him, than a mustard seed between sky and earth. Then he continued to show me of the subtleties of his beneficence and the fullness of his power and the greatness of his sovereignty what would wear out the tongue to depict and describe. Through all that, I kept saying: O my dear one! My goal is other than that which you are showing me, and I did not turn toward it out of respect for his sanctity. And when Allah Most High and Glorious knew the sincerity of my will in quest for him, he called out "To me, to me!" and said O my chosen one *(ṣafī)*, come near to me and look upon the plains of my splendor and the domains of my brightness.[77] Sit upon the carpet of my holiness until you see the subtleties of my artisanship I-ness. You are my chosen one, my beloved, and the best of my creatures.

Upon hearing that, it was as if I were melting like melting lead. Then he gave me a drink from the spring of graciousness *(luṭf)* with the cup of intimacy. Then he brought me to a state that I am unable to describe. Then he brought me closer and closer to him until I was nearer to him than the spirit is to the body.

Then the spirit of each prophet received me, saluted me, and glorified my situation. They spoke to me and I spoke to them. Then the spirit of Muhammad, the blessings and peace of God be upon him, received me, saluted me, and said: O Abu Yazid: welcome! welcome! Allah has preferred you over many of his creatures. When you return to earth, bear to my community my salutation and give them sincere advice as much as you can and call them to Allah Most High and Glorious. I kept on in this way until I was like he[78] was before creation and only the real remained *(baqiya)* without being or relation or place or position or quality. May his glory be glorified and his names held transcendent!

Abu l-Qāsim al-'Arif said: O tribes of my brothers, I have shown this vision to the most venerable among the people of *ma'rifa*. All of them support it, none deny it. Rather, they accept it as one of the levels of the people who cut themselves off in quest for him. Then they cited the word of the Prophet, the blessings and peace of Allah upon him, that "the servant remains from Allah and Allah is never from him as long as he does not panic. If he panics, then he incurs blame and reckoning." It is also related from the Prophet, blessings and peace of Allah upon him, that "of knowledge there is something like a hidden figure which is known only by the people of knowledge in Allah and which is denied only by the people of heedlessness of Allah." And were it not for a dislike of going on at too much length, we would have mentioned support of the soundness of the story through the sound reports and known and accepted accounts. However, I know that whoever is ignorant of the levels of the chosen and the people of *ma'rifa* will not know *(ya'raf)* their destiny and nobility. Multiplying proofs and elucidation will not suffice them and multiplying arguments and demonstrations will not avail them. In this regard, Allah Most High said (10:101): "Signs and warnings will not avail those who do not believe"; and (7:143): "I will turn away from my signs those who act proud on the earth without reality"; and (29:48): "These are clear signs in the breasts of those to whom knowledge is given. No one ignores our signs except the unjust"; and (29:40): "Whomever Allah does not provide light will have no light." Allah is most knowing of the right.

8

Junayd: On The Affirmation of Unity (Tawḥīd)

Introduction

Abū l-Qāsim al-Junayd was the nephew of the celebrated Sufi Sarī as-Saqaṭī, who was the student of Sahl at-Tustarī. Junayd's teachings brought the Baghdad school of Sufism to a certain culmination; his writings were widely accepted within Sufism and he became known as "Master of the Sect" (Sayyid aṭ-Ṭā'ifa). *He died in Baghdād in 297/910.*

Numerous citations of Junayd's sayings can be found in the biographies and major compendia, but only a few of his complete treatises are extant. For the most part these treatises exist in an often defective text in a single manuscript.[1] *In a poignant comment at the end of the Junayd treatises, the medieval copyist of the manuscript text complains that the text came to him through the intermediary of a non-Arabic speaker* ('ajam) *and offers a number of severe difficulties. God willing, he says, some day in the future a more reliable text can be established. However, unless other manuscript traditions are discovered, the hopes of our anonymous redactor will be further deferred.*

Beyond the poor shape of the text in its single manuscript, there are further difficulties. Even when we are fairly certain of what Junayd's words actually are, the style is often cryptic and contorted. As was shown in the comment by Sarraj (see Chapter 7, section 1 in this volume), Junayd seems to presuppose that his hearer or reader has had the experience about which he is speaking—or, even more radically, that the hearer or reader is able to enter that experience, or some re-creation of it—at the moment of encounter with Junayd's words.

Yet despite (and sometimes by means of) these difficulties, the treatises provide articulations of the Sufi concept of passing away (fanā') as theologically penetrating and intellectually challenging as any early Sufi formulation. They also express a distinctively unrelenting view of the role of balā' (trial, suffering, torment) in Sufi life and thought.

Junayd's writing—even when the text is in clear condition (as in the second essay below)—is particularly resistant to closure, even at the syntactical level. Junayd's words make an implicit but strong demand. They demand a particular and distinctive form of semantic struggle, a re-creation of the experience of trial (balā') so central to Junayd's conception of the mystical.[2]

Presented in this section are four short essays selected out of the surviving treatises on tawḥīd (affirmation of unity). Each essay is introduced with the rather academic-sounding title "Another Point (mas'ala) on Tawḥīd" or "Another Point." Yet beneath a sometimes formal and abstract language is the agonistic and dramatic clash characteristic of Junayd. The first essay is a particularly dense discussion of mystical union, with a full play on the various meanings of the w/j/d radical expounded by Qushayri (see Chapter 3 in this volume): wajd (ecstasy, finding) and wujūd (ecstatic existentiality, found existentiality, founded existentiality). It might be viewed as a kind of automatic writing, a stream of consciousness (and transconsciousness)—what someone has called "an interlocking progression along a mobius strip"[3] —that will be clarified in the succeeding essays.

The second essay is textually more secure than the others; the first two-thirds of it are found in Qushayri (see Chapter 3 in this volume). It gives an indelible and graphic account of the emotive aspects of mystical experience. Most striking is the contrast between the abstract quality of the title "Another Point on Tawḥīd" and the first-person urgency apparent in the first words of the essay: "Fear grips me. Hope unfolds me!"

The third essay furthers the discussion of tawḥīd, with emphasis on the experiential and subjective aspects of affirming unity. The essay begins with a meditation on the act of seeking or quest (ṭalab), with a cryptic discussion of the paradox of the quest: that until the object of quest frees the seeker from the seeker's own anticipation and expectation, the seeker remains trapped in a vicious circle of his own self-will. It then proceeds to the paradox of affirmation of unity. The affirmation of unity (tawḥīd) abides only insofar as the affirmer of unity (muwaḥḥid) passes away in union with the one (al-wāḥid).

The essay then takes up three grades of passing away or annihilation of the self (fanā') *in union with the divine: (1) passing away from one's attributes through the effort of constantly opposing one's ego-self* (nafs); *(2) passing away from one's sense of accomplishment, that is, passing away from "one's share of the sweet deserts and pleasures of obedience"; and (3) passing away from the vision of the reality "of your ecstasies as the sign of the real overpowers you."*

The fourth essay offers four grades of tawḥīd. *The first grade consists of the affirmation of one deity and the denial of all associates or rivals, what we might call the standard monotheistic credal affirmation. The second grade occurs on the plane of exterior acts, that is, the complete harmonization of the person to the one deity through carrying out the ritual activities and the life of shari'a. The third grade adds the harmonization of one's interior actions and life around the single center. The depiction of the fourth stage brings in a reference to a person's being "as he was before he was," that is, in the preexistent state associated with the pre-eternal compact (7:171) of "Am I not your lord? Yes, indeed!"*[4] *With the fourth stage, Junayd culminates the entire discussion within an exploration of the state of being "as one was before one was." Here his language attains a combination of lyricism, rhythm, and theological intensity that defies paraphrase.*

♦ ♦ ♦

ABŪ L-QĀSIM AL-JUNAYD SOME POINTS ON *TAWḤĪD*

ANOTHER POINT ON *TAWḤĪD* (AFFIRMATION OF UNITY)[5]

Know that the first part of the worship of Allah Almighty is knowing him. The root of the knowing of Allah is the affirmation of his unity. Affirming unity demands the negation of all attributes from him, including the how, the whereby, and the where. He indicates himself through himself.

The cause of this indication through himself of himself is his granting of success.[6] From his granting of success occurs the affirmation of unity; from the affirmation of unity occurs the affirmation of his truth; from the affirmation of truth, realization; from the realization of him, the knowing of him; from knowing him, begging a response from him to prayers; from begging a response, refinement toward him; from refinement, clinging to him; from clinging to him, declaration of him; from declaration, bewilderment *(ḥayra);* from bewilderment, the vanishing of declaration. All description is cut off from him. With the vanishing of description, one falls into the realization of existence for him *(al-wujūd lahu);* and from realization of existence one falls into the realization of witness through the vanishing of existence; with the loss of his existence his existence is purified; in his purity, he becomes hidden from his attributes; and from his hiddenness he is made present in his totality. He is nonexistent in his existence and existent in his nonexistence. He was whereby he was not and he was not whereby he was.

Then he was, after he was not, whereby he was—was![7] He was he after he was not-he. He was an existent existent after being a nonexistent existent, for he had emerged from overpowering intoxication into the clarity of waking. He was given back his witness in putting everything back down in its station *(manzil)* and placing each thing in its place, through the ascertaining of his attributes, through the abiding of his traces and the performance of his act, after attaining the culmination of what he has from him.

ANOTHER POINT[8]

Fear grips me. Hope unfolds me. Reality draws me together. The real sets me apart. When he seizes me with fear, he annihilates me from myself through my existence, then preserves me from myself. When he unfolds me in hope, he returns me to myself through my loss, then orders my preservation. When he re-collects me in reality, he makes me present, then calls me. When he sets me apart through the real, he makes me witness the other-than-me, then veils from himself. In all that, he transforms me, rather than making me secure, and desolates me, rather than granting me his intimacy. Through being made present I taste the flavor of my existence. Would that he had annihilated me from myself and compensated me! Or that he had absented me from myself, then revived me, then in annihilation made me bear witness. My annihilation is my abiding. From the reality of my annihilation, he annihilated me from both my abiding and my annihilation. I was, upon the reality of annihilation, without abiding or annihilation, through my abiding and annihilation, for the existence *(wujūd)* of annihilation in abiding, for the existence of my other in my annihilation.

Another Point[9]

Know that you are veiled from yourself by yourself. You will not attain him through yourself. You will attain him only through him. When he manifests to you the vision of clinging-to-him, when he calls you to seek him and you seek him, you will find yourself in the vision of quest through the vision of quest and in your struggle to anticipate your will in quest. You will be veiled until the need for him returns to the seeking, and he becomes your column of support in seeking: by intensification of the quest; by your carrying out the realities of the science of quest; by performance of the conditions that have been imposed upon you in him; by taking care of what has been placed in your care through him for yourself.

He protects you from yourself, and brings you to himself through the passing away of your passing away in your attainment of your aim. He abides in your abiding, that is, the unity of the affirmer of unity abides through the abiding of the one who is one, even as the affirmer of unity passes away. Then you are you. You lacked yourself, and then you came to abide insofar as you passed away.[10]

There are three passings away. The first is the passing away from the attributes, qualities, and dispositions. This passing away occurs through the performance in you of the proofs of your work, through expending effort, through your being at variance with your self, through your confining of your self by reprehending its desire.

The second is the passing away from attention to one's share of the sweet deserts and pleasures of obedience: through the perfect accord of the quest of the real for yourself in cutting you off *(inqitā'ika)* for him; that there might be no intermediary between you and him.

The third passing away is the passing away of yourself from the vision of the reality: passing away from your ecstasies *(mawājīd)* as the sign of the real overpowers you. At that moment you both pass away and abide, and are found truly existent in your passing away; through the found existence *(wujūd)* of your other; upon the abiding of your trace in the disappearance of your name.[11]

Another Point[12]

Know that affirmation of unity *(tawḥīd)* among creatures has four aspects: the affirmation of the common people; the affirmation of the people of realities in exterior knowledge; and two aspects of affirmation among the select, the masters of knowing *(ma'rifa)*.

As for the affirmation of the common people, it consists in the affirmation of unity *(waḥdāniyya)* with the disappearing of any vision of lords, rivals, contraries, forms, or likenesses; and in the reliance upon obstructing desire and fear of any other-than-he. It perfectly fulfills its acts as long as the affirmation abides.[13]

As for the affirmation of the people of realities in exterior knowledge, it consists in affirmation of unity; with the disappearing of any perception of lords, rivals, contraries, forms, or likenesses; along with the performance of the command and the refraining—to the utmost—from what is prohibited in the exterior. It brings all that forth from the springs of desire and fear, hope and want. The perfectly realized performance of deeds is due to the realized performance of truly sincere affirmation.

As for the first aspect of the affirmation of the select, it consists of the affirmation of unity with the disappearance of the things we have mentioned; along with the performance of the command in both exterior and interior; along with the abolition of the obstructions of hope and fear of any other-than-him. It causes all that to proceed from the springs of perfect accord; the witnessing or sign *(shāhid)* of the real standing alongside it; with the carrying out of the witnessing or sign of the call and the response.

The second aspect of the *tawḥīd* of the select is a phantom *(shabaḥ)* standing in his presence, without any third in-between. The dispositions of his jurisdiction flow over him in a stream of rulings *(aḥkām)* from his power; in the depths of the seas of affirmation of his unity; with the annihilation of self, and the passing away from any call of the real to him and from his response; in the realities of the existence found in his unity; in realization of his nearness, with the disappearance of all sensation and movement through the carrying out of the real in him what he wishes of him.

The emblem of that affirmation of unity is the return of the lastness of the godservant to his firstness, that he might be as he was when he was before he was.[14]

The proof of that is the saying of Allah Almighty (7:171): "When your lord took from the sons of Adam, from their loins, their progeny, and made them witness over themselves: Am I not your lord? They said: 'Yes, indeed.' "

Who was he and how was he before he was? Did any respond but the pure, sweet, sanctified spirits?—with the performance of all-infusive power and all-perfected will.

Now he was as he was before he was. This is the furthest realization of the affirmation of unity *(tawḥīd)* by the affirmer of unity *(al-muwaḥḥid)* in regard to the one *(al-wāḥid)*—with the disappearance of "he."[15]

JUNAYD

♦ ♦ ♦

ON ANNIHILATION (FANĀ')

INTRODUCTION

The text of Junayd's Book of Fanā' (Kitāb al-Fanā') *is one of the more intransigent, and one of the more rewarding, in the extant literature of early Sufism. Much of the meaning and much of the difficulty center around the play on* wajd *and* wujūd, *with the three meanings—"finding," "existence," and "ecstasy"—almost always intertwined with one another, but with different emphases in each usage. At times English neologisms are needed to bring across the contortions of the word play and the theological subtleties it entails. Existence for Junayd is fundamentally the existence of the real. When humans give up their self-existence, through the long process of "trial"* (balā'), *the painful death of the ego-self, then they exist and abide in the existence-of-the-real-for-them. In this sense, Junayd speaks of the real existence as a transitive force, of the real as "ex-isting them," or "founding them," that is, infusing them with the genuine existence of the one reality. Yet even with such translating efforts, the translator cannot recapture the complete word play on the* w/j/d *root, and can only remind the reader at this point that whenever the words "find," "ecstasy," and "existence" appear, the same Arabic root is being used and the three meanings are being evoked all at once.*[16]

The text includes an interior dialogue that evokes various states of consciousness, passing away from consciousness, ecstasy, and trial. An anonymous interlocutor periodically asks the speaker [Junayd] to clarify a point. In the course of clarifying the point, more points in need of clarification are raised. Of special interest is the way Junayd plays on the Qur'anic notion of divine deception or guile. That the Qur'anic deity would characterize itself as deceptive has been an aspect of surprise to Western commentators, but for Junayd, reality itself is filled with embedded layers of deeper meaning, but also with embedded layers of deeper self-delusion. Because all true acts come from the one actor, the real, these layers of egoism and self-delusion are in fact aspects of a cosmic drama, a test with which the real purifies its adepts for mystical union. The issue of divine deception is a particularly vivid example of the profound tension between divine predetermination and human free will embedded within the Qur'an and at the heart of Islamic theological investigation.[17]

With the issue of guile and deception, Junayd's text continually circles back on itself, as with the earlier Junayd essay, in a mobius reality (i.e., two sides, one surface) reflecting the paradox of humility: As soon as one knows one has it, one has lost it; as soon as one is conscious of having given up egoism, egoism returns with that consciousness in the "enjoyment" and self-congratulation of the giving up of egoism. Trial is the continual struggle against this spiraling circle of ego-self, which ends with the real "overpowering" the human, working through and upon the human, subjecting (istawlā 'alā) *and making the human subject to the workings of the real within the human—all in accordance with the hadith of free devotions cited by Junayd, "I [Allah] become the hearing with which he hears and the seeing which he sees." These themes are extensions of the Junaydian doctrine of affirmation of unity that was introduced in the previous section, but in them the psychological resistance to* tawḥīd *and the trials entailed by it are more deeply elaborated.*[18]

In both his first essay on tawḥīd *and the* Book of Fanā' *Junayd uses* saj' *(rhymed prose) to open the discussion. Gradually the rhymed prose and other artistic devices seem to fall away or break apart under the pressure and urgency of the discussion, and the deeper and more difficult parts of the text turn out to be the most prosaic. The use of rhymed prose in Junayd to introduce the text in a more formal manner, before turning to his most difficult and mystically charged passages, is the inverse of what we find in Hallaj's* Tawasin *(see Chapter 9 in this volume), where rhymed prose marks a heightening and intensification of the mystical language, often pushing it to the edge of communicability.*

The text begins with an apparently optimistic discussion of the knowers (ārifīn) *on the path to mystical union. Yet the tone soon turns somber, and the syntax soon turns rough. The treatise is a fascinating combination of emotive intensity and almost complete abstraction. Thus, in the most emotionally pitched passages, both the subject of the pronoun and the object of the pronoun are left unsaid, and the last stated antecedents recede into a distance. The reader is left with an enigmatic "he," "it," or "they." Although in many cases one can divine that the antecedent "he" or "it"* (hu) *is the real* (al-ḥaqq)*, and that the antecedent of the "they" is a plural reference to the spirits of the knowers, or to those on the path of* balā'*, the pronouns build up on one another in such a fashion as to keep the reader always in doubt as to who is being subjected to the acts of whom. Given the Junaydian focus on the guile of the ego-self and of the deity that is testing it, such doubt might be an authentic reflection of Junayd's view that one can never rest secure in one's identity.*

The tendency in previous translations of Junayd has been to interpolate various explanations into the particularly elliptic or obscure parts of the text. The translation practice below is to purposefully eschew interpretive interpolations and to resist the temptation to paper over the rough points in the text. This is a difficult piece, in some ways a harsh piece. Some of that harshness may be due to difficulties in textual transmission. Some of it is due, no doubt, to Junayd's infamous syntactical contortion. Some of it is due to the topics of trial and overpowering. The constant references of Junayd to his being overwhelmed, vanquished, and crushed suggest that he might consider language itself overpowered and fractured by the encounter with the real. This is not a comfortable piece to read or to translate. However, the text may offer rewards proportionate to the discomforts it engenders.

THE BOOK OF FANĀ'[19]

Praise be to God and God's blessing to Muhammad and his family, peace upon them all.
The words of the Imām Abū l-Qāsim al-Junayd ibn Muḥammad, may Allah sanctify his spirit.

Praise be to God, who cut off attachments from those who cut themselves off for him, who granted the realities to those who cling to him and rely upon him by founding them *(awjadahum)* and granting them his love.[20] He confirmed the knowers in his party, placed them in ranks of endowment, and showed them a power which he made appear from out of himself and through which he granted them of his favor, so that passing thoughts would not dominate and obstruct them.

No attribute leads to deficiency in relation, because of their relationship with the realities of *tawḥīd*, through the implementation of *tajrīd* (stripping, peeling), in accordance with the call, and the finding in him of favor, through apparitions of the unseen, in nearness to the loved one.[21]

Then I heard him say: He endowed me with himself and became hidden in me from myself. I am the most harmful of things to myself: Woe to me from myself! Did he not deceive me and through me cheat me of himself?[22] My presence was the cause of my loss. The gratification I took in witnessing turned to absolute struggle.

In the distress of my heart-secret, my powers fail. I find no taste in existence, no sweetness in mastery of witness, no bliss in bliss, no torment in torment.[23] Tastes desert me, languages fail; no attribute lights, no motive incites. In manifestation his command was as it was in origination.[24]

I said: How then does this pronouncement appear from you when no attribute comes to light and with no motive to incite?

He said: I pronounced while hidden from my own condition. Then there appeared to me an overpowering, manifest, explicit sign. He annihilated my construction just as he constructed me originally in the condition of my annihilation.[25]

I did not influence him who is pure of all influence. I did not tell of him who masters all telling. Did he not efface my trace in his attribute? In my effacement, my knowledge vanished in his nearness. He is the creator and the reviver.[26]

I said: What do you mean by saying "he annihilated my construction just as he constructed me originally in the condition of my annihilation"?

He said: Do you not know that the Almighty said (7:171): "When your lord took out from the sons of Adam, from their loins, their progeny, and had them witness over themselves: 'Am I not your lord?' They replied: 'You are! We so witness.' "

The Almighty informed us that he addressed them and that they are nonexistent but for in his existencing-of-them. He EX-isted their created nature in a sense other than their existence-in-themselves,[27] a sense that no one can know but he and no one can find but he. He was founding them, encompassing them, witnessing them in the beginning in their condition of annihilation from their own abiding, which was their condition from all eternity. That is the lordly existence and the divine understanding which belongs to no other than the Almighty. For this reason we say that, insofar as he is ex-isting the godservant, his will is carried out upon the servant, however he wills, through his exalted attribute which none can share. That existence was the most perfect existence and the most realized, without doubt; it is the first, the overwhelming, the most truly overpowering, most properly subjugating everything to which it appears, effacing every trace of every thing and extinguishing the existence of every thing. There is no human attribute or existence to maintain such an existence for the reasons we have mentioned in exalting the truth and its triumph. This is an eternal guise upon the spirits.[28]

Bliss is not any recognized kind of bliss, generosity in the real is not any known kind of generosity, because the Almighty does not perceive and is not perceived and does not change. No one knows the modality *(kayfiyya)* of his subtle graces *(laṭā'if)* for his creatures. The meaning of that is lordly, known by no other than he. No one is capable of that. So we said that the real annihilates anything to which it appears, and when it subjugates, it is first in subjugating and most real in overcoming and overpowering.[29]

I said: What do those with such an attribute find when the attribute has effaced the name of their existence and their knowledge?

He said: Their existence-through-the-real-through-them;[30] and what appears to them in an overpowering word and sovereignty; not what they sought, then recalled, and imagined after being overtaken; the real effaces them, annihilates them; it does not adhere to them and is not related to them.

How then can they describe or find what they have not undertaken, what they have not borne upon themselves, what they have not approached, that of which they have no knowledge? The proof is in the extant tradition. Is it not related from the Prophet, peace and blessings of God upon him, that he said: Allah Almighty said: "My servant continues to come nearer to me through free acts of devotion until I love him. When I love him, I am the hearing with which he hears and the seeing with which he sees"?

There is more discussion in the hadith, but I am concerned with the evidence of this particular passage. Now if he is the hearing with which he hears and the seeing with which he sees, then how can that be given a how?[31] How can it be delimited in such a way as to be accessible to a category of knowledge? Were anyone to claim such a thing, his claim would be false, because we cannot have knowledge of "that" as a being with a certain aspect[32] that can be a category of knowledge *('ilm)* or knowing *(ma'rifa)*.

This means that he helps him and supports him and guides him and allows him to witness whatever he wills, however he wills, in reaching the aim and in agreement with the real. That is the action of Allah Almighty in him and his endowments for him which are related back to him, not to the one who finds them *(al-wājid lahā)*. They are not from him or of him or through him, but they come down upon him from another. In their being other they are prior to him in their otherness. For this reason these endowments can occur with this hidden attribute, without being attributed to him [the human party], as we have explained.

I said: How can presence be the cause of loss? How can the enjoyment of witnessing become absolute struggle? People here know that they enjoy and exist [or find ecstasy *(yajidūn)*] through presence, without struggle and loss.

He said: That is accepted opinion among the masses and the familiar known path of their existence. But as for the select and the select of the select, who become alien through the strangeness of their conditions—presence for them is loss, and enjoyment of the witnessing is struggle, because they have been effaced from every trace and every signification that they find in themselves or that they witness on their own. [The real] has subjugated them, effaced them, annihilated them from their own attributes, so that it is the real that works through them, on them, and for them in everything they experience; it is the real which confirms such exigencies in-and-upon them through the form of its completion and perfection.

They find bliss hidden in it, through enjoyment of existence in the mode of nonexistence, insofar as the real has taken exclusive possession and complete subjugation. Thus, when the spirits lost the hidden bliss which ego-selves cannot perceive nor senses approach, they became accustomed to their annihilation, finding that their abiding is prevented by their passing away. But when he makes present for them their "thatness" *(anniyatahā)* and makes them find their species, they are veiled by that from what they had been in and what had been in them. They choke on their own selves and become accustomed to their delimited form, because he had caused them to lose their first perfection and their most complete nobility and they come back to the categories of discursive reason. Grief settles in upon them. The choking of loss is attached to their condition of being-present and to being of their existence.[33] They crave the satisfaction of appetite and return to their want. How could their reemergence from hiddenness and their return to craving after fullness not oppress them?[34]

From here the selves of the knowers rise up *('araja)* to verdant spaces, pleasing sights, and lush gardens. Anything else is torment for them, including that for which they are yearning from their previous state, which was encompassed by hiddenness and taken over by the beloved. Alas! Allusion to him through the attribute is allusion to that in which nothing can share. His intention in them and from them is what leaves a trace upon them. Whoever is veiled, whoever remembers them or is selected for them, must, through the intention in them, experience the presence of apparition, not the inducements from him to him. So his attribute is secure from annihilation in his realization, slipping away from the presence that he had experienced, in the position of being overwhelmed, worked through, made subject. Then, when he is brought into presence and witnessing, veiling enfolds his presence, and all traces are obliterated in his act of bearing witness.[35]

He can find no cure for the purity of existence that overwhelmed him from the real, Most High. In this way he sees into his highest attribute and his most beautiful names. Now the path of trial opens before the people of trial. They strive, stand firm, are not deceived. A pure power, highness of rank, and dignity of position took possession of them and crushed them.

I said: Amazing! You are telling me that the people of this exalted relation must go through the experience of trial! How is that? How can I understand that?

He said: Understand! When they sought him in his intention and then kept him back from themselves, they sought the veiling of their attributes beneath a shroud of trial with which he would overwhelm them. They sought trial because the pleasure they took in things veiled them from him, so that they acted according to their "thatness" and occupied themselves with their senses and found pleasure in the vision of themselves in the realms of pride, in the results of their contemplation, and even in being overpowered.

How are you to understand this? No one knows it but its adepts, no one finds it but they, no one else is capable of it. Do you see that they sought him, then refused him, then beseeched him through what appeared to him from himself, and they sought help through the realities in beseeching him against himself?—because he ex-isted them his existence-for-them, and affirmed in-and-upon them the hiddenness of the secrets leading to union with him. Then the traces were effaced and the strands were severed. Relationships continually replaced one another. The ranks were raised higher, with loss of sense and annihilation of self.

Then he made annihilation present to them in their annihilation and he had them witness existence in their existence. What he made present to them and had them witness of themselves was a hidden veil and a subtle curtain. Through it they perceived that the choke of loss and the yoke of struggle were due to the veiling of that which does not accept reasons, by making present that which accepts reasons and takes on the traces of his attribute. They sought what they sought, without knowing it from themselves. They had alighted in the way-station of power and attained the realities of precedence. So he worked in them, preoccupying them. In them was constructed a perfection from him that was and was not according to the attributed, even as the choke of their trial increased.

I said: Describe for me the transformations of trial upon them in their wondrous homeland and nearest abode.[36]

He said: They feel autonomous in what has appeared. They have emerged from their lack, leaving their ladder behind.[37] They clothe themselves in the victory through the struggle of position and the onslaught of pride. They regarded things as their own, without ascent *(ta'rīj)* to what was his. They employed distinction and difference, in what they saw and found with their own two eyes, while he subjugated them with his own two commands. When apparitions of the real appeared to them, he gave them refuge in him from themselves by stripping away mastery and position. They left it all behind, without complaint, excited by what they had been singled out to enjoy, taking liberty with him and certain of forgiveness. They saw no necessity of return, no claim against them. At that point, they were encompassed by the guile that took them unawares.

I said: You have dazed my mind and compounded my confusion. Come nearer to what I can understand!

He said: When the people of trial cling to the event of the real in them and the exercise of his decision over them, their heart-secrets are dazed and their spirits are lost for the life of eternity. They find no refuge in their homeland, no protection hiding in their positions. They yearn for the one who puts them to the trial. They sigh at the annihilation caused by a long-lost beloved. Loss grieves them. The passion they find makes them abject in thirst for him, ache for him, yearning to find him.

Thirst follows them, wrapping itself more strongly around their insides. They are troubled in knowing, lavish in loss.[38] He works his thirst in them, as if at a funeral. Of every drapery he raises for them a banner.[39] He gives them a taste of loss. He renews in them the vision of more struggle from their inclination toward the traces of hardship, their longing toward exemplars of grief, their imploring a cure, their attachment to the traces of the beloved in whatever appears, their seeing every separation through the eye of nearness.[40] They are hidden in a hidden hiddenness, hidden in the loss of the veil that hid them. He tries them. They do not flinch. How could they be veiled when they are imprisoned before him, called to account before him in his presence,[41] then pardoned before him through perishing in all that he makes appear to them out of their trial, no longer bent on their own self-concern, freed in his love, clinging to him at the way-station of nearness?

They see the measures of gazes from him in the immediacy of their waking. Their perishing drowns as his abiding flows out of them in the harshness of their trial, until the trial delights them and their abiding becomes their intimate companion in him—when they seem near to denying them, when he produces the sting.[42] Exhaustion does not divert them from bearing it. Fullness does not sate them. These are the champions—in what came over them when he gave them the secret. They abide in his overwhelming power, awaiting his command—the command of Allah be done.

The people of trial are of two kinds. There is the one who finds refuge in trial, whose intention subsides, as well as what his desire for things abides and the excitement of the pleasure in the self, and the endowment of sense-existence—all that dies down until it hurts him and he is beguiled by it, and then the beguiling ceases as if it were a momentary condition, and he reaffirms his stance in trial as a mark of nobility, seeing that to leave it is a cause of failure and weakness.[43]

The End of the Book of Fanā'

The copy from which this version was taken was foreign and very, very defective *(kathīrat as-suqm jiddan)*. Let us await a copy that would be suitable for a corrected version, God willing.[44]

Praise be to God,
and his blessings and peace upon our master, Muḥammad,
his family and companions.

9

Hallaj: Iblis as Tragic Lover (The Ṭāsīn *of Before-Time and Ambiguity*[1]*)*

Introduction

Al-Ḥusayn ibn Manṣūr Al-Ḥallāj is most commonly associated with his sensational trial and execution (309/922). Hallaj was from the Fars region of Iran. For several years he lived and studied with Sufi masters such as Tustari and Junayd, but later broke from them. It is said that Junayd refused to grant him the Sufi cloak that was the sign of initiation into the ranks of Sufi masters.

When he arrived back in Baghdad after making the pilgrimage to Mecca, he gathered a large group of followers and became enmeshed in political and theological controversy. He was imprisoned for eight years. Caught up in the political intrigue of the Abbasid court, he was ultimately sentenced to death and executed (after flogging, mutilation, and exposure on the gibbet) in the year 309 Hijra (922 C.E.).

Unlike Junayd, Hallaj cannot be considered a classical Sufi in the sense of having his teachings passed on formally through Sufi schools. But his work is classic in another sense; among some Sufis and throughout Islamic culture, the writings and the story of Hallaj have continued to generate con-

troversy and creativity down to the present day.[2] Beyond the Islamic world, Hallaj has been the subject of debate and cultural reappropriation within Europe and America.[3]

Hallaj has been characterized as a social revolutionary, an Islamic analogue to the crucified Jesus, and a wayward and confused Sufi. The historical issues surrounding his execution are complex—far more complex than the common notion that he was executed for his mystical utterance "I am the real."[4] Such utterances were not rare in Sufism, as has been seen above in the case of Bistami, and they are grounded in the concept of the deity speaking through the emptied senses of the Sufi annihilated in mystical union. Hallaj was also accused of incarnationism (ḥulūl), the basis of which charge seems to be a disputed verse in which the author proclaims mystical union in terms of two spirits in one body. Such a proclamation would be far more difficult to harmonize with Islamic understandings of mystical union, and is indeed in conflict with the poem on mystical union attributed to Hallaj in which two spirits are becoming one.[5]

It is not the notion of radical mystical union that is difficult for Islam to accept; Islamic fanā' texts are as radical in their depiction of mystical union as those of any tradition. Indeed, the problem with the "two spirits in one body" language is that it does not affirm union and unity strongly enough; there are two spirits left whereas the Sufi fanā' texts speak of utter annihilation and annihilation in annihilation (the annihilation of the consciousness of annihilation), with only one actor, the deity, left.

There seems to be a tension in the story of Hallaj, between Hallaj's Jesus-like or Socrates-like refusal to allow his executioners a face-saving way out of carrying out the execution, on the one hand, and a complex set of political intrigues on the other. What often gets lost in the discussions of Hallaj the martyr is Hallaj the author. Few texts have come down to us intact, although numerous anecdotes and aphorisms have been collected as the Akhbār al-Ḥallāj (Sayings of Hallaj). Aside from those, we have a collection of poetry attributed to Hallaj (an attribution that is controversial), and a single sustained text, the Ṭāwāsīn, with a very thin set of surviving manuscripts.

The Ṭāwāsīn is a truly remarkable work of Sufi literature. In genre and idiom, there is nothing quite like it. The work has been described as a "carefully thought out and graduated collection of at least eleven separate treatises," edited by a disciple of Hallaj who claims to be writing "under the express dictation of the master."[6] The title is a plural form of the heading for section six, which begins with the names of two Arabic letters, ṭā (t) and sīn (s). The meaning of the letters is unclear. Several Qur'anic suras also *begin with a series of two or three mysterious letters. Two of them are named after the letters: Sura 20,* Ṭ ā H ā, *and Sura 36,* Y ā S ī n. *Hallaj's title,* Ṭ ā S ī n, *works as a combination of the first term of Sura 20 and the second term of Sura 36. That these two suras are the only suras in the Qur'an named after two opening letters makes such an association particularly likely.*

The chapters vary in length and subject. Chapter 1 is an homage to the Prophet Muhammad, for example, while Chapters 4 and 5 are treatments of the Prophet's heavenly ascent or Mi'raj. Presented here is Chapter 6, The ṬāSīn of Before-Time and Ambiguity, *the longest of the chapters.* The ṬāSīn of Before-Time and Ambiguity *presents the story of Iblis (the intimate companion of the deity who is expelled from the heavens and transformed into Satan when he disobeys the divine command to pray before the newly created Adam). The chapter takes the unusual form of a set of dramatic dialogues between Iblis and Allah and Iblis and Moses, along with a number of Iblisian monologues, and some powerful commentary by an implied narrator.*

The story presumes the following two Qur'anic passages on the creation of Adam and the disobedience of Iblis:

The Creation and Regency of Adam (Sura 2:30–34)

When your lord said to the angels:[7]
I am going to place a regent (khalīfa) *on the earth,*
and they said: Will you place one there
who will corrupt it and spill blood,
while we recite your praises and exalt you?
He said: I know what you do not know.
Then he taught Adam all the names
and showed everything to the angels, saying:
tell me their names, if you are sincere.
They said: Praise be to you,
we know only what you have taught us,
you are the All-Knowing, the most wise.
He said: O Adam, tell them their names,
and when he had told them the names,
he said: Did I not tell you that I know
what is hidden in the heavens and earth,
and know what you disclose and know what you hide?
Then we told the angels
to bow before Adam

and they did, except for Iblis,
who was scornful and acted proud,
and became a disbeliever.

The Creation of Adam and the Pride of Iblis (Sura 38:71–75)

Remember when your lord said to the angels,
I am going to create a person (bashar) *from clay.*
When I have shaped it
and breathed into it of my spirit,
fall bowing before it.
All the angels fell bowing together
Except Iblis who acted proud
and became a disbeliever.
He said: O Iblis,
what has prevented you from bowing
before what I created with my two hands?
Are you too proud or are you too lofty?

The word I have translated here as "bow" is a very precise term, based on the Arabic root s/j/d, *which indicates the positions taken in formal Islamic prayer. These positions are not prostrations (which imply a complete falling to the ground), but they involve a larger set of physical motions than simple bowing, including assuming a kneeling position and touching the head to the ground. The crucial point here is that the term used is the term for Islamic ritual prayer* (ṣalāt) *and thus entails, in the argument that Iblis will give, the notion not only of respect, but of formal worship.*

The common interpretation of the Qur'anic story is that Iblis refused out of pride to bow down before a human being made of an inferior substance (mud or clay—Iblis being made of fire according to tradition) and inferior in stature. In Hallaj's retelling of the story, Iblis's pride and disobedience are clearly present, but the issue is woven deeply into the intricacies of love-madness, monotheistic loyalty, and theological meditations on divine predetermination and free will.

The Ṭāsīn of Before-Time and Ambiguity *can be divided into four sections. Section 1 (paragraphs 1–12) is a discussion of the relative merits of Muhammad and Iblis as "proclaimers" of the truth. Section 2 (paragraphs 13–17) is a dialogue between Moses and Iblis, in which Iblis continues to defend his refusal to bow before Adam. Toward the end of this part, the dialogue turns into a soliloquy by Iblis. Section 3 (paragraphs 18–19, 26–35) consists of direct comments attributed to Hallaj concerning Iblis, on the derivation of Iblis's other name, "Azāzīl," along with snatches of dialogue between Iblis and the deity. As the argument continues, the style and tone become more intense. Standard prose gives way to rhymed prose* (saj') *and the rhyming becomes increasingly more dense as the rhyming terms begin to appear in shorter refrains. At the same time, the sense becomes more and more opaque, culminating in a series of riddles.*[8]

Section 4 (paragraphs 20–25) consists of a competition among Iblis, Pharoah, and Hallaj himself over who had the first rank in futuwwa *(chivalry, valor). There is good reason to consider this section a posthumous interpolation. It cuts right into the Azazil discussion, and it ends with some dramatic quotes from Hallaj: "I am his trace. I am the real," the most famous statement attributed to Hallaj; and "I was killed and my hands and feet were cut off. Still I did not go back on my proclamation." Here the martyred Hallaj champions his own valor against Pharoah and Iblis.*

The literary form of the chapter shifts from narrative to a more dramatic genre with various interior dialogues (especially between the deity and Iblis), from loosely rhymed prose to strictly rhymed prose (saj'), *to poetry, to linguistic riddles. Iblis's monotheistic claim—that he refused to bow before an other-than-God even at the risk of eternal rejection and torment—is combined with the lyrical language of the love-mad lover from the Majnun tradition, the lover whose loyalty is so total that there is no path for him to any "other than" the beloved. The tragic paradox is already apparent: In his total loyalty, the lover is willing to risk everything—including separation from the beloved—before being disloyal. When accused of pride, Iblis acknowledges it, but justifies his pride by pointing to the intimacy he has shared with the deity.*

The unstable form of the language, the sudden shifts in theme and genre, and the heavy use of riddles, paradox, and enigma add to the richness of the text and the multiple possibilities for its interpretation. Within this exuberance of form and content, we might outline the following modes of interpretation and argument:

1. In the metaphysical mode, nothing happens without God's preknowing and predetermining will; thus God knew, predetermined, and willed that Iblis would disobey his command. This argument, implicit throughout, is explicitly formulated in paragraph 28 ("All choices, including my own, are yours.").

2. In the mode of personal, mystical knowledge (ma'rifa), *Iblis was the most intimate companion of the deity, and thus was in a position to know the inner divine will* (irāda) *and to know its difference from the command* (amr). *This level is implicit in the argumentative stance Iblis takes throughout, disputing with the deity over the status of the divine command, and interpreting the command to bow down to an other-than-God as a "test" of Iblis's loyalty to radical monotheism.*

3. In the lyrical mode, Iblis's will and discursive knowledge ('aql) *have been annihilated, and his only existence is existence for-the-beloved; thus, he implies, his bowing before Adam was inconceivable. Yet this "pure-lover" position is complemented by another aspect of Iblis's love, his jealousy toward Adam; as the oldest and closest intimate of the deity, Iblis cannot keep his jealous rage from showing. Iblis presents himself as the paradigm of the Majnun figure (the love-mad lover willing to endure all things and to perish out of love for the beloved), but this pure-hearted abjection of the lover slips almost immediately into jealousy that God would prefer a new creature, made of mud, to Iblis, his most intimate companion.*

4. In the mode of mystical union, Iblis would not be acting out of his own will, but his annihilated will would be replaced by the divine will acting through him. Significantly, Iblis does not make this argument in regard to will from the perspective of mystical union, the union of the human will with the divine will. He stays on the theological plain; all acts are forewilled by the all-knowing, all-powerful deity. However, he does make a mystical argument (paragraph 15) in regard to dhikr *or remembrance: "His remembrance is my remembrance, my remembrance, his."*

These are a few of the aspects of Iblis evoked in this text. In addition, Hallaj is quoted in the text as associating Iblis with the principle of complementarity (the implication of opposites in the definition and meaningfulness of one another)—thus, the black backing that is needed to show the white in a fine garment, the vice without which virtue would not be known (paragraph 19). The poem in paragraph 12, however, gives the position not of complementarity but of coincidence of opposites achieved through a kind of unity (tawḥīd) *of love, as the exiled Iblis exclaims: "When I have achieved certainty / nearness and distance are one / Even if I am abandoned / abandonment will be my companion / How can it be abandonment / while love is one?"*

Louis Massignon, in his monumental work on Hallaj, mentions the tradition that offers an ultimate reconciliation for Iblis. Massignon rejects such a position and interprets the figure more traditionally: "Hallaj shows that the obstinate quietism of Satan, posing as the perfect gnostic and boasting of loving God, ends up by rejecting divine union." Massignon attributed to Hallaj a final comment by his commentator Ruzbehan Baqli, which explicitly condemns Iblis.[9]

Yet in the text itself the issue remains less clear and more open. Many questions remain. What is the ʿayn *(a word that can mean essence, eye, source, or spring of water) that is said to cover and disorient Iblis? What is the relationship of his absolute affirmation of unity and his "individuation"? What is the psychological and theological significance of such individuation and its relationship to his status as God's closest confidant? Beyond these specific questions, what makes this text so memorable and compelling is the manner in which it defers or even prevents easy moral judgment. That Iblis is condemned is presented as a fact of sacred history. The theological, psychological, and mystical implications of that fact are complex and intertwined. Iblis is certainly not a "trustworthy narrator" of his own story. Yet the issues he raises are deep. The final sections of the* Ṭāsīn of Before-Time and Ambiguity *present ever more abstruse riddles, even as the rhythm of the rhymed prose and the density of similes and metaphors grow to a fever pitch. One way of viewing the final cascades of* sajʿ *rhymes is as a way of testing the boundaries of discursive reason and walking the edge of* ḥayra, *that particular intellectual perplexity which can be viewed not as a failure to achieve knowledge, but as the result of confrontations with certain questions too deep for discursive intellect to fathom.*

♦ ♦ ♦

THE ṬĀSĪN OF BEFORE-TIME AND AMBIGUITY IN THE UNDERSTANDING OF UNDERSTANDING CONCERNING THE VALIDITY OF PROCLAMATIONS WITH INVERSION OF MEANINGS

Section 1 begins with a discussion of proclamation (tadāʾi). *Iblis proclaims his absolute monotheistic fidelity and appeals to that fidelity in defending his decision not to bow before any other-than-God, including Adam. The mode of presentation is part objective narrative, part direct dialogue (between Iblis and what appears to be the divine voice). The comparison of Iblis to Muhammad (referred to by the more intimate variant on his name, Aḥmad) confronts the reader with a riddle. Iblis, we are told, fell from the* 'ayn *while Muhammad had revealed to him the* 'ayn *of* 'ayn. *Because of its rich semantic base, the Arabic word* 'ayn *is frequently difficult to translate. It can mean "eye," "source," "spring," or "essence," or even a "concrete manifestion" of something.*[10]

Iblis refused to bow and Muhammad refused to look directly at the vision that he experienced (another reference to the Qur'anic "vision" passage of Sura 53:1–18). Among all the inhabitants of heaven, Iblis was the greatest affirmer of unity (tawḥīd), *the "unifier"* (muwaḥḥid) *par excellence. He worshiped the deity "purely" or "stripped of all else"* (bi tajrīd). *He attained the status of "individuation"* (tafrīd). *When commanded to bow before Adam, he replied with the monotheistic affirmation: "to no other [than the one God]." In a famous poem, Iblis states that his refusal was in fact a form of* taqdīs, *that is, a hallowing of the deity through the affirmation of absolute transcendence and unity.*

Iblis then evokes the issue of divine predetermination. Addressing the deity, he says, enigmatically: "I have a will (irāda) *in you and you have a will in me; yours in me is prior and mine in you is prior." He then shifts to another kind of predetermination, that of inherent nature: Iblis was created from fire and fire returns to fire, so that the threat of being cast into "the fire" of divine punishment is viewed only as a return to his essential element. The section ends with a poem depicting Iblis as the loyal lover, willing to accept eternal rejection and separation if that is the beloved's will, in the face of eternal suffering refusing to betray his loyalty to the beloved.*

Muhammad and Iblis[11]

1. That strange[12] and learned master, Abū l-Mughīth Ḥusayn ibn Manṣūr al-Ḥallā—may Allah adorn his place of rest—said:

Making claims is appropriate for no one but Iblis and Ahmad, except that Iblis fell from the *'ayn* while Ahmad—God bless him—had revealed to him the *'ayn* of *'ayn.*[13]

2. Iblis was told: "Bow down!"[14] Ahmad was told: "Look!" The former did not bow and Ahmad turned neither to the right nor left.[15]

(53:17) "The eye did not swerve nor did it exceed its bounds."

3. Iblis made claims but he returned to his power.[16]

4. Ahmad made claims and returned from his power,[17]

5. With the sayings,[18] "O changer of hearts!" and "I cannot measure out your praise."

6. Among the inhabitants of heaven, there was no affirmer of unity *(muwaḥḥid)* like Iblis,[19]

7. When Iblis was veiled by *(ulbisa)* the *'ayn*, and he fled the glances and gazed into the secret, and worshiped his deity stripped of all else,[20]

8. Only to be cursed when he attained individuation and given demands when he demanded more.[21]

9. He was told: "Bow down!" He said, "[to] no other!" He was asked, "Even if you receive my curse?" He said, "It does not matter. I have no way to an other-than-you. I am an abject lover."

10. **My disavowal in you is *taqdīs* (affirmation of transcendence)**
My reason in you, befuddlement.
Who is Adam other than you?
To distinguish them, who is Iblis?
[And the one in between is Iblis].[22]

11. He said: He disdained and grew proud, turned away and backed around, and what he insisted upon, set down.[23]

He said, "You've grown proud."[24] He replied, "A moment with you would be enough to justify my pride and lording-it-over *(tajabbur)*. So how much more am I justified when I have passed the ages with you. (7:11) 'I am better than him' because of my priority in service. There is not in the two creations anyone more knowing of you than I. I have a will in you and you have a will in me. Your will in me is prior and my will in you is prior. If I bow before an other-than-you or do not bow, I must return to my origin, for (7:11) 'you have created me from fire.' Fire returns to fire. To you belongs the determination and the choice."

12. There can be no distance for me
distancing you from me
When I have achieved certainty

nearness and distance are one.[25]
Even if I am abandoned,
abandonment will be my companion.
How can it be abandonment
while love is one?
To you, praise in success,
in the pure absolute
For a servant of true heart
who will bow to no other than you.[26]

Section 2 begins with a dialogue between Moses and Iblis and evokes the "look at the mountain" theophany passage from the Qur'an. Iblis declares that he is unconcerned about the transformation and deformation he undergoes as a result of his disobedience. He also explictly distinguishes between God's command (amr) *to bow before Adam, and his will* (irāda). *The command was only a "test" (paragraph 14).*[27]

Moses and Iblis

13. Musa met Iblis on Mount Sinai and said, "O Iblis, what kept you from bowing down?" He answered, "The proclamation of only one object of worship prevented me. If I had bowed down in prayer before Adam, I would have been like you. You were called one time to 'look at the mountain!' and you looked. I was called a thousand times to 'bow down! bow down!' but I did not bow, held back by the meaning of my proclamation."[28]

14. He said, "You abandoned the command!"
He replied, "That was a test, not a command."
He said, "Of course he deformed you."
He answered, "Musa, that and that is masquerade. The condition is unreliable; it will change. Knowing remains as sound as it was before, unchanged; only the figure has been transformed."[29]

15. Musa said, "Do you remember him now?"
"O Musa," he replied, "remembrance does not remember.[30] I am the remembered and he is the remembered. His remembrance is my remembrance, my remembrance, his. Can the two rememberers be anything but together? My service is now purer, my moment freer, my remembrance

greater. Formerly I served him out of concern for my own lot; now I serve out of concern for his."

16. We took cupidity from prohibition and defense, harm and advantage. He set me apart, "extased me" *(awjadanī)* when he expelled me, so that I would not be mixed with the pure-hearted. He held me back from others because of my zeal, othered me because of my bewilderment, bewildered me because of my exile, exiled me because of my service, proscribed me because of my friendship, disfigured me because of my praise, consecrated me because of my *hijra,*[31] abandoned me because of my unveiling, unveiled me because of my union, made me one with him because of my separation, cut me off because of the preclusion of my fate.[32]

17. By his reality! I have not erred concerning the designing *(tadbīr)* nor rejected the destining *(taqdīr)* nor concerned myself with the change in imaging *(taṣwīr),* nor am I in such measures the one to be judging![33] Even if he torments me with his fire forever and beyond, I will not bow before any other than him, abase myself before a figure and body, or recognize a rival or offspring. My proclamation is the proclamation of those who are sincere, and in love I am triumphant. How not?

Section 3 consists of comments on Iblis attributed to Hallaj himself, explanation of Iblis's other name, 'Azazil, and snatches of dialogue between Iblis and the deity.

'Azazil (1)

18. Al-Ḥusayn ibn Manṣūr al-Ḥallaj, God's compassion upon him, said:

Concerning the states of 'Azāzīl there are different opinions. One is that he was the proclaimer in heaven and on earth. In heaven he was the proclaimer of the angels, showing them the virtues, and on earth he was the proclaimer of humankind, showing them the vices.[34]

19. Things are known through opposites. A fine garment is woven on a course, black backing. Similarly, the angel displays the virtues and says to the virtuous: "Perform them and you will be requited," while Iblis shows the vices and says: "Perform them and you will be requited"—symbolically. Whoever does not know vice will not know virtue.

Section 3 on Azazil is interrupted here by a thematically independent section, the depiction of the spiritual chivalry and jousting of Iblis, Pharoah, and Hallaj, with Hallaj's famous "I am the real" proclamation and comments on his own execution.

IBLIS, PHAROAH, AND HALLAJ[35]

20. Abu 'Umāra al-Ḥallaj, the strange master, said:

I competed with Iblis and Pharoah in the domain of valor.

Iblis said, "If I had bowed down, the name of valor would have fallen from me."

Pharoah said, "If I had affirmed belief in the Prophet,[36] I would have been thrown from the station of valor."

21. I said, "If I had gone back on my proclamation, I would have been thrown from the carpet of valor."

22. Iblis said (7:12), "I am better than he" when he saw no other other than he.

Pharoah said [28:37], "I know of no other lord for you than me." He knew no one among his people who could distinguish between the real and the creation.[37]

23. And as for me, I said, "If you do not recognize him, recognize his trace. I am his trace. I am the real!"[38] because I never ceased to be real in the real.

24. My friends and teachers are Iblis and Pharoah.[39] Iblis was threatened with fire but did not go back on his proclamation. Pharoah was drowned in the sea, but did not go back on his proclamation and did not affirm any mediation at all. But I said (10:90), "I believe that there is no God but he in whom the people of Israel believed." Don't you see that Allah (may he be praised) opposed Jibril at his gate and said "Why have you filled his mouth with sand?"[40]

25. I was killed and my hands and feet were cut off.[41] Still I did not go back on my proclamation.

At this point the text returns to the discussion of Azazil. The text begins to move into a very heavy rhymed prose and the rhyming prose soon becomes the dominant force in the language. In order to give the reader some sense of how the rhymed prose works here, without resorting to artificial English rhymes, some of the key Arabic terms are kept in parentheses. As the rhymed prose intensifies, the actual meaning of the text becomes more enigmatic, turning toward a sense of pure riddle. At this point the manuscripts disagree wildly as to the correct terms and the "pointing" of the Arabic. To avoid an arbitrary translator's decision on which is the "correct" reading, the various versions have been placed together in order to allow the reader to decide which might be better, and to console the reader with the fact that the original redactors of the text may have been just as puzzled as later readers.

'Azazil (2)

26. The name "Iblis" is derived from his name 'Azāzīl: the letter *'ayn* ['] corresponds to the height of his inner resolve, the *zā'* [z] to the compounding of dilation in his dilation; the *alif* [ā] to his views on his "thatness";[42] the second *zā'* [z] to his renunciation in rank *(rutba)*; the *yā'* [ī] to his seeking refuge in the knowledge of his priority; and the *lām* [l] to his disputation over his reddening *(lamiyya)*.[43]

27. He said to him: "Why did you not bow in prayer, abject one?"

He replied: "I am a lover; lover abject. You say abject [*mahīn*] // but I read in the book *mubīn* [that makes clear] // what would happen to me, O you of the power *matīn* [unbreakable] // How was I to abase myself before him when [8:2] 'you created me from fire and created him from *ṭīn* [mud, clay]? //' two contraries that cannot meet, and I am in service senior, more majestic in his favor, in knowledge more learned, in living more complete!"[44]

28. The real, be praised, said to him: The choice is mine not yours.

He said, "All choices, including my own, are yours. You have chosen for me, O Originator! If you forbid me from bowing, you are the Forbidder. If I err in speaking, don't abandon me, All-Hearer! If you will me to bow before him, I am the Obeyer.[45] I know no one more knowing of you than me."

29. Don't blame me, blame from me is *ba'īd* [far away]
    Reward me! master, for I am *waḥīd* [unique]
In your true threat, I am made true
    Desert in desert, my plight is *shadīd* [severe]
Whoever wills a speech, here is my book and testament,
    Read it and know I am a *shahīd* [witness, martyr].

30. My brother Iblis was called 'Azāzīl because he was set apart, set apart as intimate friend, not proceeding from beginning to end, but brought forth emergent from his end.[46]

31. His coming forth inverted his rootness-on-site, ignited by his blazing fire of night, from his precedence, blinding light.[47]

32. His watering pond
    dried, cracked ground
Abundance want,
        lightning fading
His rain-swords only apparitions
    Blind he wanders off the path

Alas

33. My brother, if you understand this
    you have piled up stones,
spectres of imagination,
    then returned in consternation,
and passed away in cares.[48]

34. The most eloquent of the tribe were dumbstruck at his gate
    The sages failed to appreciate;
He was more perfected than they in the position of prayer
    Nearer than they to the one existing
Spending himself in struggle, more giving
    More faithful than they in the oaths they would swear
More loyal to the master than they, more near.[49]

35. They fell before Adam in prayer as a favor
    While Iblis, because of his ancient age of witnessing, refused.

HALLAJ

His character against the horizon huge,
   his excess a refuge,
thornweeds fruitful,
   his being cut away an unfolding flower,
his return, most giving, noble.[50]

10

Niffari: Who Are You and Who Am I? *from the* Book of Standings (Kitāb al-Mawāqif)

INTRODUCTION

Some of the more intriguing works of early Sufi literature (and of mystical literature of any place or period) are attributed to a Sufi who does not appear in any of the major Sufi biographical sources and about whose life we know very little: Muḥammad ibn 'Abd al-Jabbār ibn al-Ḥasan an-Niffarī (d. 354/965). Niffari's most famous work is the Book of Standings (Kitāb al-Mawāqif), *but according to its commentator Tilimsānī, the book was actually put together in book form by Niffari's son:*

> *And this is one of the indications in favor of the assertion that the man who composed the* Mawāqif *was the son of Shaykh an-Niffari, and not the Shaykh himself. Indeed, the Shaykh never composed any book; but he used to write down these revelations on scraps of paper, which were handed down after him. He was a*

wanderer in deserts and dwelt in no land, neither made himself known to any man. It is mentioned that he died in one of the villages of Egypt. God knows best the truth of his case.[1]

The work's title and central term, mawāqif *(standings), is part of the complex Sufi semantic field. As with Junayd's use of the word* wajd, *Niffari's use of the term* mawāqif *involves a sophisticated play on the etymological and morphological possibilities of the term. Like Junayd, Niffari refashions and reconfigures those possibilities into unusual, often striking new forms. A brief look at the semantic field of* mawāqif *will provide an entrance into Niffari's distinctive conception of "standings."*

The basic radical, w/q/f, *yields the primary verb form* waqafa *(to stand, stop, halt). However, Niffari uses the less common causative form of the verb,* awqafa, *meaning "to make someone stand." He then employs the standard verbal noun* waqfa, *not in its normal sense as the act of standing, but in a causative sense, from the point of view of the one standing, as the* act of being stood *somewhere. The prefix "m" yields* mawqif *(plural* mawāqif*), as the place where the standing or being stood occurs. Though the term can be translated as "station," such a translation loses the causative force peculiar to Niffari's writing;* waqf *("standing" or "staying") is Niffari's term for the state of being riveted, as it were, in a particular place at the divine presence.*[2] *The term* waqf *resonates with the Qur'anic "standing" of each person before the revelation of his destiny during the apocalyptic moment of truth. It also echoes the poet-lover's standing before his fate of separation from the beloved at the* ghadāt al-bayn *(morning of her departure), and his standing before the abandoned ruins* (aṭlāl) *of the beloved's campsite. Indeed the prototypical opening of the classical remembrance of the beloved is with the imperative form (Stand! before the ruins . . .* waqafa/qif*). In a single "standing" Niffari condenses a full range of language worlds and a complexity of referential and antecedent play.*

Much of the literary effect of Niffari's sayings resides in their placement of the visionary moment in a bipolar world that can be interpreted as the mystical event in the present, or the apocalyptic event of the final moment of truth. Of course, almost any Sufi representation of visionary experience can be read through eschatological lenses, but Niffari's staccato series of stayings, sayings, and visions engages the interface between the mystical and the eschatological in a particularly persistent manner. The experiences oscillate between the Sufi states of qabḍ *(constriction) and* basṭ *(expansion). Standing (or being stood) before an overwhelming power and at the edge of the dissolution of ego yields expressions of terror and awe that can suddenly change into expressions of profound inner peace beneath beyond the turmoil, which can then turn back just as suddenly to expressions of terror.*

Scholars have attempted to place Niffari's revelations within a theological framework. Some consistent ideas come through the highly elusive texts. There is a clear progression suggested, for example, from 'ilm *(traditional knowledge) through* ma'rifa *(intuitive knowing or recognition) to* mushāhada *(witnessing).*[3] *At times the notion of* waqfa *seems to represent the highest of these stations; at other times it seems to be used more generically for the act of being stood, stayed, or riveted in any particular station or state.*

But more important than any set of theological conceptions is the manner in which Niffari's language destabilizes the normal boundaries of self and other, human and divine. Indeed, the moment of mystical union in Niffari is a moment of a ghostly ventriloquism; at the moment of union there is only one "being" left, but in Niffari's dialogues there are still two voices. At times, as in Standing 44 (Who are You and Who am I?), the voices seem to switch identity, to run past one another and invert, as it were, at the moment of fanā'. *It becomes difficult to know who is speaking to whom, and the identities seem to shift at the center of the standing.*[4] *In almost all of the standings, there occur moments of a terrifying sense of fixed identity, duality, and absolute otherness before an overpowering divine reality. Finally, there are those extended passages in which the real announces itself within a symbolic vocabulary made particularly intense by the use of apocalyptic language and by the distinctive poetic symbolism of Niffari, which has been compared to the symbolist verses of Rimbaud.*[5]

Presented below are six standings: (5) The Standing "My Time Has Come"; (6) The Standing of the Sea; (43) The Standing between His Hands; (44) The Standing "Who are You and Who am I?"; (59) The Standing in the Reality of Knowing; (67) The Standing of the Presence Chamber and the Letter. There are two pairs (5 and 6, 43 and 44) with radically alternating movements and modes—or in Sufi terminology, moments (awqāt) *and conditions* (aḥwāl)*—internal to each standing within a pair, and between the two standings that make up a pair.*

♦ ♦ ♦

NIFFARI, FROM THE BOOK OF STANDINGS (*KITĀB AL-MAWĀQIF*)

5. The Standing "My Time Has Come"

He stood me, saying:

If you cannot see me, you are not with me
If you see an other-than-me, you do not see me

Intimations of me in anything
 efface the meaning of meaning within it,
 and affirm it from, not through [6]

In you is something
 that cannot be relinquished
 that cannot be turned away

When you are silent of yourself
 the proclaimer must speak[7]

In everything is a trace of me
 If you speak of it, you change it

Put remembrance of me behind you,
 Or you'll revert to the other-than-me,
  between you and it, nothing

My moment has come
 The time has come for me to unveil my face
  and manifest my splendor

My light will reach the courtyards
and what is beyond
Eyes will gaze upon me,
hearts will gaze
You will see my enemy
loving me,
my intimate companions
judging

I will raise up thrones for them
They will send away the fire
never to return
I will inhabit once more
my ruined abodes
adorning them with the real
You will see how a measure of me
expels otherness

I will gather all people into well-being
Never again will they be divided or abased
Take out my hidden treasure
Realize my tidings
my readiness,
my imminent rising
I will rise and the stars will gather around me
I will bring sun and moon together
I will enter every dwelling
"Peace to you," they will greet me
"And to you, peace," I will reply
At my beckon, the hour will rise
I am the Almighty, the Compassionate.

6. The Standing of the Sea

He stood me in the sea
I saw the ships sinking and the planks floating
I saw the planks sinking
He said to me
No one on board will be saved.

Peril for one who throws himself in and does not come on board

Destruction for those who come on board and do not accept danger

He said: In peril is a portion of salvation.
  Then the wave came
    and lifted what was beneath it
      and ran along the shore.

He said to me:
    The surface of the sea is an unattainable brilliance
    Its depth is an unfathomable darkness.
    Between them are sea-creatures that offer no refuge

    Do not sail on the sea, or the vessel will veil you
    Do not throw yourself in, or the sea itself will veil you

    In the sea are brinks. Which will support you?

    When you grant yourself to the sea and drown,
      you become like one of its creatures

    I deceive you if I guide you to an other-than-me

    If you perish in an other-than-me,
      you belong to that in which you perish

    This world belongs to the person I have turned away from it,
      and from whom I have turned away the world

    The afterworld belongs to whomever I turn it,
      to whomever turn to me.

43. The Standing between His Hands

He stood me between his hands[8] and said to me
I approve you for nothing
I approve nothing for you

Glory be to you!
It is I who glorify you
  You cannot glorify me!
It is I who act upon you and make you act
  How could you act on me?

I saw the lights as darkness
  contrition as contention
    the path leading nowhere

He said to me
Praise yourself, exalt yourself, glorify yourself
  conceal yourself from me!
Do not expose yourself to me
  If you do, I will set you afire
    concealing you from yourself

He said to me
Unveil yourself for me
  Do not conceal
If you conceal,
    I will tear the cover from you
      If I tear it from you, I will not veil you

I concealed myself and did not show forth
I unveiled myself and did not conceal
I saw him approving what he did not approve
  and disapproving what he approved

He said:
  If you become a believer, you're a deviate[9]
  If you become a seeker, you're a believer

  I saw him and recognized him
  I saw and recognized myself

He said to me:
  You've found the way
  When you come to me, none of all-that will be with you
      You will not know me
  You will not know yourself.

44. THE STANDING "WHO ARE YOU AND WHO AM I?"

He stood me in place, saying
    Who are you and who am I?

I saw the sun, moon, stars, and all the lights

He said to me
    In my sea stream nothing remains you have not seen

Everything came toward me—
    Nothing remained that did not—
        Kissed me between the eyes
            Blessed me
                    And stayed in the shadow
He said
    You know me but I know you not

I saw him clinging to my robe not me

He said to me
    This is my devotion

I did not incline
    Only my robe inclined

He said Who am I?

Sun and Moon were veiled
    The stars fell
        The lights died out
            All save he enveloped in darkness

My eye did not see
    My ear did not hear
        My perception failed

Everything spoke saying
Allahu Akbar!

Came toward me lance in hand

He said to me: Flee!
I said: Where?
He said
Fall into the darkness

I fell into the darkness
And beheld myself

He said
Behold yourself only yourself forever

Never will you leave the darkness

But when I release you from it
I will reveal myself

You will see me
And when you do
You will be the farthest of those most far away.[10]

59. The Standing in the Reality of Knowing

He stayed me in the reality of knowing and said to me:

As for now,
above,
below,
and everything that appears is world
—all of it
and all in it—
awaits the hour.

On all of it
and all in it
is written the faith.
The reality of faith:
(42:11) "There is nothing like his like."

He said to me:
Witness Gabriel and Michael,
witness the throne and the bearers of the throne,
witness every angel and every being that has knowing
as it bears witness that
there is none like his like,
seeing that its knowing
is its experience
and its experience is its knowing,
seeing that as the range of its knowing,
seeing that that is the real, the reality,
seeing that that is the knowing of realized vision, not the vision.
Behold them all.
awaiting the hour!—
waiting on the unveiling
of the veil
from that,
waiting on the lifting
of the curtain
on that
and on that!
But *that*
cannot abide
the conditions of reality
from behind the veil
except through it
—and how when the veil tears?

He said to me:
the veil will be torn
and in the tearing
overpowering
that the nature of created beings
will not withstand.

He said to me:
    If the veil were lifted
        not torn,
those beneath it
    would find rest.
It will be torn.
    When it is torn,
        the knowing of the knowers
            is baffled.
        In its bafflement,
            it will be clothed in a light
        enabling it
            to bear what appears
                when the veil is torn.

        Knowings of the veil
            cannot bear what appears
                when the veil is torn.

67. The Standing of the Presence Chamber and the Letter

He stood me in the presence chamber and said to me
    The letter is a veil. The veil a letter.

He said to me:
    Stand at the throne.
    I saw the sanctuary.
    No gaze attained it.
    No cares entered it.
    In it I saw the doors of every reality.
    I saw the doors on fire.
    In the fire was a sanctuary.
    Nothing could enter it but the sincere act.
    When it entered, it came to the door.
    When it came to the door, it stood for the reckoning
    I saw the reckoning
        single out what was for the face of God
        from what was for the other-than-him.
    I saw the reward was other-than-him.

NIFFARI

I saw that the act, sincere in him and for him alone,
  raised from the door to the highest plane of vision.
When it was raised, there was written upon the door:
"It has passed the reckoning."

Eat from my hand,
Drink from my hand
  Or you will not be equal to my obedience.

If you do not obey me on my account,
  You will not be equal to my worship.

If you cast off your fault
  you will cast off your ignorance.

If you recall your fault
  you will forget your lord.

In the garden
  is everything thought can bear
  and behind it more.

In the fire
  is everything thought can bear
  and behind it more.

What blocks you from me in the world
will block you from me in the afterworld.

I made the letter stand before creation.
I made the deed stand before the letter.
I made knowing stand before the deed.
I made sincerity stand before knowing.

The letter does not know me.
What knows me is neither from the letter nor in the letter.

The letter speaks with the tongue of the letter.
The tongue has not witnessed me.
The letter has not known me.

Pure bliss knows me not.
Pure torment knows me not.

If bliss knew me
  it would no longer enrapture.
If torment knew me,
  it would no longer torment.

The messenger of mercy
  cannot encompass knowing me.
The messenger of punishment
  cannot encompass knowing me.

What appears, appears to you
  from the species of its fixed form.

Fixed knowledge
  is fixed ignorance.

The whispering whispers in ignorance.
  Conceits conceive in ignorance.

Your worst enemy strives to remove you from ignorance
  not from knowledge.

He blocks you from knowledge
  to block you from ignorance.

Those with me do not understand through a letter addressed to them.
They do not understand within a letter that is placed for them
  and is their knowledge.
I made them bear witness to my rising *(qiyāmī)* through the letter
  and they saw me in what they witnessed.[11]
They saw me directly.
They witnessed a side of it.
They heard me and knew it instrumentally.

You will be born to me,
  with what you have known and what you have ignored,
  what you have taken and what you have left behind.

I will ask you about my term.
My case will bind.
Then through compassion I will pardon.

The letter is their place; in it he appeared.
The letter is their knowledge; through it he appeared.
The letter is their standing; before it he appeared.

From the letter there emerges the range of the knower;
 he is within that range even if the letters veil him.

The knower's range is his fixing.
His fixing is such that, if he is not in it, he cannot be at home.

The letter does not enter ignorance and cannot.

The letter is the mark of knowledge.
 Knowledge is the mine of the letter.

The masters of letters are veiled from the unveilings *(kushūf)*.
They stand with their meanings between the ranks *(ṣufūf)*.

The letter is the pass *(fajj)* of Iblis.

When knowledge abides, danger abides; when the heart abides,
 danger; when intellect abides, danger; when anxiety abides, danger.

Your meaning is stronger than the heaven and the earth.

Your meaning perceives without a glance and hears without hearing.

Your meaning finds no home in dwellings, no nourishment in fruits.

Your meaning is not gathered in by night
 nor let out by day to wander.

Your meaning is not encompassed by minds
 nor adhered to by causes.

This is your meaning. I created it;
these its attributes I actualized for it;

this adornment, I placed upon it;
this the goal, I allowed it to attain.

I am who is behind it.
I am the one behind what you have come to know.
Its knowledges do not know me, its visions do not witness me.
If I do not come to your aid, you will not hold fast.
If you do not hold fast, I will not make myself known to you.

Remember me. You will know me.
Help me. You will witness me.

I am the near, with no sign of nearness.
I am the far, with no sign of distance.

I am the apparent, without appearance.
I am the hidden, without hiddenness.

Say: Absolve me from being absolved from you.
Release me from what eludes you.
Winnow me not with the letters in knowing you.
Stay me not except in you.

Attain to knowledge for my countenance.
You will strike the real in my presence.
When you strike the real in my presence,
I will praise you with my self-praise.

When I make myself known to someone,
  I take possession of his bliss and torment.
  I draw out the bliss from his bliss and the torment from his torment.

The name is a bent *alif*.[12]

Knowledge is behind the letters.

Presence is select. For everything select, there is the common.

Presence burns the letter.
In the letter is ignorance and knowledge.

NIFFARI

In knowledge is this world and the next.
In ignorance this world and the next are dawning.
Dawn is the goal of everything apparent and hidden.
The goal is effacement in an apparition of presence.

The letter does not enter presence.
The people of presence pass by the letter.
They do not stay.

You will be estranged beneath the earth as you were estranged
above it.

The people of presence negate the letter and its conceits.

If you weren't of the people of presence,
a conceit would conceive itself in you.
Everything other-than is a passing inclination.
Only knowledge can negate it.
In knowledge are contraries.
You will not be sincere except through struggle.[13]

No struggle except through me.
No knowledge except through me.
Stand through me. You will be among the people of my presence.

Look into your grave.
If knowledge enters it with you, ignorance enters with it.
If the deed enters with you, reckoning enters with it.
If the other-than *(as-siwā)* enters with you
then its contrary in otherness enters with it.

Enter your grave alone.
You will see me alone.
You will not hold firm in me with the other-than-me.

When I make myself known to you,
beware of my torment in your limbs
have hope for a doubling of my favor in honor of you.

The people of presence are those who are with me.

Those who have left the letter are the people of presence.

Those who have left themselves have left behind the letter.

Leave knowledge. You will leave ignorance.
Leave the deed. You will leave the reckoning.
Leave loyalty *(ikhlāṣ)* and you will leave infidelity *(shirk)*.
Leave unification behind in favor of the one.
Leave unity and you will leave estrangement.
Leave remembrance and you will leave neglect.
Leave gratitude *(shukr)* and you will leave ingratitude *(kufr)*.

Leave the other-than. You and you will leave the veil.
Leave the veil. You and you will leave separation.
Leave separation. You will leave nearness.
Leave nearness and you will see God.

If I make myself known to you through knowing of seizure
you will lose all knowledge and sense.

The presence-chamber doors
are numerous as the doors of heaven and earth.
It is one of the doors of presence.

The first door of presence is the standing of the question.
I will make you stand to be questioned.
I will teach you and you will respond,
holding firm through my self-disclosure.
You will recognize your knowings as of my core being[14]
knowings that announce me.

He said to me: What is the fire?
I said: A light of the lights of seizure.
He said: What is the seizure?
I said: One of the properties of majesty.
He said: What is majesty?
I said: One of the properties of all-might.
He said: What is all-might?

I said: One of the properties of sublimity.
He said: What is sublimity?
I said: One of the properties of sovereignty.
He said: What is sovereignty?
I said: One of the properties of exaltation.
He said: What is exaltation?
I said: One of the properties of identity.
He said: What is identity?
I said: You, God, there is no God but you.
He said: You've spoken the real.
I said: You spoke through me.
He said: Look at my clear proof![15]

He said to me:
The first rank are tormented through seizure,
the second through majesty,
the third rank through all-might,
the fourth rank are tormented through glory,
the fifth rank are tormented through sovereignty,
the sixth rank are tormented through exaltation,
the seventh rank are tormented through the identity.

Torment from below to the people of the fire,
bliss from above to the people of the garden.

He said to me: What is the garden?
I said: One of the properties of comforting.
He said: What is comforting?
I said: One of the properties of grace.
He said: What is grace?
I said: One of the properties of compassion.
He said: What is compassion?
I said: One of the properties of generosity.
He said: What is generosity?
I said: One of the properties of sympathy.
He said: What is sympathy?
I said: One of the properties of affection.
He said: What is affection?
I said: One of the properties of love.
He said: What is love?

I said: One of the properties of contentedness.
He said: What is contentedness?
I said: One of the properties of chosenness.
He said: What is chosenness?
I said: One of the properties of the gaze.
He said: What is the gaze?
I said: One of the properties of identity.
He said: What is identity?
I said: You, Allah.
He said: You have spoken the real.
I said: You spoke through me. He said: Behold my bliss.[16]

He said to me:
The first rank find bliss in comforting,
the second in generosity,
the third in sympathy,
the fourth in affection,
the fifth in love,
the sixth in contentedness,
the seventh in chosenness.
The eighth rank find bliss in the gaze.

He said to me: You have seen how torment spreads and bliss spreads
(2:210) "To me returns the order entire"
Stand with me and you will stand beyond all description or property.

If you do not stand beyond property, property will take you.

If the higher property takes you,
  the lower property will take you.

If the lower property takes you,
  you are no longer of me nor of my knowing.

I dignified you, then made you my regent,
exalted you, then made you my servant,
honored you, then encountered you face-to-face,
loved you, then tested you.

I gazed at you, then intimated to you,
turned to you, then commanded you,

was jealous of you, then prohibited you,
singled you out for my affection, then made myself known to you.

The Qur'an constructs.
Remembrances plant.

The letter circulates according to the quest:
the "h" heaven and the "h" hell.[17]

When the word of the pronouncers reaches me,
I confirm it there where they find peace.

If I take hold of you with your fault,
I do so with all of your faults
until I have questioned you about the return of your glance
and the innermost thought of your heart.[18]

If you accept the good, I render all evil deeds good.

He said to me: Who are the people of the fire?
I said: The people of the exterior letter.
He said: Who are the people of the garden?
I said: The people of the hidden letter.
He said to me: What is the exterior letter?
I said: Knowledge that does not lead to act.
He said: What is the hidden letter?
I said: Knowledge that leads to reality.
He said: What is the act?
I said: Sincerity.
He said: What is reality?
I said: That through which you disclose yourself.
He said to me: What is sincerity?
I said: Toward your countenance!
He said: What is self-disclosure?
I said: What you encounter in the hearts of your friends.

He said to me: The pure word is stayed upon the deed.
The deed is stayed upon the appointed time.
The appointed time is stayed upon peace-of-heart.
Peace-of-heart is stayed upon eternal abiding.[19]

NIFFARI

Niffari's writings are opaque, enigmatic, and open to a variety of interpretations. Their openness makes them a fit ending for this book. In many ways, such a book, like Sufi writings themselves, aims to be circular. After reading Niffari, the reader might wish to return to Sufi writings presented earlier in this volume and come back to Niffari again. The textures and subtleties of Niffari's Standings *should offer new disclosures with each new reading.*

Epilogue: "If They Only Knew" from the Dīwān *Attributed to al-Hallaj*

What earth is this
so in want of you
they rise up on high
to seek you in heaven?

Look at them staring
at you
right before their eyes,
unseeing, unseeing, blind.

* * *

I was patient,
but can the heart
be patient of
its heart?

My spirit and yours
blend together
whether we are near one another
or far away.

I am you,
you,
my being,
end of my desire.

EPILOGUE

The most intimate of secret thoughts
enveloped
and fixed along the horizon
in folds of light.

How? The "how" is known
along the outside,
while the interior of beyond
to and for the heart of being.

Creatures perish
in the darkened
blind of quest,
knowing intimations.

Guessing and dreaming
they pursue the real,
faces turned toward the sky
whispering secrets to the heavens.

While the lord remains among them
in every turn of time
abiding in their every condition
every instant.

Never without him, they,
not for the blink of an eye—
if only they knew!
nor he for a moment without them.[1]

Appendix. Shahrastani: Scholastic Theology (Kalām) *on Unity and Justice*

Introduction

By the time of the death of the ascetic and theologian Hasan of Basra (110/728), two issues in the Qur'an had set off an increasingly sophisticated argument. Much of early scholastic theology in Islam has come down to us in fragmented form, in quotations and pieces of lost works. These quotations are often exceedingly difficult, thrusting the reader into a highly technical discussion without the necessary context to understand clearly all of the terms. One of the clearest introductions to theological debates in early Islam is given by the historian and comparativist of religions, Muḥammad ibn 'abd al-Karīm ash-Shahrastānī (d. 548/1153).[1] *Shahrastani divides the theological schools according to positions on key issues, and offers us an overview of those positions. The sections from Shahrastani's discussion that are most relevant to early Sufism have been translated below. No attempt is made here to give a full picture of scholastic theology. The examples are meant to offer the reader a sense of what was at stake in the debate, and how the debate underlies much of Sufi discussion, albeit transformed by Sufis into a new mode of inquiry and expression.*

In introducing Shahrastani, I will first offer a general overview of the two key theological issues and a deductive interior debate meant to show some of the ideal positions one can take. This debate should allow more immediate access to Shahrastani, who will then show us how these positions spread out historically into theological schools.

The first issue was tawḥīd, *the affirmation of absolute divine unity. This affirmation is of course one of the two bases of Islamic belief, as codified in the* shahāda *or Testimony (which is itself encoded in the call to prayer and recited five times a day): "No God but God, and Muhammad is his Messenger"* (la ilāha illa llāh wa muḥammad rasūluhu). *The common meaning of such affirmation is of course that there is only one deity. To affirm any other deities is to be guilty of* shirk, *"associationism," that is, associating other deities with the one God. The most obvious interpretation of* shirk *is the worship of various idols. The Qur'anic story of Abraham's destruction of his father's idols and the story from the life of Muhammad of the Prophet's destruction of the idols at the Ka'ba in Mecca (clearly in parallel to Abraham's act) were viewed as the key testaments to prophetic* tawḥīd. *Indeed, in this sense Abraham was considered the father of monotheist belief, the prototypical* ḥanīf *(upholder of one deity).*

To the theological mind, however, tawḥīd *raised further questions. If there is only one deity, how do the divine attributes in the Qur'an (seeing, hearing, knowing, having compassion) relate to the deity? Are they part of the divine essence? If so, are we to imagine a multiplicity of powers (knowing, hearing, seeing) existing from all eternity, and would that not be a subtle form of* shirk, *asserting the existence of multiple, eternal powers? However, if the attributes are not part of the deity's essence, then does the deity change? Is it in a state of not-hearing at one time, and hearing at another? Is it then subject to accident and contingency?*

Is not the literal interpretation of Qur'anic references to a deity that sees, hears, creates "with two hands," and "sits on a throne" the construction of an image based on humankind, a form of "likening" (tashbīh) *the deity to human characteristics, an anthropomorphism as idolatrous as idols of wood and stone? Should we not use interpretation (ta'wīl) with such expressions, explaining them as figures of speech for the one divine power? Or should we not distinguish between attributes, rejecting all attributes that are shared by humans (seeing, hearing, etc.) as implicitly anthropomorphic, and affirming those attributes that, in our view, belong only to the deity? But is not such explanation an "explaining away" of the Qur'anic text based on the preferences of human rationalizing, and a stripping* (ta'ṭil) *of the deity of the attributes it has affirmed for itself in its own word?*

The second major theological issue centers on divine predetermination and human free will. Several passages in the Qur'an emphasize the all-powerful nature of the deity in a way that seems to preclude human will or choice; the deity is said to "stop up the ears" of those who have rejected the Qur'anic message, for example. Other passages are urgent prophetic appeals to the hearer to choose the path of prophetic wisdom over that of "going astray." If the response of the listener has already been predetermined by an all-knowing, all-powerful deity, what is the status of such appeals and is it just for the deity to then reward and punish humans on the basis of a decision made from all time by that deity? As Wāṣil, the most famous theologian of the Mu'tazilite school of theology, put it in rejecting divine predetermination: "It is not possible for him to will for his servants what is in disagreement with his command—to control their action and then punish them for what they did." Or as another theologian, 'Amr, said: "Does he predestine me to do something and then punish me for it?" The deity is all-wise (ḥakīm) *and therefore must act in the interests of his creatures and with justice* ('adl). *Human beings have an innate capacity for understanding justice, right and wrong, without which they could not receive prophetic revelation in the first place. For their opponents, such statements are denial of divine power and knowledge; what the deity does is, by nature, just—the deity cannot be held accountable to fallible human understandings of what is just; and what the deity imparts by way of revelation is in fact the only knowledge of right and wrong, and the only understanding of justice, available to humankind.*

Ironically, and confusingly, those who rejected divine predetermination (qadar) *were called by the epithet "the Determinists"* (qadariyya). *Those who affirmed predetermination were called the Compulsionists* (jabriyya). *Those who appealed to the interpretations of the earliest companions of the prophets and rejected the theological attempt to apply formal human reason to such questions were called "the Traditionalists"* (salaf), *but even this group finally accepted a form of theological discourse to defend their original antitheological stance.*[2] *Another major group was called the "Attributionists"* (ṣifātiyya). *This group originally sprang from the position of the theologian al-Ash'ari, who vehemently maintained both the literalness of the attributes and the reality of divine predetermination. However, his school, the Ash'arites, later tried to walk a middle ground on both issues and came to be the most widely accepted theological school in Islam. It is important to point out, however, that the term "orthodoxy" should not be applied without serious reservations to Ash'arite thinking. Although Ash'arite thought is predominate in many Islamic circles, there is no official body to declare the official creed, and the Islamic practice of consensus means that at any time a new form of interpretation can become prevalent.*

The Sufis dealt both explicitly and implicitly with the positions of the theological groups described above. On the one hand, some Sufis took explicit theological positions; Kalabādhī (d. 380/990), for example, offers a point-by-point affirmation of what he considers to be the proper Ash'arite line.[3] *These formulaic statements, however, are less interesting, from the point of view of Islamic spirituality, than the way in which Sufi discourse mirrors and transforms the key theological dilemmas into a new register of discourse. The dynamic factor in this transformation is* fanā', *the passing away of the ego-self in mystical union. From the perspective of* fanā', *as grounded in the divine saying: "I am the hearing with which he hears, the seeing with which he sees," the attributes are neither affirmed nor denied in relation to an objective deity. Rather, the attributes (seeing, hearing, etc.) are seen as being actualized and realized within human consciousness at the moment that the ego-self and separate identity of the human is annihilated. Similarly, the issue of predestination and human free will is transformed. In mystical union, standard divisions of time and temporal sequence are transformed, with important implications for the entire issue of predeterminism.*

The most explicit and theologically sophisticated Sufi transformation of scholastic theology into the register of mystical union occurs in the later period, with figures such as Rumi, 'Attar, and Ibn 'Arabi. The theological issues are deeply embedded in an implicit way, however, within every text translated in this volume, from Rabi'a's redefinition of tawḥīd *as the complete obliviousness to anything other than the divine beloved, through the theory of the "one actor," to Niffari's shattering of normal linguistic and grammatical dualisms at the point of mystical union.*

♦ ♦ ♦

FROM SHAHRASTANI: ON THE SCHOLASTIC THEOLOGIANS

THE MU'TAZILITE MOVEMENT

In his introduction to the first large category of theologians, the Mu'tazilites, Shahrastani begins with the confusing name given to those who denied divine predetermination, "the determinists" (qadariyya). *The introduction offers a condensed and cogent discussion of the problems of divine unity and divine predetermination. He then moves to a discussion of several schools of Mu'tazilite thought. Presented here is a complete translation of Shahrastani's account of the first school of Mu'tazilites, the followers of Wāṣil, known as the* Wāṣiliyya *(Wasilites).*

The account of the Wasilites also explains the origin of the word mu'tazila *(Mu'tazilites: i.e., those who cut themselves off). It occurred during a theological session led by the famous ascetic and theologian Hasan of Basra. Hasan asked about the issue of "capital sins," and whether the commission of capital sins made a person an "unbeliever." This was an explosive issue, because some Muslim groups had wished to overthrow the Caliphate on the grounds that a particular Caliph had committed capital sins and was thus not a believer and could not be the leader of the community of believers. One group, the* murji'a, *insisted that if one declared himself a Muslim, no act or lack of action could make him an unbeliever. Wasil offered an opinion that a declared Muslim who committed a capital sin was neither a believer nor an unbeliever. He then got up and isolated himself from Hasan's group, thereby generating the term Mu'tazila (those who cut themselves off).*

Shahrastani details two controversial issues in addition to divine unity and divine predetermination: the question of reward and punishment at the end of time and the question of one's view on the Sunni-Shi'ite split (exemplified in the battle of the Camel between the followers and opponents of 'Ali, who would become the first Shi'ite Imam). (Because this last issue has little relevance for the texts in this volume, I will place the comments on it in the notes, except those necessary to give context to the crucial story of Wasil's "cutting himself off" and forming the Mu'tazilite movement.)

The Mu'tazilites

The Mu'tazila were called the people of justice and unity *(tawḥīd).* They were also given the name "the Qadarites" (al-Qadariyya, the determinists). However, they themselves claim that the term Qadarites would in that case be ambiguous. They maintain that the term should be applied to those who maintain that the determination *(qadar)* of things—both for good and evil—is from God. They are wary of the disgrace implied by the name due to the low esteem it has received from the saying of the Prophet: "The Qadarites are the Magians of the community." The Attributionists opposed the attempt of the Qadarites to disclaim the term "Qadarite" ["determinists," *qadariyya*]. The Attributionists appealed to the general usage in which the Jabrites (compulsionists) and the Qadarites are opposites. How then, could one term [Qadarite] be applied to its opposite [Jabrites: those who affirm divine compulsion or predetermination]?[4]

The Prophet, peace upon him, said that the Qadarites were the opponents of Allah in predetermination *(qadar).* Opposition in divine predetermination and the dividing of good and evil between the act of Allah and the act of the servant are inconceivable in the school of those who affirm submission, trust in God *(tawakkul)*, and the procession of all states according to the determination sealed and the decree ordained.

The belief that unites all Mu'tazilites as a single group is the claim that Allah Most High is eternal and that eternity is the unique characteristic of his essence *(dhāt)*.[5] They completely deny the [divine] attributes, saying that God is knowing through his essence, powerful through his essence, living through his essence, not through knowledge, power, and life, which would be eternal attributes and meanings subsisting in him.[6] If the attributes shared *(shārikat)* in his eternity, which is his unique characteristic, then they would share in his divinity.[7]

They are agreed that his words are originated,[8] created in a substratum *(maḥall)* which consists of letter and sound, the likenesses of which are composed in books as stories from him. Whatever exists in a substratum is only an accident that passes away *(fāniya fīḥāl)*. They are agreed that will, hearing, and seeing are not meanings that subsist in his essence, but they disagree on the manner of their existence and the loci of their meanings—as will be seen.

They are agreed in denying any perceptual vision of Allah in the final abode, and denying any likeness of him in terms of directions, place, form, body, position, motion, coming to an end, change, or passibility. They demand a figurative interpretation *(ta'wīl)* of any anthropomorphic verses and they call this mode of interpretation "*tawḥīd.*"

They are agreed that the servant is powerful, creator of his own acts, both good and evil, and deserving of the reward and punishment he receives in the after abode. They agree further that the lord Most High is exalted beyond any attribution to the lord of evil, oppression, or any act of unbelief or disobedience, because if he created oppression he would be oppressive, in the same way that if he creates justice he is just. [The Mu'tazilites] agree that the All-Wise does only what is beneficial and good. He must act, in accordance with his wisdom, in the interest of his servants. They disagree, however, on the necessity of his acting in the best interest of his servants and with special grace. They call this mode of interpretation justice *('adl)*.

They agree that the believer, when he leaves the world in a state of obedience and repentance, deserves reward and requital, while special favor *(tafaḍḍul)* is something other, beyond due reward. When he departs without repentance for major sins he has committed, he merits an eternity in the fire. His punishment is less severe than the punishment of the unbeliever. They call this mode of interpretation the promise and threat *(wa'd wa wa'īd)*.

[The Mu'tazilites] agree that the principles of intuition *(ma'rifa)* and the gratitude for well-being are necessary even before the reception of revelation *(sam')*. They also agree that a rational intuition *(ma'rifa bi l-'aql)* of what is right and wrong, as well as the embracing of the right and avoiding of the wrong, is also necessary before revelation. The reception of divine ordinances is a special favor of the creator, Most High, sent to servants through the intermediary of the prophets, peace upon them, as a test and a forewarning (8:42), "so that one who perishes, perishes after a clear sign, and one who lives, lives after a clear sign."

They disagree on the Imamate [leadership of the Islamic community], and upon its being founded upon special designation *(naṣṣ)* or upon choice *(ikhtiyār)*, as will be shown in the discussion of each individual group. Now we will specify, group by group, what distinguishes the followers of each group [of Mu'tazilites].

The Wāṣiliyya

The Wāṣiliyya are the disciples of Abū Ḥudhayfa Wāṣil ibn 'Aṭā' al-Ghazzāl. He was a student of Ḥasan of Baṣra. He studied religious sciences and traditions with Ḥasan. The two lived in the time of 'Abd al-Mālik and Hishām ibn 'Abd al-Mālik. There is still a small party of the Wasiliyya in the West, in the province of Idrīs ibn 'Abdullāh al-Ḥasanī, who led a rebellion in the West in the period of Abū Ja'far al-Manṣūr. So they are called the Wasiliyya.

The Wasiliyya are said to have four basic doctrines.

1. The first doctrine consists of the denial of the attributes of the creator, Most High, such as knowledge, power, will, and life. This position was at first undeveloped. Wasil ibn 'Ata' formulated it in popular terms as an affirmation of the impossibility of the existence of two pre-eternal and everlasting deities. He said: Whoever affirms an eternal mode *(ma'nā)* or attribute is affirming two deities.[9]

However, after the circulation of the books of the philosophers,[10] Wasil's students reformulated the position and ended up affirming the view that reduced all attributes to the deity's being "knowing" and "powerful," with the provision that these two attributes were essential and were attributes of the eternal essence *(dhāt)*. This was the position of Al-Jubā'i, whereas Abū Hāshim considered these two [i.e., the qualities of being "knowing" and "powerful"] as two states *(ḥālatān)*. Abū l-Ḥusayn of Baṣra inclined toward reducing them to a single attribute, that of knowingness, which is exactly the position of the philosophers. We will give the details of this position later. The Traditionalists opposed the Wasiliyya in this [denial of the attributes] on the grounds that the attributes are mentioned in the Book [the Qur'an] and the tradition *(sunna)*.[11]

2. The second doctrine [of the Wasiliyya] is the affirmation of free will [*qadar*, the word that means "predeterminism" but that comes to mean, confusingly, its opposite, free will]. In this they followed the line of Ma'bad al-Juhanī and Ghaylān of Damascus. Wāṣil ibn 'Atā' insisted upon this doctrine even more than he had insisted upon the doctrine of attributes. He said: The creator, Most High, is all-wise *(ḥakīm)* and just *('ādil)*. Evil and oppression cannot be properly attributed to him, nor is it possible for him to will for his servants what is in disagreement with his command—to control their action and then punish them for what they did. The servant himself is the actor *(fā'il)* of good and evil, faith and disbelief, obedience and disobedience, and he is requited according to his actions. The lord Most High gives him the power to do all that. The acts of godservants are confined to motion and rest, applications, speculation, and knowledge. He said that it is impossible that God should enjoin action upon his servant without the servant being able to act and sensing that the ability *(iqtidār)* and the act resided within himself. Whoever denies this denies the necessary truth. Wasil would appeal to various verses of the Qur'an in his discussion.

I [Shahrastani] saw a letter that Hasan of Basra is said to have written to 'Abd al-Malik bin Marwan, who had asked him about the affirmation of *qadar* (free will) and *jabr* (compulsion). Hasan's reply was in agreement with the school of free will *(qadariyya)*, and appealed to verses from the Book and to logical proofs. However, perhaps the letter was really by Wasil ibn 'Ata', since Hasan was not one to oppose the position of the Traditionalists, who were in complete consensus that all determination *(qadar)*, for good and for evil, was from God Most High.

It is remarkable that with this issue they [the Wasiliyya] applied the relevant expression [on divine predetermination] from the tradition to suffering *(balā')* and well-being *('āfiya)*, difficult times and times of ease, sickness and health, death and life, and other such acts of Allah Most High, but not to good and evil, acts of charity and acts of wickedness originating in the acquisition of servants. Thus in the issues examined in this treatise, the entire party of the Mu'tazilites has based themselves on the position of this group [the Wasiliyya].[12]

3. The third doctrine is the affirmation of the mean between two extremes. The source of this position is as follows: Someone paid a visit to Hasan of Basra and said:

> O Imam of the faith. In our time there are those who dispute the affirmation of the reality of capital sins *(kabā'ir)*. For this group, a capital sin does not take away from one's faith. According to them, action is not a pillar of faith. Disobedience does not mar one's faith and obedience is of no use if one lacks faith. These are the *murji'a* of the community. What is your judgment of what should be believed in this matter?

Hasan began to think over the question, but before he could respond, Wasil ibn 'Ata' said: "I maintain that one who commits capital sins is neither an absolute believer nor an absolute unbeliever. Rather, he is in a position between the two extremes, neither believer nor unbeliever." Then he rose and went off to another pillar in the mosque, repeating [to the new group] what he had said to Hasan's group. Hasan said: "Wasil has gone off *(i'tazala)* from us." Thus he and his followers came to be called the Mu'tazlila [i.e., those who cut themselves off or go off by themselves].[13]

The point of his position is the claim that faith is a manifestation of virtuous characteristics *(khiṣāl khayr)*. When they are brought together, a person is said to be a believer, and that is a name of praise. The ethically corrupt does not bring together the traits of the good, does not merit a name of praise, and therefore is not a believer. However, he is not an unbeliever, either, because the Testimony of belief *(shahāda)* and the other good acts exist in him and there is no point in denying them. However, when he departs from this world with a capital sin and without repentance, he is condemned eternally to the fire, since in the afterworld there are only two groups, one group in the garden and one in the blaze *(sa'īr)*. However, his torment will be lighter and his level higher than that of the unbelievers. Wasil was followed in this view by 'Amr ibn 'Abid, who also agreed with him on the issue of *qadar* and on denying the attributes.[14]

THE COMPULSIONISTS

Shahrastani's second major category of scholastic theologians is the category of the Compulsionists (jabriyya/*Jabrites*). *The Compulsionists upheld absolute divine power. They maintained that all human activity is in fact carried out by the one God who, alone, has power to act. Although humans might think they have a choice, they are in fact acting (or shadow-acting) under the divine compulsion.*

After a short introduction, Shahrastani moves into specific schools of Jabrites. I have translated his essay on the school of Jahm, the founder of which, Jahm ibn Safwān, was executed by political authorities on the charge of bid'a *(innovation)—that is, innovating or adding on to what is taught in the divine revelation completed with the Qur'an. Also translated here is a section from the essay on the school of* an-Najjār, *which followed the Mu'tazila in denying attributes, but adopted a position of moderate compulsionism and a middle-of-the-road position on the possibility of humans' acquiring a vision of the deity.*

The Compulsionists (Jabriyya)

Jabr (compulsion) is the denial that any act can be attributed to the servant. Instead, the act is attributed to the lord Most High. There are different kinds of Jabrites (compulsionists). The pure Jabrites refuse to attribute to the servant any act or power *(qudra)* to act whatsoever. Moderate Jabrites attribute to the servant a power, but a power that is not in any way effective. If anyone attributes to that originated power any effect upon the human act and calls such an effect "acquisition" *(kasb)*—such a person is not a Jabrite.[15]

For the groups who believed in the doctrine of "acquisition" whereby the human acquires a responsibility for the act even as the deity actually carries it out, see the section on the Ash'arites, below.

A. *The Jahmites* (Jahmiyya)

The Jahmites are the followers of Jahm ibn Ṣafwān, who was a pure compulsionist. His innovation *(bid'a)* first appeared in the city of Tirmidh. He was executed at the command of Sālim ibn Aḥwaz al-Māzinī in Marw at the end of the Umayyad dynasty.

Jahm agreed with the Mu'tazila in denying the eternal attributes, but went beyond them in certain respects. First, he claimed that one cannot attribute to the creator, Most High, attributes that are attributed to creatures, because that would be a form of *tashbiyya* (the "likening" of the deity to the creature). Therefore he denied that the creator was living and knowing, but affirmed that he was powerful *(qādiran)*, acting, and creating, because to none of his creatures can be attributed power, act, and creation.

Second, he claimed that cognitions *('ulūm)* belonging to the creator, Most High, are originated, and have no substratum *(maḥall)*. He said that it is not possible that the creator would know a thing before he creates it, because if he knew it and then created it, either his knowledge would remain as it was or it would not. If it remained as it was, then it would be ignorance, for the knowledge that he was about to create is not the same as the knowledge that he had created. If it did not remain, then it would change, but what changes is what is created, not the eternal. In this position, he was in agreement with the school of Hishām ibn al-Ḥakam. . . .

He said, further, that once the originated nature of such cognition is acknowledged, then there are the following possibilities. If it is originated in his essence, Most High, that would entail change in his essence and make his essence a substratum for new occurrences. If it occurs in a substratum, then it would be an attribute of the substratum, not the creator, Most High. Thus it can be seen that divine cognition can have no substratum. For Jahm, then, there are as many originated cognitions as there are existent objects of knowledge.

Third, Jahm claimed concerning the originated power that the human being has no power over anything, cannot be attributed capability, and is compelled in his acts. He has no power or will or choice of his own. God Most High creates the acts in him just as he creates them in all the inanimate objects. Acts are ascribed to the human being figuratively, in the same way they are ascribed to inanimate objects, as when a tree is said to bear fruit, water to run, a rock to move, the sun to rise and set, the sky to cloud over and rain, the earth to quake and to sprout, and the like. Just as the acts are compelled, so are reward and punishment compulsory. Once compulsion is affirmed, then *taklīf* (the imposition of particular obligations upon the human) is also compelled.[16]

Fourth, Jahm maintained that the movements of the people of the two eternal afterworlds *(ahl al-khālidayn)* come to an end. The garden and the fire will pass away after the people enter them, after the people of the garden enjoy its bliss and the people of the fire suffer its burning. We cannot conceive of motions that have no end, any more than we can conceive of motions that have no beginning. His words, Most High (11:107), "eternal in it," should be taken as hyperbole and emphasis, not as literally true in reference to eternity. We say, for example, "May God make so-and-so's dominion eternal." Jahm also cited in full his saying Most High (11:107), "Eternal in it as long as the heavens and earth endure, except by the will of your lord." The verse contains a condition and an exception, but eternity and everlastingness are unconditioned and accept no exception.

Fifth, he maintained that one who achieves *ma'rifa* and then verbally abjures the faith is not an infidel because of his abjuration. Knowledge and *ma'rifa* do not come to an end with an abjuration, so that he is still a believer. He said, faith is not divisible into parts. It cannot be divided up into contract *('aqd)*, word, and act. People cannot be placed in different degrees of faith, for the faith of the prophets and the faith of the community are of the same kind, because religious understandings *(ma'ārif)* cannot be put one above the other. The upholders of the old tradition *(salaf)* refuted him vehemently and accused him of *ta'ṭīl* (stripping the deity of its attributes). Jahm also agreed with the Mu'tazila in denying the final vision, in affirming the createdness of the words [of the Qur'an], and in maintaining the necessity of rational, religious understandings for the acceptance of audition (of revelation).[17]

B. The Najjāriyya

Here Shahrastani discusses a school that denies the divine attributes but affirms a moderate version of divine predetermination according to which the deity creates and determines all acts but the human servant ('abd) *"acquires" them and thus acquires a certain capability in performing them. This doctrine of acquisition* (kasb) *will be discussed in more detail in the summary of the thought of al-Ash'ari that follows.*

The Najjariyya were the followers of Ḥusayn ibn Muḥammad an-Najjār. Most of the Mu'taziles in Rayy and its environs are of this school. Even though they might differ in some areas (dividing into the schools of the Barghuthiyya, Za'afraniyya, and Mustadrika), they do not disagree on the basic issues discussed here.

They agree with the Mu'tazila in denying the attributes of knowledge, power, will, life, hearing, and sight, but they agree with the Attributionists in affirming that actions are created. The Najjariyya affirm that the creator, Most High, is a willer-for-himself *(murīd li nafsihi)* just as he is a knower-for-himself. Najjar extracted the necessary conclusions, and was in turn compelled by them to admit that the Most High was a willer of good and evil, benefit and harm. Najjar also said that the meaning of God's being a willer is that he is not subject to coercion or oppression. He also maintained that he [the deity] creates of the deeds of servants, both good and evil, praiseworthy and blameworthy, and that the servant acquires the deeds. He thus affirmed an influence on the part of the created power and called it "acquisition" *(kasb)* in accord with what al-Ash'ari maintained. He also agreed with al-Ash'ari in affirming a capacity with the act.

In regard to the question of the vision (by the human of the deity), he denied the possibility of a vision of Allah Most High through any perceptive faculty, although he granted that Allah Most High could transform the power of knowing *(ma'rifa)* within the heart to a kind of eye with which Allah could be seen, and that would be a kind of vision.[18]

THE ATTRIBUTIONISTS

Shahrastani's third and last major category is the Attributionists (Ṣifātiyya). *His naming of the categories is thus oblique. The Qadariyya (free willers) and the Compulsionists were named (however paradoxically in the case of the Qadariyya) after the position of divine predetermination. The Attributionists are named after their position of the question of divine unity and the reality of multiple attributes.*

Shahrastani introduces his essay on the Attributionists by speaking first of the Traditionalists, (salaf), *such as Mālik ibn Anas. The Traditionalists argued that the divine attributes mentioned in the Qur'an should be accepted, "without asking how"* (bi lākayfa). *If it says in the Qur'an that God is a seer and a hearer, one accepts these attributes without asking "how," without asking how it can be that an infinite being without organic sense organs "sees," or whether his seeing and his hearing are two eternal powers threatening absolute divine unity.*

Shahrastani then traces the birth of the Ash'arite school, the most famous school of Attributionists, in the famous theologian al-Ash'ari's rejection of Mu'tazilite positions and embracing of the traditionalist school.

Shahrastani then shows how the followers of Ash'ari modified his doctrine and brought back formal, rationalistic investigation of the issues of attributes, so that they came to be viewed as the moderate position between the Mu'tazilites and the Traditionalists. The full essay on the Ash'arites is far too long and complex to be included here. Representative samples are given here to demonstrate how Ash'arite thinking was viewed within medieval Islam.

The Attributionists (Ṣifātiyya)

Know that most of the Traditionalists affirmed that Allah Most High has eternal attributes of knowledge, power, will, hearing, seeing, speech, beauty, munificence, generosity, bestowal, glory, and majesty. They did not distinguish between attributes of essence and attributes of act, but spoke in the same way of them all. They also affirmed the "announced" *(khabarī)* attributes, such as "the two hands" and "the face," and did not interpret them figuratively. Instead they said: "These attributes have come to us in the divine ordinance *(shar')*, so we call them announced attributes."[19]

Because the Mu'tazila denied the attributes and the Traditionalists affirmed them, the Traditionalists were named "attributionists" *(ṣifātiyya)* and the Mu'tazila were named "vacators" *(mu'aṭṭila)* [for vacating the deity of its attributes]. In their affirmation of the attributes, some of the Traditionalists crossed the boundary into "likening" *(tashbīh)*, by applying to the deity attributes of creatures. Others limited themselves to attributes implied by the acts [of the divine] and those that were announced. They divided further into two camps. One camp would employ a moderate contextual interpretation *(ta'wīl 'alā wajh yaḥtamil al-lafẓ)*. The other stopped short of interpretation, saying: "We know through the dictates of reason that concerning Allah 'there is nothing like his like,' that he is like no creature and no creature is like him. Of that we are certain."

Then a later group went beyond what the Traditionalists had said and maintained that such expressions must be taken literally *('alā ẓāhirihā)* and should be explained (through *tafsīr*) as they appear without *ta'wīl*. However, they did not stop at the literal meaning, but fell into pure anthropomorphism *(tashbīh)*, which was contrary to the belief of the Traditionalists.

A very pure form of anthropomorphism existed among the Jews, not all of them, but among the Qaraites who found in the Torah many expressions suggesting anthropomorphism. Then the Shi'ites in our religion [i.e., Islam] fell into either *ghuluw* or *taqṣīr*. *Ghuluw* is the likening *(tashbīh)* of the Imams to the deity and the affirming of their transcendence *(taqaddus)*. *Taqṣīr* is the likening of the deity to one of the creatures.

With the appearance of the Mu'tazila and the Mutakallimun among the Traditionalists, some of the Shi'ites went back on their *ghuluw* and *taqṣīr* and fell into the Mu'tazilite belief. At the same time, a group of the Traditionalists went beyond literal explanation and fell into anthropomorphism.

Among the Traditionalists who neither accepted *ta'wīl* nor fell into anthropomorphism was Mālik ibn Anas (May God be pleased with both father and son). He affirmed that the "settling" [upon the throne] is known but "how" it occurred is unknown, that faith in it is incumbent, but the asking about it is innovation *(bid'a)*. Others include Aḥmad ibn Ḥanbal, Sufyān, Da'ūd al-Isfahānī, and their followers, and more recently, 'Abdullāh ibn Sa'īd al-Kilānī, Abū 'Abbās al-Qalānisī, and Ḥārith ibn Asad al-Muḥā sibī.[20] These latter were of the Traditionalists, except that they propagated scholastic theology and supported the dogmas of the Traditionalists with scholastic proofs and basic arguments *(barāhīn uṣūliyya).* Some wrote and some taught, until a debate took place between Abu al-Hasan al-Ash'ari and his teacher over a question concerning interest and best interest *(ṣalāḥ* and *aṣlaḥ).* They disagreed and al-Ash'ari went over to the Traditionalists. Ash'ari supported their positions with scholastic methods, and that became a school for the people of *sunna* (tradition) and *jamā'a* (community). Thus the name "Attributionists" came to be applied to the followers of Ash'ari. Inasmuch as the anthropomorphists *(mushabbiha)* and the Karramites also affirm the attributes, we have numbered them as two groups within the larger category of "Attributionists."[21]

The Ash'arites

Selections from the section on the Ash'arites focus on the issues of divine unity (tawḥīd) *and divine predetermination* (qadar). *They emphasize the doctrine of* kasb *(acquisition) whereby all acts are created and predetermined by the deity, but the human "acquires" a power* (qudra) *over the act as it is enacted and thus also acquires a responsibility for the act.*[22]

[Abū l-Ḥasan] al-Ash'arī said:

If you reflect upon your creation, from what thing it began, and how it proceeded in the development, phase by phase, until arriving at the completed creature, and you know with certainty that it could not on its own have planned out the process, moved itself through its stages, and raised itself up from the lowest stage to the stage of completion, you will know necessarily that it has a maker, who is powerful and knowing. It is inconceivable that these acts, reflective of a directive wisdom, could have proceeded from nature. The appearance of traces of choice in the innate disposition, the clarity of the traces of judgment, and the masterful construction of the creature all negate the notion that such developments proceeded from nature.

[The creator] must therefore have undeniable attributes as indicated by his acts. Just as his acts indicate his being knowing, powerful, and willing, they also indicate knowledge, power, and will. Such indication is not dependent upon whether [the acts] are witnessed or hidden. There would not be any authentic meaning to "the knower" unless he were the possessor of knowledge, nor to "the powerful" unless he possessed power, nor to "the willer" unless he were the possessor of will. With knowledge comes judgment and perfect mastery. With power comes the act of establishment *(al-*

wuqūʿ) and origination. With will comes the determination of one time over another time, one determination over another, one form over another. Nor can we conceive of the essence *(adh-dhāt)* unless it be living through life, for the reasons we have mentioned.

He [Ashʿari] inextricably bound up the deniers of attributes in his proof, saying: You have granted, and the proof exists, that [the creator] is knowing and powerful. Therefore what is meant by these two attributes must be either one or plural. If they both mean the same thing, then he must know through his power and be powerful through his knowing, and from the simple knowledge of his essence we would be able to know that he was knowing-powerful—which cannot, of course, be the case.

Know that the two expressions are different, and that difference must be either to the expressions themselves, to their state *(ḥāl)*, or to the attribute. The difference cannot be based on the difference in the expressions alone; reason would demand a difference in what was understood and intellected. Even if there were not expressions, reason would have no doubt about the meaning of the two concepts. Nor can the difference be in their state. Affirmation of an attribute cannot fall in some intermediary between existence and nonexistence, or between affirmation and denial. That was the position of his school.[23]

Abu l-Hasan [al-Ashʿari] said that the creator, Most High, was knowing through his knowledge, powerful through his power, living through his life, willing through his will, speaking through his speech, hearing through his hearing, seeing through his sight. Regarding the rest [of the attributes], he had a different opinion.[24]

He said that these attributes [knowledge, power, life, will, speech, hearing, and sight] are eternal, established in the essence of the Most High. They cannot be said to be he, nor other-than-he. They cannot be said to be not-he nor not-other-than-he. The proof that he is a speaker through an eternal speech and a willer through an eternal will is that he is the master and the master is one who commands and prohibits and has control of command and prohibition. Now either he does this in his essence or in a substratum or in a nonsubstratum. It is impossible that he does this in his essence, because that would lead to it [his essence] being a substratum for originations *(ḥawādith)*, and that is impossible. It is impossible that it occur in a substratum because that would entail that the substratum be characterized by him [the creator], which cannot be the case. Nor can it happen in a nonsubstratum, because such a thing is absurd. Therefore it is determined that he is eternal, carrying out his attributes by himself, and that is the case with will, hearing, seeing.

He said: His will is one, everlasting, connected to all willings from his own actions, and the actions of his servants insofar as they are created for him, not insofar as they are acquired for them. From that, he said that he willed everything, good and bad, beneficial and harmful, just as he willed and knew it to be. He willed from his servants what he knew and what he commanded his pen to write on the preserved tablet.[25] That is his decree, ruling, and predetermination which never changes and can never be replaced. It is impossible for anything to be against what is known and predetermined in form in this manner.

According to his [Ash'ari's] school, it is possible [for the deity] to enjoin upon someone an act that that person cannot carry out. Such a situation is possible for the reasons we have mentioned, and also because capability for him [Ash'ari] is an accident and does not remain for two moments. In the condition of being assigned an act, the person assigned it might be incapable of completing it because the one assigning it will not have predetermined the carrying out of what he has assigned. But it cannot possibly happen that a person would be assigned something which that person has no ability to carry out, fundamentally. Such a thing is impossible even if it were found in the text of the Book.[26]

Al-Ash'ari said: The servant is capable of carrying it out because the human being finds in himself a necessary distinction between movements such as quaking and trembling and movements that come about through choice and will. The distinction is due to the fact that motions that are chosen occur under the power dependent upon the choice of the one who has power. In this sense he maintained that the acquired was determined to happen through and occurred under the created power.

In the principle of Abu l-Hasan [al-Ash'ari], the originated power has no influence on events because the meaning of "being originated" is one. It cannot vary in respect to essence and accidents. If the originated being exerted an influence in respect to the world of origination, it would exert an influence in the origination of every originated being, even to the point of originating colors, tastes, scents, and the origination of substances and bodies—and following the same logic—to the establishment of heaven and earth through an originated power. But it is Allah Most High who has carried out his custom *(sunna)* in such a way as to create subsequent to the originated power, or under it and with it, the act that occurs when the servant frees himself for it. That act is called an acquisition; it is creation by Allah Most High and brought forth, occurring, and acquired by the servant, occurring under his power.[27]

Chronology of Some Important Figures in the Development of Sufism

Ḥasan al-Baṣrī	d. 110/728
Ja'far aṣ-Ṣadiq	d. 145/765
Rābi'a al-'Adawiyya	d. 185/801
al-**Muḥāsibī,** al-Ḥarith	d. 243/857
al-**Bisṭāmī,** Abū Yazīd (Bāyezid)	d. ca. 261/875
Sahl at-Tustarī, Ibn 'Abdullāh	d. 283/896
Ibn Sālim, Muḥammad Abū 'Abdullāh	d. 297/909
al-**Junayd,** Abū l-Qāsim, Muḥammad	d. 297/910
al-**Ḥallāj,** Ḥusayn ibn Manṣūr	d. 304/922
ash-**Shiblī,** Abū Bakr	d. 334/946
an-**Niffarī,** 'Abu l-Jabbār	d. 354/965
as-**Sarrāj,** Abū Naṣr aṭ-Ṭūsī	d. 378/988
al-**Makkī,** Abu Ṭālib, Muḥammad	d. 386/966
as-**Sulamī,** Abū 'Abdu r-Raḥmān	d. 412/1021
Ibn Sīna (Avicenna)	d. 428/1037
al-**Qushayrī,** Abū l-Qāsim	d. 465/1074
Abū Ḥamid al-**Ghāzalī**	d. 505/1111
Shahrastānī	d. 548/1153
Ruzbehān Baqlī	d. 606/1209
Fariduddīn **'Attar**	d. 627/1230
Muḥyiddīn **Ibn al-'Arabī**	d. 638/1240
Jalāluddīn **Rūmī**	d. 672/1273

Notes

NOTES TO THE INTRODUCTION

1. Muḥammad Sahl ibn ʻAbdullāh at-Tustarī, *Tafsīr al-Qur'ān al-ʻAẓīm* (Cairo: Dār al-Kutab al-Gharbiyya al-Kubrā, 1329/1911), pp. 40–41.

2. These generalizations were common throughout Orientalist literature, and often reflected similar generalizations about classical Judaism. See, for example, the chapter on Sufism in Ignaz Goldziher, *Vorlesungen uber den Islām* (Heidelberg: Carl Winter, 1910; *Introduction to Islamic Theology and Law,* trans. by Andras Hamori and Ruth Hamori [Princeton, N.J.: Princeton University Press, 1981]). At the same time, Islamic reformers and modernists, many of them influenced by nineteenth-century European thought, imposed a similar dichotomy; Sufism was viewed as a foreign import, a repository of superstition and encrustation on the originally pure Islam of the shariʻa. Sufi spirituality was viewed as a form of irrationality. For a typical example, see the section on Sufism in Ismail Al-Faruqi, *Cultural Atlas of Isla*m (New York: Macmillan, 1986). In many cases a popularized version of the "spirit versus the law" is imposed on Islam as the spirit (Sufism) versus the law (Shariʻa).

This dichotomy continues to exist and can be found as an unexamined premise in recent texts meant to introduce Islam to the Western reader. See the discussion of Sufism in John Esposito, *Islam: the Straight Path* (Oxford: Oxford University Press, 1994).

3. According to the presentation of her life and sayings given by authors of a much later period.

4. From Bukhārī, 81:38. For a discussion of the hadith of free devotions *(ḥadīth an-nawāfil)*, see William Graham, *Divine Word and Prophetic Word in Early Islam* (The Hague: Mouton, 1977), p. 173. Note that the last phrase, "the tongue with which he speaks," occurs only in some versions of the hadith.

5. For transmission as a formal rite, see Carl Ernst, *Eternal Garden: Mysticism, History, and Politics at a South Asian Sufi Center* (Albany: SUNY Press, 1992), and Mathew W. Simonds, "The *Musalsalāt* Literature in the 18th Century" (paper presented at the annual meeting of the Middle East Studies Association, Research Triangle Park, North Carolina, 11/13/93). In this paper, the notion that *"baraka"*

or blessing is passed on through the official rites of transmission is introduced with evidence from an entire genre of literature discussing such *isnad baraka.*

6. A fourth writer deserves to be placed alongside Sarraj, Sulami, and Qushayri: Abū Ṭālib al-Makkī (d. 386/996). Makki's "Food for the Hearts" *(Qūt al-Qulūb)* combines the perspective of Tustari and his disciples (known as the Sā limiyya after Tustari's disciple Muhammad ibn Sālim and his son), the moral and psychological rigor of Muhasibi, and the intellectual sweep of Sarraj with a careful and continual demonstration of not only the compatibility, but the essential grounding of Sufism within ritual Islam. However, because there is no critical edition and because the printed editions that exist are extremely difficult to use, I have not been able to translate any part of it for this volume. Makki's work was appropriated in part by the more famous Abu Hamid al-Ghazali (d. 505/1111) and became the basis for much of Ghazali's magnus opum, *The Revival of the Religious Sciences (iḥyā' 'ulūmi d-dīn).* How much of Ghazali's work is truly original is difficult to ascertain until a much more thorough study of Makki has been made.

7. Cf. Carl Ernst, "Mystical Language and the Teaching Context in the Early Lexicons of Sufism," in *Mysticism and Language,* ed. S. Katz (Oxford: Oxford University Press, 1992), pp. 181–201.

8. Not all influential Sufis are represented; there are others that could have been included, such as at-Tirmidhi, whose writings were influential on later Sufi ideas of saintship, and Abu Talib al-Makki, mentioned in note 6, above. I hope that these selections here may be of use to readers in investigating the rich and complex world of early Islamic spirituality, and may encourage others to edit, translate, and make accessible more of this heritage.

CHAPTER 1. SOURCES OF ISLAMIC MYSTICISM

1. The point is made by Michel Chodkiewicz in connection with the later mystic, Ibn 'Arabi *(Ocean without Shore* [Albany: SUNY Press, 1993]).

2. I need to say a word specifically about the problems of translating the Qur'an. According to Islamic belief, the Qur'an is an "inimitable" text, and that belief is applied to the Qur'an in its original Arabic form. Thus from the point of view of the doctrine of inimitability, the notion of a "translation" of the Qur'an is problematic, at the very least. From the point of view of this translator, there are other, more practical issues, that make translating the Qur'an a deeply problematic exercise. The particular Qur'anic phonological parallelism and Arabic "sound patterns" have never been successfully translated or recreated in other languages, and these sound patterns are intimately interwoven with the semantic patterns of the text. Though it is of course written down, the Qur'an is both an oral text and a performed text in Islamic cultures; it is heard before it is read, it is heard constantly, recited by those trained in bringing out and lingering over the interior sound patterns of the text. From this point of view, the emphasis in Qur'anic education on

learning the sounds first, on memorizing the text with emphasis on exact pronunciation, *before* studying the grammar and vocabulary of classical Arabic is not—as it has so often been interpreted by Western writers and some modernist Muslim intellectuals—a form of mere "rote" learning. Rather, it is beginning with first things first. What is needed, ultimately—and new changes in the way we receive and communicate information will make this possible soon—is a presentation of the Qur'an, one that brings it across as performed recitation.

3. My interpolate commentary (in italics) is meant only to highlight a few themes. There is no way to do justice to these passages in an interpretive sense without exploring their multiple resonances with other passages throughout the Qur'an.

4. The Arabic dual construction demands the translation "two of you." What the "two" are has been a matter of debate within the tradition of Qur'anic commentary; some suggest it refers to humans and jinn. I prefer to see it in the context of the notion of polarity signs (male and female, night and day, odd and even). The fact that the antecedent for "the two of you" is never specified places the hearer within that world of polarity signs, but without any fixed representation.

5. *Jinn* is the plural of *jinnī* (genie), a semi-spirit being of the desert that in pre-Islamic poetry was identified with poetic inspiration, love, and madness. The Qur'an affirms the existence of the jinn, but emphasizes that unlike poets, the Prophet Muhammad was not inspired by jinn, but rather was given the word of God. The notion that the jinn were made of fire was used by early Qur'anic commentators to contrast them to the angels, who were made of light. The notion of jinn prevalent in the West comes from the much later Arabian Nights tradition, with its urban and sea-trade contexts.

6. The precise meaning of the "two weighty ones" (*al-thaqalān*) has been a matter of debate within the exegetical tradition. Some commentators suggest the two weighty ones are the two major earth-beings, the humans and the jinn.

7. In pre-Islamic Arabia, satans were a group of semi-spirits related to jinn and ghouls. In the Qur'an, the focus is on a single individual, *the satan*. The term is cognate to the Hebrew for Satan and does appear to be used as a proper name, justifying the use of the upper-case *S*. In some Sufi texts the older understanding of shaytān appears, with references in both the singular and the plural. In those texts I use the expressions "the satan" and "satans."

8. See the commentary on Qur'an 2:30–33 in Tabari: Abū Ja'far Muḥammad ibn Jarīr at-Ṭabarī, *The Commentary on the Qur'ān*, abridged translation by W. F. Madelung and A. Jones, Vol. 1 (Oxford: Oxford University Press, 1987).

9. As mentioned in the introduction to this passage, the Qur'an suddenly shifts voices when referring to the deity. Some commentators try to explain the frequent use of the plural "we" for the divine speaker by saying it refers to the deity and the angels, but this passage, where the "we" voice speaks directly to the angels, seems to rule out that possibility. Other commentators suggest versions of the "royal we." My own view is that the breakup of reference to the divine speaker into several

different voices resists any simple explanation and requires an investigation into the psychodynamics of Qur'anic discourse. One of the few recent examinations of this neglected topic is that of Andrew Rippin, "Celestial Stammering: 'Point of View' in Qur'anic Discourse" (paper presented at the American Oriental Society, Cambridge, Mass., March 30, 1992).

10. Cf. *Sura 15:28–31:*

When your lord said to the angels
I am going to create a person from hard-dried clay.
  When I have shaped him
and have blown into him of my spirit
fall bowing before him.
  All the angels fell bowing together
Except Iblis who disdained to bow.

11. See the selections from Junayd's *Book of Fanā'*, Chapter 8, below.

12. The lote tree is one of several important trees: the tree of life discussed in early Islamic sacred histories, the tree under which Maryam found nurture and comfort before giving birth to Jesus, the firmly rooted tree as an analogue for the true sign of reality, and the blessed olive tree, neither of the East nor of the West, that is at the center of the most famous mystical passage of the Qur'an, the verse of light. In much later literature, these trees overlap in a multivalent and multireferential tree-symbol.

13. See Norman K. Brown, "The Apocalypse of Islam," *Social Text* 3, no. 8 (1983–1984): 155–171, a rich and original reading of Sura 18.

14. The term for "person" here, *nafs*, is grammatically feminine. As I have argued in detail elsewhere, grammatical gender is not merely grammatical in the Qur'an. Thus, I have tried to more accurately reflect gender balance in the Qur'an, not by imposing feminine constructions, but by breaking with the tradition—which has no Qur'anic or linguistic justification—of repressing them. See M. Sells, "Sound, Spirit, and Gender in *Sūrat al-Qadr*," *Journal of the American Oriental Society* 111, no. 2 (April-May 1991): 239–259.

15. The ways in which these feminine "sound figures" are stressed is demonstrated throughout Sells, "Sound, Spirit, and Gender in *Sūrat al-Qadr*," and "Sound and Meaning in *Sūrat al-Qāri'a*," *Arabica* 40, no. 3 (1993): 403–430.

16. For the various meanings and levels of meaning involved in *tawḥīd*, see, for example, the discussion of Junayd, in Chapter 8, below.

17. For some of the issues surrounding this term, see Uri Rubin, "*Al-Ṣamad* and the High God: An Interpetation of *sūra* CXII," *Der Islam* 61 (1984): 217.

18. From this point, I will simply use the anglicized form, Mi'raj, without diacriticals.

19. *Ṣaḥīḥ Muslim bi Sharḥ an-Nawawī*, vol. 1 (Cairo: Al-Maṭba'a al-Miṣriyya, 1924), pp. 209–232.

20. Cf. Gn 2:10–15: "There was a river flowing from Eden to water the garden, and when it left the garden it branched into four streams. The name of the first is Pishon; that is the river which encircles all the land of Havilah, where the gold [or frankincense] is. The gold of that land is good; bdellium and cornelians are also to be found there. The name of the second river is Gihon; this is the one which encircles all the land of Cush. The name of the third is Tigris; this is the river which runs east of Asshur. The fourth river is the Euphrates." (*The New English Bible* [New York: Oxford University Press, 1971], p. 2).

21. "As far as": the Arabic term is *muntahā*, an apparent lexical allusion to the Qur'anic phrase "lote tree of the furthest limit" (*sidrat al-muntahā*).

22. The commentators have trouble explaining the precise meaning of this point, repeated throughout the Mi'raj accounts. Choosing "the innate character" or *fiṭra* could refer to Muhammad's choosing the drink that accorded with his own innate disposition, or with a more universal innate religion, but the context does not seem to allow a definitive interpretation.

23. *'Araja* (he took me up)—the verb from which the verbal noun *mi'rāj* (rising, ascent) is derived.

24. In later Islamic literature, the Qur'anic prophet Idris is identified with the biblical Enoch, partially on the correlation of the Qur'anic verse 19:57 (*We took him up to a high station*) with Gn 5:24. Enoch's death is never recounted; instead he departs the earth (or at least the scene) in a distinctive manner: "Enoch walked with God, and he was no more, for God took him." In some philosophical and esoteric circles, Idris/Enoch was identified in turn with Hermes Trismegistus and the philosophical perspectives of the Hermetic Corpus, especially the Poimandres and Asclepius.

25. *Ṣaḥīḥ Muslim*, pp. 218–222. This account of the rise through the heavens contains the formulaic question and response between Jibril and the guardian (*khāzin*) of each heaven. Muhammad's account seems to reflect the dazed condition of the Prophet: he remembers only the prophets Adam, Jesus, Idris, Moses, and Abraham, and cannot place them in their normal heavens. Indeed, he remembers only Adam in the first heaven and Abraham in the sixth.

26. *Ṣaḥīḥ Muslim*, pp. 222–223. The word translated as domes, *janābīdh*, is obscure in Arabic, and an-Nawawi offers some even more obscure possibilities. It may be an Arabized, broken plural form of the Persian word for dome, *gumbad*[*h*].

27. Ibid., p. 223, lines 1–7.

28. Ibid., pp. 224–225.

29. The grammatically feminine pronoun *hā* is without a stated antecedent, unless we interpret the antecedent as the seventh heaven. But the commentators have no qualms whatsoever in identifying it as the lote tree. See ibid., p. 224, gloss.

30. There follows here a phrase: "And when they leave, they don't return *akharu mā 'alayhim*" that even the inveterate commentator an-Nawawi admits is obscure (see ibid., p. 225).

31. From *Kitāb Sīrat Rasūl Allāh* (The Book of the Sira of the Messenger of God): *Das Leben Muhammed's nach Muhammed Ibn Isḥāk bearbeitet von Abd el-Malik*

Ibn Hischām, ed. Ferdinand Wüstenfeld (Göttingen, 1858) I: 263–271. I have translated those passages relevant for Islamic mysticism. I have omitted the original apology of Ibn Isḥāq in which he lists his sources and defends the veracity of the incidents reported (Wüstenfeld 263) and other sections, as noted below, that are of little relevance to the Sufi tradition.

32. Interpreted by some as Gabriel.

33. There occurs here a report by Qatāda describing how Jibril calmed the refractory Buraq by telling him he should respect the Prophet of God, thus allowing Muhammad to mount him.

34. (He said:) Then the Envoy, peace and blessings on him, turned back to Mecca. When he approached the Quraysh the next morning and reported to them what had happened, most of the people said "By God, the matter is clear! A camel train takes a month to go to Sha'm [Syria] and a month to return. Does that Muhammad there go and return to Mecca in a single night?" (He said:) Many of those who had given themselves to Islam went back on it. The people went to Abu Bakr and said: "What do you make of your companion claiming that he went in a single night to the *bayt al-muqaddas*, performed the prayer there, and returned to Mecca?" (He said:) Abu Bakr said: "You're lying about him!" They said: "To the contrary, there he is in the prayer enclosure telling people about it!" Abu Bakr replied: "By God, if he said it, it is true (*ṣadaqa*). What by God! are you so amazed about? By God, he has told me that a communication comes to him from Allah all the way from the heaven to the earth in a single hour of day or night and I believed him to be true—and that goes beyond what you find so amazing."

Then he came forward all the way to the Envoy of God, peace and blessings on him, and said: "Prophet of God, you have told these that you went to the *bayt al-muqaddas* last night." He answered "Yes." He said: "Prophet of God, describe it for me, for I have been there."

(Al-Ḥasan said:) The Envoy of God, peace and blessings on him—and I [Hasan] was lifted up so that I could see him as he spoke—began to describe it to Abu Bakr. Abu Bakr was saying "You have told the truth. I testify that you are the Rasul Allah." Every time he described anything for him, he would say "You have told the truth. I testify that you are the Envoy of God." When he was finished, the Envoy of God, peace and blessings on him, said to Abu Bakr: "You, Abu Bakr, are the Ṣiddīq [the one who testified to the truth, *ṣaddaqa*]" and from then on he called him the Ṣiddīq (Ibn Hishām, *Kitāb Sīrat Rasūl Allāh* 1: 265).

35. Here occurs a report by Sa'īd al-Musayyab with some unusual details about the appearance of Moses (thin, curly-haired, hook nosed), Jesus (freckled and looking as if he had come from a bath) and looking like a certain 'Urwa b. Mas'ūd. This report is followed by an extended report from Umm Hāni bint Abī Ṭalib (Hind) in which the Prophet describes various moments in his journey through Syria, the valleys he passed, the caravans he met, etc.

36. The text of Ibn Hishām continues with detailed depiction of the ascent through the seven heavens and the reception of the obligation of five prayers. The

accounts are basically consistent with the hadith accounts, but much more elaborate, with an emphasis on reward and punishment, physical characteristics of the prophets, and other details that have relatively little relevance for the mystical texts that are presented in this volume.

37. More detailed discussions can be found in the following recent works: Suzanne Stetkevych, ed. *Reorientations: Studies in Arabic and Persian Poetics* (Bloomington: Indiana University Press, 1994); Jaroslav Stetkevych, *Zephyrs of Najd: The Poetics of Nostalgia in the Classical Arabic Nasīb* (Chicago: University of Chicago Press, 1993); Mustansir Mir, ed., *The Literary Heritage of Classical Islam* (Princeton: Darwin Press, 1993); M. Sells, "Like the Arms of a Drowning Man: Simile and Symbol Worlds in the *Nāqa* Sections of Bashama's *Hajarta Umāma*," in *A Festschrift in Honor of Professor Ewald Wagner, 2 volumes*, ed. W. Heinrichs and G. Schoeler (Beirut/Istanbul: Beiruter Studien, 1994), pp. 18–41; idem, *Desert Tracings: Six Classic Arabian Odes by 'Alqama, Shanfara, Labid, Antara, Al-A'sha, and Dhu ar-Rumma* (Middletown: Wesleyan University Press, 1993); idem, "Ibn 'Arabi's *Alā Yā Hamāmāti l-Arākati wa l-Bāni*, A Modern Translation," *Journal of the Muhyiddin Ibn 'Arabi Society*, 10 (1991): 1–11; and Emil Homerin, *From Arab Poet to Muslim Saint: Ibn al-Fāriḍ, His Verse and His Shrine* (Columbia: University of South Carolina Press, 1994).

38. In translating place-names and personal names from poetry, I mark English accentual accents rather than the quantitative transliterations, in order to allow the rhythm of the poetic translations to come through.

39. From M. Sells, *Desert Tracings*, pp. 35–36.

40. Ibid., p. 36.

41. Ibid., pp. 36–37.

42. See John Seybold, "The Earliest Demon Lover: *The Ṭayf al-Khayāl* in *al-Mufaḍḍalīyāt*, in Stetkevych, ed., *Reorientations*, pp. 180–189.

43. From M. Sells, "Along the Edge of Mirage: The *Mufaddaliyya* of Mukhabbal as-Sa'dī, an Interpretation," in Mir, ed., *Literary Heritage of Classical Islam*, pp. 119–120. The water imagery in this poem, as in all the other nasībs, brings together an eroticized world of sexual waters with a purified world of ablutionary waters. See M. Sells, "Guises of the Ghul: Dissembling Simile and Semantic Overflow in the Classical Arabic *Nasīb*" in Stetkevych, ed., *Reorientations*, pp. 103–164.

44. Sells, *Desert Tracings*, p. 14.

45. Sura 26:225. Though often interpreted as a kind of Platonic criticism of poetry, the Qur'anic depiction here could also be viewed as simply stating what the poets themselves would freely admit.

46. From the elegy of Ḥassān ibn Thābit, translated by Stetkevych in *The Zephyrs of Najd*, p. 61.

47. Sells, *Desert Tracings*, p. 18.

48. See Homerin, *From Arab Poet to Muslim Saint*, pp. 33–54.

49. The people of 'Ad, the city of Iram: a fabled Arabian civilization whose destruction is recounted in the Qur'an as an example of the fate of those civilizations that reject their prophets.

50. Name given to Sassanian Persian kings (derived from Caesar).

51. See the Sarraj passages on Bistami, below.

52. Reading *wa annī anti* for *wa annī 'anki*: the reading of K and A (in which this reading is written in above the text). The alternative reading would give: "I search my heart secret for desire for you/ but find only myself, that you are separate, and the inner essence greater."

53. See Qushayri's "On the Interpretation of Expressions," below.

54. Sells, *Desert Tracings*, pp. 67–76. For the Arabic text of the passage cited here, see *Dhū al-Rumma, the Dīwān of Ghaylān ibn 'Uqba*, ed. Carlile Henry Hayes Macartney (Cambridge: Cambridge University Press, 1919), pp. 80–83.

CHAPTER 2. EARLY SUFI QUR'AN INTERPRETATION

1. These translations of selected sections are based on the text of Paul Nwyia. See his, "Le Tafsīr Mystique Attribué a Ga'far Ṣādiq: Édition critique," *Mélanges de l'Université Saint-Joseph* 43 (Beirut, 1968): pp. 181–230. Nwyia collected the various interpretations attributed to Ja'far (d. 148/765) from the *Ḥaqā'iq at-Tafsīr (Realities of Interpretation)* of Sulamī (d. 412/1021), basing the edition on three manuscripts from Istanbul. I have selected those passages that offer a distinctively Sufi interpretation, with special emphasis on the more extended sections of commentary. Nwyia discusses the thorny issue of whether the commentary is correctly attributed to Ja'far in his introduction (pp. 181–185).

Ja'far was born and lived his entire life in Medina and lived during the transition between the Umayyad Caliphate of Damascus and the Abbasid Caliphate that became centered in Baghdad.

2. See Paul Nwyia, *Exégese coranique et langage mystique* (Beirut: Dar al-Machreq Editeurs, 1970), pp. 158–159. Nwyia lists two manuscripts: Bankipore, n. 1460, 232 fol (v. Catalogue of the Arabic and Persian mss., t. XVIII, 2, pp. 143–144) and Istanbul, Nafiz Pasa 65, 154 fol. For a close discussion of Ja'far's Qur'anic exegesis, see pp. 156–208 of *Exégese coranique.*

3. Ibid., p. 159. The manuscript is listed as Yeni Cami 43.

4. Because the Yeni Cami manuscript is not available to me, I have translated this passage from Nwyia's French translation of it on p. 159 of *Exégese coranique,* no. 3.

5. For an example of *du'ā* and *munājāt,* see Imam Zayn al-'Abidin, *The Psalms of Islam (Al-Sahifat al-Sajjadiyya),* trans. William Chittick (London: Muhammadi Trust, 1988).

6. While Moses' encounter with the burning bush and his experience on Mount Sinai are distinct events in the narrative of Exodus, the Qur'an tends to give various versions of a single encounter that has elements analogous to each of the two Exodus episodes. Western polemicists have found such differences between Qur'anic and biblical accounts a way of portraying Muhammad as a copier of biblical

traditions who just could not get them right. In Islamic tradition, the discrepancies are a result of errors in the Jewish and Christian transmission of the original prophetic revelations, and the Qur'an is viewed as offering the original and correct version of the story.

7. "Humanity": *bashariyyatihi*. The antecedent of "him/it" here is not clear. The most probable reading is that it refers to the deity: Moses heard words from his own self and attributed them to the deity. The meaning is clarified below when Moses' experience is compared to that of Muhammad. God spoke to Moses through Moses' human attributes, but to Muhammad through the attributes of Muhammad's lord.

8. The ambiguity is even more acute here than in previous instance. Does the "his" refer to the words of the deity or the words of Moses? The grammatical ambiguity is enhanced by and enhances the meditation on the fine line between unmediated revelation and that which passes through the medium of one's own consciousness or sensibility. Some manuscripts then read redundantly: "In this he confided in him."

9. "Face-to-face," and below, "eye witness": *'ayyānan;* "Face-to-face vision in respect to the servant": *mu'āyanat ru'yati llahi li 'abdihi.*

10. An alternative translation would be: The eyewitness of the lord belongs to the servant while the servant passes away; witnessing the servant belongs to his lord while the servant endures in his lord.

11. "Manifestation": *tajallī;* "contact": *wusla;* "knowing": *ma'rifa*; "innate disposition": *fiṭra*; "interval of distance": *masāfa*; "apparition": *mubāyana.* Yet another elusive Sufi aphorism.

12. The implication of this cryptic comment is that, because the deity cannot be seen, Moses must believe without seeing.

13. The passage then turns (verses 15–16) to a discussion of the apocalyptic final hour, and then (verses 17–24) with Moses being given the power to turn his staff into a snake as a sign to show before the Pharoah.

14. *Jabarūt:* a technical term that designates one of the higher realms of reality, related to the Arabic *jabr* (power, compulsion), but non-Arabic in morphology, probably borrowed from Aramaic, Syriac, or Hebrew.

15. A lyrical and elusive point. It is not clear whether this "fall" represents Muhammad's birth and prophecy on earth, and thus suggests the preexistent Muhammad discussed more explicitly in later Sufi writings, such as those of Ibn 'Arabi (d. 638/1240), or perhaps the death of the Prophet.

16. "How-it-was" or its "howness": *kayfiyya.* When the vision approaches the peak of nearness and intensity, the mode or manner of its being is no longer accessible as the seer is totally overcome.

17. The commentary skips over the "lote tree" part of the vision passages (53:13–17), perhaps because they have been discussed in the earlier comparison of the vision of Moses to that of Muhammad.

18. "Those with *taqwā*," that is, with the quality of being on-guard and vigilant against the wiles of one's own ego-self.

NOTES

19. "Friendship with the divine": *wilāya.* The word has a complex lexical field. See Michel Chokiewitz, *Le Sceau des saints: prophetie et saintité dans la doctrine d'ibn 'Arabi* (Paris: Gallimard, 1986).

20. *Wa ḥaṣluhu fī mīdān as-sarūr wa l-ḥuḍūr wa l-qabḍa.* Another difficult phrase, the obscurity of which is attested by variant manuscript readings.

21. That which is annihilated in *fanā'* is then reconstituted and endures through the enduring *(baqā')* of the divine.

22. An early example of the attitude known as *malāmatiyya,* the regarding of blame in the eyes of the wider society as a protection against self-admiration, and conversely, the regarding of praise as dangerous. The point draws on a number of Qur'anic passages explaining to the Prophet Muhammad and to the general hearer of the message why the wicked are sometimes allowed to prosper and be praised. The two Ja'farian statements on this verse offer a good example of the anthology character of the text. The first Ja'far interpretation was primarily concerned with Sufi notions of passing away and enduring, with a focus on the synchronic notion of annihilation, that it can occur in the present moment, mystically. The second quotation is more concerned with the reason that exterior reality, in which the good are sometimes disdained while the wicked prosper, is allowed to continue; in other words, in which the annihilation and renewal (in the more conventional sense of the final judgment and resurrection) do not take place immediately.

23. *B* (the Arabic *bā'*), *s* (the Arabic *sīn*), and *m* (the Arabic *mīm*).

24. For an excellent view of twentieth-century letter symbolism, see Martin Lings, *A Sufi Saint of the Twentieth Century* (Berkeley: University of California Press, 1971).

25. "Column": *'amūd.* The first letter of *'amūd* is the /'/ (the arabic *'ayn*), not *a,* equivalent to the Arabic *alif,* which begins the word "Allah." The correspondence depends on the shape of the *alif,* which as a vertical straight line represents a column.

26. *Mā'īya,* i.e., its quiddity or whatness (from the Arabic pronoun *mā*—"what").

27. *Kayfiyya,* i.e., its "howness" (from the Arabic *kayfa*—"how").

28. These translations are based on selected passages from the following Arabic printed text: Muḥammad Sahl ibn 'Abdullāh at-Tustarī, *Tafsīr al-Qur'ān al-'Aẓī m* (Cairo: Dār al-Kutub al-Gharbiyya al-Kubrā, 1329/1911). For a full discussion of Tustarī and his tafsir, see Gerhard Böwering, *The Mystical Vision of Existence in Classical Islam: The Qur'ānic Hermeneutics of the Ṣūfī Sahl at-Tustarī (d. 283/896)* (Berlin: Walter de Gruyter, 1980).

29. The milieu in which Tustari lived and taught has been described by Böwering (*Mystical Vision,* p. xx) as follows:

> Tustari, a native of Tustar in the Persian province of Khuzistan, who died at Basra, the Arab metropolis of Lower 'Iraq, lived in a region where for centuries the Iranian civilization of Susian had bordered on the cultural traditions of Southern Mesopotamia. His own life-span arches these two

areas at a time when, in the 3rd/9th century, the 'Abbasid Caliphate absorbed the Iranian and Hellenistic traditions under its domain, moulding them into the Arabic matrix of the nascent civilization of Islam.

30. The verse begins with the distinctive Qur'anic "when," which would normally open a relative clause but which is never followed by an independent clause. Thus it is ungrammatical by conventional standards. Interpreters and translators frequently interpret a phrase such as "remember when . . ." in order to put this locution into conventional grammar.

31. The use of the word "glass" *(zujāj)* in Tustari's commentary connects his theory of Muhammadian light directly to the Qur'anic light verse.

32. Here we have another example of the Qur'anic unfinished when-clause.

33. The verse continues: "And Ibrahim, Musa, 'Issa (Jesus) the son of Maryam, a covenant that binds."

34. Page 40, line 11: *an yablighu 'an allāhi ta'ālā amrahu wa nahyahu.*

35. "Power": *qudrā*; "design": *murād.* Böwering (*Mystical Vision*, p. 155, lines 5–6) paraphrases this section as "God gathered His design *(murād)* from his creation and apprised them of the origin *(ibtidā')* and the final outcome *(intihā')* which he keeps in store for them." The language of the text (p. 40) at least does not seem to offer direct evidence that the deity "apprised" the progeny of their destinies, though it does not rule such a possibility out either.

36. This is a homonymic pun on *balā*, a grammatical particle that means "yes, indeed" used after a negatively phrased question, and *balā'* and the word derived from it, *ibtilā'*, both of which mean "trial," "test," or "torment."

37. The immediate cause for this citation is of course to show the relationship between trial and testing *(balā', ibtilā')* and the partial homonym "yes indeed" *(balā)*. But the existence of the divine throne on water is a key motive in early Islamic mysticism (as it is in early Jewish mysticism). See M. Sells, "The Semantics of Mystical Union in Islam," in *Mystical Union and Monotheistic Faith,* ed. M. Idel and B. McGinn (New York: Macmillan, 1989), pp. 101–108, and the imagery in the Mi'raj of Abu Yazid al-Bistami, Chapter 7 in this volume.

38. Tustari uses the oblique Qur'anic syntax to distinguish between the prophets and the progeny (i.e., the preexistent souls of all humankind), interpreting the verse as having the prophets bear witness against all the preexistent souls. The reflexive (against themselves) seems to be justified implicitly by the prophets being a voice both on behalf of the deity and a collective voice of humankind.

39. As mentioned in the introduction to Sahl above, this passage—a homily on virtues—whether originally here or placed here by a later editor or compiler, seems digressionary and it is not clear how, if at all, it fits into the issue of the preeternal covenant. Grace as nourishment: reading *rizq as-sa'āda.* The text reads, if read as passive, *wa yurzaqu as-sa'āda*: "and that one be given grace for nourishment." "Self-vigilance": *taqwā*; "gaze": *naẓar.*

40. Muhammad then not only is the seal of the prophetic tradition, the prophet who brings it to its final culmination; he also prefigures the entire history and sequence of prophets.

41. The hadith is cited in somewhat different forms in the standard sources.

42. "People of the bench": *ahl aṣ-ṣuffa*. The *ṣuffa* was an enclosure with a palm-stick roof near the first mosque in Medina, where refugees and the homeless (the people, *ahl*, of the *ṣuffa)* would be given food and shelter. See Edward Lane, *An Arabic-English Lexicon,* part 4 (Beirut: Librairie du Liban, 1980, reprint of the 1872 edition), p. 1694. Some have argued that this term may have been behind the origin of the term *ṣūfī* to designate the early Islamic ascetic and mystic. The point of this interpretation of the hadith seems to be that the reference to Muhammad eating and drinking is not to be taken literally. The hadith is meant to emphasize Muhammad's uniqueness and his generosity, but according to this interpretation, Muhammad would be beyond the need for food and drink—a spiritualizing interpretation consonant with the primordial Muhammad being developed by Tustari at this point in the tafsir.

43. Böwering (*Mystical Vision,* p.152) seems to have access to a different text where the creation of Adam from the light of Muhammad is stated more directly.

The famous Sufi hadith: I was a prophet when Adam was between water and mud *(kuntu nabiyyan wa Adam bayna al-mā' wa ṭ-ṭīn)* is not found in the standard hadith collections, and was attacked by Ibn Taymiyya as "innovation" *(bid'a)*. A similar hadith is found in the standard collection of Ibn Hanbal, as well as in Hakim at-Tirmidhi: "When did you become a prophet?" "When Adam was between spirit and body *(bayna ar-rūḥ wa l-jasad)*" (Ahmad IV, 66, V 59, 379, Tirmidhi, *Manāqib* 1). See M. Chodkiewicz, *Le Sceau des saints* (Paris: Gallimard, 1986), pp. 80–87; and William Chittick, *The Sufi Path of Knowledge* (Albany: SUNY Press, 1989), p. 405, n. 8. Another noncanonical Sufi hadith goes as follows: *inna qurayshan kānat nūran bayna yaday Allah . . . qabla an yukhlaqa ādam . . . fa lammā khalaqa Allāhu ādama, alqā dhālika n-nūra fi ṣulbihi.* "The [tribe] of Quraysh was a light close to God before Adam was created. When God created Adam, he placed that light within his loins." See Chodkiewictz, *Le Sceau des saints,* pp. 80–87.

44. "Seeker": *murīd;* "guide": *murād.*

45. The Bal'am ben Be'or of the Hebrew Bible *(Numbers* xxii–xxiv, xxxi 8). Bal'ām is not mentioned by name in the Qur'an, but later commentators evoke him to explain the rather obscure reference in 7:176: *If we wished we would have raised him on high.*

46. A *rak'a* is one set of bodily motions and positions—a single act of standing in prayer with one position of bowing of the head and two prostrations—within the performance of the prayers. The number of *rak'a*s required varies with the five daily prayer times.

The *taslīm* is a short invocation, offering praise, prayers, and good works to God, with invocations of peace, mercy, and blessings on Muhammad, and peace *(salām)* on all true worshipers of God. See Lane, *An Arabic English Lexicon*, part 4,

p. 1413, and idem, *The Manners and Customs of the Modern Egyptians* (New York: Everyman's Library, 1966, originally published in 1860), p. 80.

47. Sahl at-Tustarī, *Tafsīr al-Qur'ān al-'Aẓīm*, pp. 40–41, continuous.

48. The word *satan (shayṭān)* can take singular or plural forms in Arabic. Sometimes I have translated as Satan, other times as the satan, depending on the context.

49. The plural "us" refers back to the Qur'anic "we," which is the dominant Qur'anic mode of divine self-reference.

50. As light in the form of a column of light: *nūran fī 'amūd an-nūr*. Reading *'amūd* for *'āmūd* (Ibid., p. 95).

51. "Oncomings": *mawārid.* The section on oncomings in Chapter 3.

52. Sahl at-Tustarī, *Tafsīr al-Qur'ān al-'Aẓīm*, pp. 95–96.

Chapter 3. Qushayri

1. Two other major precursors of Qushayri in writing synoptic works on Sufis were Kalabādhī (d. 380/990) and Abū Ṭālib al-Makkī (d. 386/996). Qushayri's *Treatise* was followed in turn by the *Ḥilyat al-Awliyā'* of Abū Nu'aym al-Isfahānī (428/1037) and the *Kashf al-Maḥjūb* of Hujwīrī (d. 466/1074).

2. Abū l-Qāsim 'Abd al-Karīm al-Qushayrī, *Al-Risāla al-Qushayriyya fī al-Tasawwuf* [The Qushayrian Treatise on Sufism], ed. 'Abd al-Kalīm Maḥmūd and Maḥmūd ibn ash-Sharīf (Cairo: Dār al-Kutub al-Ḥadītha, 1966). Qushayri's *Treatise* contains: (1) a synoptic introductory discussion; (2) a section consisting of the hagiographies of eighty-three early Sufis; (3) a short section, the "interpretation of expressions" *(Tafsīr Alfāẓ)*, giving interpretations of twenty-seven key Sufi terms and expressions; (4) and a section of fifty-seven longer essays on Sufi states, stations, beliefs, and practices. For a complete translation, see *Das Sendschreiben al-Qushayrīs.* Übersetzt, eingeleitet und kommentiert von Richard Gramlich (Freiburger Islam studien, Band 12) (Wiesbaden: Steiner, 1989), with the section on the "interpretation of expressions" translated on pp. 106–145. For the final, longer essays on Sufi belief and practice, see al-Qushayri, *Principles of Sufism*, trans. B. R. von Schlegell (Berkeley: Mizan Press, 1992).

3. Like other Sufi writers, Qushayri uses the term "folk" *(qawm)* to designate those we might call Sufis. The term is an important indication of the effort by Sufi thinkers to avoid isolating and selecting Sufis out as a distinct and possibly elite element; for them, they were simply *qawm*. Throughout this volume, wherever the term "folk" occurs it translates *qawm* used in this particular sense. Sometimes Qushayri simply refers to "them" without specifying "them" as Sufis. Although it can sound strange in English at first to use this unspecified "they," I have used it rather than interpolating in words like "Sufis," to avoid setting up the kind of separate category Qushayri deliberately avoided.

4. Indeed, in the later theosophical philosophy of the moment found in Ibn 'Arabi, the moment becomes an "eternal moment" in which it is, indeed, such a totality.

5. "Realized masters": *ahl at-taḥqīq.*

6. "The teacher": *al-ustādh;* "The afterworld": *al-uqbā.*

7. "One who embraces poverty": *al-faqīr.*

8. As will be the case throughout this section from Qushayri's *Treatise,* the antecedent of "they" is often unclear in itself, and in its relationship (the same as or different than) to previous unspecified speakers.

9. "Dispositions of the real": *taṣrīf al-ḥaqq.*

10. "Magianism" can refer narrowly to the religion of the Magi, the Zoroastrian priestly class, but is used here derogatorily to refer to any false or misguided religious activity.

11. "Behavior": *taṣarruf;* "standing": *iqāma;* "contentedness": *iqnā'a*; "trust-in-god": *tawakkul;* "surrender": *taslīm;* "repentance": *tawba;* "contrition": *ināba;* "watchfulness": *war;* "renunciation": *zuhd.*

12. "Entrance": *mudkhal;* "exit": *mukhraj.* In Sufism, the terms *maqām* and *muqām* are sometimes used interchangeably. Qushayri appeals to the morphology of the *mu* prefix *muqām, mudkhal, mudhraj* to argue that *muqām* indicates the verbal gerundive act of being placed in a particular station. Behind what seems to be a grammatical quibble is an important theological point: Although the station is initially viewed as a result of an individual's personal endeavor, in fact it is also the result of a person's "being stationed" (i.e., by the deity, the one true actor). The tension between divine predetermination and human endeavor is never allowed to rest for long in a static position; so Qushayri moves to complicate the issue of the station by returning to the ultimate source of all action.

13. Here we see Qushayri's concern to place in context a statement that might sound outrageous when taken out of context. Rather than preaching that one should ignore ritual obligations, al-Wāsiṭī was demanding a total immersion in the obligations themselves, to the point that one was no longer concerned with or aware of one's own "acting" in carrying them out.

14. As will be seen below, Sarraj places contentedness among the stations, rather than the states.

15. At times, Qushayri refers to *ḥāla* (with the added "a" at the end), which I translate as "condition." The term is closely related to the *ḥāl* and seems to be used almost interchangeably.

16. "Freely given": *min al-jūdi.* I have used the reading given in three manuscripts cited by Gramlich, *Sendschreiben,* p. 110, over the readings in the two printed versions I have been following. The printed versions have: "States come from existence *(wujūd).*"

17. "Notion": *ḥadīth an-nafs.*

18. There is an etymological play on the two terms, *ḥāla* (to change, be transformed) and *ḥalla* (to alight at). Though the radicals of the two words are

different *(ḥ/w/l* vs. *ḥ/l/l)* in some cases the weak verbs such as *ḥ/w/l* are in fact related to verbs with a doubled consonant (like *ḥ/l/l).* Whatever the etymological justifications for the play, the association of the state of the lover (or beloved) and the "alightings" (usually of the beloved in her journey away from the poet) were well established in pre-Islamic poetry.

19. Sarraj, however, places contentedness among the stations rather than the states (see Chapter 6 in this volume). Given that most Sufis imply that one can only be in one state at a time, Sarraj's categorization seems to make more sense. If contentedness is a state, then al-Hiri was in a "long state" of contentedness during which he presumably experienced many other "shorter" states. Qushayri solves the problem in the next paragraph by introducing the notion of the "continuous state" that is a portion or taste of something to be realized more fully later.

20. At times, Qushayri's analysis comes close to collapsing the distinction between the station (as more permanent and product of individual endeavor) and state (as ephemeral and bestowed), especially in his insistence that even the station is ultimately bestowed and in his discussion of states that are at least relatively stable. As with most of the key Sufi concepts, the analysis begins by clarifying them, and then pushes them to the point of dissolution, as if the final answer to their meaning could be understood only through the reader's own experience.

21. See Wensinck, *Concordance* 5, 38b; 4, 537b, and Gramlich, *Sendschreiben,* p. 111.

22. "Truly realized attainment": *al-wuṣūl ilayhi bi t-taḥqīq.* Here Qushayri undermines the very phrase he uses so frequently: "realized masters" *(ahl at-taḥqīq).* In the dynamic world of Sufi psychology, complete mastery can never be attained, since the path is infinite, and the modes of consciousness can be infinitely deepened and expanded. In this particular notion, we might be reminded of Gregory of Nyssa's *epektasis,* the ever-continuing movement toward reality in which absence and presence oscillate even as the two states grow in intensity. See Bernard McGinn, *The Presence of God: A History of Western Mysticism,* Vol. 1, *The Foundations of Mysticism* (New York: Crossroad, 1991), pp. 139–142.

23. The *wārid,* for which I have coined the term "oncoming," is the "coming down upon" a person of a particular state or mode of consciousness. It is more active and invasive than an "occurrence" or a "happening," though it shares with them an independence from the will and intention of the person on which the state alights. Qushayri introduces the term in this essay, and later explains it in a separate essay.

24. Qushayri engages in a play on the near homonyms for that which is final or deferred to the future *(ājil)* and that which is imminent *('ājil),* a play that derives from Qur'anic meditation on the day of resurrection and judgment *(yawm al-qiyāma, yawm ad-dīn)* and its deferral.

25. Or al-Qaḥṭabī.

26. These same comments appear in the treatises *(al-rasā'il)* of Junayd, in a series of analyses of the concept of *tawḥīd* (affirmation of unity). The analyses are both lucid and powerful, but they occur in a third-person, discursive context. Each

of the eight analyses is labeled "another point *(mas'ala ukhra).*" Thus from the rather emotionless title "another point," the reader plunges with shock into Junayd's first-person discourse: "Fear grips me. Hope unfolds me. Reality draws me together. The real sets me apart."

The text from the *rasā'il* contains a number of subtle differences, and some sentences in the end that are absent from Qushayri. Those ending sentences are: "My annihilation is my abiding *(fanā'ī baqā'ī).* From the reality of my annihilation, he annihilated me from my abiding and from my annihilation. I was, upon the reality of annihilation, without *baqā'* and without *fanā'*, through my *baqā'* and my *fanā'* for the finding/existence *(wujūd)* of the *fanā'* and *baqā'*, for the *wujūd* of my other, in my annihilation."

For references and translations, see Chapter 8 in this volume.

27. Rudolf Otto, *The Experience of the Holy* (London: Penguin, 1959), an English version of *Das Heilige* published in 1917.

28. For a detailed argument, see M. Sells, "Sound and Meaning in *Sūrat al-Qāri'a,*" *Arabica* 40, no. 3 (1993): 403–430.

29. The final sentences of this anecdote are elusive in the original Arabic.

30. Abū Sa'īd al-Kharrāz, a famous practitioner of *khalwa* (ascetic isolation). "One of the people of true existing": *min ahl al-wujūdi ḥaqīqatan. Wujūd* here takes on the notion of ecstatic existentiality, but such an English expression is obviously inappropriate poetically. I have tried to bring across the Qushayriyyan sense of *wujū d* by using the verbal noun in an unusual way within a poetic context that relates it to absence from even the highest consciousness (as symbolized by the worlds, the throne, and the footstool). The verses fit the common Sufi theme of criticizing the world-abandoner for not abandoning attachment to various states of mind and feeling.

31. The final verses suggest—as Muhasibi claimed (see Chapter 5 in this volume), that the person immersed in remembrance of the one God need not fear being led astray. With Muhasibi, the fear was of being led astray by inclinations *(khaṭarāt)* from the self or Satan. With Kharraz, it was the company of humans that was the object of fear.

32. The early Sufis did not use the term "unity of existence" *(waḥdat al-wujūd)* used by later Sufi theosophists, and their concept of the "one existence" was expressed without the metaphysical framework and focus of later Sufi theosophy. They did assert the oneness of existence—but that assertion is made here in the experiential mode.

33. A gerund *(tafā'il* form) of the sixth verbal form, based on the *ta* prefix and the addition of a long *a* after the first radical.

34. The morphology of *tawājud,* i.e., taking the original radical and adding to it the prefix "ta," a first vowel of *a* and a second vowel of *u.* For those unfamiliar with Arabic grammar, a simple example with the English letters *x/y/z* might be helpful. If there were such an Arabic radical, the morphology of *tawājud* would be *taxāyuz.*

35. "Made as if I were squint-eyed": *takhāraztu*. The meaning of "made as if I were" is all in the morphology of the word.

36. "Ecstatic mode of consciousness": *ma'nā al-wijdān.*

37. "Audition" *(samā')* involves the use of chants and singing as a meditative practice to bring on various trance-like states.

38. Here is yet another example of word play, in this case between *wird* (the devotions carried out at the prescribed times) and *wārid*, the "oncoming" of a state, moment, or mode of consciousness.

39. "He encounters": *yunāziluhu;* "encounters": *munāzalāt.* The precise meaning of these rare expressions remains obscure.

40. "Ecstatic existentiality": Here Qushayri uses the term *wujūd* with a verbal force in a manner that can only be fully translated by the awkward phrase ecstatically and existentially experiencing. Mortal, mortal human: *basharīyya.* As opposed to the Arabic *insān* (human, humankind), *basharīyya* has stronger connotations of the human in its embodied, mortal condition. Another possibility would be to translate the term as "the flesh"; the Arabic is in fact etymologically related to the word for skin, *bashara.* However, the Arabic term, while denoting humankind in its embodied, mortal state, does not imply the theological framework of Christian notions of sin that the English term "flesh" has taken on.

41. For the ambiguity of the antecedent of "he" here (the seeker or the real) see the comments in the general introduction, above.

42. A reference to the famous hadith of free devotions.

43. This vocabulary is imbued with the classical Arabic *nasīb*: light of longing *(nīrān al-ishtiyāq)*, vestiges *(āthār)*, make an apparition *(talūḥu)*, a term that is terribly weakened when translated only as "appeared"; "body-temples": *hayākīl*: body-temples. See Chapter 1 in this volume.

44. The people of 'Ad, the city of Iram—a fabled Arabian civilization whose destruction is recounted in the Qur'an as an example of the fate of those civilizations that reject their prophets. Khusraw: the name given to Sassanian Persian kings (from Caesar). Ibn al-Mu'tazz (d. 296/908), the famous poet of Baghdad who was made Caliph for a day during a revolution. In addition to composing his own widely admired verse, Ibn al-Mu'tazz also collected an anthology of wine-poems. For the full five-verse poem, see Ibn al-Mu'tazz, *Diwān* (Beirut: Dar Sadir, n.d.), p. 76.

45. There are major confusions over the names here. Some manuscripts give the second name of ad-Duqqī to both Abu Bakr and Jahm, making the story almost incomprehensible when only the second name is used. I have followed the reading of Gramlich, *Sendschreiben,* in this case.

46. "How are you and how is your condition": *kayfa anta wa kayfa ḥāluka.* The phrase would normally simply be translated as "how are you, how are you doing." *Kayfa* (how) is your state *(ḥāluka)* is simply the common way of greeting someone. But in an essay and a story where the term *ḥāl* is used with such intense consciousness of its technical meaning of mystical state or condition, this more technical and literal translation is appropriate.

The story never reveals explicitly whether the absence was death, disappearance, or mystical trance in the literal sense.

47. Qushayri is making a continual argument, in this passage and elsewhere, that although mystical practice can cause a person to be "absent," it will not cause him to neglect the obligation of Islamic ritual practice. For a very interesting parallel, see Muhasibi's argument (in Chapter 5 of this volume) that if one concentrates only on God, one will still be prepared for dangerous thoughts and inclinations, just as a sleeping person can wake himself up at an unusual time, even though when he is asleep, he has no conscious intention of doing so nor any conscious keeping of time.

48. "Acquired by the servant": *kasban lahu.* In the theology of the Mutakallimun, *kasb* is a technical term referring to the way in which the human being acquires the responsibility for his acts even though the acts are created by the all-powerful deity. Here it takes on a more subjective sense of a person viewing his acts as his own.

49. The texts read *ibdā'* or *ibtidā'*.

50. "Sign": *shāhid.* See below for Qushayri's essay on this key term. Once again Qushayri uses a foreshadowing technique by inserting a term to which he will later devote a full essay.

51. The Qur'anic verse is called "His words," i.e., the words of the deity. In this case the actual quotation is a prayer on the part of the worshiper direct *to* the deity, but the prayer is ultimately the word of the deity because it is part of the Qur'an, which defines itself as the divine word.

52. "In remorse": *mutanaṣilan.*

53. "That he might see him": reading *wa arāhu* for *wa arādahu.*

54. In the Arabic, the final *u* [the first person singular marker] or *a* [the second person singular marker] is usually not written and can in many cases be the occasion for deliberate ambiguity or the source of interpretive controversy.

55. It is not clear from the text whether Qushayri intends the following section on the "union of union" as a subcategory of separation and union, or as a separate category. The phrase "union of union" comes to complete the sentence "Then there is."

56. As throughout my translations, I vary the pronoun referring to "the real" between "he" and "it" in order to avoid reifying it into a masculine-personal, or neuter-impersonal entity.

57. "Carnal desires": *shahawāt*; "intention": *niyya*; "appetitive nature": *raghba.*

58. "Vestige": *athar*; "trace": *rasm*; "ruin": *ṭalal.* See Chapter 1 in this volume for the poetic associations of these terms.

59. "People of fire": *ahl an-nār*, i.e., those who will be condemned to the fire at the final judgment.

60. Gramlich, *Sendschreiben*, p. 125, identifies that state of being *mabsūṭ* with *basṭ*, the formal state of expansion. While such a reading is certainly reasonable, I

have chosen the more informal reading, translating *mabsūṭ* as "high" (in the slang sense), a usage that continues to the present day.

61. "Would-be drunk": *mutasākir*, or "one who is trying to get drunk" or "one who is making as if drunk." The grammatical form is parallel to the earlier "making ecstatic" *(tawājud, mutawājid).*

62. Qushayri devotes a later essay (below) to his definition of "oncomings" *(wāridāt).*

63. "Conduct": *mu'āmalāt*; "descents": *munāzalat*; "intimacies": *muwāṣilāt.*

64. "Freed": *mu'taqa.* There may be a pun or play here on the possibility of *mu'attaqa* (mellowed).

65. "Power of divine decree": *qudra.* The term *qudra* means power, but its association with Qur'anic usages of the term, and the close connections to *qadr* (the decree or destiny association with the deity in the Qur'an) and *qadar* (the predetermination, again associated by traditional Muslims with the deity), makes it evident to the Muslim reader that the subject of the predication is the deity.

66. Gramlich, *Sendschreiben,* reads *nafā* (rejects, denies) here. In either case, the meaning is clear. Effacement is the act of the real in effacing those states of act, mind, and heart that it rejects or from which it purifies the Sufi. This intense, continual effacement of the *nafs* and the various acts, thoughts, and modes of consciousness associated with it, is a distinctive mark of the moral seriousness of Sufism.

67. "Divine will": *mashī'a.* As with *qudra,* the Qur'anic and theological contexts in which this term was embedded in early Islamic literature make it clear that it is divine will that is meant, although no explicit specification of the "divine" is given.

68. The meaning of this passage is particularly elusive.

69. Another fine example of the unspecified antecedent of intimacy.

70. "Sign": *shāhid.* Whatever a person "witnesses" becomes for that person her sign, and becomes constitutive of her identity. See Qushayri's essay devoted to the *shāhid,* below.

71. See the section above on the "condition" *ḥāl,* for this hadith. In the present context, Qushayri's use of it seems puzzling since with the "select" it is the self-manifestation that is overpowering and, as Qushayri says, it is the veil or cover that *is* a mercy. So for one already shrouded to ask for mercy seems redundant.

72. *Ṣaḥīḥ Muslim* 1:161–162, Ibn Hanbal, *al-Musnad* 4:401; 4:405, and other references are given in Gramlich *Sendschreiben*, p. 130.

73. I.e., the signs, attributes, and identity *(dhāt)* of the deity: the reference seems to be to the deity in all three cases here, another occurrence of the sense of familiarity and intimacy engendered by the nonspecified, assumed antecedent of "his."

74. The point seems rhetorical here, an emphatic affirmation of the necessity of passing-away or annihilation of the ego-self, expressed through the medium of

the blood vein. In Sufi thought, the egoism of the self and of Satan was often associated with the blood, and blood with the self of the human being.

75. "They say": Some manuscripts have *qālā,* which would give "he said" and would be interpreted as a probable reference to Nuri.

76. The morphological form of *mushāhada* is expressed in Arabic as *mufā'ala,* with the Arabic root *f/'/l* (for the verb *fa'ala,* to do) used as the example for all forms.

77. This is a fundamental theological point that should not get lost in the grammatical details. In Sufi understanding of mystical union, there is no "meeting of two parties," but rather one party disappears and the other emerges, an understanding that is intensified by Qushayri's oscillating play of polarities.

78. The point here is that the verb "travel" *(sāfara)* generates the noun "traveling" *(musāfara),* which does not imply more than one party; likewise with the compound "to line a boot" *(ṭaraqa n-na'l).*

79. Particularly that of the classical Arabic *nasīb.* The reader may wish to consult the storm scene in the poem of Al-A'sha, for a strong parallel. See M. Sells, *Desert Tracings* (Middletown: Wesleyan University Press, 1989), pp. 62–63.

80. Up to this moment, the text has been primarily in the voice of Qushayri, who cites previous masters, such as his own teacher Al-Daqqaq. Here, a student or editor places Qushayri in the third person and cites Qushayri's sayings. This kind of switch in frame-narrator is common to classical Islamic literature.

81. *Lam tarid ma'a wajhihi l-'aynu illā shariqat qabla rayyihā bi raqībin* (p. 229).

Gramlich, *Sendschreiben,* p. 132, offers this version:

Nicht erreicht das Auge das Wasser seines Antlitzes, ohne sich
An einem Aufpasser zu verschlucken, noch bevor es sich sattgetrunken hat.

82. Again, the antecedent of the pronoun *hu* (him/it) is ambiguous; it could refer reflexively to the light or to the real.

83. Moses' veil.

84. The story of how the Pharaoh's wife tricked the women by giving them knives and then presenting them suddenly with the sight of the beautiful Joseph is told in Sura 12:30–33.

85. The first group interprets the notion of an angel shaking the hand of a human as impossible. Thus Muhammad's words "If you had remained in the experience you had with me, the angels would have shaken your hand" suggests that fixity or remaining in such a state is fundamentally impossible for humans. The second group argues that the angels' shaking of human hands is not impossible; indeed, it is less than the promise in the saying of Muhammad that the "angels will lower their wings for the seeker of knowledge."

86. "Possibilities": *maqdūrāt.* "In each breath": reading *nafas.*

87. This concept is explained in a discussion devoted to it later in the essay, below.

88. Or as Dhū l-Rumma puts it, in reference to the beloved: "She is the cure, she the disease." See Chapter 1 in this volume.

89. Again the antecedent of "him" or "it" (hu) is both assumed and obvious. For this use of a pronoun whose antecedent is unspecified, and for the manner in which it creates a particular tone and feeling within the text, see the general introduction, above.

90. A version of the famous union hadith or *ḥadīth an-nawāfil* (hadith of free devotions). The "he" in "he said" is of course the Prophet Muhammad, as is signaled by the phrase "peace and blessings upon him." The "we" within the hadith is the deity, who speaks, as the deity frequently speaks within the Qur'an as well, in the first-person plural form "we."

91. The antecedent here seems ambiguous. It could be the servant's constant attentiveness to the deity, or the deity's constant watchfulness over the servant, through the "watchers" mentioned in the following sentence.

92. Qushayri moves back subtly to the notion of mystical union provided within the hadith of free devotions. When a person draws near to the deity and the deity loves that person, the deity becomes the "hearing with which he hears, the seeing with which he sees." Insofar as anyone has vision or hearing or even breathing of their own, that person has not been brought into such a state of intimacy and nearness. For a later Sufi discussion of the significance of viewing even one's breaths as breaths of the divine, see M. Sells, "Ibn 'Arabi's Garden among the Flames: A Reevaluation," *History of Religions* 23.4 (1994): 287–315, and idem, *Mystical Languages of Unsaying* (Chicago: University of Chicago Press, 1994), Chap. 4.

93. The precise meaning of the Qur'anic term *ṣamad* has been a matter of debate for centuries. The Qur'an calls Allah *aṣ-ṣamad*, and the word can be interpreted as "the goal," "the refuge," or "that which perdures forever." Allah's *ṣamadiyya*, then, would be his quality of being *aṣ-ṣamad*, in whichever way the interpreter wishes to understand that enigmatic term.

94. "Essences": *dhawāt*.

95. Again, Qushayri structures his essay in part on the phonological word play between *sharī'a* and *ḥaqīqa*, each of which is built on the *CaCīCa* form.

96. For a more cosmic perspective on this notion of counting breaths with the deity as articulated by the later Sufi Ibn 'Arabi (d. 638/1240), see M. Sells, "Ibn 'Arabi's Garden among the Flames," and idem, *Mystical Languages of Unsaying*, Chap. 4.

97. I preserve here in my translation the distinctive and precise form "the satans" *(shayāṭīn)* and "the satan" *(ash-shayṭān)*. As with the biblical tradition, so with the Qur'anic tradition, the transformation of "the satan" into the proper noun "Satan" is a late addition.

98. Cf. Muhasibi's analysis of "inclinations" or "passing thoughts" in Chapter 5 in this volume.

99. This is through a condition of traditional knowledge: "*wa hādhā bi sharṭ al-'ilm.*"

100. "Traces": *āthār.*

101. The meanings of the word *shāhid* include: present; witness; piece of evidence; attestation; quotation serving as textual evidence; testimony; an oblong, upright tombstone.

102. "Material substrate": *al-qālib al-mawḍū'.*

103. "Acquired": *kasban lahu.* The point here is that actions in this category are not intrinsically blameworthy or base (as in the following category), but they are blameworthy because they disobey sacred law.

104. "The prohibition of sacred law": *taḥrīm*; "the more rigorous standards of complete integrity": *tanzīh.* This particular sense of the two terms is articulated more fully in 'Arūsī, who suggests the standard division between those things considered *ḥarām* (clearly prohibited) and those considered *makrūḥ* (something to be avoided). See Gramlich, *Sendschreiben,* p. 144.

105. "Status": *qadr.* The word could also be voweled as *qadar*, in which case the translation would read: "the delusion that it deserves [to be considered] the determiner of its own acts." Though more awkward grammatically, this second reading is more consonant with the theological controversies over the divine creation of acts and thus predetermination *(qadar).*

106. "Idolatry": *shirk*, i.e., by seeing itself as a source of good and as a free source of action, the self holds itself up as another ultimate metaphysical principle, another god.

107. "Norm": *'āda.* The notion of the norm is important in Islamic theology, particularly in its defense of miracles. Denying any natural causal necessity, the Ash'arite theologians spoke of natural processes as involving a norm; in each instance the deity recreates the world and can at any moment diverge from that norm. A miracle, then, is simply a diverging from the norm *('āda)*, not a violation of any natural law or necessity.

108. "Whole": *jumla*, i.e., the entity made up of both body and spirit.

109. "Subtle essences": *'ayān laṭīfa.* "Subtle essence": *laṭīfa*; "bodily mold": *qālib.*

110. "The heart-secrets have been formed from the bondage of the others, from traces and ruins": *al-asrār mu'taqatun min raqqi l-aghyāri min al-āthāri wa l-aṭlāl.* Qushayri is clearly drawing on the *aṭlāl* motif of the *nasīb* here.

Chapter 4. Rabi'a

1. Paul Losensky translated the text based on textual considerations discussed in note 7, below. The introduction and notes are by Michael Sells. Special gratitude is due to Birch Miles for the assistance, patience, and insight he offered during the preliminary work on this chapter.

2. Shams ad-Dīn Aḥmad Aflākī, *Manāqib al-'Ārifīn* (Virtues of the Knowers), Vol. 1 Tehran: Dunyā-yi Kitāb, 1983), p. 396.

3. See Julian Baldick, "The Legend of Rābi'a of Baṣra: Christian Antecedents, Muslim Counterparts," *Religion* 20 (1990): 233–247.

4. Similarly in medieval Christendom, female mystics frequently engaged in a dialectic of the weak and the strong. Hildegard of Bingen (d. 1179), who wielded major political influence, stated "I am a little, poor, feminine form" *(Ego paupercula feminea forma sum)*. Marguerite Porete continually evoked a somewhat different dialectic, of having nothing and having all, in asserting a less accepted form of power. She challenged the inquisition and its backers in the papacy and the French monarchy for the right to author and publish her own work. She was burned at the stake in 1310. See M. Sells, *"The Pseudo-Woman and the Meister: 'Unsaying and Essentialism,'"* in *Meister Eckhart and the Beguine Mystics*, ed. Bernard McGinn (New York: Continuum, 1994), pp. 114–146.

5. Hasan appears in sections 15–23 and 46. Ibrāhīm Adham appears in one of the more extended anecdotes (9). Other participants in these jousts include Mālik Dīnār (45, 46), 'Abd al-Wāḥid 'Amir (44), Sufyān Thawrī (44, 49), Shaqīq Balkhī (46), Ṣāliḥ Murrī (21, 31), Muḥammad ibn Aslam aṭ-Ṭūsī and Na'imī Ṭarṭusī (57). For the spiritual joust or "boasting contest" *(mufākhara, munāqara)* in Sufism, see Carl Ernst, *Words of Ecstasy in Islam* (Albany: SUNY Press, 1985), p. 39. In the anecdotes of Rabi'a, the irony of the spiritual joust is continually evoked: Each "combatant" tries to emphasize the notions of humility, denial of the ego-self *(nafs)*, and of course however subtly, each statement itself can be viewed as a form of "return of the repressed" egoism.

6. This absolute annihilation of self-will, or merging of the human will with the divine will—to the point of rejecting any petition to the deity (see number 21, below)—was being articulated by 'Attar's contemporaries, the Beguine mystics, Mechthild of Magdeburg (d. ca. 1297), Hadewijch of Antwerp (fl. ca. 1240), Marguerite Porete (d. 1310), and by Meister Eckhart (d. ca. 1328). Porete is most emphatic in rejecting any self-will "to do anything for God or refrain from doing anything for God." See M. Sells, *Mystical Language of Unsaying* (Chicago: University of Chicago Press, 1994), Chaps. 5–7.

7. There are four editions of the Persian text of 'Attar's *Tadhikrat al-'Awliyā'*. The earliest of these was edited by Reynold A. Nicholson (2 vols. in 1; London: Luzac, 1905, Rābi'a, 1: 59–73). This text was extensively revised and its spelling modernized by Muḥammad Khān Qazvīnī (2 vols. in 1; Tehran: Kitābkhānah-'ī Markazī, 1336/1957, 1: 64–77). An entirely new edition was prepared in 1967 by Muḥammad Istislāmī (Tehran: Zavvār, pp. 72–88). The edition that is introduced by Nāṣir Hayyirī does not credit an editor, but appears to be based primarily on Istislamī's edition (Tehran: Intishārāt-i Gulshā'ī, 1361/1982, pp. 42–51).

This translation is based on the Istislāmī and Hayyirī editions; certain readings from Nicholson and Qazvīnī will be indicated in the notes. Without entering into the complexities of the manuscript transmission of this work, the Istislāmī edition appears preferable on literary grounds. It lacks most of the explanatory comments and elaborations found in Nicholson and Qazvīnī, resulting in a leaner, more laconic text that is closer to 'Attar's narrative style in verse.

NOTES

To my knowledge, there are no complete translations into any Western language of this great work. Selections in English can be found in Farid al-Din ʻAttar, *Muslim Saints and Mystics, Episodes from the Tadhkirat al-Auliya'* (Memorial of the Saints), trans. A. J. Arberry (London: Arkana, 1990; first published London: Routledge & Kegan Paul Ltd., 1966). Arberry's version is selective, not only in the particular lives that he translated, but in the choice of texts from each life translated. As he points out in his introduction (pp. 16–17), he focuses on the "miracles" of each Godfriend, and excludes the sayings. Many sections of ʻAttar's life of Rabiʻa are translated or paraphrased in Margaret Smith, *Rābiʻa the Mystic & Her Fellow-Saints in Islām* (Cambridge: Cambridge University Press, 1928, 1984). The Ouigour text has been translated by A. Pavet de Courteille: "Farid-ud-Din ʻAttar," *Le mémorial des saints* (Paris: Editions du Seuil, 1976). Short German selections from ʻAttar, including six on Rabiʻa, can be found in *Frühislamische Mystiker aus Faridud-din ʻAttars "Heiligenbiographie,"* translated from the Nicholson text by Gisela Wente (Amsterdam: Castrum Peregrini Presse, 1984). Selections appear in the translation of Charles Upton: Rabiʻa al-ʻAdawiyya, *Doorkeeper of the Heart: Versions of Rabia* (Putney, Vt.: Threshold Books, 1988). Cf. Suʻād ʻabd ar-Rāziq, *Rabiʻa al-ʻAdawiyya: Bayn al-Ghinā' wa l-Baqa'* (Cairo: The Anglo-Egyptian Bookshop, 1982). Numerous passages from ʻAttar are translated in Javad Nurbakhsh, *Sufi Women* (New York: Khaniqahi-Nimatullahi Publications, 1983), pp. 25–73.

8. Nicholson-Qazvīnī: *gumshudah-i viṣāl.*

9. ʻAttar's final position is ambiguous here. The various anecdotes validate his inclusion of a woman in what was called at the time the "ranks of [Sufi] men," but no theological statement is made about the status of women, such as the famous statement of Augustine that a woman in her sexual and procreative roles should be an object of contempt but insofar as she becomes "dewomanized" as it were and gender-neutral, she takes on the image of God. Such Augustinian theology led to the medieval Christian notion of the virago, the woman who by denying her sexual and procreative roles becomes manlike and thus can achieve saintliness. ʻAttar engages in no such theologizing, and uses arguments that allow him to place Rabiʻa in the ranks of men, leaving the issue of women as women open. Of course almost every anecdote concerning Rabiʻa is a refutation of implied attitudes toward the "weak woman."

10. ʻAttar includes this story in his earlier account of Hasan of Basra:

> Hasan would hold meetings and speak once a week. Whenever he ascended the pulpit and found that Rabiʻa was not present, he came back down. Once he was asked, "So many important and honored people are present, so what if an old woman's not here?"
>
> "How can the drink that we have prepared for elephants be poured out for mice?" he replied.
>
> Whenever the meeting heated up, when hearts were afire and eyes were swimming in tears, he would turn to Rabiʻa and say, "O noble lady,

> this is from the embers of your heart." In other words, "All this warmth is from one sigh from the depths of your being."

11. Seventy-thousand is a key number in Islamic cosmology. The most famous occurrence of it is in the depiction of the "house of life" *(al-bayt al-ma'mūr)*, the celestial archetype of the Ka'ba, which Muhammad encounters at the culmination of his Mi'raj. Into that house of life, it is said, 70,000 angels enter each day, not to return until the end of time.

12. A hadith qudsi (transcendent hadith), that is, a hadith in which the speaker is Allah. Arabic: *idhā taqarraba l-'abdu ilayya shibran, taqarrabtu ilayhi dhirā'an.* Among the many references, see *Ṣaḥīḥ Bukhārī*, Tawḥīd, 50; *Ṣaḥīḥ Muslim*, Dhikr, 2, 3, 20–22, Tawba, 1.

13. A station in the *ḥajj* pilgrimage, the scene of Muhammad's last sermon, and the place where all the pilgrims assemble and stand, as at the final day of judgment, saying "*labbayka*" (Here I am lord).

14. A series of reflexive pronouns make it difficult to know just who owns what house. I have followed Istislāmī's basic text while adopting Qazvīnī's distinction between *khvud* (referring, in this case, to God) and *khvīsh* (referring to Rabi'a).

15. Nicholson and Qazvīnī clarify where this "reed" came from by including *ḥaṣīr*, "reed mat."

16. Nicholson and Qazvīnī also include *gūrān*, "wild asses," in this list of animals.

17. 'Attar includes this incident in his account of Hasan of Basra:

> It is related that one day Hasan had wept so much on the roof of his meditation cell that water had run out from the rain spouts and dripped on someone who asked, "Is this water ritually pure or not?" Hasan said, "No, go wash. This is the tears of a disobedient rebel."

18. Pavet de Courteille, "Farid-ud-Din 'Attar," has: "Maître, dit-elle, sont-ce les choses de cette terre que tu vas montrer aux gens de l'autre monde? Fais-nous voir une chose que le commun des mortels soit impuissant á exécuter" (p. 90).

Arberry's translation has: "Hasan," Rabi'a replied, "when you are showing off your spiritual goods in this worldly market, it should be things that your fellow-men are incapable of displaying" (p. 44; see note 7).

Smith, *Rābi'a the Mystic*, has: "O Hasan, was it necessary to offer yourself in the bazaar of this world to the people of the next? . . . This is necessary for people of your kind, because of your weakness" (p. 35).

19. The Nicholson text and the Arberry translation reverse the point (see note 7). "Come up here, Hasan, where people can see us!" (Arberry translation, p. 45). The Istilām ī-Hayyirī and Pavet de Courteille's translation based on the Ouigour (p. 90) all have Rabi'a asking Hasan to come up where they can*not* be seen, that is, to quit engaging in feats to show off in front of human beings, a motive that is rooted

in conceited self-display (*riyā'*). For the subtle problems of self-display, see Chapter 5 in this volume.

20. See the Qur'an 20:22 for the story of Moses' receiving "signs" of his prophetic mission, including the staff that becomes a snake, and of his hand, which turns white after he holds it to his breast. The "white hand" of Moses became a common, if enigmatic, allusion in Sufi writings.

21. This notion of the "without how" parallels in a significant way the "without how" and "without why" that was developed in Europe only a few decades later by the mystics Mechthild, Hadewijch, Porete, and Eckhart.

22. The Qur'an refers to the moment of truth or day of judgment when those whose "book" (of deeds in their lifetime) is given to them. Those who are given the book in the right hand or who are led off to the right are those who are given the garden *(janna)*. Those whose book is given into the left hand or are led off to the left are those who are given the fire *(nār)*.

23. Earlier (see note 17, above) Rabi'a had berated Hasan's public weeping as a whim of the ego-self *(nafs)*. The contrast between his weeping and hers, in 'Attar's story, resides in both the issues of public vs. private devotions (and the vice of *riyā'* or showing one's devotion), and in the incomplete quality of Hasan's weeping, a less-than-total immersion.

24. The neighbor, then the house: *al-jār thumma d-dār*. An Arabic proverb here used to emphasize that it is the person rather than the abode that is of primary importance, a point that recurs in a number of the Rabi'a stories in 'Attar.

25. "I am your highest lord": Pharoah's claim to Moses as depicted in this Qur'anic passage becomes an epitome of human arrogance and self-delusion within the later Islamic tradition.

26. In Arabic: *huwa yarzuqu man yasubbuhu, fa lā yarzuqu man yuḥibbuhu?* The Persian translation of the Arabic moves from the terse syntax and vocabulary of the proverb ("If he provides for someone who insults him, will he withhold daily bread from someone who loves him?") to a more emotive language: "who seethes with love for him."

27. Another Arabic proverb: *man aḥabba shay'an akthara dhikrahu.*

28. Istislāmī-Hayyirī add the two following sentences from the Qur'an: "Enter among my servants, enter my garden."

29. Munkir and Nakir: The two fearsome angel-guardians of death in Islamic lore.

CHAPTER 5. MUHASIBI

1. His full name is Abū 'Abd Allāh al-Ḥārith al-Muḥāsibī (pronounced in English with the accent on the second syllable, Muhásibi).

2. Muhasibi's influence was both direct and indirect. It was passed on directly through his pupil as-Sarī as-Saqatī (the uncle of Junayd). Muhasibi's psychol-

ogy can be found in particularly strong form in the works of Abū Ṭālib al-Makkī, who grounded his own synoptic view of Sufism in Muhasibi's unflinching exposé of the subtleties of human egoism. Al-Makkī in turn was a decisive influence on the encyclopedic works of Abū Ḥāmid al-Ghazzālī (d. 1111), which are among the most popular works of Sufism in the Islamic world today.

3. I have based all translations from *The Book on the Observance of the Rights of God* on the editions of Smith (1940) and 'Atā (1970). See Abū 'Abdallāh Ḥārith ibn Asad al-Muḥāsibī, *Kitāb al-Ri'āya li Ḥuqūq Allāh*, ed. Margaret Smith (London: Luzac & Co., E. J. W. Gibb Memorial, 1940), and idem, *Kitāb al-Ri'āya li Ḥuqūq Allāh*, ed. 'Abd al-Qādir Aḥmad 'Atā (Cairo: Dār al-Kutub al-Ḥadītha, 3rd printing, 1970). All citations begin with the page numbers in Smith and then give the page numbers in 'Aṭā.

The standard secondary works on Muhasibi are: Margaret Smith, *Al-Muḥāsibī A.D. 781–857: An Early Mystic of Baghdad* (Amsterdam: Philo Press, 1974, a reprint of the original 1935 Sheldon Press version); Louis Massignon, *Essai sur les origines du lexique technique de la mystique musulmane* (Paris: Librairie Orientaliste Paul Geuthner, 1922, 1954), pp. 11–25; and Josef van Ess, *Die Gedankenwelt des Ḥārith al-Muḥāsibī* (Bonn: Selstverlag des Orientalischen Seminars der Universität Bonn, 1961).

4. For the discussion of pride as the servant taking the role of master, the human taking the role of God, see Muhasibi, *Kitāb al-Ri'āya*, pp. 232 ff. /446 ff.

5. *Mubāha, ḥubb al-ghalaba, takāthur* and *tafākhur*, respectively.

6. From the chapter on what the intuition of the self entails, along with an explanation of vanity *('ujb)* and being conceited *(al-idlāl)* in acts of devotion: Muhasibi, *Kitāb al-Ri'āya*, p. 208/398.

7. Al-Muḥāsibi, *Kitāb al-Waṣāya (The Book of Counsels)*, ed. 'Abd al-Qādir Aḥmad 'Aṭā (Beirut: Dār al-Kutub al-'Amaliyya, 1986).

8. A reference to the battle of *Ḥunayn* in which the Muslim army was almost destroyed.

9. See Muhasibi, *Kitāb al-Ri'āya*, pp. 208ff./399ff., for his Qur'anic and hadith citations and his dissection of vanity into its various types.

10. Another Arabic word commonly translated as "sincerity" is *ṣidq*. When discussing intention *(niyya)*, Muhasibi defines *ṣidq* in precisely the same way he defines *ikhlās*: acting with regard for the deity alone, without regard for human praise or blame. See *Kitāb al-Waṣāya*, p. 254.

11. Muhasibi uses different words for human praise *(maḥamada)* and divine praise or favor, and human blame *(dhamm)* and divine wrath.

12. "Relationship of transaction": *mu'āmala.*

13. *Kitāb al-Waṣāya*, p. 259.

14. Ibid., p. 262.

15. The first section is to be found in Muhasibi, *Kitāb al-Ri'āya*, pp. 44–46/105–108.

The 'Aṭā version varies little from the Smith version, but 'Aṭā makes fuller use of section and chapter headings and breaks, allowing for a clearer sense of contents.

16. Muhasibi has switched order here from the original statement, which listed the inclination from the self as the first kind.

17. The reference in Sura 12 is to the story of Isaac (Isra'il) and his sons, the gifting of Joseph with the gift of interpretation of dreams and reality (see Chapter 1 in this volume), and the plot against him by his jealous brothers. For other Qur'anic references to enticement *(taswīl)*, see 12:18, 20:96, and 48:25.

18. It would be tempting here to translate less literally: "And he allowed himself to . . . ." But such a translation, although more idiomatic, loses the crucial notion that it is the self *(nafs)* that in this Qur'anic expression and subsequent Sufi psychology is the *agent* of the enticement, not the passive recipient of it.

19. "The self that dominates with wrong": *an-nafsu l-'amāratu bi s-su'*. This phrase became one of the Qur'anic foundations for Sufi division of the "self" into three phases: the phase of ego-domination *(an-nafsu l-'amāra)*, the phase of self-blame *(an-nafsu al-lawāma)*, and the phase of peace and security *(an-nafsu al-muṭma'inna)*.

20. For other Qur'anic references of the insinuations *(nazgh)* of Satan, see 12:100; 17:53, and 41:36.

21. "Holding in check the ego-self": *ḥafs an-nafs*.

22. Massignon, *Lexique*, p. 223.

23. Muhasibi, *Kitāb al-Ri'āya*, pp. 73–76/154–159.

24. "Interior illness": *baṭn*; "decrepitude": *haram* for *hadam*.

25. Although the term *al-akhira* is usually translated as "the afterlife," Muhasibi is using it here in a way that brings out its etymological connotations of finality, termination, the end of all activity, justification, and appeal.

26. Muhasibi, *Kitāb al-Ri'āya*, p. 75/158—the syntax of this sentence is broken and I have supplied what seems like the most reasonable reading.

27. Luqmān: The ancient Arabian prophet associated with a body of proverbial wisdom.

28. Muhasibi, *Kitāb al-Ri'āya*, pp. 109–110/223–224. The term used for an act failing, *yaḥbutu 'amaluhu*, is used throughout the *Book on the Observance* to indicate the existential and moral failure of an act, regardless of its apparent success.

29. Following Smith's *lam yu'min* rather than 'Aṭā's *lam yu'mar*.

30. If he were truly repentant of the conceited thought, he would simply expel it. His lingering with it to engage in what he puts forward as a worthwhile struggle is a self-delusory justification for his lack of sincerity.

31. The difference between the second and third stations appears to be that the person in the third station does not even have to actually reject the inclination. He just continues his proper activity, oblivious to any counter-suggestions.

32. Muhasibi, *Kitāb al-Ri'āya*, pp. 115–117/233–236.

33. "Populate": *na'muruhā*

34. Reading *aḥalla* for *akhalla*.

35. Reading *dhikr* for *dhālika.*

36. Muhasibi, *Kitāb al-Ri'āya*, pp. 120–123/241–247, in the chapter entitled: "On the Stations (*manāzil*) of Conceit and their Moments (*awqāt*)."

37. Muhasibi, *Kitāb al-Ri'āya*, pp. 129–132/258–264.

38. Most probably an allusion to the transmission of hadith—how many hadiths has he had transmitted to him.

39. The syntax here is rough, as Muhasibi parodies the thoughts and sayings of the self-vaunter, but seems to switch persons and in and out of direct discourse.

40. The question is rhetorical, meaning: I am not the kind of person sleeping at dawn, but am awake (performing the ritual prayer, or performing a vigil, etc.).

41. Muhasibi, *Kitāb al-Ri'āya*, pp. 140–141/278–279.

42. "Inauthenticity": *sahw*. Although this word is frequently translated as silliness, it has a graver meaning in Muhasibi. It refers to a fundamental lack of sincerity or authenticity, to a state of moral and existential superficiality.

43. I.e., his fear about any egoism that may have entered after he began his act and that he has forgotten, but that would be known to the deity.

CHAPTER 6. SARRAJ

1. I have translated these sections from Abū Naṣr 'Abdallah B. 'Alī al-Sarráj al-Ṭusi, *The Kitáb Al-Luma' Fi 'l-Taṣawwuf*, ed. R. A. Nicholson (Leiden and London: Gibb Memorial Series, 1914), pp. 423–454. For an outstanding translation and commentary on the entire work, see Richard Gramlich, *Schlaglichter über das Sufitum: Abū Naṣr as-Sarrājs Kitāb al-luma'* (Stuttgart: Franz Steiner Verlag, 1990).

2. Among the more celebrated figures cited by Sarraj in this short section are:

Muḥāsibī (d. 243/857)
Dhū n-Nūn (d. c. 246/861)
Sārī as-Saqaṭī (d. 253/867)
Sahl ibn 'Abdallah [at-Tustarī] (d. 283/896)
Nūrī (d. 295/908)
Muḥammad ibn Sālim (d. 297/909)
and son, Aḥmad ibn Muḥammad ibn Sālim (d.350/960)
Junayd (d. 297/910)
Shiblī (d. 334/946)
Other figures cited by Sarraj in the section include:

Abu Sulayman ad-Dārānī (d. 215/830)
Abū Ya'qūb as-Sūsī
Yaḥyā ibn al-Mu'ādh (d. 258/871)
Yaḥyā ibn 'Abdullāh al-Jallā' (d. 258/871)
Abū Sa'īd al-Kharrāz (d. c. 286/899)
Abū Bakr at-Tūsī
Ibrāhīm al-Khawwāṣ (d. 291/904)
Ruwaym (d. 303/915)
Abū Bukr al-Wāsiṭī (d. 320/932)
Abū l-Ḥasan al-Qannād (d. c. 330/941)

3. The reference to the Shaykh is a reference to Sarraj as the author of the book. The form is that of a transcriber writing down the words of the author and therefore referring to the author in the third person.

4. "Venturers": *mut'arriḍin*; "those who have achieved realization": *muta-ḥaqqiqīn*; "neglect": *ghafla*.

5. This hadith does not occur in the major canonical collections. For other attributions of this saying, including that to a descendant of 'Ali, see Gramlich, *Schlaglichter*, p. 89.

6. "Contrives": *yaḥīku*; "sin": *al-ithm*. This hadith is found in Ibn Ḥanbal, *Musnad*, 5, 252, 256.

7. For the hadith, see Ibn Ḥanbal, *Musnad*, 4, 228.

8. A typical example of the way in which Sufi authors tend to immerse any possible implication of autonomy of the human will back into the complex and paradoxical tension between divine predetermination and human responsibility.

9. This hadith is also unattested in the canonical collections. See Gramlich, *Schlaglichter*, p. 93, for other references, including the attribution of the saying to Ibn An'um al-Ifrīqī (d. 156/772).

10. "Bestowal of God to his friends": *karāma li awliyā'ihi*.

11. "Tribulation": *balwā*. The syntactical ambiguity here reflects a similar ambiguity in the original Arabic. Is the second element in true poverty the hiding of the trace of *balwā* or the refraining from the hiding of the trace of *balwā*?

12. "The true": *ṣiddīqīn*.; "free gift": *ṣadaqa*. This is a difficult passage. Gramlich (*Schlaglichter*, p. 94) reads "its sincerity," *ṣidquhu*, for the manuscripts' *ṣadaqa (Die Sühnegabe für ihr Betteln ist dann ihre Ehrlichkeit)*, and cites a statement in Abū Ṭālib al-Makkī's *Qūt al-Qulūb*: "The atonement for the request is the sincerity in the request of the one making the request." My translation follows the manuscripts. The logic would appear to be that by confiding in someone he knows will rejoice in his confidence, the poor person will in fact be giving that person the gift of his confidence.

13. "In his love": *fī ḥubbihi*. I have translated it as subjective genetive. It is possible to read it as an objective genetive (in the love for him, i.e., for God). Though there is no immediate antecedent, the Sufis often used the pronoun without immediate antecedent, generating thereby the intimacy of a personal referent who does not need to be named.

14. "Trace": *rasm*. The trace can refer to the last vestige of the ego-self *(nafs)* that prevents the Sufi from full passing away or extinction in the divine beloved, but Sarrāj's elliptic sentence does not offer a contextual certainty to the meaning here.

15. The full verse reads: "He provides sustenance for him from where he does not reckon. Whoever trusts in God, he is his sufficiency. Allah sees to it that his command is fulfilled. Allah has allotted for each thing its determined measure *(qadran)*." The first part of the verse underlies the notion of *tawakkul*: The deity provides from where one does not reckon.

16. The immediate point of verse 9:72 is to state that simple divine acceptance of the human is a greater reward than all the goods of paradise and the garden of Eden promised to the faithful godservant.

17. The Decree: *al-qadā'*. I have treated *al-qadā'* as a proper noun here. It is used to refer to the decree, i.e., the divine decree.

18. Discontent: *sakhṭ*. Acceptance is an active virtue, as opposed to mere resignation, and the Sufi is warned not to allow acceptance to become a mode of passivity or pleasure.

19. "Anxiety": *jaz'*; "conditions": *aḥwāl;* "heart-secrets": *asrār;* "self-observance": *murāqaba.* The various stations and conditions tend to be categorized differently according to different authors, and what for some is a station, for others is a condition. The Qushayri essay (Chapter 3 in this volume) discussed conditions in detail (though not the first condition mentioned here by Sarraj, self-observance).

Chapter 7. Bistami

1. I have translated these sections from Abū Naṣr 'Abdallah B. 'Alī al-Sarráj al-Ṭusi, *The Kitáb al-Luma' Fi 'l-Taṣawwuf,* ed. R. A. Nicholson (Leiden and London: Gibb Memorial Series, 1914), pp. 380–395.

For an important discussion of the role of *shaṭḥiyāt* in Sufi discourse and in Islamic history, see Carl W. Ernst, *Words of Ecstasy in Sufism* (Albany: SUNY Press, 1985). See pp. 9–36 in this work for translation and analysis of passages of Sarraj and later writers on the issue of *shaṭḥiyāt*, not included in the selection here.

2. As is frequently the case, the "book" of a Sufi writer is written in the voice of an auditor or transcriber who often refers to the author in the third person.

3. As-Sarraj seems to be referring here to a formal commentary *(tafsīr)*, which he had heard about but which evidently he was not able to find.

4. To avoid quotes within quotes within quotes, I have not placed the comments of Junayd in quotes, because they frequently have other quotations embedded within them.

5. "Well": *mustaqāh.*

6. "The rapture he found": *f īm ā wajada minhā.*

7. R. Gramlich, *Schlaglichter über das Sufitum: Abū Naṣr as-Sarrājs Kitāb al-Luma'* (Stuttgart: Franz Steiner Verlag, 1990), p. 521, reads this clause differently: *Und da hat der einer daraus in Argument für Abū Yazīd's Nichtigkeit gemacht.*

8. "Unity": *waḥdāniyya*; "subjectivity": *anāniyya* (literally, "I-ness"); "oneness": *(aḥadiyya).* Sufis divide unity into various degrees, usually with *aḥadiyya* as the culmination.

9. "Faultfinder": *al-muta'annitu; 'anita a:* to fall on evil days, suffer adversity, commit sin, commit fornication; *ta'annata*: to cause vexation, annoyance, or distress; bring trouble, harass, press, molest, seek to confuse (with questions); pick a quarrel; be out for a fight, stickle, be pigheaded, insist stubbornly. Sarraj uses this

term as his key epithet for critics of Bistami. Gramlich, *Schlaglichter*, uses translations based on the term *lästig*: troublesome, annoying, uncomfortable, inconvenient.

10. A particularly powerful use of the demonstrative, similar in its semantic intensity to the "that" of the Upanishadic "That thou art" *(tat tvan asi)*. In Bistami and Sarraj's case, the "that" could refer to the personal deity, to absolute reality beyond the distinction between person and nonperson, or to the vision of deity or reality. For a detailed discussion of what is at stake in the indeterminacy of the referent at the moment of mystical union, see M. Sells, *Mystical Languages of Unsaying* (Chicago: University of Chicago Press, 1994), Chap. 3.

11. For a different translation and interpretation of these verses, see Gramlich, *Schlaglichter*, p. 523.

12. This comment seems to be a comment by the medieval editor of the text on the comment of Sarraj on the utterance of Abu Yazid. After Sarraj's exquisite and powerfully concise discussion of intimate conversations between lover and beloved, it is a comment that can only be called a grand understatement.

13. "Detachment": *tajrīd.*

14. This version of the union hadith differs from the more standard versions by using "eye" for seeing (a distinction the later Sufi Ibn 'Arabi was to make into a major theological point) and by leaving out the reference to the "feet with which he walks." Cf. Sells, *Mystical Languages*, Chap. 4

15. These verses, attributed to an anonymous "someone"—as is the case with many poetic verses cited by Sufis—are mentioned by Sarraj earlier (120:106). Elsewhere they are attributed to Hallaj (see Chapter 9 in this volume), though in some cases with an important variant for the second verse. Sarraj seems to be trying to attenuate their theologically controversial character by insisting that they refer only to two human lovers. As mentioned in Chapter 9 in this volume, the theological controversy was probably more concerned with the issues of *ḥulūl* (the incarnationism associated with Christianity) that might be found in verse 2 than it is with the issue of mystical union per se, which was standard Sufi doctrine by this time.

16. "Everlastingness": *daymūmiyya.*

17. A difficult Qur'anic passage that becomes a touchstone for theological examination of the issue of divine predetermination versus human free will.

18. Reading *wa annī anti* for *wa annī 'anki*: the reading of *K* and *A* (in which this reading is written in above the text). The alternative reading would be: "I examine the secret of my heart for desire for you/but find only myself, apart from you."

19. The syntax of the original Arabic here is fragmentary.

20. Gramlich (*Schlaglichter*, p. 526) omits the phrase *hawā' al-kayfiyya* (ether of *kayfiyya* or "howness") though the phrase is not listed by Nicholson as being lacking in any of the manuscripts.

21. *Itighlāl bi l-mulāḥaẓati ilā:* Gramlich (*Schlaglichter*, p. 527 and n. 12) follows the reading in manuscript *wa l-mulāḥaẓata.*

22. Following manuscript (see Gramlich, *Schlaglichter,* p. 527, n. 14), which reads *lam ara* for the ungrammatical *law anna* of NA.

23. "Air": *hawā'*; "field": *mīdān.* The syntax in the original is extremely loose and amenable to differing translations. Gramlich (*Schlaglichter,* p. 527) offers a different reading, linking the following phrase (his saying "I learned that it was all a cheat") to the previous list, and breaking the sentence after "cheat." My reading avoids the ungrammatical sentence opening with *li'anna.* It also suggests that this last statement is a remark by Sarraj and an attempt by him to put a more positive spin on Bistami's statement by excepting the last phrase—"I saw that all was a cheat"—from Junayd's criticism or, at best, his damning with faint praise.

24. The "Master of the First and the Last" is clearly an epithet for Muhammad. This hadith is widely attested in the hadith collections. It is found in Aḥmad ibn Ḥanbal, *al-Musnad* 2.248, and Bukhārī, *Ṣaḥīḥ, adab* 90, to name only two examples. The verse of Labīd is in the *ṭawīl* meter. Labīd was one of the most famous classical poets, the author of one of the seven Mu'allaqat. He is said to have lived to be over 100 years old, to have converted to Islam, and, after his conversion, to have ceased composing poetry. The *ṭawīl* meter was the major meter of pre-Islamic poets. The verse is also found in the standard collection *(Diwān)* of Labīd. In the Brockelmann edition it is in poem number 41, verse 9.

25. From nothing through nothing in nothing: *min laysa fī laysa bilaysa.*

26. "Searching": *istidrāk*—the word could also mean "rectification."

27. "Initiated": *ahlihi* (I am indebted to Gramlich, *Schlaglichter,* p. 529, for this way of expressing the concept).

28. Nicholson reads here: *min al-mazīd kāīna (sic)* and suggests no variants. Gramlich *(Schlaglichter)* offers no explanation either. 'Abd al-Ḥalīm Maḥmūd, ed. Kitāb al-Luma fī t-Taṣawwuf (Cairo: Dār al-kutub al-Ḥaditha, 1380/1960), has *kā 'ina,* which seems to make more sense, but leaves the syntax questionable.

29. "Position of homeland": *waṭanuhu fī makānihi.* The sentence is difficult because, in addition to the awkward syntax, the *waṭan* or homeland, which would normally be the goal toward which the journey is made, here becomes what attains or reaches the final place.

30. This is somewhat obscure. Gramlich *(Schlaglichter)* suggests that the foot refers to the foot of Jahannam, which is being figured here as a beast, in which case *qadamahu* (its/his foot) should read *qadamahā* (its/her foot), since *jahannam* is feminine.

31. Their essences: *ma'ānīhā:*—i.e., essences in the sense of their primary meanings or contents. In usages like this, the term *ma'ānī hā* seems close to the notion of quiddities, which in more philosophical terminology is rendered as *māhiyyāt.*

32. Some might think this buildup of defenses to be counterproductive. First Abu Nasr defends the propositions, then he says that the people of Bistam do not recall Bistami ever saying them, then he says he himself would not recall them if they were not demonstrably authentic.

33. "What he intended in what he said": *irādatahu fī mā qāla.*

34. The section suggests that Bistami aroused controversy for seeming to declare (and assume the authority to declare) that the Jews were "forgiven." It is difficult to reconstruct the context. It could be that certain Muslim groups were overemphasizing Qur'anic passages critical of the Jews. Perhaps Bistami was led to counter such hostile positions. Sarraj suggests that Bistami simply meant that Jews were destined to feel the wrath of God and were not personally responsible for it, and that they could not be forgiven retroactively by Bistami for the criticisms leveled against them (for all time) in the eternal Qur'an.

35. This apparently dismissive remark about the sacred notion of remembrance was to become a standard remedy for those who were viewed to be so concerned with the techniques and process of remembrance that they forget the beloved being remembered. Sarraj shows Ibn Salim that this remark of Ibn Salim's own beloved teacher, Sahl, taken out of context, sounds just as scandalous as those of Bistami. Indeed, Sahl at-Tustari was forced to live out his final years in exile because of theological attacks on his positions.

36. It is not clear whether this is the comment of Sarraj on his recounting of the conversations, or of the editor of the text on his writing down of Sarraj's account.

37. Abu Yazid observed the Ramadan fast every day of the year except the one festival day *('īd)* of fast-breaking that is the official end of the month of Ramadan. For such accounts of Abu Yazid, see the next section, the biographies of Sulami and Qushayri.

38. Of course, charges of undue asceticism and antinomian excess can frequently go together, as one finds in the Christian tradition with polemics against the Gnostics and inquisitorial charges against alleged twelfth- and thirteenth-century heretics.

39. See John Esposito, *Islam: The Straight Path* (Oxford: Oxford University Press, 1988), pp. 104–105, for a typical example. There "ecstatic rebels" like Abu Yazid and Hallaj are contrasted to the "doctrinally safe followers of the law."

40. Abū 'Abd ar-Raḥmān as-Sulamī, *Ṭabaqāt aṣ-Ṣufiyya*, ed. Nūr ad-Dīn Shurayba (Cairo: Maktabat al-Khanaji, 1953), pp. 67–74; and *Kitāb Ṭabaqāt Al-Ṣūfiyya*, ed. Johannes Pedersen (Leiden: Brill, 1960), pp. 60–67. Cf. Meddeb, *Les Dits de Bistami* (Paris: Fayard, 1989).

41. The Sulami text has "Ummayy," but Gramlich (*Das Sendschreiben*, see note 58) has shown that the more likely reading is 'Ammī.

42. "That you would have people be content with": *turḍī n-nās*; "bestowal": *rizq*. The saying places in opposition the vice of resentment *(sukht)* and the virtue of acceptance *(riḍā).* Those who resent Allah and resent their own lives lack "certainty," and thus are unable to attain active acceptance in life. This vice of resentment is linked here to the error of assuming that those who suffer in life are suffering because in the view of the deity they somehow deserve it, and those who prosper, prosper because in the divine view they deserve prosperity. True acceptance, on the

other hand, means that one accepts the good times and the bad times with certainty in the ultimate worth of the all-powerful deity, without making judgments about the moral meaning of prosperity and poverty, and without making assumptions about what one deserves oneself or what others deserve.

43. Cf. Meddeb, *Les Dits de Bistami*, p. 146, no. 340.

44. The point seems to be that if a person has the quality of *ma'rifa*, mystical knowing, the knowing itself is sufficient. It is not necessary to obtain possession of that which one has experienced through mystical knowing.

45. "Trial": *ibtilā'*. A rather laconic remark; the point seems to be that those who lead people into trial and mystical knowing should bear responsibility for the carrying out of the ritually enjoined acts of devotion.

46. The ablution with sand *(tayammun)* is allowed in cases where there is no water for ablutions, such as travel in the desert.

47. Here we have the same *matn* as Qushayri 3 and same isnad except that Qushayri has Muhammad ibn Husayn at the very beginning. Cf. Meddeb, *Les Dits de Bistami*, p. 152, no. 364.

48. "Craving of appetite": *shahwa*.

49. "Inner resolve": *himma*; "sounder": *aslama*. There is an untranslatable play here on the root *s/l/m*, which is also the root for the word "Islam": "the infidelity of the people of inner resolve is sounder/more authentically Islam, than the faith . . ." "People of tradition": *ahl as-[sun]na*. The first part of the word is missing in the edition of Shurayba, p. 71. The Pedersen version (see note 40), p. 64, has *ahl al-minna* (the people of goodwill).

50. Cf. Meddeb, *Les Dits de Bistami*, p. 147, no. 342

51. The objective pronouns, translated here as "him," refer to the deity. Though it is confusing at first to translate them without explicitly flagging the deity as their referent, it is in fact more faithful both to the text and to the quality of intimacy that the text achieves by refusing to flag the referent and by assuming that the reader will understand what it is. See the discussion of this issue in Chapter 3 in this volume.

52. "Robe of honor": *khil'a*. Cf. Meddeb, *Les Dits de Bistami*, p. 74, no. 130.

53. This report forms one of the selections from Bistami in Margaret Smith, *Readings from the Mystics of Islam* (London: Luzac and Company, 1950), p. 26 (first part of selection 24). Cf. Meddeb, *Les Dits de Bistami*, p. 90, no. 175, the last part of which differs from the version given here.

54. "Essence of the real": *dhāt al-ḥaqq*; "referring": *ishāra*, a term that can also mean to allude to or point to; "idolatry": *shirk*, the associating of another entity with the one deity.

55. See no. 2 in Qushayri's biography of Abu Yazid.

56. That is, distracts the knower from the one object of his knowing.

57. "The Book": *al-kitāb*, an apparent reference to the Qur'an as "the" book within the tradition.

58. Abū l-Qāsim ʿabd al-Karīm al-Qushayrī, *Al-Risāla al-Qushayriyya fī at-Taṣawwuf* [The Qushayrian Treatise on Sufism] (Cairo: Dār al-Kutub al-Ḥadītha, 1988). Cf. al-Qushayri, *Das Sendschreiben al-Qushayrīs*. Übersetzt, eingeleitet und kommentiert von Richard Gramlich. (Freiburger Islamstudien, Band 12: Wiesbaden: Franz Steiner Verlag, 1989), pp. 50–52.

59. "Affirmation of unity": *tawḥīd*. See the same *matn* (content) and almost identical isnad in Sulami 10, above.

60. "The direction of Mecca": *qibla*. Cf. Meddeb, *Les Dits de Bistami*, p. 40, no. 21; This version specifies that the event took place in the region of Qūmis.

61. The God-sent refers to Muhammad, who had several wives, the most famous of whom are his first wife, Khadija, and his younger wife Aʿisha, who was a major political and cultural leader in early Islam.

62. "You will not be able to endure being with us": the apparently divine voice speaks in the first person plural, as the divine voice is accustomed to speak in the Qur'an. "You've found": *wadajta*, the exact equivalent of the expression "eureka" (Greek for I've found). In both cases the object is left off, making the expression more powerful than "I found it," because the object is not delimited. Cf. Meddeb, *Les Dits de Bistami*, pp. 127–128, no. 298.

63. Again, the portrayal of Bistami shows him simultaneously engaged in feats of asceticism and devaluing ascetic feats in relation to other aspects of spiritual struggle. Cf. Meddeb, *Les Dits de Bistami*, p. 95, no. 185.

64. A similar saying appears in ibid., p. 45, only in the second person: When you station yourself before Allah Most High, act as if you were a Magian who wished to cut his *Zunnār*.

65. I will be able to touch upon only a few of these parallels here: the green bird that takes Bistami through the heavens and the "wings of the Shekhina" that bear Enoch to the highest heaven; angels in ranks "with feet through the stars" (3Enoch7, 3Enoch22); the angel with four faces (Bistami's third heaven, 3Enoch21); the gift of languages by which Bistami is able to greet the angels, as did Muhammad in seventy languages, the number of languages the angels speak in 3Enoch and other Merkevah texts; Bistami's encounter with an angel the height of a journey of 500 years and Enoch's encounter with an angel (Sarapi'el) the height of a journey of 502 years along with Sandalphon *(BTHag. 13b)*, who is taller than his companions by a distance of, precisely, 500 years; the repeated use of the number 100,000 or a thousand thousand as a culmination of the experience of reduplicating and increasingly intense expansion of spatial dimensions; enlargment of Bistami and the very similar enlargement of Enoch (3Enoch9); angels with eyes "equal in number to the stars" as an almost exact parallel to 3Enoch26 where Seraphiel's body is described as full of eyes "like the stars of heaven, beyond reckoning"; the culmination of Bistami's ascent with his being called "the chosen" *(safī)* and the culmination of Enoch's ascent with the epithet "the choicest of them all." A detailed discussion in M. Sells, "Bistami's Miʿraj and the Jewish Merkevah Tradition" (revised version of a paper entitled "*3Enoch* and the *Miʿraj* of Bistami," presented at the annual meeting of the American Academy of Religion, Anaheim, California, November 11, 1993).

For a study of the Merkevah tradition, with an excursus devoted to some Islamic parallels, see David Halperin, *Faces of the Chariot: Early Jewish Responses to Ezekiel's Vision* (Tubingen: J. C. B. Mohr, 1988). See also Elliot R. Wolfson, *Through a Speculum That Shines: Vision and Imagination in the Medieval Jewish Mysticism* (Princeton: Princeton University Press, 1994).

66. A nonromanticized understanding of textual development does not assume any pure "urtext." Borrowings, therefore, do not threaten or diminish the originality of a tradition. Indeed, all traditions are made of elements borrowed from elsewhere. When a term or an image is borrowed, the choice of the term or image, and the manner of its new contextualization and any transformations it undergoes, is key to the concerns that motivate such a borrowing. Nor do classical exegetes of the Qur'an have a problem acknowledging that terms or stories within the divine revelation exist in previous traditions; the revelation was offered as an "Arabic Qur'an" and made use of the language (in the full sense of the term) that was available and understood at the time. The postulation of pure urtext turned nineteenth-century and early twentieth-century discussions of borrowing into needlessly tendentious arguments over the alleged lack of originality of the later tradition.

Complicating all efforts to more precisely locate the various authors and schools involved in such symbolic transformations and contentions is the fact that the key Hebrew text, 3Enoch or the Book of the *Hekhalot* (Palaces), belongs to that category of mystical literature, the hekhalot texts, whose provenance and date are completely unknown, with estimates ranging from the third century to the fourteenth century CE. See Peter Schäfer, *Synopse zur Hekhalot-Literatur* (Tubingen: J. C. B. Mohr, 1981); H. Odeberg, *3Enoch or the Hebrew Book of Enoch* (Cambridge: Cambridge University Press, 1928, reprinted by KTAV, 1973); and P. S. Alexander, *3Enoch: The Book of Enoch by Rabbi Ishmael the High Priest*, in *The Old Testament Pseudepigrapha*, ed. J. H. Charlesworth, Vol. 1: *Apocalyptic Literature and Testaments* (Garden City, N.Y.: Doubleday, 1983), pp. 255–315.

67. See M. Sells, "The Semantics of Mystical Union in Islam," in *Mystical Union and Monotheistic Faith*, ed. M. Idel and B. McGinn (New York: Macmillan, 1989), pp. 101–108.

68. This translation is based on the text found in R. A. Nicholson, "An Early Arabic Version of the Mi'raj of Abu Yazid al-Bistami," *Islamica* 2, no. 3 (1926): 403–408.

69. "Related from": reading *'an* for *an.*

70. A clear parallel to the four-faces angel or beast found in the Enoch ascents and grounded in Ezekiel.

71. "Cessation": *farāgh.* The day of cessation is another of the many terms used for the final day of reckoning or moment of truth, each term emphasizing a different aspect of that ultimate moment. The cessation points to the ending of all work, argument, struggle. It is a day of emptiness, of termination of all activity except for each human's realization of his ultimate and final destiny.

72. As pointed out by Frederick Colby, the author of the text is making a play

on the term *ta'ālā* (most high, he is most high, may he be exalted) and the imperative verb spoken to Bistami, *ta'āli* (come up!). The play mirrors the famous *shaṭḥ* or mystical utterance of Bistami, *subḥānī*—"glory to me." The word *subḥānahu* is commonly placed with *ta'ālā* after reference to the deity. The play on the famous mystical utterance of Bistami is of the highest degree of finesse and subtlety, yet the implications of the imperative *ta'āli* in close proximity to the term *ta'ālā* are not less extreme than Bistami's more direct expression of mystical union in his utterance of *subḥānī*. The term *ta'āli* means "rise up!" but also, given the context and the standard pairing of *subḥānahu wa ta'ālā*, evokes the famous ecstatic utterance of Bistami. See Frederick Colby, "The Flight of the Innermost Heart: Sufi Terms, Images and Concepts in the Mi'raj of Abu Yazid al-Bistami" (B.A. Thesis, Haverford College, 1991), pp. 37–38.

73. Reading *ilayhim* for *ilayhi*. One would expect a plural "them" here (the yearning angels) or the demonstrative "that," because there is no single angel or entity tempting Abu Yazid at this point.

74. "The two heavy ones": *ath-thaqalān*. This enigmatic Qur'anic expression has been interpreted in a number of ways, as referring to the jinn and human beings (the two heavy "earth creatures"), or as referring to Jupiter and Saturn, to give two common interpretations.

75. The exact size of the angel Sandalphon in the Babylonian Talmud *(BTHag. 13b)*.

76. *Malakūt* and *jabarūt* are technical terms in Islamic philosophical and mystical literature. Their meaning varies according to the particular context and writer. In general, there is a hierarchy of divine essence *(lāhūt)*, the world of power *(jabarūt*, related to *jabr*, the term used for absolute divine determination), and the world of sovereignty *(malakūt*, related either to *mālik*, king, or *ma'lak*, angel), all of which are beyond the normal earthly sphere. Although *malakūt* and *jabarūt* have clear Arabic cognates, their morphology is not Arabic and they are generally considered to be non-Arabic imports from related Semitic languages: Hebrew, Aramaic, and/or Syriac sources.

77. As with Muhammad and Enoch, so with Bistami, the culmination of the ascent is being designated the chosen one.

78. Nicholson (see note 1) places after this ambiguous *hu* the parenthesis ("the worshiper of God"), but I would argue that at this point of culmination of *fanā'*, the ambiguity of antecedent (Allah or worshiper, divine or human) should not be explained away by interpolated parentheses.

Chapter 8. Junayd

1. These texts were published, along with a translation and introduction, by A. H. Abdel Kader in *The Life, Personality and Writings of Al-Junayd* (London: Luzac, 1962).

2. I would call this re-creation the "meaning event" of the encounter between the text and its hearer or reader. For a detailed elaboration of the role of such an event in mystical literature, see M. Sells, *Mystical Languages of Unsaying* (Chicago: University of Chicago Press, 1993).

3. Krista Woodbridge, editorial comment on the margin of my translation, August 1993.

4. For precise Christian counterparts of this notion of return to "what one was before one was," see Sells, *Mystical Languages,* pp. 131–134, 199–203.

5. Abdel Kader, *The Life, Personality and Writings of Al-Junayd*, Arabic Text, pp. 51–52.

6. There is an intricate *saj*ʿ (rhyme prose) here: Through this *tawfīq* occurs his *tawḥīd*, from his *tawḥīd*, *taṣdīq*, from his *taṣdīq*, *taḥqīq*, from his *taḥqīq* is drawn knowing him.

7. *Thumma kāna baʿda mā lam yakun ḥaythu kāna kāna.*

8. Abdel Kader, *The Life, Personality and Writings of Al-Junayd*, p. 53.

9. Ibid., pp. 54–55.

10. Abdel Kader, p. 175, translates these last two sentences as follows: "At this stage you are your true self because you have lost the shackles of your human individuality and you achieve eternal life with God because you are obliterated." The Arabic reads: *Fa ḥīn ā'idhin anta anta, idh kunta bilā anta, fa baqiyat min ḥaythu fanayta.*

11. "Upon the abiding of your trace in the disappearance of your name": *ʿinda baqā'i rasmika bi dhibābi ismika.*

12. Abdel Kader, *The Life, Personality and Writings of Al-Junayd*, pp. 55–57.

13. "As long as the affirmation abides": *bi baqā' al-iqrār.*

14. "That he might be as he was when he was before he was": *an yakūn kamā kāna idh kāna qabla an yakūn.*

15. "With the disappearance of 'he' ": *bi dhahbi huwa.*

16. See below, where I translate *awjadahum wujūdahum lahum* as "he EXisted them his existence-for-them."

17. Emily Camp has written of this text: "Even in the discussion of existence of the human versus annihilation within the divine, the source of action is key to a determination of whether the human is totally subsumed or not, as well as to whether Allah never intended total annihilation of the human or an action of the human's own power prevented annihilation. The tension created by this question of human or divine action and obstruction resounds through Junayd's discourse, never being fully resolved" ("The Action, Power, and Tension of and in Junayd's Linguistic Feat," *Kitāb al-Fanā'*, unpublished paper, May 1992).

18. Cf. Muhammad Abdul Haq Ansari, "The Doctrine of One Actor: Junayd's View of *Tawḥid,*" *Muslim World* 73, no. 1 (1983): 33–56; and Muḥammad 'Abdu r-Rabb, *Al-Junayd's Doctrine of Tawḥīd: An Analysis of his Understanding of Islamic Monotheism* (M.A. Thesis, McGill University, 1967).

19. Abdel Kader, *The Life, Personality and Writings of Al-Junayd*, pp. 31–39.

In addition to the translation by Abdel Kader in the same volume, there exists another English version of this text, by R. C. Zaehner, *Hindu and Muslim Mysticism* (New York: Schocken, 1960), Appendix B, pp. 218–224.

20. "Those who cling to him": *al-muttaṣilīn ilayhi.*

21. Through the implementation of *tajrīd* (stripping, peeling), in accordance with his *da'wā* (call) and the finding/existing in him of *ḥazwa* (favor) in apparitions of the *ghuyūb* (hidden things) and the nearness of the *maḥbūb* (beloved). By ignoring the *saj'* here, Zaehner (*Hindu and Muslim Mysticism,* p. 218) seems to misconstruct the statement structure, breaking the sentence in the middle where the *saj'* would indicate a series of parallel statements.

22. "Did he not deceive me": cf. Qur'ān 86:16.

23. "Existence": *wujūd*; "witness": *wujūd*; "bliss": *na'īm;* "agony": *ta'dhīb.*

24. "It was": *kāna l-amru fī.* This expression is both highly particular in its Qur'anic allusions and impossible to translate word for word. I have used an expression ("was as it was") that parallels both the rhetorical solemnity and the referential comprehensiveness of the term *amr*, a term that combines the divine "command" with the "state of affairs" or "whatever is as it is." "Disclose": *tabdū;* "incite": *tahdū;* manifestation: *ibdā'ihi*; "origination": *ibtidā'hi.*

25. "My construction": *bi inshā'ī.* "In the condition of my annihilation": Junayd plays on the ambiguity of annihilation here: (1) as the negative condition of human existence, the lack of necessary or true existence; (2) as the possibility of mystical annihilation in the deity through which existence or ecstatic existentiality (*wujūd*) is realized.

26. "The reviver" *(al-mu'īd).* The Qur'anic reviving or "second creation" is the re-creation of each human on the final day of truth *(yawm ad-dīn);* Junayd makes particularly explicit the parallel between the apocalyptic day of truth and the mystical moment of annihilation in union with the deity, a parallel that can be found more implicitly as a subtext in many Sufi writings on *fanā'*.

27. Reading *wujūdihā li anfusihā* for *wujūdihu li anfusihā.*

28. "This is an eternal guise upon the spirits": *innamā hadhā talabbus 'alā al-arwāḥ* [*mā lahā min al-azaliyya*]. This is a puzzling passage. Abdel Kader (*The Life, Personality and Writings of Al-Junayd*, p. 154) gives: "Now hand in hand with this spiritual metamorphosis." Zaehner (*Hindu and Muslim Mysticism*, p. 219) has: "However this is only metaphorically applied to souls."

29. "Overcoming": *ghalaba*; "overpowering": *qahr.*

30. "Their existence-through-the-real-through-them": *wujūdahum bi l-ḥaqqi bihim.*

31. "Then how can that be given a how": *fa kayfa takayyafa dhālika bi kayfiyyati*, that is, how can any modality be conceptualized outside the divine self-revelation itself? Again, see the extraordinary parallels with the thirteenth-century Christian mystical puns on "without a how" and "without a why" in Sells, *Mystical Languages.*

32. "As a being with a certain aspect": *kā'inan bi jihatin min al-jihāt.* This passage recalls Plotinus's statement that the one cannot be known as a some-thing, a *tode ti*, or as a "thus" or a "not-thus."

33. For the concept of presence or being-present (*ḥuḍūr*), see the discussion by Qushayri (in Chapter 3 in this volume). "The reification of their existence": *kā'in wujūdihā.* The term *kā'in*, sometimes translated as "being," has the connotation of a delimited, created entity.

34. Reading: *yaẓlimuhā* for what appears to be *yukallimuhā.*

35. This passage, beginning with "Alas!" (lines 12, 18, p. 35, of the Arabic text), is even more fragmented grammatically than the rest of the text, filled with ambiguities of pronominal antecedents and syntactical breaks.

36. "Transformations": *talwīn.* This is a key Sufi term, but one that is seldom explained explicitly. The transformations indicated by *talwīn* entail the various states that the self is brought through during mystical experience. A related term, *talawwun*, especially as used by later Sufis, indicates the transformation through various modes of understanding the deity, and such transformation is viewed positively. *Talwīn*, on the other hand, tends to refer more to the various postures and objections of the ego-self in the process of its annihilation in mystical union.

37. "Ladder": *maṭāli'.* The word can also mean beginnings or first stages: "leaving their first stages behind."

38. "Troubled in knowing": *fa hiya al-kulfa bi ma'rifatihā.* Another example of grammatical roughness in this text.

39. "Drapery": *kiswā.* This is also the term for the drapery that is hung over the Ka'ba in Mecca.

40. "Exemplars": *mathalāt.* This plural form is not found in the classical lexicons.

41. "Called to account before him in his presence": *Mutaḥsiba lahu bayna yadayhi.* Or one might read *muḥtabisa* for *mutaḥsiba*: confined by him in his presence. See Zaehner (*Hindu and Muslim Mysticism*, p. 224) and Abdel Kader (*The Life, Personality and Writings of Al-Junayd*, p. 159).

42. Zaehner (*Hindu and Muslim Mysticism*, p. 224) gives a more irenic rendition: "for they see that he is near to ward off their suffering and to draw out its sting." There is little grammatical justification for such a rendition; the pronouns and prepositions do not support it. Zaehner could appeal to other, only slightly less ungrammatical usages to defend his interpretation. A more troubling difficulty, in my view, is that the notion of the divine nearness warding off suffering and drawing its sting is not consistent with Junayd's implacable avoidance of such consolatory sweetness throughout this treatise and throughout his other treatises.

43. The last paragraph in the text of Abdel Kader, *The Life, Personality and Writings of Al-Junayd*, is quite difficult, and seems to have been cut off in mid-stream. Abdel Kader translates it (p. 159), while Zaehner, *Hindu and Muslim Mysticism*, omits it from his translation. The passage begins by saying that there are two kinds of people of trial, but only one kind is depicted. Either the text is corrupt, or Junayd,

in a manner jarring even for him, simply stops at the point where language is of no avail.

44. As mentioned above, this is the comment of the medieval copyist.

CHAPTER 9. HALLAJ

1. *Ṭāsīn al-Azal wa l-Iltibās*. This translation is based on two texts: the edition of L. Massignon (Paris: Geuthner, 1913) and the later edition of Paul Nwyia, Hallāj, *Kitāb at-Tawāsīn* (Beirut: Imprimerie Catholique, 1972). Massignon based his edition on the single manuscript known to him at the time (henceforth M) as well as the Persian translation and commentary of Ruzbehān Baqlī from the latter's *Sharḥ ash-Shatḥiyāt* (henceforth MBaq). Cf. Ruzbehan Baqlī's *Sharḥ-i Shatḥiyāt* (Commentary on Mystical Utterances), ed. Henry Corbin (Tehran: Bibliothèque Iranienne, 1966), pp. 508–527. Nwyia was able to obtain access to three other manuscripts: B (British Museum 12937, fol. 16b–23a), T (Riḍawiya Library of Meshhed, Hikmat), and V (Veliyuddin Library of Istanbul; see Nwyia, pp. 188–189). I will follow the edition of Nwyia unless otherwise indicated. Although Nwyia's edition clarifies many problems, many other problems are left unresolved and, in some cases, where the manuscripts diverge, I choose a different version from that of Nwyia. Such choices will be indicated in the notes.

2. Thus the modern Egyptian poet, Salāḥ 'Abd aṣ-Ṣabūr, composed a play on social revolution and justice entitled *Mas'āt Ḥallāj* (The Tragedy of Hallaj).

3. The works of Massignon, only a few of which are cited below, and the recent original works of Herbert Mason offer some notable examples.

4. The essential work is Louis Massignon, *The Passion of al-Hallaj: Mystic and Martyr of Islam*, 4 vols., trans. Herbert Mason (Princeton: Princeton University Press, 1982). Despite the apologetic distortions caused by Massignon's overtly Christological perspective on Hallaj, his work remains valuable for its detail, insight, and precision.

5. For the poem, see the Epilogue in this volume.

6. Massignon, *The Passion of al-Hallaj*, Vol. 3, pp. 280–281. For Massignon's translation and analysis of the *Ṭawāsīn*, see Vol. 3, pp. 279–327.

7. The opening of a particular narration or pericope in the Qur'an frequently includes a hanging temporal clause that is never completed: "When . . ."

8. In this paragraph the manuscripts diverge completely, and it is clear that the scribes themselves had trouble making out the intended meaning. Rather than impose a unilateral interpretation here, I have translated the various versions together, allowing the reader to decide which makes more sense.

9. Massignon, *Passion*, 3:307. On pages 306–307 Massignon offers a condensed summary of theological positions on the issues raised by Iblis's self-defense.

10. In many cases, the context will make clear which meaning is operative, but Hallaj never defines his term and the text can be read with all three major mean-

ings in mind. In order to preserve this semantic openness, I have not translated the term here.

11. These division headings are my own interpolations, meant to help show more clearly the various segments of the text.

12. "Strange": *gharīb.* The anonymous writer of the conventional frame text, in which the author is introduced in the third person, qualified Hallaj here with this epithet. Although Hallaj was certainly unusual, even by the standards of early Sufis, many of whom (such as Shibli) were themselves quite unconventional, the exact purport of the epithet is unclear. It most likely relates to the comparison, implicit throughout much of what follows, of Hallaj to Iblis.

13. *'Ayn*: as mentioned earlier, the word means "eye," "essence," and "source" and it is clear that the text is playing on its various meanings.

14. "Bow down!": *usjud.* The term *sajada* (to bow down, to prostrate oneself) is impossible to translate precisely into English. It refers to the actions Muslims make in ritual prayer *(ṣalā)*, in which the posture goes beyond a simple bow, but does not extend to full "prostration," a term that implies a horizontal position and a sense of abjectness lacking in the *salā.*

15. The Persian manuscript has a fuller version of this sentence: "and Ahmad looked neither to the right nor left and did not turn . . . ." This version has the advantage of making the connection of the statement to the Qur'anic text more clear, but the Arabic version is in fact more faithful to the wording of the Qur'an here, a wording that is difficult to interpret precisely and does not necessarily mean that Muhammad did not turn to the right or left.

16. Numbers 3 and 4 are of great difficulty. "Power": *ḥawl.* The term is particularly associated with the common proverb: "There is no power *ḥawl* and no force *(quwwa)* except in (or with) Allah": *lā ḥawla wa lā quwwata illā bi llāh.* The Persian and Arabic texts are inconsistent here. The Persian has "from *(az)* his power" while the Arabic has "to *(ilā)* to his power." Al-Tarjumana follows Massignon in interpolating a "not" *(mā)* into the text: "He did not return to his first power." See Mansur al-Hallaj, *The Tawasin*, translated by Aisha Abd ar-Rahman al-Tarjumana (Berkeley: Diwan Press, 1974), p. 41.

17. In this verse and the previous verse, Nwyia's text (following B) places specific objects to the claims into the text: "Iblis proclaimed his pride *(takaburrahu)* and Ahmad proclaimed his humility *(taḍarra'ahu).*" However these words are absent in T and M, and only the first appears in V. On general literary grounds, particularly the tendency for later versions to try to fill in the semantic blanks and read in a strong moral, I prefer the reading in M and T, which leaves the object open to be demonstrated by the drama that follows. Al-Tarjumana has "he returned to his power" (Ibid., p.41), though both the Persian and Arabic versions have "from" *(az, 'an).*

18. In addition to the two sayings mentioned in T, B, and V, M has here "In you I am transformed and in you I find my origin." *Bika aḥulu* (In you I am transformed) is a pun based on the saying mentioned about "no power," playing

upon the words *ḥawl* (power, might) and *ḥawala / ḥala* (to change, be transformed), from which is derived the Sufi term *ḥāl* (a momentary condition or state).

19. A *muwaḥḥid (unifier)* would be one who affirms that Allah is one *(aḥad)*, from the root *(w/ḥ/y)* of the divine. The common translations of this term are problematic: "unitarian" because of its common usage as the name for a Christian denomination, and "monotheist" because it is used here in a much more specific sense than implied by the usual sense of the term monotheist.

20. *Ulbisa* is a pun on the word Iblis, a metathetic play on the three consonants *b/l/s* of Iblis, with a shift in order to *l/b/s*. The verbs *albasa* and *labisa* mean to cover, clothe, or conceal, but are closely related to *labasa* and *labbasa*, which means to confuse or disorient. I have chosen the term "veil" in order to evoke both meanings. "Stripped of all else": *'alā t-tajrīd.* We have an interesting counterpoint here between veiled and reveal. His insight is veiled so he is only satisfied with worshiping Allah in a stripped form. (My acknowledgement to Krista Woodbridge for her helpful thoughts on this verse, unpublished comments, 7/93.)

21. "To be given demands when he demanded more": Nwyia follows B in reading *ṭurida* for *ṭuliba*: "to be expelled when he asked for more." Though such a reading is clearer, it is not supported by the other manuscripts and the more enigmatic pun on being asked (as petition and interrogation) sounds more Hallajian to me.

22. This Arabic poem is not found in the Arabic version, but only in the Persian translation and commentary of Ruzbehan. Even so, it has been attributed to Hallaj in versions of his Diwan. I have placed it in bold print to indicate its uncertain status. The last verse—*wa man fi l-bayni iblīs*—can be translated two ways, and I have given the alternate translation in brackets.

23. Here the text breaks into a rhymed prose *(saj'): abā wa stakbar, tawallā wa adbar, wa aqarra mā aṣarr*. For the Qur'ānic subtext:

2:34	*fa sajadū*	*illa iblīs a*	*abā wa stakbara wa kāna min al-kāfirīn.*
15:31		*illā iblīsa*	*abā an yakūna ma'a s-sājid īn*
20:116	*fa sajadū*	*illā iblīsa*	*abā*
70:17		*tad'ū man*	*adbara wa tawallā.*
74:23		*thumma*	*adbara wa stakbara*
80:1-2			*'abasa wa tawallā in jā'ahu l-a'mā*
20:60			*fa tawallā fir'awnu*
20:48; 75:32; 92:16			*kadhaba wa tawallā*

There are twenty instances of the term *tawallā* in the Qur'an according to 'Abd al-Bāqī. The text alludes through the use of *tawallā* (turned away), the general short *saj'* scheme, to the famous Qur'anic sura beginning (80:1-2): "He frowned and turned away that a blind man approached him." This sura is a divine reproach to Muhammad for growing proud and disdaining to receive a blind man who had wished to speak with him.

24. Preceding this passage, Ruzbehan has the following poetic gloss: "He fell from the sea of majesty and was blinded."

25. The first verse is built on an extravagant and untranslatable example of *jinās*, word play or root play. In this case the root *b/'/d* is used to construct the words for distance and the word for after *(ba'da mā).*

26. Again, what seems to be Iblis's most arrogant claim of intimacy and even union with the deity is at the same time his lover's claim of total servitude to the beloved, a paradox found in the poetic tradition but heightened by Iblis's mixing of the poetic tradition with the theology of fate and free will and with Sufi meditations on mystical union.

27. Hallaj's authorship of extra-Qur'anic dialogues among Qur'anic characters is audacious in a tradition with such an emphasis on the closing of prophecy with the Qur'an. Although extra-Qur'anic stories were commonly told, they were usually associated with the legends of the Jews *(Isrā'īliyyāt)* or attributed to other historical authors. And although it was common for Sufis to write "divine-human" dialogues (see the examples from Niffari, Chapter 10 in this volume), to write a dialogue among such Qur'anic characters was unusual.

28. Iblis chides Moses for giving in too easily to a command that—as is explained elsewhere—may have been a "test" rather than a reflection of the deeper divine will.

29. "That and that is masquerade": i.e., my appearance before and after the deformation is a masquerade. "Command": *amr*; "test": *ibtilā'*; "he deformed you": *ghayyara ṣūrataka*; "condition": *ḥāl*; "figure" *shakhṣ*; "That and that is masquerade": *dhā wa dhā talbīs*. Baqli's Persian paraphrase has *ān talbīs bud wa īn iblīs ist*: "that was masquerade and this is Iblis." Baqli is playing on a metathesis of the word Iblis, where the *b/l/s* root becomes *l/b/s*. This metathetic pun was well known in Iblis lore, and indeed become the title of a famous book, *Talbīs Iblīs (The Masquerade of Iblis)* by Ibn al-Jawzī. See Abū l-Farāj 'Abd ar-Raḥmān Ibn al-Jawzī, *Talbīs Iblīs*, ed. Khayr ad-Dīn 'Alī (Beirut: Dār al-Wa'ī al-'Arabī, n.d.). Of course in most traditions Iblis's masquerade refers to the wily deceptiveness of Iblis, rather than to the philosophy of transformation (itself common in Sufism) that Iblis claims at this point: that appearance and form are a matter of masquerade, because the condition *(ḥāl)* is always changing.

The same *l/b/s* radical that forms *talbīs* (clothing, masquerade) also forms the word *iltibās* (ambiguity or equivocation), which figures in the title to this section ofHallaj's *Ṭawāsīn*, The Ṭs of Before-Time and Ambiguity: *ṬāSīn al-Azal wa l-Iltibās.*

30. Nwyia (*Hallāj*, p. 206) vocalizes this sentence as "remembrance is not remembered" *(lā yudhkuru)*. However, the sense seems to me to be active: "remembrance does not remember" *(lā yadhkuru)*, expressing the mystical idea of the merging in mystical union of the active subject and the activity into an intensity beyond subject-predicate expression. Massignon's translation (*Passion* 3:312) approaches

this latter sense, even though he was reading *fikra* for *dhikr (la tadhkaru,* "Pure thought does not need to remember.").

31. As Massignon points out (*Passion* 3:312), there is a strong antithesis between consecration *(iḥrām,* the placing of one[self] within the consecrate state of the pilgrim undertaking the *hajj)* and the *hijra*, the foresaking of Mecca by Muhammad and his followers and their emigration to Medina, in which the movement is reversed, now a movement away from Mecca. Nwyia's translation (*Hallāj*, p. 222), *"Il ma'a mis en interdit parce que je l'ai abandonné,"* seems to me to read too much into the text *(aḥramanī li hijratī)* and to lose the specific reference to the *hijra.*

32. "Preclusion of my fate" *(mani' maniyyatī).* Nwyia's more explicit translation of *maniyya* as "death" (*Hallā*, p. 222), *"parce que je ne pouvais mourir,"* is also quite plausible.

33. I have used the participial forms to bring across the *saj'* based on the second form verbal participals in Arabic.

34. For Sufi traditions on Iblis as the one from whom the most advanced Sufis can seek the deepest knowledge of their own vices, see Peter Awn, *Satan's Tragedy and Redemption: Iblis in Sufi Psychology* (Leiden: Brill, 1983). Awn's book is the essential guide for anyone interested in the Iblis traditions in Islam and Hallaj's interpretation of them.

35. This section, which contains Hallaj's famous expression *"anā l-ḥaqq"* (I am the real), is considered by Massignon to be an interpolation. The expression "I am the real" is of course one of the most famous of the Sufi *shaṭaḥat* or ecstatic utterances, defended by later Sufis as examples of the deity speaking through the Sufi whose ego-self has been annihilated in *fanā'*. See Carl Ernst, *Words of Ecstasy in Islam* (Albany: State University of New York Press, 1985), pp. 63–72.

36. "Prophet": *rasūl.* Technically the term should be translated as messenger as opposed to the term *nabī*, which is usually rendered as prophet. Here the distinction is not central enough to warrant using an English term that is distracting and difficult to use in a graceful diction.

37. Massignon's translation (*Passion* 3:356) of Pharoah's response, "I did not teach you of any other divinity than me" is problematic. Later in the same passage, after the Pharoah and his troops are drowned, the Qur'an (28: 42) states that "a curse lies upon them in this world, and on the day of resurrection they will be among the despised *(min al-maqbūḥīn).*" This is the only instance in the Qur'an of the Arabic radical *q/b/ḥ* found in the term *qabīḥ*, which is used by Hallaj in reference to Iblis's changed form, his deformation, and the deformations, vices, or uglinesses that Iblis proclaims to humans on the earth.

38. "I am the real": *anā l-ḥaqq.* As pointed out by Nwyia (*Hallāj*, p. 223), manuscript B contains a less radical variant: "I see the real" *(arā l-ḥaqq).*

39. It is not clear if both Iblis and Pharoah are both friends and teachers, or if Iblis is the friend and Pharoah the teacher. The notion of Iblis as a "teacher" is discussed by Awn (*Satan's Tragedy*). Hallaj was not the only one to give an unusual and seemingly scandalous interpretation of Pharoah. For Ibn 'Arabi's even more

appreciative remarks on Pharoah, see Ernst, "Controversy over Ibn 'Arabi's *Fusus*: The Faith of Pharoah," *Islamic Culture*, 1985.

40. "Why have you filled his mouth with sand": *limā ḥashawta fā hu ramlan?*

41. Massignon's version (*Passion* 3:51–52) has the very interesting reading "Even if I am killed . . ." (reading *wa in* for *wa anā*).

42. "Thatness": *anniyatihi.* A philosophical term derived from the Arabic particle *anna.* A similar term was coined from the Arabic pronoun *mā* (what), the term *māhiyya* (quiddity or "whatness"). As opposed to quiddity, "thatness" is the ipseity, that is, any thing's fact of existing.

43. For this kind of letter symbolism, cf. the Qur'anic commentary attributed to Ja'far as-Sadiq in Chapter 2 of this volume. The manuscripts here are in sharp disagreement over many of these letter-word explications. I have followed the version in Nwyia, *Hallāj.* Thus, for the final term corresponding to the *lām* ("l"), the Massignon text (*Kitāb aṭ-Ṭawāsīn*) has *baliyya* (which would be a rather weak symbolic connection, placing the "l" in the middle of the word it symbolized), while the Nwyia text gives *lamiyyatihi,* which has the advantage of putting the symbol-letter at the beginning, where it is more commonly found, but whose meaning, "his reddening," is obscure; it may refer to the deformation of Iblis after his disobedience. Yet here Nwyia's alternative manuscripts offer yet a third possibility, *kamiyyatihi* (his quantification). The manuscripts diverge as badly on the other symbol words. Baqli's Persian paraphrase takes what some might consider the better part of wisdom and omits the entire passage.

44. The *saj'* rhymes: "And I am in service *áqdam* [senior] // and in favor *á'ẓam* [greater] // and in knowledge *á'lam* [more knowing] // and in living *atámm* [more complete]."

45. "*O badī'* [O originator]. If you forbid me from bowing, you are the *manī* ' [the forbidder], and if I err in speaking, don't abandon me, for you are the *samī'* [the all-hearer], and if you wish me to bow before him, I am the *maṭī'* [the all-obeyer]."

46. "O brother" (Arabic), the rest of the translation follows the Persian. The key Arabic *saj'* words are *wilāya* (intimate friendship with the deity) and *nihāya* (end): "My brother, Iblis was called 'Azāzīl because he was set apart. He was set apart in *walāya* [intimate friendship, share in sovereignty]; and he did not arrive from his beginning to his *nihāya* [end]; because he was made to emerge from his end."

47. "His coming out was inverse in the fixity of his *ta'rīs* (rootedness), ignited by the fire of his *ta'rīs* (ardor or night camp); and the light of his *tarwīs* (precedence)." "Precedence": *tarwīs*, probably from *r/'/s*, with nouns *ra'īs* and *rayyis* (chief).

48. "O my brother, if you understood, you have piled up stones *raḍman* [piling them up], imagined an imagining *wahman* [in imagination], have come back *ghamman* [anxious] and have passed away *(fanayta) hamman* [out of cares]." "Piled up stones": *taraḍḍamta r-raḍma raḍman*: The *Munjid* gives three meanings for *raḍama*: to build a structure of stones, to stay in a place, and to till the earth. M gives:

taraṣṣamta r-raṣma raṣman while the Persian gives *taraṣṣamta r-rasma rasman.* There is no radical, *r/ṣ/m* in the Arabic lexicons. Massignon, *Passion* 3:315: "O brother! if you have understood, you have pondered the narrow pass in its very narrowness; you have shown the imagination in its very unreality, and you have returned from it (to reality) through sorrow filled with anxiety." Tarjumana (*The Tawāsīn*, p. 49) gives: "O my brother, if you have understood, you have considered the narrow pass in its very narrowness, and have represented the imagination to yourself in its very unreality, and you have returned distressed and full of anxiety." Kamran gives for the whole section: "O my brother! by understanding this you saved yourself, or had met detachment, separation, sorrow; and bitterness, and death in sharp regrets." The Persian text has *'amman* and *ghamman* for the last two *tasjī* 's. See Gilani Kamran, *Ana al-Haqq Reconsidered* (Lahore: Naqsh-e-Awwal Kitab Ghar, 1398 H), p. 91.

49. "The most eloquent of the Sufis at his gate *kharisū* [were dumbstruck], and the sages failed in what they *darisū* [learned]. He was more learned than they in *sujūd* [bowing, prostrating], nearer than they to the *mawjūd* [the existent], more spendthrift than they in *majhūd* [exertion], more faithful than they in *'uhūd* [oaths], closer than they to the *ma'būd* [object of worship]."

50. I offer the following alternative translation to show how the *saj'* operates in the text: "They fell in prayer before Adam as a favor [*masā'ida*], while Iblis refused to bow because of the length of witness he made [*mashā'ida*]. His customs stood large [*mashkhāṣ 'wā'iduhu*], his excess was a refuge [*manāṣ zawā'iduhu*], his thornweeds fruitful [*natīja abramahu*], his needs are fertile [*munattaja alzimuhu*], his gentleness cutting [*mahīluhu ṣarima*], his manners giving [*'ādatuhu karīma*]."

Massignon, *Kitāb at-Tawāsīn*, had originally placed in the text of Hallaj a comment by Baqli that Iblis had erred and was condemned justly to eternal punishment.

Chapter 10. Niffari

1. Translated by A. J. Arberry. The commentator, 'Afif ad-Din at-Tilimsānī (d. 690H), says in another place that it was actually the son of the Shaykh's daughter who put the sayings into their present order. See *The Mawáqif and Mukhátabát of Muḥammad ibn 'Abdi l-Jabbār al-Niffarí, with Other Fragments*, edited, with translations, commentary, and indices, by Arthur John Arberry (London: Luzac, for the "E.J.W. Gibb Memorial," 1935), p. 1. All translations below will be based on Arberry's edition, hereafter referred to simply as *The Mawāqif.* For a brief biography of Niffari, see A. J. Arberry's entry "Niffari" in *The Encylopaedia of Islam*, 1st ed. (Leiden: Brill, 1936), p. 910.

2. Another disadvantage to "station" is that it is the same term used to translate other, more common Sufi terms such as *maqām* and *manzil.*

3. In the translation passages, "knowledge" translates *'ilm* and "knowing" translates *ma'rifa*, which Niffari consistently sees as more of a process and a continual activity rather than a body of knowledge.

4. For a more detailed analysis of this standing, see M. Sells, "Bewildered Tongue: The Semantics of Mystical Union in Islam," in *Mystical Union and Monotheistic Faith: An Ecumenical Dialogue*, ed. M. Idel and B. McGinn (New York: Macmillan, 1989), pp. 108–115. For a discussion of key vocabulary in Niffari within the tradition of Junayd, see David Martin, " *'Al-Qayyūmiyya'* (Self-Existence) in the Work of Al-Niffarī" (Expanded version of a paper read at the annual meeting of the American Oriental Society, Austin, Texas, March 1982).

5. Paul Nwyia, "Al-Niffari ou l'homme en dialogue avec Dieu," *Les Cahiers de l'Oronte* 1965, pp. 13–27.

6. The pronominal antecedents are ambiguous. All the pronouns are *hu* (it/he). Arberry, in *The Mawāqif*, introduces a distinction among the antecedents, interpreting some instances of the pronouns as referring to the thing, and others as referring to the deity: "My indications in a thing annihilate in it the real reality, and establish it as belonging to God, not as existing through itself" (p. 31).

7. "Proclaimer": *nāṭiq*.

8. "Between his hands": *bayna yadayhi*—an idiomatic expression for being near to or intimate with someone, but with Niffari the latent, concrete meanings (such as the actual sense of being between two hands) are shaken free, and so I have translated it strictly. In other words, what might be called "dead metaphors" are used in a context that reminds the reader and imposes on the sense of the text the original sense of the term.

9. "Deviate": *mulḥid*. The term is frequently translated as "unbeliever" or "heretic," but the root meanings of the radical *l/ḥ/d* go back from wandering off the path or deviation. Another root meaning goes back to the act of digging a grave.

10. I have translated this passage from the Arabic text found in ed. and trans. A. J. Arberry, *The Mawāqif* (Cambridge, 1935), Arabic Text, 73.

11. Reading the manuscript variant *fīmā* for *qayyiman*.

12. *Alif* is the first letter of the Arabic alphabet, formed of a straight vertical line.

13. "Passing inclination": *khāṭir*; "struggle": *jihād*.

14. "Of my core being": *min ladunnī*. The reference is to the Qur'anic story of Moses and Khidr (18:16–82). The unnamed "servant" of God, later known as Khidr, is given the "knowledge of my [the deity's] core being. " See Chapter 1 in this volume.

15. "Seizure": *saṭwa*; "majesty": *'izza*; "all-might": *jabarūt*; "sublimity": *kibriyā'*; "sovereignty": *sulṭan*; "exaltation": *'aẓama*; "identity" (*dhāt*); "clear proof": *bayyina*.

16. "Comforting": *tan'īm*; "grace": *luṭf*; "compassion": *raḥma*; "generosity": *karam*; "sympathy": *'aṭf*; "affection": *wadd, wudd, widd*; "love": *ḥubb*; "contentedness": *riḍā*; "chosenness": *iṣṭifā'*; "the gaze": *naẓar*.

17. Or as Arberry puts it (p. 115): *jīm* of the *janna*, the *jīm* of *jehennam*.
18. "Innermost thought": *ḍamīr*.
19. "Appointed time": *al-ajal*; "eternal abiding": *dawām*.

Epilogue

1. Poems number 1, 22, and 12 from the *Diwān* of al-Hallaj. See *Le Dîwân d'al-Ḥallâj*, ed. L. Massignon, published in *Journal Asiatique* (Janvier-Mars 1931): 1–158.

Appendix: Shahrastanī

1. Abū al-Fatḥ 'Abd al-Karīm Shahrastānī, *Kitāb al-Milal wā an-Niḥal* [Book of Religious and Philosophical Sects], edited by William Cureton, 2 vols. (London: Society for the Publication of Oriental Texts, 1846). I have also consulted the Badrān edition, Shahrastani, *Kitāb al-Milal wa n-Niḥal* (Cairo: Maṭba'at āl-Azhar).

2. Throughout this translation, "Traditionalists" with an upper-case T will be used for the particular group known as the *salaf*, while "tradition" (lower-case) will be used for the much broader notion of *sunna*, that is, the accumulated traditions based on the sayings of Muhammad that become the model for the Islamic community among the vast majority of Muslims of whatever theological school.

3. See Abū Bakr al-Kalābādhī, *The Doctrine of the Ṣūfīs*, trans. A. J. Arberry (Cambridge: Cambridge University Press, 1935, 1978).

4. The Attributionists (the followers of Al-Ash'ari) refuted the Qadarites' attempt to disown their own confusing name. The Qadarites said that the term "determinist" (Qadarite) should be applied to those who maintain divine predeterminism, the group called compulsionists or Jabrites. The Attributionists appeal (in what seems like a rather nasty argument) to common usage. If the Qadarites and Jabrites are opposites, how can the term "Qadarite" be applied to the Jabrites?

5. In the discourse of scholastic theology, the translation "essence" is most appropriate. However, in many Sufi texts that are consciously "nonessentialist," the term *dhāt* takes on a different meaning, one that is quite difficult to translate—identity, self, the transcendent aspect of the real that is beyond all distinction, all quiddity, and all description.

6. "Meanings": the term *ma'nā* can be used in this discourse to mean "meaning," or "mode."

7. And, of course, any affirmation that another power "shares" in the divinity of the one God is association *(shirk)*, the primary theological error in Islam.

8. In Islamic theology originated *(muḥdath)* means having a temporal origin; the opposite of eternal *(qadīm)*.

9. The point is that if one affirms a deity, and then eternal attributes, those eternal attributes exist eternally, uncreated by the deity, and thus there is more than one deity; in a theological context where all things must be either creatures or deities, anything uncreated must be, by nature, divine. If Allah had eternal attributes of knowledge, will, power, and life, each of these attributes would be deities and such a position would fall into the error of association *(shirk)*.

10. "The philosophers": *al-falāsifa*. As the Greek origin of the term suggests, the *falāsifa* were those thinkers in Islam who were influenced by the newly translated texts of Plato, Aristotle, Plotinus, and other Greek thinkers, and who wrote under the particularly strong influence of Aristotle, although with their own original perspectives and contributions.

11. "The traditionalists": *as-salaf*, i.e., the school of the "predecessors" or early ones—i.e., those who claimed to represent the earliest understanding of Islam.

12. Shahrastani's point here is that the Wasiliyya were willing to acknowledge the Qur'anic and hadith affirmation of absolute divine predetermination in a variety of areas, from a person's situation in life to the appointed moment of death. But they refused to acknowledge the deity as the source of good and evil actions on the part of humans, separating this category out from divine predetermination on the grounds that if such were the case, God would require people to do what he ordains that they cannot or will not do, and such a deity would be unjust.

13. The story may be apocryphal. Others have suggested that the Arabic radical *'/z/l* within Mu'tazila suggests that Mu'tazile theology emerged among ascetics (those who had isolated themselves from society).

14. Shahrastani, *Kitāb al-Milal wa n-Niḥal* 1: 29–34. The text continues with the fourth category concerning the conflicts between the followers of 'Ali (later to be called Shi'ites) and those who did not recognize 'Ali's claim to succeed Muhammad, a conflict that came to a climax when the Caliph 'Uthman was assassinated by members of an 'Alid faction. The fourth doctrine concerns the two opposing parties at the battles of the Camel and Ṣiffin. "He said that one side was in the wrong, but not essentially *(bi 'aynihi)*. Similarly, concerning those who assassinated him and those who deserted him, he maintains that one of the parties had to be sinful, just as one of the two groups cursing one another is sinful, but the sinfulness is not essential. One cannot accept the testimony of 'Ali, Talha, and Zubair (the parties to the conflict) even concerning a bundle of onions. 'Ali and 'Uthman might both be wrong."

This is the position of the head of the Mu'tazila and the founder of this particular school on the most famous companions of the Prophet and members of his family. 'Amr ibn 'Abid agreed with him in his position and affirmed even more strongly than he [Wasil] that the determination of which of the two parties was sinful is not an essential determination. According to 'Amr, even if one saw two men from one of the parties, such as 'Ali and one of his soldiers, or Talha and Zubayr, their testimony and declaration of which party was in the wrong and destined for the fire could not be accepted. 'Amr was a master of hadith and known for his renunciation. Wasil was famous for his virtue and behavior."

15. There follows a technical discussion of how different groups should be classified: "The Mu'tazilites consider a Jabrite anyone who denies that the originated power has influence in the initiation or production [of acts]. They are therefore obliged to consider as Jabrites those of their own circle who claim that engendered acts *(mutawallidāt)* are acts without any actor, since this claim denies any effect to the originated power. Those who compose treatises of classification have numbered the Najjāriyya and the Ḍirāriyya among the compulsionists, while placing the Kullā biyya among the Attributionists. Sometimes they call the Ash'arites Ḥashwiyya, sometimes they call them Jabrites. We have heard them (the Jabrites) affirm as their colleagues the Najarriya and the Dirariyya and have numbered them among the Jabrites. We did not hear them acknowledge as their own any other groups, so we have numbered the others among them and we have numbered them among the Attributionists *(ṣifātiyya)*."

16. The implication seems to be that once the principle of compulsion is affirmed, the human response to its obligations will be compelled.

17. Shahrastani, *Kitāb al-Milal wa n-Niḥal* 1: 59–61.

18. At this point, Shahrastani discusses Najjar's position on the createdness of the divine word, a topic that was highly controversial but does not affect Sufi discussions in the same manner as the controversies over *tawḥīd* and *qadar*.

19. That is, announced in the word of God, the Qur'an.

20. Al-Muhasibi, the famous exponent of Sufi moral psychology of self-examination. See Chapter 5 in this volume.

21. Shahrastani, *Kitāb al-Milal wa n-Niḥal* 1: 64–65.

22. This section begins with an anecdote concerning a certain Musa al-Ash'-ari, who was supposedly an ancestor of Abu l-Hasan al-Ash'ari:

> The Ash'arites are the followers of Abu l-Hasan 'Ali ibn Isma'il al-Ash'ari who was descended from Musa al-Ash'ari, May Allah be pleased with him. I have heard of the amazing coincidence that Abu Musa Abu l-Hasan al-Ash'ari used to maintain the same thing as Abu l-Hasan al-Ash'ari in his school. There was a dispute between 'Amr ibn Al-'As and Abu Musa. 'Amr said: "Do I find anyone with whom I can dispute about my lord?" Abu Musa said: "I'll judge the issue." 'Amr said: "Does he predetermine *(yuqaddir)* me to do something and then punish me for doing it?" Abu Musa said: "Yes." 'Amr said: "Why?" Abu Musa said: "Because he does you no injustice." 'Amr was silent, finding nothing to reply.

23. At this point Shahrastani discusses the modifications of Ash'ari's position made by Baqilani. I have proceeded directly to the next statement of Ash'ari's position.

NOTES

24. I am reading *al-baqiyya* here for *al-baqā'*; *al-baqā'* would lead to the translation: as for the [attribute] of abiding, he had a different opinion.

25. "Preserved tablet": *al-lawḥ al-maḥfuẓ*, that is, the eternal archetype of the Qur'an.

26. Evidently a reference to the Qur'an; a rather strong statement.

27. Shahrastani, *Kitāb al-Milal wa n-Niḥal* 1: 66–69.

Selected Bibliography

The formative period of Islamic Mysticism is still largely unexplored. There are few English translations or works devoted to it. Below are some of the studies and texts consulted in the preparation of this volume.

Abdel Kader, A. H. *The Life, Personality and Writings of al-Junayd.* London: Luzac, Gibb Memorial Series, new series 22, 1976.

'Afīfī, Abu'l-'Alā'. *Al-Malāmatiyya wa aṣ-Ṣufiyya wa Ahl al-Futuwwa.* Cairo: Dār Iḥyā' al-Kutub al-'Arabiyya, 1364/1945.

Aflākī, Shamsuddīn Aḥmad. *Manāqib al-'Ārifīn.* Tehran: Dunyā-yi Kitāb, 1983.

———. *Manāqib al-'Ārifīn.* Ankara: Turk Tarih Kurumu Basimevi, 1976.

———. *Manāqib al-'Ārifīn (Virtues of the Knowers).* Translated by Idris Shah under the title *The Hundred Tales of Wisdom.* London: Octogon Press, 1978.

Anawati, G. C., and Gardet, L. *Mystique musulmane; aspects et tendances, expériences et techniques.* Paris: J. Vrin, 1961.

Andrae, T. *In the Garden of Myrtles.* Albany: State University of New York Press, 1987.

———. "Islamische Mystiker." Stuttgart: Kohlhammer, 1960.

-Anṣārī, 'Abd Allāh. *Manāzil as-Sā'irīn.* Ed. and tr. S. de Beaurecueil. Cairo: Institut Français d'Archeólogie Orientale, 1962.

-Anṣārī, Muḥammad 'Abdul Ḥaqq. "The Doctrine of One Actor: Junayd's View of *Tawḥid.*" *Muslim World* 73, no. 1 (1983): 33–56.

-Anṣārī, Zakarīya. *Sharḥ ar-Risāla al-Qushayrīya.* Būlāq, 1290 H.

Anṣārī-i Harawī, 'Abdullāh. *Ṭabaqāt aṣ-Ṣūfīya.* Kabul: The Historical Society of Afghanistan, 1962.

Arberry, A. J. *Aspects of Islamic Civilization.* Ann Arbor, 1967.

———. "Bisṭāmiāna." *Bulletin of the School of Oriental and African Studies* 25 (1962): 28–37.

———. "A Bisṭāmī Legend." *Journal of the Royal Asiatic Society,* January, 1938: 89–91.

———. "Did Sulamī Plagiarize Sarrāj?" *JRAS*, July, 1937. pp. 461–465.

———. *The Doctrine of the Sufis*. Cambridge: Cambridge University Press, 1935, 1977. Translation of Kalābādhī's *Kitāb at-Ta'arruf.*

———. *An Introduction to the History of Ṣūfism*. London: Longmans, Greene and Co., 1943.

———. "Junaid." *JRAS*, July, 1935, pp. 499–507.

———., ed. *The Mawáqif and Mukhátabát of Muhammad ibn 'Abdi l-Jabbár al-Niffarí, with other fragments*. London: Luzac, E. J. W. Gibb Memorial, 1935.

———. *Muslim Saints and Mystics*. London: Routledge and Kegan Paul, 1966. [Excerpts from 'Aṭṭār's *Tadhkirat al-Awliyā'*.]

———. "Niffari." *The Encylopaedia of Islam*, first ed. Leiden: Brill, 1936.

———. *Pages from the "Kitāb al-Luma' of Abū Naṣr al-Sarrāj*. Being the lacuna in the edition of R. A. Nicholson. Edited from the Bankipore MS., with Memoir, Preface, and Notes by A. J. Arberry. London, 1947.

———. *Revelation and Reason in Islām*. London: Allen & Unwin, 1965.

———. *Ṣūfism: An Account of the Mystics of Islām*. London, 1947, 1963. From the Bankipore manuscript.

Archer, J. C. *Mystical Elements in Muḥammad*. New Haven: Yale University Press, 1924.

'Aṭṭār, Farīduddīn. *Les Mémorial des Saints*. Translated by A. Pavet de Courteille from the Ouigour Text of *Tadhkirat al-Awliyā'*. Paris: Editions du Seuil, 1976.

———. *Tadhkirat al-Awliyā'*. Ed. Reynold A. Nicholson. 2 vols. London: Luzac, Gibb Memorial Series, and Leiden: Brill 1905–7. Reprint. London: Luzac and Leiden: Brill, 1959.

———. *Tadhkirat al-Awliyā'*. Ed. Muḥammad Khān Qazvini (2 vols. in 1). Tehran: Kitabkhānah-'i Markazi, 1336/1957.

———. *Tadhkirat al-Awliyā'*. Ed. Muḥammad Istislāmī. Tehran: Zavvār, 1967.

———. *Tadhkirat al-Awliyā'*. Intro. Nāṣir Hayyirī. Tehran: Intisharāt-i Gulshā'i, 1361/1982.

———. *Tadhkirat al-Awliyā'*. Translated by A.J. Arberry as *Muslim Saints and Mystics* (Episodes from the Tadhkirat al-Auliya'). London: Arkana, 1990, first published London: Kegan Paul Ltd., 1966.

Awn, Peter. *Satan's Tragedy and Redemption: Iblis in Sufi Psychology*. Leiden: Brill, 1983.

Badawī, Abdur Raḥmān. *Shāhidat al-'Ishq al-Ilāhī, Rābi'a al'Adawiyya*. Cairo: Maktabat al-Nahdat al-Miṣriyah, 1946.

———. *Shaṭaḥāt aṣ-Ṣūfiyyah*. Cairo: Maktabat an-Nahḍat al-Miṣriyyah, 1949.

———. *Shaṭaḥāt aṣ-Ṣūfiyyah*, vol 1: Abū Yazīd al-Bisṭāmī. Cairo: Maktabat an-Nahḍa al-Miṣriyya, 1949.

Baldick, Julian. "The Legend of Rābi'a of Baṣra: Christian Antecedents, Muslim Counterparts." *Religion* 20 (1990) 233–247.

Baqlī, Rūzbihān. *Sharḥ-i Shaṭḥiyāt*, *Les paradoxes des soufis*. Ed. Henri Corbin. Paris: Librairie Paul Geuthner, 1966. In Persian.

Böwering, Gerhard. *The Mystical Vision of Existence in Classical Islam: The Qur'ānic Hermeneutics of the Ṣūfī Sahl at-Tustarī*. Berlin: Walter de Gruyter, 1980.

Brown, Norman K. "The Apocalypse of Islam." *Social Text* 3, no. 8 (1983–4): 155–171.

Burckhardt, Titus. *An Introduction to Sufi Doctrines*. Trans. D. M. Matheson. Lahore: Sh. Muhammad Ashraf, 1959.

Casper, R. "Muslim Mysticism: Tendencies in Modern Research." *Studies in Islam*, ed. and tr. Mi.I. Swartz, 164–184. New York: Oxford University Press, 1988.

Colby, Frederick. "The Flight of the Innermost Heart: Sufi Terms, Images and Concepts in The Mi'raj of Abu Yazid al-Bistami." B.A. Thesis, Haverford College, 1991.

Corbin, Henri. "Quiétude et inquiétude de l'âme dans le soufisme de Rū zbihān Baqlī de Shiraz." *Eranos Jahrbuch* 27 (1950).

Courteille, A. Pavet de. "Farid-ud-Din 'Attar." *Le mémorial des saints*. Paris: Editions du Seuil, 1976.

Deladrière, R. "Abū Yazīd al-Bisṭāmī et son enseignement spirituel." *Arabica*, 14, Part 1 (1967): 76–89.

Dhū r-Rumma. *The Dīwān of Ghaylān ibn 'Uqba*. Ed. Carlile Henry Hayes Macartney. Cambridge: Cambridge University Press, 1919.

Ernst, Carl W. "Mystical Language and the Teaching Context in the Early Lexicons of Sufism." In *Mysticism and Language*, ed. S. Katz, pp. 181–201. Oxford: Oxford University Press, 1992.

———. *Words of Ecstasy in Sufism* . Albany: SUNY Press, 1985.

Ess, Joseph van. *Die Gedankenwelt des Hārit al-Muḥāsibī*. Bonn: Selstverlag des Orientalischen Seminars der Universiẗat Bonn, 1961.

Field, Claud H. *Mystics and Saints of Islām*. London: Francis Griffiths, 1910.

Gardet, Louis. "La mention du nom divin, dhikr, dans la mystique musulmane." *Revue Thomiste*, 1952–53.

Goldziher, Ignaz. "Materialien zur Entwickelungsgeschichte des Ṣufismus." *Vienna Oriental Journal* 13 (1899): 35–65.

Graham, W. A. *Divine Word and Prophetic Word in Early Islam*. Paris: Mouton, 1977.

Gramlich, Richard. *Schlaglichter über das Sufitum: Abū Naṣr as-Sarrājs Kitāb al-Luma'*: Stuttgart: Franz Steiner Verlag, 1990.

———. *Das Sendschreiben al-Qushayrīs. Übersetzt, eingeleitet und kommentiert von*. Freiburger Islamstudien, Band 12, Wiesbaden: Steiner, 1989.

Ḥallāj, Ḥusayn ibn Manṣūr. *Akhbār al-Ḥallāj. Recueil d'oraisons et d'exhortations du martyr mystique de l'Islam*. Ed. and tr. by Louis Massignon and Paul Kraus. Etudes Musulmanes, IV. 3rd ed. Paris: Vrin, 1957.

———. "*Dīwān*. Essai de reconstitution by Louis Massignon." *Journal asiatique* 218 (January-July) 1931: 1–158.

———. *Dīwān*. Ed. and tr. Louis Massignon. Paris: Editions du Sud, 1954.

———. *Kitāb aṭ-Ṭawāsīn*. Texte arabe . . . avec la version persane d'al-Baqlī. Ed. and tr. Louis Massignon. Paris: Librairie Paul Geuthner, 1913.

———. *Kitāb aṭ-Ṭawāsīn*. Ed. and tr. Louis Massignon. 2nd ed. Paris, 1957.

———. *Kitāb aṭ-Ṭawāsīn*. Ed. Paul Nwyia. *Mélanges de l'Université Saint-Joseph* 47: 183–238.

———. *The "Tawasin" of Mansur al-Hallaj*. Tr. Aisha Abd ar-Rahman at-Tarjumana. Berkeley: Diwan Press, 1974.

Hartmann, Richard. "Die Himmelreise Muhammads und ihre Bedeutung in der Religion des Islam." In *Vorträge der Bibliothek Warburg*. Hamburg, 1928–29.

———. *Al Kuschairis Darstellung des Sufitums*. Berlin: Türkische Bibliothek 18, 1914.

———. "As-Sulamī's *Risālat al-Malāmatīya*." *Der Islam* 8 (1918).

Heath, Peter. *Avicenna*. Philadelphia: University of Pennsylvania Press, 1992.

Heer, Nicholas. "Some Biographical and Bibliographical Notes on al-Ḥakīm at-Tirmidhī." In *The World of Islam: Studies in Honour of Philip K. Hitti*. Ed. by James Kritzeck and R. Bayly Winder. London, 1960.

———. "A Sufi Psychological Treatise." *Moslem World* 51 (1961).

Homerin, Emil. *From Arab Poet to Muslim Saint: Ibn al-Fāriḍ, His Verse and His Shrine*. Columbia: University of South Carolina Press, 1994.

———. "Preaching Poetry: The Forgotten Verse of Ibn al-Shāhrazurī." *Arabica* 38 (1991): 87–101.

-Hujwīrī, 'Alī ibn 'Uthmān. *Kashf al-Maḥjūb.* Ed. V.A. Zukovskij. Leningrad, 1926.

______. *The "Kashf al-Maḥjūb," the Oldest Persian Treatise on Sufism* by al-Hujwiri. Tr. Reynold A. Nicholson. London: Luzac, Gibb Memorial Series, no. 17, 1911. Reprint London: Luzac, 1959, 1976.

Ibn al-Jawzī, Jamāl ad-Dīn. *Talbīs Iblīs aw Naqd al-'Ilm wa al-'Ulamā'.* Cairo: Idārat aṭ-Ṭibā'ah al-Munīriyya, 1950.

Ibn al-Jawzi, Sibt. *Mir'āt al-Zamān.* In *Shaṭa ḥāt aṣ-Ṣūfiyyah*, ed. 'Abd al-Raḥmān Badawī. Cairo: Maktabat an-Nahḍat al-Miṣriyyah, 1949.

Ibn Hishām/Ibn Isḥāq. *Kitāb Sīra Rasūl Allāh* (The Book of the Sira of the Messenger of God). *Das Leben Muhammed's nach Muhammed Ibn Isḥāk bearbeitet von Abd el-Malik Ibn Hischâm*, ed. Ferdinand Wüstenfeld. Göttingen: Dieterich, 1858–1860.

______. *The Life of Muhammad.* Tr. A. Guillaume. Karachi: Oxford University Press, 1955.

Ibn Sīnā, Abū 'Alī. *Al-Ishārāt wa at-Tanbīhāt.* With commentary by Naṣīr ad-Dīn at-Ṭūsi. Cairo: n. pub., 1958.

______. *"Risāla fi'l-'ishq": Traitée sur l'amour.* Ed. A. Mehren. Leiden, 1894.

-Iṣfahānī, Abū Nu'ayn. *Ḥilyat al-Awliyā' wa-Ṭabaqāt al-Aṣfiyā'.* 10 vols. Cairo: Maktabat al-Khanjī, 1351–1357/1932–1938.

Ja'far aṣ-Ṣādiq. *Le Tafsīr Mystique attribué à Ja'far Ṣādiq.* Edition critique by Paul Nwyia. Mélanges de l'Université Saint-Joseph 43, no. 4 (1968): 181-230.

-Junayd, Abu l-Qāsim. *Kitāb al-fanā'.* In *The Life, Personality and Writing of al-Junayd*, ed. A. H. Abdel-Kader. London: Luzac, Gibb Memorial Series, 1962.

Jurbakhsh, Javad. *Sufi Women.* New York: Khaniqahi-Nimatullahi Publications, 1983.

-Kālābādhī, Abū Bakr. *The Doctrine of the Sufis.* Tr. A. J. Arberry. Cambridge: Cambridge University Press, 1935, 1978.

______. *At-Ta'arruf li-Madhhab Ahl at-Taṣawwuf.* Ed. A. J. Arberry. Cairo: Maktabat al-Khanji, 1934.

______. *Kitāb at-Ta'arruf li-Madhhab Ahl at-Taṣawwuf.* Cairo: Dār Iḥyā' Kutub al-'Arabiyyah, 1960.

Kamran, Gilani. *Ana al-Haqq Reconsidered.* With a translation of *Kitab al-Tawasin* by Husain b. Mansur Hallaj. Lahore: Naqsh-e-Awwal Kitab Ghar, 1398H.

Khan, K. S. K. *The Secret of Anā al-Ḥaqq.* Lahore: Sh. Muḥammad Ashraf, 1965.

-Kharrāz, Abū Bakr. *Kitāb aṣ-Ṣidq: The Book of Truthfulness.* Ed. A. J. Arberry. Oxford: The University Press, 1937.

Krymsky, A. E. "A Sketch of the Development of Ṣūfīsm down to the End of the Third Century of the Ḥijrah." Tr. from the Russian by N. S. Doniach, *Islāmic Quarterly* 5 (1957–1960): 109–125; 6 (1961–1964): 79–106.

Lings, Martin. *A Sufi Saint of the Twentieth Century.* Berkeley: University of California Press, 1971.

-Makkī, Abū Ṭālib. *Qūt al-Qulūb.* 4 vols. Cairo: Maktabat al-Ḥusayniyya, 1932.

______. *Qūt al-Qulūb fī Mu'āmalāt al-Maḥbūb.* 2 vols. Cairo: al-Maṭba'a al-Maymaniyya, 1310H/ 1892–1893.

Martin, David. " *'Al-Qayyūmiyya'* (Self-Existence) in the Work of al-Niffarī." Expanded version of a paper read at the annual meeting of the American Oriental Society, Austin, Texas, March 1982.

Massignon, Louis. *"Anā al-Ḥaqq," Der Islām* 3 (1912): 248–257.

______. "Le Dîwân d'al-Ḥallâj." *Journal Asiatique.* Janvier-Mars 1931, pp. 1-158.

______. *Le Dîwân d'al Hallâj.* Nouvelle édition avec additions et corrections. Paris: Cahiers du Sud, 1955.

______. *Essai sur les origenes du lexique technique de la mystique musulmane.* Paris: Librairie Paul Geuthner, 1922. 2nd ed. Paris: Vrin, 1954.

______. *Opera minora; textes recueillis, classés et présentés.* 3 vols. Beirut: Dā r Ma'ārif, 1963; Paris: Presses Universitaires de France, 1969.

______. *The Passion of al-Ḥallāj: Mystic and Martyr of Islam* 4 vols. Tr. Herbert Mason. Princeton: Princeton University Press, 1982.

______. *Parole Donnée.* Paris: Union General D'Editions, 1962.

______. *Receuil des textes inédits concernant l'histoire de la mystique en pays d'Islam.* Paris: Librairie Paul Geuthner, 1929.

Massignon, Louis, and Kraus, Paul. *Akhbār al-Ḥallāj, texte ancien relatif à la prédication et au supplice du mystique musulman al-Ḥosayn b. Manṣour al-Ḥallaj.* Paris: Editions Larose, 1936. 3d ed. Paris: Vrin, 1975.

Meddeb, *Les Dits de Bistami.* Paris: Fayard, 1989.

Meier, Fritz. *Abū Sa'īd-i Abū l-Khayr. Wirklicheit und Legende.* Leiden: Brill, Teheran: Bibliotheque Pahlavi, 1976.

______. "Khurāsān und das ende der klassischen ṣūfik." In *Atti del Convegno Internationale sul Tema: La Persia nel Medioevo,* pp. 545–570. Rome: Accademia Nationale dei Lincei, 1971.

______. "Qushayrīs Tartīb as-Sulūk." *Oriens* 16 (1963), 1–39.

Molé, M. *Les Mystiques musulmans*. Paris: Presses Universitaires de France, 1965.

-Muḥāsibī, Abū 'Abdallāh Ḥārith ibn Asad. *Kitāb al-Ri'āya li Ḥuqūq Allāh*. Ed. Margaret Smith. London: Luzac, E. J. W. Gibb Memorial, 1940.

———. *Kitāb al-Ri'āya li Ḥuqūq Allāh*. Ed. 'Abd al-Qādir Aḥmad 'Atā. 3rd printing. Cairo: Dār al-Kutub al-Ḥadītha, 1970.

———. *Kitāb al-Waṣāya (The Book of Counsels)*. Ed. 'Abd al-Qādir Aḥmad 'Aṭā. Beirut: Dār al-Kutub al-'Amaliyya, 1986.

Muslim ibn al-Ḥajjāj. *aṣ-Ṣaḥīḥ*. Beirut: Dar Ihyā' at-Turāth al-'Arabī, 1972.

———. *Ṣaḥīḥ Muslim bi Sharḥ an-Nawawī*, Cairo: al-Maṭba'a al-Miṣriyya, 1924.

Mustansir Mir, ed., *The Literary Heritage of Classical Islam*. Princeton: Darwin Press, 1993.

Naṣr, Seyyed Husein. *Sufi Essays*. Albany: State University of New York Press, 1973.

———. *Three Muslim Sages: Avicenna-Suhrawardi-Ibn 'Arabi*. Cambridge: Harvard University Press, 1964.

-Nawawī, Abū Zakarīyā Muḥyī ad-dīn Yaḥyā b. Sharaf ash-Shāfi'ī. *Matn al-'Arba'īn an-Nawawīya*. Cairo: Matba'at 'Isā al-Bābī al-Ḥalabī, n.d.

Nicholson, Reynold A. "An Early Arabic Version of the Mi'rāj of Abū Yazī d al-Bisṭāmī." *Islamica* 2 1925: 403–408.

———. "The Goal of Muhammadan Mysticism." *JRAS* 1913.

———. *The Kashf al-Mahjūb. The Oldest Persian Treatise on Sufism*. London: Luzac, Gibb Memorial Series 17. Reprint London: Luzac, 1959.

———. *Studies in Islamic Mysticism*. Cambridge: Cambridge University Press, 1921.

-Niffarī, Muḥammad ibn 'Abdi'l-Jabbār. *The Mawāqif and Mukhāṭabāt, with other fragments*. Ed. and tr. by A. J. Arberry. London: Luzac, Gibb Memorial Series, new series 9, 1935.

Nwyia, Paul, S.J. *Exegése coranique et langage mystique*. Beirut: Dar al-Machreq, 1970.

———. *"Ḥallāj: Kitāb at-Ṭawāsīn." Mélanges de l'Université Saint-Joseph* 47 (1972): 183–238.

———. "Al-Niffari ou l'homme en dialogue avec Dieu." *Les Cahiers de l'Oronte* (1965): 13–27.

———. *Trois oevres inédites de mystiques musulmans: Shaqīq al-Balkhī, Ibn 'Aṭā, Niffarī*. Beirut: Dār al-Mashriq, 1973.

Pedersen, Johannes. *Muhammedansk mystik*. Copenhagen: Nordist Forlag, 1952.

-Qushayrī, Abū l-Qāsim 'Abd al-Karīm ibn. Hawāzin. *Arba' Rasāīlfī at-Taṣawwuf*, 1969.

______. *Laṭa'if al-Ishārāt*. Cairo: Dār al-Kātib al-'Arabī, 1968–71.

______. *Kitab al-Mi'rāj*. Ed. 'Alī Ḥasan 'Abd al-Qādir. Cairo: Dār al-Kutub al-Ḥadītha, 1384/1964.

______. *Naḥw al-Qulūb aṣ-Ṣaghīr*. Libya: al-Dār al-'Arabīya lil-Kitāb, 1977.

______. *Principles of Sufism*. Trans. B.B. Von Schlegell [the last section of the *Risālah al-Qushayriyy)a*.]. Berkeley: Mizan Press, 1992.

______. *Ar-Risālah al-Qushayrīah fī 'ilm al-Taṣawwuf.* Cairo: Muhammad 'Alī Ṣubayḥ, 1966.

______. *Ar-Risālah al-Qushayrīah fī 'Ilm al-Taṣawwuf.* Damascus: Dār al-Khayr, 1988.

______. *Ar-Risāla al-Qushayriyya fī at-Taṣawwuf.* Ed. 'Abd al-Ḥalīm Maḥmūd and Maḥmūd ibn ash-Sharīf. Cairo: Dār al-Kutub al-Ḥadītha, 1966.

______. *Ar-Risālah al-Qushayriyya*. Tr. from the Arabic by Richard Gramlich as *Das Sendschreiben al-Qushayrīs Über das Sufitum*. Stuttgart: F. Steiner Verlag, 1989.

______. [Essays. Selections] *Thalāṭh Rasāīl lil-Qushayrī*. Cairo: S. N., 1988.

-Rabb, Muḥammad 'Abdu. *Al-Junayd's Doctrine of Tawḥīd: An Analysis of his Understanding of Islamic Monotheism*. McGill University, Montreal, M.A. Thesis, 1967.

______. *Persian Mysticism: Abu Yazid al-Bistami*. Dacca: The Academy for Pakistan Affairs, 1971.

Rabi'a al-'Adawiyya. *Doorkeeper of the Heart: Versions of Rabia*. Tr. Charles Upton. Putney, Vt.: Threshold Books, 1988.

Radtke, B. *Al-Ḥakim at-Tirmidhī*. Freiburg: Klaus Schwarz, 1980.

-Rāziq, Su'ād 'abd. *Rābi'a al-'Adawiyya: Bayn al-Ghinā' wa l-Baqā.'* Cairo: The Anglo-Egyptian Bookshop, 1982.

Reinert, Benedikt. *Die Lehre vom tawakkul in der älteren Sufik*. Berlin: de Gruyter, 1968.

Ritter, Helmut. "Die Aussprüche des Bāyazīd Bisṭāmī." In *Westöstliche Abhandlungen, Festschrift für Rudolf Tschudi*, ed. Fritz Meier. Wiesbaden, 1954.

______. "Ḥasan al'Baṣrī, Studien zur Geschichte der islamischen Frömmigkeit." *Der Islam* 21 (1933).

______. *Das Meer der Seele: Gott, Welt und Mensch in den Geschichten des Fariduddin 'Aṭṭārs*. Leiden: Brill, 1955; Leiden, 1978; Brill, 1978.

-Sahlagī, Abū al-Faḍl Muḥammad. *Kitāb an-Nūr min Kalimāt Abī Tayfur*.

In *Shaṭāhāt aṣ-Ṣūfiyyah*, ed. 'Abd al-Raḥmān Badawī. Cairo: Maktabat an-Nahḍat al-Miṣriyyah, 1949.

-Sāmarrā'ī, Qāsim. *The Theme of Ascension in Mystical Writings*. Baghdād: The National Printing and Publishing Co., 1968.

-Sarrāj, Abū Naṣr. *Kitāb al-Luma' fi t-Taṣawwuf*. Ed. Reynold A. Nicholson. London: Luzac: Gibb Memorial Series, no. 22, 1914.

———. *Kitāb al-Luma' fi t-Taṣawwuf*. Ed. 'Abd al-Ḥalīm Maḥmūd. Cairo: Dār al-Kutub al-Ḥaditha, 1380/1960.

Schimmel, Annemarie. *Al-Halladsch, Märtyrer der Gottesliebe*. Cologne: J. Hegner, 1969.

———. *Mystical Dimensions of Islam*. Chapel Hill: University of North Carolina Press, 1976.

Schrieke, Bernherd. "Die Himmelsreise Muhammads." *Der Islam* 6 (1961).

Sells, Michael. "Along the Edge of Mirage" in *Literary Heritage of Classical Islam*, ed. Mustansir Mir, pp. 119–136. Princeton: Darwin Press, 1993.

———. "Bewildered Tongue: The Semantics of Mystical Union in Islam" in *Mystical Union and Monotheistic Faith: An Ecumenical Dialogue*, ed. M. Idel and B. McGinn, pp. 108–115. New York: Macmillan, 1993.

———. *Desert Tracings: Six Classic Arabian Odes by 'Alqama, Shanfara, Labid, Antara, Al-A'sha, and Dhu ar-Rumma*. Middletown: Wesleyan University Press, 1993.

———. "Guises of the Ghul: Dissembling Simile and Semantic Overflow in the Classical Arabic Nasīb" in *Reorientations: Arabic and Persian Poetry, ed. Suzanne Stetkevych*, pp. 130–164. Bloomington: Indiana University Press, 1993.

———. "Like the Arms of a Drowning Man" in *A Festschrift in Honor of Professor Ewald Wagner*, ed. W. Heinrichs and G. Schoeler, 2:18–41. Beirut/Istanbul: Beiruter Studien, 1994.

———. *Mystical Languages of Unsaying*. Chicago: University of Chicago Press, 1994.

———. "Sound and Meaning in *Sūrat al-Qāri'a*." *Arabica* 40, no. 3 (1993): 403-430.

———. "Sound, Spirit, and Gender in *Sūrat al-Qadr*." *Journal of the American Oriental Society* 111.2 (April-May 1991): 239–259.

———. "3 Enoch and the Mi'raj of Bistami," presented at the annual meeting of the American Academy of Religion, Anaheim, Nov. 11, 1993.

Seybold, John. "The Earliest Demon Lover: The Ṭayf al-Khayāl in al-Mufaḍḍalīyāt," in S. Stetkevych, ed. *Reorientations*.

-Shahrastānī, Abū al-Fatḥ 'Abd al-Karīm. *Kitāb al-Milal wā al-Niḥal.* Ed. Muhammad al-Badran. Cairo: Maṭba'at al-Azhar, 1951.

______. *Kitab al-Milal wa al-Niḥal* [*Book of Religious and Philosophical Sects*]. Ed. William Cureton, 2 vols. London: Society for the Publication of Oriental Texts, 1846.

-Sha'rānī, 'Abd al-Wahhāb. *Ṭabaqāt al-Kubrá.* Cairo: Maṭba'at al-'Amirat al-'Uthmāniyyah, 1898.

-Shaybī, Kāmil Muṣtafā, ed. *Sharḥ Diwān al-Ḥallāj.* Beirut, 1393/1973.

Singh, S. O. J. *The Persian Mystics: The Invocations of Sheikh 'Abd Allāh Anṣā rī of Herāt, A.D. 1005–1090.* London: John Murray, 1939.

Smith, Margaret. *An Early Mystic of Baghdād.* London, 1935.

______. *Al-Muḥāsibī A.D. 781–857: An Early Mystic of Baghdad.* Amsterdam: Philo Press, 1974, a reprint of the original 1935 Sheldon Press version.

______. *The Persian Mystics: 'Aṭṭār.* London: John Murray, 1932.

______. *Rābi'a the Mystic and Her Fellow Saints in Islām.* Cambridge: Cambridge University Press, 1928, 1984.

______. *Readings from the Mystics of Islām.* London: Luzac, 1950.

______. *Studies in Early Mysticism in the Near and Middle East.* London: The Sheldon Press, 1931.

Stetkevych, Jaroslav. *Zephyrs of Najd: The Poetics of Nostalgia in the Classical Arabic Nasīb.* Chicago: University of Chicago Press, 1993.

-Sulamī, 'Abdu'r Raḥmān. *Ḥaqā'iq at-Tafsīr.* Hs. Fatih 262/Hs. British Museum Or. 9433.

______. *Jawāmī' ādāb aṣ-ṣūfīya wā-'Uyūb an-nafs wa-mudāwātuha.* Ed. Etan Kohlberg. The Max Schloessinger Memorial Series. Texts 1. Jerusalem, 1976.

______. *Kitāb al-Arba'īn fī at-taṣawwuf.* Ḥaydarābād: Maṭba'at Majlis Dārisāt al-Ma'ārif al-'Uthmāniyya, 369/1950.

______. *Kitāb ādāb aṣ-Ṣuḥba.* Ed. M. J. Kister. Jerusalem: Israel Oriental Society, 1954.

______. *Ṭabaqāt aṣ-Ṣūfiyya.* Ed. J. Pedersen. Leiden: Brill, 1960.

______. *Kitāb Ṭabaqāt aṣ-Ṣūfiyya.* Ed. Nūr ad-dīn Shurayba. Cairo: Maktabat an-Nahḍat al-Miṣriyah, 1953.

______. *Risālat al-malāmatīya.* In: *al-Malāmatīya wa- ṣ-Ṣūfiya wa-Ahl al-Futūwa*, ed. 'Afīfī, Abu l'Alā'. Cairo: 'Īsá al-Bābī al-Ḥalabī 1364/1945.

-Ṭabarī, Abū Ja'far Muḥammad ibn Jarīr. *The Commentary on the Qur'ān.* Abr. tr. W. F. Madelung and A. Jones, Vol. 1. London: Oxford University Press, 1987.

-Tirmidhī, Abū 'Abdallāh Muḥammad b. Alī b. al-Ḥasan al-Ḥakīm. *Khatm al-Awliyā'*. Ed. 'Uthmān Ismā'īl Yaḥyā. Beirut: al-Maṭba'ah al- kāthū likiyya, 1965.

-Tustarī, Muḥammad Sahl ibn 'Abdallah. *Tafsīr al-Qur'ān al-'Aẓīm*. Cairo: Dār al-Kutub al-Gharbiyya al-Kubrā, 1329/1911.

Wente, Gisela, tr. *Frühislamische Mystiker aus Fariduddin 'Attars "Heiligenbiogrphie."* Amsterdam: Castrum Peregrini Presse, 1984.

Widengren, E. *Muḥammad, the Apostle of God and his Ascension*. Uppsala: Lundequistska bokhandeln, 1955.

Yaḥyā, Osman. "L'oeuvre de Tirmidhi, essai bibliographique." In *Mélanges Louis Massignon*. 3 vols. Damascus: Institut francais de Damas, 1956–57.

Zaehner, R. C. "Abū Yazīd of Bisṭām: A Turning Point in Islamic Mysticism," *Indo-Iranian Journal* I (1957): 286–301.

———. *Hindu and Muslim Mysticism*. New York: Schocken, 1960.

Zayn al-'Abidin, Imam. *The Psalms of Islam (Al-Sahifat al-Sajjadiyya)*. Tr. and intro. William Chittick. London: Muhammadi Trust, 1988.

Index of Topics

INDEX OF TOPICS

INDEX OF TOPICS

INDEX OF TOPICS

INDEX OF TOPICS

Index of Names

INDEX OF NAMES

INDEX OF NAMES

Other Volumes in this Series

Julian of Norwich • SHOWINGS
Jacob Boehme • THE WAY TO CHRIST
Nahman of Bratslav • THE TALES
Gregory of Nyssa • THE LIFE OF MOSES
Bonaventure • THE SOUL'S JOURNEY INTO GOD, THE TREE OF LIFE, AND THE LIFE OF ST. FRANCIS
William Law • A SERIOUS CALL TO DEVOUT AND HOLY LIFE, AND THE SPIRIT OF LOVE
Abraham Isaac Kook • THE LIGHTS OF PENITENCE, LIGHTS OF HOLINESS, THE MORAL PRINCIPLES, ESSAYS, AND POEMS
Ibn 'Ata' Illah • THE BOOK OF WISDOM and KWAJA ABDULLAH
Ansari • INTIMATE CONVERSATIONS
Johann Arndt • TRUE CHRISTIANITY
Richard of St. Victor • THE TWELVE PATRIARCHS, THE MYSTICAL ARK, AND BOOK THREE OF THE TRINITY
Origen • AN EXHORTATION TO MARTYRDOM, PRAYER, AND SELECTED WORKS
Catherine of Genoa • PURGATION AND PURGATORY, THE SPIRITUAL DIALOGUE
Native North American Spirituality of the Eastern Woodlands • SACRED MYTHS, DREAMS, VISIONS, SPEECHES, HEALING FORMULAS, RITUALS AND CEREMONIALS
Teresa of Avila • THE INTERIOR CASTLE
Apocalyptic Spirituality • TREATISES AND LETTERS OF LACTANTIUS, ADSO OF MONTIER-EN-DER, JOACHIM OF FIORE, THE FRANCISCAN SPIRITUALS, SAVONAROLA
Athanasius • THE LIFE OF ANTONY, A LETTER TO MARCELLINUS
Catherine of Siena • THE DIALOGUE
Sharafuddin Maneri • THE HUNDRED LETTERS
Martin Luther • THEOLOGIA GERMANICA
Native Mesoamerican Spirituality • ANCIENT MYTHS, DISCOURSES, STORIES, DOCTRINES, HYMNS, POEMS FROM THE AZTEC, YUCATEC, QUICHE-MAYA AND OTHER SACRED TRADITIONS
Symeon the New Theologian • THE DISCOURSES
Ibn Al'-Arabī • THE BEZELS OF WISDOM
Hadewijch • THE COMPLETE WORKS
Philo of Alexandria • THE CONTEMPLATIVE LIFE, THE GIANTS, AND SELECTIONS
George Herbert • THE COUNTRY PARSON, THE TEMPLE
Unknown • THE CLOUD OF UNKNOWING
John and Charles Wesley • SELECTED WRITINGS AND HYMNS
Meister Eckhart • THE ESSENTIAL SERMONS, COMMENTARIES, TREATISES AND DEFENSE
Francisco de Osuna • THE THIRD SPIRITUAL ALPHABET
Jacopone da Todi • THE LAUDS
Fakhruddin 'Iraqi • DIVINE FLASHES
Menahem Nahum of Chernobyl • THE LIGHT OF THE EYES

Early Dominicans • SELECTED WRITINGS
John Climacus • THE LADDER OF DIVINE ASCENT
Francis and Clare • THE COMPLETE WORKS
Gregory Palamas • THE TRIADS
Pietists • SELECTED WRITINGS
The Shakers • TWO CENTURIES OF SPIRITUAL REFLECTION
Zohar • THE BOOK OF ENLIGHTENMENT
Luis de León • THE NAMES OF CHRIST
Quaker Spirituality • SELECTED WRITINGS
Emanuel Swedenborg • THE UNIVERSAL HUMAN AND SOUL-BODY INTERACTION
Augustine of Hippo • SELECTED WRITINGS
Safed Spirituality • RULES OF MYSTICAL PIETY, THE BEGINNING OF WISDOM
Maximus Confessor • SELECTED WRITINGS
John Cassian • CONFERENCES
Johannes Tauler • SERMONS
John Ruusbroec • THE SPIRITUAL ESPOUSALS AND OTHER WORKS
Ibn 'Abbād of Ronda • LETTERS ON THE SŪFĪ PATH
Angelus Silesius • THE CHERUBINIC WANDERER
The Early Kabbalah •
Meister Eckhart • TEACHER AND PREACHER
John of the Cross • SELECTED WRITINGS
Pseudo-Dionysius • THE COMPLETE WORKS
Bernard of Clairvaux • SELECTED WORKS
Devotio Moderna • BASIC WRITINGS
The Pursuit of Wisdom • AND OTHER WORKS BY THE AUTHOR OF THE CLOUD OF UNKNOWING
Richard Rolle • THE ENGLISH WRITINGS
Francis de Sales, Jane de Chantal • LETTERS OF SPIRITUAL DIRECTION
Albert and Thomas • SELECTED WRITINGS
Robert Bellarmine • SPIRITUAL WRITINGS
Nicodemos of the Holy Mountain • A HANDBOOK OF SPIRITUAL COUNSEL
Henry Suso • THE EXEMPLAR, WITH TWO GERMAN SERMONS
Bérulle and the French School • SELECTED WRITINGS
The Talmud • SELECTED WRITINGS
Ephrem the Syrian • HYMNS
Hildegard of Bingen • SCIVIAS
Birgitta of Sweden • LIFE AND SELECTED REVELATIONS
John Donne • SELECTIONS FROM *DIVINE POEMS,* SERMONS, *DEVOTIONS AND PRAYERS*
Jeremy Taylor • SELECTED WORKS
Walter Hilton • *SCALE OF PERFECTION*
Ignatius of Loyola • *SPIRITUAL EXERCISES* AND SELECTED WORKS
Anchoritic Spirituality • *ANCRENE WISSE* AND ASSOCIATED WORKS
Nizam ad-din Awliya • MORALS FOR THE HEART
Pseudo-Macarius • THE FIFTY SPIRITUAL HOMILIES AND THE *GREAT LETTER*
Gertrude of Helfta • *THE HERALD OF DIVINE LOVE*
Angela of Foligno • COMPLETE WORKS

Margaret Ebner • MAJOR WORKS
Marguerite Porete • *THE MIRROR OF SIMPLE SOULS*
John Henry Newman • SELECTED SERMONS
Early Anabaptist Spirituality • SELECTED WRITINGS
Elijah Benamozegh • ISRAEL AND HUMANITY
The Classic Midrash • TANNAITIC COMMENTARIES ON THE BIBLE
Vincent de Paul and Louise de Marillac • RULES, CONFERENCES, AND WRITINGS
Isaiah Horowitz • THE GENERATIONS OF ADAM